American Drama
From the Colonial Period
Through World War I:
A Critical History

TWAYNE'S CRITICAL HISTORY OF AMERICAN DRAMA

Jordan Y. Miller
GENERAL EDITOR
University of Rhode Island

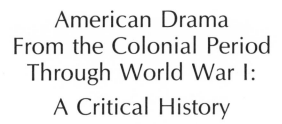

American Drama
From the Colonial Period
Through World War I:
A Critical History

Gary A. Richardson
Mercer University

Twayne Publishers ◊ New York
Maxwell Macmillan Canada ◊ Toronto
Maxwell Macmillan International ◊ New York Oxford Singapore Sydney

American Drama from the Colonial Period Through World War I:
A Critical History
Gary A. Richardson

Twayne's Critical History of American Drama Series

Copyright © 1993 by Twayne Publishers

Twayne Publishers   Maxwell Macmillan Canada, Inc.
Macmillan Publishing Company 1200 Eglinton Avenue East
866 Third Avenue   Suite 200
New York, New York 10022   Don Mills, Ontario M3C 3N1

Macmillan Publishing Company is part of the Maxwell
Communication Group of Companies.

Library of Congress Cataloging-in-Publication Data

Richardson, Gary A., 1949–
    American drama from the colonial period through World
War I : a critical history / Gary A. Richardson.
        p.   cm. — (Twayne's critical history of American
drama series)
    Includes bibliographical references and index.
    ISBN 0-8057-8956-1
    1. American drama—History and criticism.   I. Title.
II. Series.
PS332.R53   1993
812.009—dc20   92-36497
                                                            CIP

10 9 8 7 6 5 4 3 2 1

The paper used in this publication meets the minimum
requirements of American National Standard for Information
Sciences—Permanence of Paper for Printed Library Materials.
ANSI Z3948-1984.♾™

contents

prologue

My subject is the critically marginal, for drama has always been the stepchild of American literary culture. Whether out of religious, aesthetic, or ideological bias, the nation's cultural arbiters have traditionally been, at best, ambivalent about America's drama and its functions. This is especially true of drama before O'Neill, about which the prevailing opinion seems to be that the less said the better. As Ethan Mordden phrased it in justifying his pointedly brief survey of the first 150 years of the country's drama, the early years are "more fun than intelligent."[1] This volume seeks to prompt a wholesale rethinking of that attitude.

For both theoretical and pragmatic reasons, however, this volume is not offered as a totalizing, teleological narrative tracing the development of the national drama. While such narratives have their appeals, as a class they tend to find and emphasize connections, links, and progressions. In investigating American drama, especially after the Revolution, when its authors became increasingly self-conscious, I have been more often struck by disjunctions, discontinuities, and variety than any organic history could hope to explain.

Though this volume touches upon a formally varied group of works, practical considerations have necessitated the omission of numerous categories of dramatic representation. Native American rituals, treaty ceremonies, farces, minstrel shows, vaudeville skits, musical theater, civic pageants, and non-English language ethnic drama have received, at most, passing reference. Many of these theatrical forms merit individual investigation, and any generalizations about the total dramatic output of the American nation should surely include thorough examinations of them. Neither have I attempted to address the merits—however they might be defined—of every play produced within what are generally considered "legitimate" theaters between 1665 and 1917. The tens of thousands of plays written and produced in the period make such an undertaking impossible at the current time.

As a consequence of the inevitable selectivity of this project, this volume does not seek to address issues of canonicity, though I do occasionally note my lingering distrust of the historical, critical, and economic forces that have shaped the canon of American drama. Instead, I have taken plays that are, in the main, fairly well known and readily accessible to students of early American drama. The contribution that I hope this volume will make emerges from the interplay of the premises on which I have based my readings: that these works are worthy of serious critical consideration; that they have much to tell us about the era in which they were written and produced; that they can provide some insight into what, if anything, is particularly American about this drama. These premises have taken me on occasion far afield from the traditional aesthetic grounds on which this drama has been judged. Versions of the nation's fluid social, economic, and political realities have served not merely as background or context for these plays' composition and production but as distinct voices with which the plays have been in dialogue. The general politics of culture, issues of racial and ethnic identity, the import of race and ethnicity upon the nation's sense of itself, anxieties about economic dislocation, and conflicts surrounding gender configurations—all these topics found their way onto the American stage long before the social protest theater of the 1930s or the 1960s.

This volume falls into three general parts. The first section is composed of the initial three chapters and discusses roughly the period between the founding of the English colonies in America and the early nineteenth century. It seeks to trace the growth and circumstances of drama until the outbreak of the American Revolution, to examine the ways in which drama served as a means of political and cultural intervention during the Revolution itself, and to analyze the efforts of three early republican dramatists to establish a new national drama in the wake of independence. The second portion, chapters four and five, suggests the tensions between elite and populist dramatic culture in the first half of the nineteenth century and examines both the manner in which European romantic drama was Americanized and the emergence of certain national character types which have persistently remained part of our culture. The final three chapters discuss the increasingly complex dramatic practice after the Civil War. Chapter six seeks to outline the various cultural uses to which melodrama, the dominant dramatic form of the later nineteenth century, was put by a host of extremely diverse writers. Chapter seven outlines the emergence of the realist aesthetic among American literary artists and charts realistic drama's complicated and fitful growth as an aesthetic, political, and formal alternative to melodrama. Chapter eight encompasses discussions of turn-of-the-century comedy of manners, the drama of progressivism, neoromantic drama, and the gender problem-play and seeks to suggest the richly textured dramatic antecedents of O'Neill, Odets, Rice, Anderson, Howard, Sherwood, and Behrman.

As I suggested above, this book can only begin to discuss the formal diversity and cultural complexity of American drama before O'Neill. But as we approach the end of another century confronted by a host of political, social, economic, and cultural conundrums, we would do well to turn our attentions to our cultural heritage with renewed seriousness of purpose. Though unlikely to furnish any ultimate solutions to contemporary problems, such an examination may provide us with a valuable historical perspective on the ways analogous concerns have been perceived by our forebears and also the consequences of configuring issues in certain ways. If we would know who we are, we should understand who we have been—or who we thought we were.

A project of this length does not come to fruition without the collective efforts of numerous collaborators, and I have been especially fortunate to receive the generous aid of many friends, colleagues, students, and institutions. A series of research grants from the College of Liberal Arts of Mercer University provided resources and time at crucial points. Institutional libraries and their staffs have readily shared their resources and expertise. I am especially grateful to the British Library, the National Library of Ireland, the Library of Congress, the New York Public Library, the Folger Shakespeare Library, the Newberry Library, the William Andrews Clark Library of UCLA, the Huntington Library, and the libraries of the University of Illinois, Vanderbilt University, the University of Georgia, and Mercer University. Special thanks to Elizabeth Hammond, Valerie Edmonds, and Virginia Cairns, three Mercer University librarians, who proved again and again that with diligence one can almost always find someone somewhere willing to share the necessary tools of scholarship.

Over the long evolution of this work several friends and colleagues answered specific questions, discussed theoretical issues, read sections of the early drafts of the book, or provided criticisms and suggestions, and I am grateful to acknowledge them: James Hurt, Marian Janssen, Gerrit Janssens, Walter Kalaidjian, Vincent Leitch, Stephen Watt, and Edward Weintraut. Additionally, I am especially grateful to the general editor of this series, Jordan Y. Miller, for his faith, prodding, and scrupulous reading of the entire manuscript. Whatever errors of judgment and infelicities of expression are to be found in this book persist despite their collective efforts. Finally, I thank my editors at Twayne, especially Elizabeth Traynor and John Fitzpatrick, for their consideration, efficiency, and flexibility.

For permission to reprint sections of this study that appeared first elsewhere, in somewhat different forms, I wish to thank *Theatre Journal* and the University of Georgia Press. For permission to reproduce the photographs I am grateful to the British Library, the Library of Congress, and the New York Public Library.

My greatest debts are to those closest to me. To my children, Matthew and Kathleen, who suffered with amazing grace the intrusions of their textual sibling, and to my wife, Mary Alice Morgan, who gave enormously of her energies, intellect, and love to see me through to this project's completion, I gratefully dedicate this book.

1

Colonial Drama

W hen in "Bermudas" Andrew Marvell came to express English optimism at the unfolding possibilities of the New World, he presented his hope in an image that interestingly juxtaposes the secular and religious worlds of the day. The travelers of the poem are, according to Marvell, delivered by God to a "grassy Stage / Safe from the Storms, and the Prelat's rage."[1] The evocation of the Edenic garden is common to much seventeenth-century English religious poetry, but Marvell's use of the image is especially interesting because of the tension he creates by linking this traditional religious trope with the preeminent emblem of secular license—the stage. Almost from the construction of Burbage's first playhouse in 1576, the theater was, in large measure, an anathema to those like Marvell's persona whose central concern is the state of the individual soul. Serious-minded Englishmen, such as Marvell's friend John Oxenbridge (who twice left England for religious reasons, first immigrating to Bermuda and later to New England), had little use for their theatrical heritage. Nevertheless, the cultural impulses which had grown for five centuries in England, had transmogrified an extension of liturgy into a secular entertainment, and had been expelled from the churches only to find a home in Southwark, could not be resisted indefinitely, even on the decidedly austere frontier of early America. While American drama would not occupy a central concern in colonial life, it would be turned to serve the purposes of the day. Despite reaction in the colonies that ranged from indifference to vociferous antagonism, the advent of the theater in America was inevitable. While the development of a truly national drama awaited more talented practitioners, the early dramatists of the colonies provided a firm sense of the appropriateness of drama as a means of translating and interpreting the experience of the New World. America's initial impact on the course of world drama was not to be as revolutionary as its influence on governmental institutions, but the process which was to produce O'Neill, Williams, Miller, and other major figures of twentieth-century American and international drama did not begin in this century. The roots of American drama are deep and strong.

Colonial Attitudes and the Beginnings of Theater in America

When the first English settlers arrived in America, the commercial theater in England had already become a vital part of English life. Despite moral objections, occasional financial difficulties, and governmental interference, the theater of the English Renaissance had thrived in a country whose people had grown to love the entertainment and pageantry associated with the playhouses. Thus, the English Puritans' rise to power and their institution of a sober Commonwealth society resulted in only a temporary interruption in the growth of English theater and drama. Indeed, within months of his Restoration in 1660, Charles II had granted William Davenant and Thomas Killigrew royal patents to revive the London theater companies that had been closed by the Puritans in 1642. Charles II's proclivity for dramatic entertainment (not to mention actresses) guaranteed the survival of the revitalized companies during his reign, and neither wars, neglect by Charles II's successors, nor periodic economic woes would be sufficient to inhibit for long the growth of the theater in eighteenth-century England.

In America the story was quite different. The cultural attitudes of colonial Americans were prescribed by prejudices for hard work, frugality, and piety that the immigrants had brought to the New World and that they thought contributed to their physical and spiritual survival in an inhospitable land. The antagonism of early American settlers to the theater stemmed from many sources. In New England, the most obvious of these was a rigid Puritan theology.[2] Speaking in the characteristically hysterical manner of both English and American Puritans on the subject, Philip Stubbes assures his readers that plays are "sucked out of the Devills teates to nourish us in ydolatrie, hethenrie, and sinne" (Solberg, 52). In addition to their theological objections, the Puritans had economic and social difficulties with the theater. Actors not only took money that the Puritan ministers saw as rightfully theirs but also encouraged idleness and seduced the upright from their work. Moreover, the playhouse itself was a venue of depravity where prostitutes and thieves plied their trades with seeming impunity. In sum, as a host of Puritan writers argued, theaters were responsible for "emptying the churches, aiding the Pope, . . . corrupting maidens and chaste wives, and providing a market place for harlots and their customers" (Rankin, 2).

While the Puritans and Pilgrims who settled New England were the most strident in their opposition to the theater, the inhabitants of the ostensibly more liberal colonies to the south tended initially to be every bit as reluctant to build permanent theaters or to allow itinerant actors to practice their craft. Indicative of early attitudes is the history of the first recorded theatrical performance in the English colonies. In August 1665 in Accomac County, on the eastern shore of Virginia, three residents were brought before the local justices of the peace for acting the now lost *Ye Bare and Ye Cubb*. While the actors were exonerated and their accuser was forced to pay court costs, the fact is that the laws of the Roundhead Parliament which had forbade public acting in England continued to find proponents in America—five years after the Restoration of Charles II and the Stuart monarchy.

But the American colonists did not rely solely upon the injunctions of English parliaments to deal with the perceived corrupting influence of theater. Indeed, with the exceptions of Maryland and Virginia, all the American colonies at one point or another had laws whose effects were to discourage, and in some cases prohibit, theatrical activity in America. While the most stringent of these laws were in New England, even the Quakers of Pennsylvania, who usually relied upon suasion rather than punitive laws, enacted a statute in 1682 which provided that anyone found guilty of introducing or attending " 'such rude and riotous sports and practices as prizes [prize-fights], stage plays, [and] masques' " would be sentenced to hard labor (Wright, 243–44).

Despite the inhibitions, both legal and social, drama and theater grew by fits and starts in the later colonial period. The development of population centers within the various colonies, especially the colonies south of New England, brought an increasing interest in cultural matters including the theater. A growing awareness that theatrical entertainments would be permitted in the colonies, if not encouraged, is indicated by the erection of theaters by entrepreneurs such as William Levingston, who built the first colonial theater in Williamsburg, Virginia between 1716 and 1718. By 1767, Charleston, Philadelphia, and New York had permanent theaters and several other colonial cities had structures that served that capacity for traveling companies such as those of Lewis Hallam or David Douglass. Perhaps even more illustrative of the changing attitudes of Americans toward drama was the steady incorporation of dramatic materials into the intellectual and social life of students at American colleges and universities.

The College Exercises and Dialogues

American colleges in the eighteenth century were a natural locus for dramatic activity, despite the occasional misgivings of school authorities. Students who foresaw careers in business, law, and the ministry were naturally drawn to activities that simultaneously provided an opportunity to perfect oratorical skills useful after graduation and an escape from the rigors of a stringent classical education. Just as southern cities were the first to permit dramatic performances, so the colleges of the South led the way in academic drama. As early as 1702 students at the College of William and Mary performed a "pastoral colloquy." Such theatrical endeavors apparently became perennial, for in 1736 the same college's students advertised productions of Addison's *Cato* and *The Drummer* (Rankin, 19–20). Although academic drama first found an audience in the South, collegians at the College of New Jersey (Princeton), Yale, the College of Philadelphia (University of Pennsylvania), Dartmouth, and Harvard all performed dramatic pieces, both sanctioned and unsanctioned.

The dramatic quality of pieces written expressly for or by collegiates is uniformly poor, for in most instances they were not designed as dramas at all. The majority are odes or formal poetic dialogues which speak about some event or person through characters (usually pastoral).

Despite their formulaic and subdramatic natures, the collegiate exercises and dialogues served an essential function in the development of the fledgling American drama. They provided American students with opportunities to see and participate in dramatic productions and thereby not only encouraged would-be dramatists and prospective audiences by providing an aesthetic training ground, but also gave intellectual credibility and social acceptability to dramatic endeavors. For example, Thomas Godfrey, whose *The Prince of Parthia* in 1767 became the first play written by a colonial to be produced by a professional company in America, was a protégé of William Smith, Provost of the College of Philadelphia. Smith actively supported dramatic presentations and, in fact, wrote several himself. In all probability Godfrey saw his mentor's production of *The Masque of Alfred* presented during the Christmas holidays in 1756–57. Certainly Godfrey's tragedy displays the same rhetorical treatment of subject and stems from the same didactic impulse that underpins Smith's college pieces.

The collegiate exercises are most important, however, because of the evidence they provide of the adaptation of the dramatic impulse to colonial American experience. At least a few of the writers of these dramatic poems and dialogues transcend mere rhetorical exercise and begin to reflect critical American attitudes and to deal with decidedly American issues. While in 1762 Francis Hopkinson, later a signer of the Declaration of Independence, could pen a rather conventional ode to "celebrate in Notes divine" the ascension of George III, by 1771 Henry Hugh Brackenridge and Philip Freneau were implicitly suggesting the supplanting of English authority by arguing that the westward progress of civilization and empire since ancient times seemed to foreshadow the inevitable ascendancy of America (Hopkinson, 6). Though not an overtly revolutionary poem, their "The Rising Glory of America" does reflect the pervasive colonial attitude that the essential element of progress is liberty, "Without whose aid the noblest genius fails, / And Science irretrievably must die" (Freneau, 13). Although it is tempting to pass off Freneau and Brackenridge's ode as the understated grumblings of young men forced by the Stamp Act to pay a two-pound fee in order to graduate, their poem intimates, however mildly, the growing dissatisfaction with the relationship between England and her colonies.

Two more overtly dramatic pieces written by Dartmouth professor John Smith illustrate the diversity of later collegiate dialogues. In "A Dialogue between an Englishman and an Indian," written in 1779, Smith presents a disputation on the humanity of Native Americans and the relative "merits" of exterminating them. The Englishman, after three years of the Revolutionary War, is presented as a bloodthirsty racist whose prejudices extend so far beyond reason and good conscience that he would "chearfully contribute powder and bullets" for the destruction all Native Americans.[3] On the other hand, the Native American is portrayed as an enlightened Christian gentleman who has overcome the "disadvantages" of his birth through education at the hands of Eleazer Wheelock, a pious Dartmouth teacher. After enumerating the atrocities committed against the indigenous population by Europeans, including the English, the Native American caps his argument by pointing out the Christian faith's abhorrence of the vicious attitude expressed by the Englishman. He concludes his presentation by expressing the hope that his adversary "will yet exhibit a meek, merciful, and benevolent temper of mind" (8). Given the rules of the form, the Englishman is, of course, overwhelmed and admits that he has perhaps been "too much prejudiced against the Indians" (8). This dialogue is interesting not only as an excellent example of the traditional rhetorical exercise, but also as an illustration of the manner in which contemporary social and political issues inevitably became part of a seemingly mundane oratorical piece.[4] More important, however, is the parallel drawn between Native Americans and the English colonists that forms the political subtext of the dialogue. The insightful Native American contends that the Englishman wishes to destroy the native population merely because they are not civilized in the way the Englishman conceives of the term, and that given "sufficient power," the Englishman "would be as fierce a destroyer of mankind, as cruel a tyrant as ever existed" (8). While Smith neatly displaces revolutionary outrage and allows the nameless Native American spokesman to indict the English, many in the audience no doubt found the Native American's view of potential English despotism too kind an assessment given the perceived tyrannies inflicted upon the colonies. The cultural, intellectual, and moral superiority of the Native American suggests that American, both native and colonial, need no longer accede meekly to an English rule on the assumption that English attitudes inherently reflect civilized norms (Rugg, 56).

Two years later Smith turned his clear eye to the fiscal consequences of the revolution in "A Little Teatable Chitchat." On the whole this seems a lighthearted satire on the greed of erstwhile colonials within and without local governments who were attempting to turn the economic hardships of the general populace to their advantage. Sharp, the main character, has paid off his debts with the nearly worthless paper currency issued by local colonial governments during the revolution. Having subsequently secured debtors, he is determined to see that the local assembly revalues its currency so that it is equal to gold. Sharp's guest, Pendulum, who obviously suggests the self-interested profiteers of the period, applauds Sharp's business acumen and wholeheartedly endorses Sharp's plan to abolish supports to ministers. The piece ends on an ironic note when Pendulum, averring that he has had enough tea and bacon, echoes the proverb, "Enough is as good as a feast." Whether Smith knew the Tudor interlude of the same title or was referring solely to the proverb, the intent of the line is obvious. Pendulum and Sharp are both guilty of the worldly wisdom which does not recognize "enough"; they will inevitably glut themselves physically while starving spiritually. Though they may temporarily prosper in this world, their fate is assured in the judgment of the afterlife.

However tentatively, the collegiate dialogues represent the American desire to turn a basic tool of culture—drama—to the service of colonial life. As the works of William Smith, Francis Hopkinson, Philip Freneau, Hugh Henry Brackenridge and John Smith testify, the collegiate oratorical tradition provided the means by which many of the brightest and most privileged of America's young colonists might examine their world. Molding English university traditions to their own needs and desires, the American academicians and their followers grasped "opportunities for creating images of social difference and social interaction, for personification of basic norms and the rejection of rival symbols" (Martin, 25).

Colonial Comedy

While collegiate dialogues provided one outlet for American dramatic impulses, they were by no means the only vehicles through which Americans found their dramatic voices. As colonial life became more subject to reflection, colonials began to vent their frustrations at individuals and institutions in comedy, and a healthy comedic tradition combining elements of folk humor, literary comedy, and satire grew up rather quickly. Most of the extant plays speak to specific issues and personalities and are, thus, of more historical than literary interest. Nevertheless, Robert Hunter's *Androboros* and two anonymous plays, one dealing with Jonathan Belcher's succession to the governorship of Massachusetts and the other with the Paxton Boys episode in Pennsylvania, indicate the persistent use of drama as a means of simultaneously chronicling events and shaping public response to them. These three plays are overtly propagandistic and freely utilize the tools of the satirist to savage their specific targets. In contrast, *The Trial of Atticus, Before Justice Beau, for a Rape*, while definitely satiric, is more a generalized indictment of colonial institutions than an attack upon particular individuals or groups. Finally, Robert Munford's *The Candidates*, though not published until 1798, focuses satiric attention on the electioneering procedures of the Virginia frontier in the early 1770s. Though there is no specific evidence that any of these plays was ever produced, it is perhaps unwise to label them as closet drama. They are, for the most part, suited to the stage, and internal evidence suggests that their authors conceived of stage action as an integral part of the dramas. These plays are not, in other words, mere poetic set pieces, and thus mark a substantial advance in American drama. For the first time, action is joined to language to delineate both character and event.

The first play written and printed in America, *Androboros: A Biographical Farce in Three Acts*, was composed in 1714 to vent Robert Hunter's frustration at the political situation in the royal colony of New York. Hunter, who had assumed the governorship in 1710, had struggled with a variety of problems: a long-standing and bitter factionalism rooted in the ill-fated Leisler rebellion of 1689–91; a strained relationship with the New York Assembly which steadfastly refused to implement royal instructions concerning the operation of the colony's government (including the governor's salary); a large number of disgruntled creditors who had lost money subsidizing, at Hunter's request, a Crown plan to resettle in New York Palatine refugees displaced by Louis XIV's victories in the Rhineland; and a running battle with various Anglican ministers in New York and New Jersey who demanded that Hunter give them certain parcels of land and desist from carrying out a royal decree that he install as parish ministers only those credited by the Bishop of London[5]. Hunter's opponents sought to unite behind General Francis Nicholson, the Royal Commissioner of Accounts, a man whose vile temper, violent manner, and close affiliation with Queen Anne's Tory ministers made him a considerable political opponent (Leder, 156–59).

Hunter's response to the crisis precipitated by Nicholson's impending arrival was *Androboros*, in which he not only lampooned the pompous Nicholson in the title character but also enumerated his other adversaries' shortcomings and offered his vision of the world they seemed intent upon creating. Set in an insane asylum (the colonial Assembly) in an unnamed colony (New York) overseen by Keeper (Hunter), the play follows the various stratagems of the inmates to overthrow the lawful authority of Keeper. Having located his action in a site appropriate to enthusiasts of all types, Hunter presents a set of masterfully chosen incidents whose absurdity is heightened by the malapropian commentary of Tom of Bedlam and the pointed fables of Aesop, both of whom are Keeper's allies.

The playwright first insinuates the nature of the Assembly's operation by opening the play with the chaotic convening of the inmate's Senate. Initially, all that the members can agree upon is that neither the Senate nor its constituents are bound by any laws whatsoever, that the Senate recognizes no authority but its own, that it controls the property of its voters, and that it is the court of final resort for all conflicts and recognizes no other court's right to rule on any issue. Hunter thus deftly suggests an affinity between the New York Assembly and the Long Parliament which had brought on the English Civil War, beheaded Charles I, instituted the Commonwealth, and abrogated the rule of law for a period of eighteen years after taking to itself many of the same powers the inmates' Senate claims. When one member dares to dissent and is expelled, Hunter extends his analogy by symbolically re-enacting the founding of the Rump Parliament after Pride's Purge and suggests that the effects of factionalism in the colony will be the same as they were in England—reason and moderation will give way to fanaticism, itself merely a disguised self-interest. Hunter next indicates his adversaries' lack of political and military astuteness by having them commission Androboros to attack the *Mulo Machians* (the French). Instead of waging war, the vainglorious Androboros concludes a peace which effectively guarantees the subjugation of the inmates' state. They naturally vote him a triumph. Finally, Hunter attacks the political ambitions and religious bigotry of his ministerial foes in the persons of Flip and Fizle, whose antics range from smearing their garments with excrement in a futile attempt to suggest that Keeper and his allies do not properly reverence the clergy to attempting Keeper's murder. Their assassination attempt fails and the play ends as they sink through the floor in the company of Androboros.

A man of obvious wit and wide reading, Hunter utilized his talent to effect in *Androboros*. While the scatological element common to much early eighteenth-century English satire has been seen by one nineteenth-century critic as a flaw, modern readers will find the play as a whole a delight (Ford, 675). Hunter borrows widely and well. From Shakespeare he secures both the "wise fool," Tom of Bedlam, who gives linguistic spice to the play, and the walking ghost motif from *Hamlet*, which serves as the vehicle for Androboros's final humiliation. From Aesop he borrows not only a name but also the tradition of folk wisdom embodied in beast fables. Hunter's imagery, while not terribly original, is consistent and effective. The major patterns surround the inmates who are constantly associated with the excremental, the animalistic, and the fantastically irrational. Tom of Bedlam's explanation of his hieroglyphic minutes of the Senate's first meeting illustrates admirably the relationship among the three: "The *Castle Renvers'd* and in the Air, denotes the independency of our House; The *Wind-Mill* without Sails, an Expedition without Means or Leader; and the *Ram* butting the *Shephard on the Breech*, or in other words, dismissing him from having any further Authority over him."[6] The knockabout action of the play extends its appeal to those incapable of recognizing its literary merits and, at the same time, suggests that Hunter conceived of the play for the stage, whether it was produced or not. Whether viewed or merely read, the play had its desired effect. Within three years of the play's penning, Nicholson's appointment had been revoked, and Hunter had reached a *rapprochement* with the colonial Assembly.

Though written by an English governor, *Androboros* foreshadows in significant ways the American drama that was to follow it. Its strong-minded condemnation of perceived political corruption and its choice of satiric humor to attack that venality began an American theater tradition which has persistently found expression in moments of local and national crisis. In addition, the play's mixture of linguistic play and farcical action served to Americanize a substantial part of the English comedic practice, which from its beginnings had been the common ground of the learned and the unlettered. Finally, in its implicit faith in the audience's ability to respond "correctly" to a well-drawn dramatic indictment the play evidences the idealism about both the playwright's ability to bring about social change and the good-heartedness of the American people that characterized American dramatic responses to political and social issues throughout the nineteenth and much of the twentieth centuries.

The untitled and anonymous play concerning Jonathan Belcher's rise to power in colonial Massachusetts and the anonymous farce *The Paxton Boys* are of significant historical interest. The Massachusetts piece, which appears to have been written in Boston in 1732, traces the career of Belcher from his days as a staunch opponent of Governor William

Burnet to his own assumption of the governorship in 1730. The play operates along lines common to much Augustan satire, though with a twist: in this American satire, the Whig government of Robert Walpole, usually pilloried by Tory satirists as unthinkingly egalitarian and liberal, is attacked by American Whigs as too conservative. The play's basic conflict revolves around the issue of the royal governor's salary. Like the colonists of New York under Hunter, Massachusetts assemblymen under Burnet were reluctant to grant the royal governor a salary at the behest of the Crown. Belcher is sent to London to persuade the English colonial ministry that royal governors should be paid according to the wishes and abilities of those they govern and that the Crown is unjustly attempting to compromise the rights of freeborn Englishmen by ordering payments of a specific amount. While in London, Belcher is corrupted and, upon the death of Burnet, agrees to become governor. He repudiates his former stance on the salary issue and the play ends with Belcher swearing to enslave the colonists if they do not submit to his will, "For he's a Fool that e're pretends / To serve Mankind, but for his own Ends."[7]

As the play's prologue makes clear, the subject of the piece is colonial liberty, and much of the language forms a discourse on that topic. The major tropes are appropriately centered in Roman history and culture, with the colonials portrayed as Catos resisting the impinging despotism of Tarquin or Caesar. Appeals to a tradition of liberty grounded in ancestral virtue and sacrifice abound, and the play's epilogue speaks of the colonists' "Roman like" determination to "preserve our Libertie" (139). These classical elements are supplemented by Biblical references which picture the colonists and their resistance to tyranny as part of God's plan to "Overthrow Antichrist by Warrs of the Lamb" and to raise "in these Western parts of the world" Christ's millennial kingdom (135–37).

The characters are not well drawn even by the standards of political satire. Among the minor characters, Phebe, Belcher's loyal wife, and the would-be-wit Achmuty, a lawyer, offer a few interesting plot possibilities. The attorney's winks, leers, and vain attempts to seduce Belcher's wife are slightly diverting and provide the non-political humor in the play. Even the historical personages at the play's center—Burnet, Belcher, and Elisha Cook, Jr.—are little more than two-dimensional figures spouting political slogans. As Robert Moody has commented, Cook's sole qualification as the play's hero is his painfully consistent willingness to be the voice of the common man (119). In fact, even the central character, Belcher, is poorly developed. The viewer is left to ponder, for example, whether Belcher has been seduced by the corrupt English court after his arrival in London or whether he had merely managed to hide his true nature previous to his departure. The text, through negligence rather than design, supports both positions. The plot is of little aid in resolving the ambiguity since Belcher's transformation occurs offstage and we are presented evidence of the change without explanation.

The importance of this play resides almost solely in its historical position. Its narrow political appeal, lack of literary merit, and the fact that it was unpublished limits its possible influence. While the mere existence of this play will not counter the general truth that New England was hostile to the drama, it does suggest that the people of Massachusetts recognized the political potential of drama much earlier than Mercy Warren's anti-British pieces in the 1770s. The play also states explicitly for the first time in American drama the feeling that British and American perspectives on colonial matters were in seemingly irreconcilable conflict and that, though they continued to consider themselves Englishmen, the colonists were regarded by the British as being the victims of what Belcher calls "darkned . . . American Views" (138).

The Paxton Boys (1764) presents a farcical picture of the citizenry's reaction to a near-invasion of Philadelphia by frontiersmen demanding governmental aid in their ongoing conflicts with Native Americans. Historically, the situation was a great deal more serious than the play suggests, for the Paxton Boys had massacred a group of peaceful Christianized Native Americans and there promised to be more bloodshed until Benjamin Franklin and others negotiated a solution (Meserve, 46). With the situation resolved, the anonymous author took the opportunity to satirize the backwoodsmen, their Presbyterian allies, and certain citizens of Philadelphia. The piece is an odd mixture of narrative, dialogue, and action. The stage directions that are liberally sprinkled throughout the text testify to the author's theatrical conception. For example, when a group of reinforcements comically arrive, the author concisely directs "A Glorious Parade through the City, Night comes in, some Guard, while others rest after their Fatigue."[8] On the other hand, the play opens with the narratized observation "The Inhabitants alarm'd for several days" (2). Nevertheless, the play is effective in conveying in its seven brief scenes the source of the conflict, the nature of the combatants, and the author's attitude toward the situation.

The first four scenes are straightforward farce. The play opens with the arrival of an express rider bringing the news that the Paxton Boys are on their way. In quick succession come scenes which detail the reactions of the townspeople, the ludicrous preparations of the local militia, the cowardly attitudes of particular individuals, and the near massacre of local citizens by their own terrified soldiers when a "Dutch Company of Butchers" is mistaken for the Paxton Boys (6). The last three scenes seek to explore the roots of the rebellion and are, perhaps inevitably, more seriously rendered. The pivotal fifth scene presents two Presbyterians who reveal that the Paxton Boys are merely the means by which they hope to overthrow the Quaker government. While the fanaticism of the major Presbyterian speaker makes him a fit target for ridicule, there is little doubt that the author wishes his audience to take the threats seriously. After linking himself to his "Forefathers *Oliverian* Spirits," the zealot contends, "I would freely Sacrifice my Life and Fortune for this Cause, rather than those Misecrants of the Establish'd Church of *England*, or those R——ls [Rascals?] the Q——s [Quakers], should continue longer at the head of Government" (7). The sixth scene introduces a Quaker counterpoint whose reasonable manner naturally infuriates the Presbyterian further. The Quaker's observation that the Presbyterian seems "possess'd of a Spirit of Madness" precipitates the rabid reply: "Bless'd shall that Man be call'd, / That takes thy Children young / To dash their Bones against the Stones, / That lye in the Streets among" (11). The final scene introduces an Anglican who instantly becomes another target of the fanatic. Although the play makes obvious the author's antipathies, the Presbyterian's indictment of Quaker pacifism provokes an admonition from the Quaker character to the audience to "Rouse up yourselves take Arms and quell the Riot" (16).

Like the Boston play, the importance of *The Paxton Boys* is almost wholly historical. While the play's popularity (it went through three editions) indicates that it was widely read, there is no evidence that its success marked a change in Philadelphians' general attitude toward drama. The citizenry's fondness for the play seems to indicate only that in Philadelphia, as in Boston, the power of drama as a political tool was recognized early. The only noteworthy dramatic development in the play is the advent of the theme of sectarian antagonism and religious intolerance. Though this issue is not treated seriously in *The Paxton Boys*, the topic continued to be a concern of American playwrights. While this is certainly not Barker's *Superstition*, it is a step in that direction.

The loosely structured *The Trial of Atticus* (1771) is a fairly effective dramatic indictment of the colonial court system. The ostensible issue in the play is whether Atticus has raped Sarah Chuckle. But as we quickly discover, the Chuckles have brought the charges (two years after the supposed attack) only after Sarah's revelation of her "encounter" with

Atticus has constrained Atticus to threaten to sue them for slander. Any doubt as to Atticus's innocence disappears as the trial progresses through ludicrous assertion and blatant falsehood. The patent absurdity of the case is indicated by the fact that Atticus mounts no real defense and that he speaks on only five occasions during the course of the entire play. Initially, he enters a plea of "not guilty" and refuses to settle the case before the trial begins; later he three times casts doubt on the validity of witnesses' testimony; and, finally, he refuses to pay court costs when Justice Beau attempts to salvage some financial advantage from a hopelessly compromised case. Though taciturn, Atticus emerges through the testimony of his accusers as the typical hero of satire—plainspoken, honest, and unwilling to accommodate his fellow citizens' idiocies.

The satire's main targets are judges, lawyers, and a colonial judicial system which allows the Chuckles's ridiculous case to come to trial. Justice Beau, who would be at home in the pages of Fielding or Gay, is portrayed as an officious, pompous, corrupt, and ignorant justice of the peace. Like many another country justice, Beau is not "versed in all points and niceties of law," though he makes great pretensions to learning.[9] He works hand-in-hand with Rattle, his kinsman, to secure a living through the operation of the court. Rattle is a typical avaricious lawyer of the eighteenth century whose interest is his fee ("It is direct in the face of the law to hear a case, or give advice without one," he tells Chuckle) rather than justice (49). He will indulge any impropriety, including suborned witnesses, in order to win his cases. With these two men in authority, the court system is doomed to be a corrupt, money-making enterprise rather than an instrument of justice. Thus, Atticus's refusal to pay court costs is a thoroughly appropriate response in the satiric world of the play.

Although the legal system and its practitioners are the primary butts of the satiric attack, the trial allows the author to exhibit and ridicule other members of colonial society as well. Using classical as well as contemporary English and continental models, the author lampoons male and female gossips and intriguers, astrologers, gullible and hypocritical clergymen, sharp-practicing innkeepers, quacks, and pompous, unlearned schoolmasters. The author attempts to give added weight to his attack by using the familiar satiric device that the whole play is merely a transcription of court records.

While neither its techniques nor targets are new within the English satiric tradition, this play marks the first American dramatic satire on so broad a scale. Unlike the plays we have examined previously, the assumption that underlies this work is not that individuals or groups are the sources of particular problems, but rather that humanity as a whole is corrupt. Ranged against the pettiness and potential evil embodied by his fellow citizens, Atticus stands alone, the classical ideal man in danger of obliteration. Thus, in this early and seemingly unlikely play we find clear evidence of a prominent American mythic character type—the individual whose sense of right and integrity inevitably brings him into conflict with a corrupt society.

As tension with England grew, Americans, perhaps subconsciously, began to consider possible reforms that might be necessary to effect a democratic government. Four years before the American Revolution broke out at Lexington and Concord, Robert Munford presented a stark picture of colonial politics in *The Candidates; or, The Humours of a Virginia Election*. Probably composed between 1770 and 1771, the play traces the campaign of Mr. Wou'dbe for a seat in the House of Burgesses, a process that Munford, himself elected a Burgess in 1765, knew well. The election setting allows Munford not only to examine the workings of democracy on the frontier, but also to raise fundamental questions about the efficacy of representative democracy as a method of government. Additionally, the play provides an interesting insight into the context within which major political decisions of the day were made.

Whether portrayed as a government conspiracy to deprive freemen of their rights or merely as an emblem of broader social and political decay, electoral corruption was a popular target of satirists on both sides of the Atlantic in the eighteenth century.[10] The catalogue of abuses including the self-centered naiveté of the electorate and candidates' willingness to play upon that ignorance with outlandish campaign promises, the verbal and physical assaults on candidates and supporters, and candidates' attempts to buy votes by "treating" voters to food and drink, were all well-documented in both England and America. Munford's contribution to this body of literature lies, therefore, in the Americanized particulars of his treatment and the artistry of his effort rather than in the development of new material.

Voter ignorance is cited endlessly by satirists in the period, and Munford echoes the concern of other writers. Early in the play, the depth of that ignorance is indicated by Guzzle's assertion that a successful Burgess need only be able to eat, drink, sleep, fight, and lie. When pressed to explain the inclusion of fighting and lying, the freeholder maintains that a Burgess needs to protect himself from other legislators in order to transact business and that he must be able to tell his constituents a convincing story of legislative accomplishment, even when he has done nothing. While one may be tempted to attribute Guzzle's comments to cynicism about colonial politics, a later discussion among several voters and their wives makes it obvious that these men and women have little more insight into the workings of government than does Guzzle. Initially, they judge a candidate's worthiness not at all on political philosophy and only minimally on character. Instead, a candidate's social grace, physical appearance, and supposed cleverness are determinative. Only after the timely intervention of Wou'dbe, who attempts to dispel the voters' misunderstandings about the legislative process, does the focus shift from superficialities to more reasonable political concerns. Even then, Wou'dbe is forced to counter his opponents' outrageous campaign promises which are designed to play on the voters' ignorance. The vows of Sir John Toddy to lower the price of rum and of Strutabout to reduce taxes are obviously pledges that they cannot redeem. As Wou'dbe notes, laws, good or ill, are enacted by whole legislatures which are constantly balancing private interest against public good. Despite Wou'dbe's explanations, some of the voters refuse to give over their self-interest and blindly embrace the assurances of the other candidates. Thus, Munford intimates, while voters assert their desire to choose "the wisest, and the best," they may lack the ability to make an informed choice.[11]

As the Paxton Boys incident served to remind us, the American frontier in the eighteenth century was a rough-and-tumble, sometimes violent world. One might naturally assume that with its subject matter and especially its setting, Munford's play would be liberally sprinkled with physical violence and verbal abuse. Such is not the case. The violence of factional party politics in England has no parallel in Munford's Virginia backwoods. The play presents its political contest as a series of individual battles. At most, a loose affiliation is sometimes formed by candidates, but this "ticket" does not seem to have the divisive effect of Whig and Tory politics in England. This is not to suggest that Munford's play is totally devoid of confrontation. In fact, Wou'dbe is challenged to a fistfight by two opponents. But in that instance—and in a later episode when Guzzle attempts to bully a group of voters—offers to fight are met with superior scorn. Wou'dbe points out the disparity between civilized and barbaric methods of settling disputes and forming public policy when he asks rhetorically, "Are candidates to fight for their seats in the house of burgesses" (21). While the only physical violence in the entire play is a farcical beating given a tipsy Sir John by Guzzle's equally drunken wife, Joan, there is a fair amount of verbal abuse, especially from such characters as Sir John, Guzzle, and Strutabout, all of whom resort to insults or threats of violence when their wits fail them.

The major target of Munford's satire is the wooing of the electorate with food and alcohol. Perhaps taking his cue from Hogarth's famous "Election" series (1753–54), Munford paints a vivid picture of the drunken feasting which attended many eighteenth-century English and American campaigns. Most of Munford's stout Virginia freeholders enjoy, but are not swayed by, the traditional "treating" which accompanies the election. As Captain Paunch, a local justice, makes clear, candidates who attempt to buy the voters have supporters only "as long as the liquor is running" (24). But the potential for abuse is embodied by Guzzle, who makes it plain that he will support "the first man that fills my bottle" (17). Guzzle later decides to support Sir John, an equally notorious drunkard, solely because Sir John promises to lower the price of rum. Like most stage drunks in the period, Sir John and Guzzle are played primarily for humor, the assumption being that laughter is the proper response to a man's decision, as Wou'dbe phrases it, to "debase the workmanship of heaven, by making his carcase a receptacle for pollution" (17). But Sir John's venture into politics offers the possibility that private failing may be translated into public disaster. Again, Wou'dbe assumes the proper posture when he repudiates Sir John's bid for election, commenting rather bluntly, "since his folly has induced him to offer himself for a place, for which he is not fit, I must say, I despise him" (19). But Sir John, who is "an honest blockhead" rather than a knave, has some inkling of his actual merit—even in a drunken haze he retires from the campaign when Worthy, the former Burgess and a friend of Wou'dbe, comes out of retirement to stand for election again (22).

As drama *The Candidates* has much to recommend it. The characters are generally well drawn, especially Wou'dbe and his major adversaries, Sir John and Guzzle. A fairly broad spectrum of the colonial backwoods citizenry and attention to linguistic nuances add realism to the play.[12] Much if not all of the action would make entertaining theater. The slapstick scenes between the drunken Guzzles and the besotted Sir John would play particularly well, and the general electioneering scenes at the racetrack offer the type of spectacle which has always appealed to audiences.

But it is as a reflection of American attitudes about democracy and democratic institutions that *The Candidates* has the most to offer. Pointing to the victory of Worthy and Wou'dbe, several critics have maintained that Munford was basically optimistic about the future of democracy in America (Richard Moody, 12; Meserve, 87). But the final quatrain's assurance that legislatures will enact wholesome laws only if the voters elect men rather than coxcombs is less than reassuring given the action of the play and the commentary of some of the characters. Wou'dbe expresses his own reservations in the very first speech in the play: "Must I again be subject to the humours of a fickle crowd? Must I again resign my reason, and be nought but what each voter pleases? Must I again cajole, fawn, and wheedle, for a place that brings so little profit" (14). Worthy intensifies Wou'dbe's point by describing public service as a variety of punishment, a "troublesome office [the voters] have . . . imposed upon me" (23). Worthy, it seems, is only willing to serve because of his regard for Wou'dbe, and that service extracts a severe price: "Myself I'd punish for the man I love" (24). Such rhetoric suggests the ideals of mythic friendship rather than frontier reality. The conflict between such an idealized code of behavior and the actualities of Virginia elections during Munford's life leads Beeman to argue that the play "seems more a description of the way Munford thought things *ought to be* than a description of the way things actually were" (175–76). Historically, Munford's support of Patrick Henry's arguments for freedom in the Virginia House of Burgesses leaves little doubt the backwoods legislator, who later served in the Continental army, was an advocate of democracy. But *The Candidates* suggests that Munford recognized the dangers of the system he embraced and that he assumed his stance with some trepidation.

The comedy of colonial America was in many ways supremely of its time. Less concerned with the traditions of literature than with expressing what was perceived as the new reality of the New World, the comedies of the period are marked by their energy and their exuberance. While appropriating forms from the Old World, these writers turned those borrowings into something uniquely American. Behind these pieces are strong voices, loudly announcing their beliefs, prejudices, fears, and aspirations. Comedy, even satiric comedy, is an essentially hopeful artistic form which acknowledges the flaws in humanity and attempts through laughter to make life more bearable, more enjoyable, or both. As America moved inexorably toward its conflict with England, America's comic dramatists had to some extent provided both models of individual behavior and definitions of national identity. At the war's arrival, both contributions would prove invaluable in forging a new nation.

Colonial Tragedy

Perhaps because colonial life was often filled with distress and suffering, perhaps because most colonial writers deemed contemporary events unworthy of elevated treatment, tragedy as a form had few practitioners in the period. In addition, the three tragedies written during the period all present certain problems for the historian of American drama. Thomas Godfrey's *The Prince of Parthia* was written in 1759 and presented in Philadelphia by David Douglass in 1767, making it the first play by a native colonial American to be produced by a professional company. As the title suggests, however, the American nature of the play is not immediately evident. George Cockings's *The Conquest of Canada; or, The Siege of Quebec,* published in London in 1766 but later produced in Philadelphia by Douglass, can only incidentally be considered American at all. The play celebrates British heroism in what is perhaps best described as a dramatic eulogy for General Wolfe. In both subject and attitude *The Conquest of Canada* is a pro-British historical tragedy, written by an Englishman who happened to be living in America at the time of its composition. Robert Rogers, who was born in Massachusetts, grew up in the New Hampshire backwoods, and was a Ranger during the French and Indian War, wrote what, on the basis of its subject matter, must be considered the first tragedy written on an overtly native topic, *Ponteach; or, The Savages of America.* During the American Revolution, however, Rogers chose to follow the Union Jack. He departed America for England in 1780 and died there in 1795.

Even if one dismisses Cockings's play, the question of what characterizes American tragedy in the colonial period remains. Despite the obvious differences one expects between a play written by a former student of Provost William Smith and one written by a frontiersman, *The Prince of Parthia* and *Ponteach* share several basic attitudes and issues. Both plays start from the premise that history, whether ancient or modern, is instructive. Both provide a discourse on honor and serve to define the nature of manhood for their audiences. Finally, both choose to examine the nature of governance and suggest that despotism inevitably inspires a desire for freedom and a willingness to die rather than compromise that aspiration.

The Prince of Parthia and *Ponteach* are founded on the popular eighteenth-century premise that history is one of the primary means by which man learns to improve himself and his institutions. On both sides of the Atlantic, the eighteenth century rang with the praises of history as a method of obtaining practical knowledge of social and political affairs. Bolingbroke contended that history is "philosophy teaching by examples," while Hume, whose *History of England* began to appear in 1754, maintained that history was "the greatest mistress of wisdom" (Colbourn, 5). These British attitudes were, if anything, amplified by American politicians and thinkers. Notwithstanding the fervent belief of many New Englanders in such Calvinist doctrines as total depravity and predestination, Americans as a whole were firmly committed to the Enlightenment ideal that man's reason would allow him to create a better world. Assured by Whig historians of the unreasonable and ongoing diminution of their constitutional rights as Englishmen, the colonists had taken the first step in what they saw as an attempt to recapture their liberty by separating themselves physically from the oppression of the Old World. Immigration to the New World proved insufficient, however, for most settlers still felt strongly the ties to Great Britain, and the British government, intent upon solidifying its North American holdings, sought to limit colonial freedoms. Cut off from the possible mediating influences of family, friends, and countervailing intellectual forces, the colonists thus came even more fully under the sway of Whig historians such as Burnet, Care, Hulme, and Macaulay.

Adding to the colonists' feelings of estrangement was a pervasive sense that England was infected with a moral corruption which if unchecked would spread to the colonies. To this issue Whig histories spoke loudly. Equally as important as the legal relationship between the people and the Crown was the genuine sense that public action was indivisible from private virtue. Thus, Benjamin Franklin, when contemplating the education of the youth of Pennsylvania, argued forcefully that history would "fix in the Minds of Youth deep Impressions of the Beauty and Usefulness of Virtue of all kinds" (Colbourn, 5–6). Of course, the most famous colonial American pairing of political history and public virtue was made by Patrick Henry who reminded his fellow Burgesses in 1765 that "Caesar had his Brutus; Charles the First his Cromwell; and George the Third—may profit by their example!" With such avid interest in history, it is little wonder that both Godfrey and Rogers chose to dramatize historical events. While one produced a largely fictionalized tale of oriental intrigue and the other an account of parochial happenings on the American frontier, both men were instinctively drawn to a form which spoke with unique authority to the colonists before the Revolution.[13]

It is only by an accident of history that *The Prince of Parthia* became the first play written by an American to be produced professionally in the colonies. David Douglass originally intended to produce *The Disappointment; or, The Force of Credulity* by Thomas Forrest during his 1767 season in Philadelphia. *The Disappointment*, which is more ballad-opera than drama, was pulled from rehearsal by Douglass after certain citizens objected that the play satirized them personally. In fact, it did.

Forrest had set out to ridicule a group of Philadelphians who, believing tales that the pirate Blackbeard had buried treasure on the banks of the Delaware River, had engaged in treasure hunting. Forced to withdraw a colonial piece whose "personal reflections," according to the *Pennsylvania Gazette* (16 April 1767), rendered it "unfit for the stage," Douglass substituted Godfrey's romantic tragedy.

In his oriental tale of romantic and political intrigue, Godfrey conflates the issues of love and honor by using a conventional plot formula. The essential problem of Arsaces—how to balance often conflicting demands of love and honor in a politically and morally corrupt world—is one often examined in Restoration heroic drama. Like Dryden's *Aureng-Zebe*, for example, Arsaces must preserve the woman he loves from the undesired affections of his father, the King, without violating any of his filial or political obligations. Following the practice of Shakespeare, to whom he is obviously indebted for much in the play, Godfrey chooses to explore this dilemma through several characters' parallel predicaments.[14] Godfrey, probably unconsciously, hits on undercurrents in American political life and symbolizes them in the unresolved tensions of the play. The desire for political autonomy, or at the very least equality with Englishmen living in Great Britain, takes the form of the hero's desire to unite with Evanthe and establish himself fully in the adult community. Colonial allegiance to England, on the other hand, is represented in Arsaces's wish to please his father. Godfrey's unconscious conflicts between the urge for independence and fidelity to the homeland create a problematical hero in Arsaces and necessitates a *deus ex machina* ending to conclude the plot.

Godfrey makes the customary distinctions between honorable and dishonorable love but is unable finally to decide which love—that owed to a parent or that felt for a lover—should have precedence. The most obvious example of dishonorable love in the play is Vardanes's lust for Evanthe. While Vardanes, Arcase's younger brother, is capable of uttering all the romantic clichés, he leaves no doubt that Evanthe's reluctance will not deter him. Having failed at romantic overtures and blackmail, Vardanes finally attempts physical assault, an option he does not shun: "Hence coward softness, force shall make me blest."[15] Only slightly more acceptable than Vardanes's lust is the passion of King Artabanus. The aged King attempts to justify his desire on two grounds—his basic nature and the overpowering quality of his love—but Evanthe (as well as the reader) ultimately remains unconvinced. Cast in pastoral hues, the romantic love of Arsaces and Evanthe is, of course, whole-heartedly endorsed. Arsaces, bemoaning his royal obligations, longs for a world in which he is "some humble Peasant's son" and Evanthe is "some Shepherd's daughter on the plain" (27). Such is obviously not to be. That recognition and the specter of the corrupting power of the court (illustrated by the dissolving relationship of Artabanus and his new Queen, Thermusa) mitigates the audience's unreserved acceptance of the young lovers' future happiness. This idyllic love is complicated, moreover, by the lovers' affections for their parents. If Arsaces and Evanthe's love represents a vision of independence, Godfrey suggests that vision is intriguing but dangerous.

Just as honor may, filial devotion may conflict with romantic love. Vardanes, who proves least capable of true romantic love, also lacks any real affection for his father. Though Vardanes focuses his hatred on Arsaces, his comment that "Ambition, glorious fever! mark of Kings, / Gave me immortal thirst and rule of Empire" leaves little doubt about Artabanus's fate if Vardanes becomes his immediate heir (10). When Lysias, a disaffected courtier and confidant of Vardanes, murders the king, Vardanes's desires are merely fulfilled more quickly and violently than Vardanes would have preferred. Godfrey's anxiety about colonial independence becomes, momentarily, emblemized in the ruthless patricide. Paradoxically, Vardanes also represents the kind of despotic ruler the colonists most feared. In contrast, Evanthe and Arsaces are models of filial devotion. In fact, they seem almost willing to abandon their own desires and needs in order to please their fathers. For example, having secured Evanthe from his father as a reward for his military feats, Arsaces is astounded by Evanthe's revelation that his father loves her. Interestingly, his reaction focuses on the effects on his father rather than its impact on his own future happiness: "Ye cruel Gods! I've wrecked a Father's peace, / Oh! bitter thought" (26). Throughout the play Arsaces remains torn between his duty to his father and his love for Evanthe. Godfrey is unwilling or unable to resolve the tension that exists between the characters' conflicting desires for adult love on the one hand and parental approval on the other, between political independence and patriotic loyalty. Artabanus's murder and Arsaces's death are thus *deus ex machina* devices which untangle the plot but do not answer one of the play's pivotal questions.

As a hero and embodiment of the ideals of manhood, Arsaces is something of an odd mixture. As the court officer Phraates's catalogue of Arcases's virtues indicates, Arcases seems to have all of the requisites of the traditional hero: "He's gen'rous, brave, and wise, and good, / Has skill to act, and noble fortitude / To face bold danger, in the battle firm, / And dauntless as a Lion fronts his foe" (7). But while the audience is given little reason to doubt this portrait of the brave warrior prince, the action of the play shifts the focus to Arsaces's personal life. By presenting the issues of love, marriage, and filial devotion as private concerns with public consequences, Godfrey tries to enforce a disjunction between public and private life that his Whiggish principles will not sustain. Godfrey's attempt to generate sympathy for his protagonist by portraying him as a Parthian man of sensibility ironically undermines Arsaces's stature as a public leader. Arsaces's reliance upon and fondness for his emotions is obvious in such lines as "sympathetic passion / Falls like a gushing torrent on my bosom" (20). Though his emotionality and his willingness to believe the best of those around him seem to make Arsaces an admirable man in Godfrey's estimation, they also generate a remarkably passive hero. In fact, Arsaces's passivity compromises his heroism, at least heroism as traditionally defined in heroic literature. While Arsaces's lack of despotic ambition is portrayed positively, his suicide at the end of the play bespeaks a disturbing lack of concern for the public welfare. His death is no final act of defiance and no mere acknowledgment of personal defeat. His is a desire not only to embrace oblivion but also to force upon all of humanity his own egocentric emotional reality: "Now burst ye elements, from your restraint, / Let order cease, and chaos be again" (41). In Arsaces's suicide Godfrey finally resolves the political consequences within his veiled allegory by an infantile wish for anarchy.

While Godfrey's attitude toward his hero seems problematic, his speculations about governance and the effects of tyranny are straightforward. Though not a strict allegory of political possibilities, *The Prince of Parthia* enunciates relatively clearly many of the colonists' concerns and gives "dramatic form to Whiggish ideas" (Silverman, 106).[16] The picture drawn of monarchy stops short of indictment, but illustrates many of its abuses in Artabanus's reign—rule by personal whim rather than law, lack of impartial legal redress, neglect of the public good in favor of personal desire. These abuses are not, of course, directly responsible for the demise of the King. But for Godfrey, "absolute monarchs inhabit a world of suspicions and jealousies" which inevitably erupts in violence (Shuffelton, 20). Vardanes, a nightmare version of Artabanus, exemplifies this world of violence and lust. Arsaces seems to provide a realistic and positive alternative. Unlike Vardanes who sees the common people as a "manyheaded monster multitude," Arsaces unites the populace during the general uprising following his father's murder (10). But Arsaces abandons his people through suicide. Gotarzes, who inherits the throne, is presented throughout the play as a younger and untested version of Arsaces and thus may offer an improvement in the government of Parthia. But the monarchical system, with its endless potential for abuse, remains unchanged. Godfrey's Whiggish critique is obvious but crucial: the quality of any monarchy is contingent almost totally on the personality, good or bad, of the ruler.

As a romantic tragedy in blank verse, Godfrey's play is at best second-rate. Its characters, plot, and images are all conventional for the eighteenth century, and the whole appears a patchwork of material taken from better dramatists. But the play does indicate that colonists were beginning to think of tragedy as an appropriate form through which to express their vision of the world. Like English dramatists before them, American tragedians might displace the action to some remote corner of the globe, but the characters who trod the boards were at their cores Americans.

In both substance and technique, Robert Rogers's *Ponteach* is a much more direct play than *The Prince of Parthia*. Written and published in 1766 while Rogers was in London, the play presents a fictionalized account of Pontiac's rebellion, 1763–66.[17] The play has a split plot with the main action detailing the causes of the war, the Native Americans' preparations, representative events of the conflict, and the eventual defeat of Ponteach's forces. The secondary, romantic plot traces the doomed triangle of Ponteach's two fictional sons, Philip and Chekitan, and Monelia, the daughter of a rival chief. Rogers's penchant for the melodramatic serves to simplify greatly his dramatic universe. Assuming the point of view of the Native Americans, the play is an indictment of English ineptitude and greed on the American frontier. The first scene of the play exposes the basic attitude of the English. McDole, an Indian trader, tells Murphey, a newcomer to the business, "Our fundamental Maxim, is this, / That it's no Crime to cheat and gull an Indian."[18] Herein, suggests Rogers, is the fundamental problem with European activity in America. Europeans are interested in exploiting the inhabitants without regard to the long-term moral or cultural effects on either the indigenous population or themselves. The episode in which Orsbourn and Honnyman cavalierly murder two Native Americans whom they see as "mere savage Beasts" illustrates that the supposed distinctions between the barbarity of the "savages" and the civilized actions of the Europeans were already in danger of disappearing (122). Native American culture is presented as primitive, but enviable in the basic dignity that it assures the individual, the honesty with which its members treat each other and outsiders, and the honorable code of behavior it instills in its men. Ponteach exercises more wisdom and restraint than the British are capable of when he argues that Britain's only justification for usurpation of his lands is that it has something to exchange culturally for what it takes. Ponteach reproaches the British, saying, "If Indians are such Fools, I think / White Men like you should stop and teach them better" (127). Having no honor and no ability to recognize its existence in persons of another culture, the Europeans in the play are obviously inferior. In essence, "the Indian, embodying all the virtues of the noble savage, is set up as a model for white Americans to emulate" (Anderson, 226).

Ponteach, the embodied rustic ideal, foreshadows a host of American frontier heroes. As Winton has noted, "Pontiac . . . is possessed of the Roman virtues as the eighteenth century saw them: magnanimity, generosity, love of country and of liberty" (89). But those "Roman virtues" do not spring from Roman civilization, nor are they the results of his contact with the British. Ponteach, while not strictly speaking Rousseau's "noble savage," does seem to have absorbed from his daily intercourse with Nature a dignity of person and clarity of vision which no one else in the play shares. The contrast with the British is obvious. Less overt but more instructive are the distinctions between Ponteach and his two sons. Chekitan, while sharing his father's sense of duty and desire for freedom, is incapable of gaining the necessary objectivity to be an effective leader. Philip, on the other hand, has the tactical ability of all villains, but his orientation is personal glory and power rather than community good. Philip's European name may be more than mere coincidence. His thirst for power is reminiscent of any number of European despots and would-be tyrants.

While it is tempting to read *Ponteach* as a displaced indictment of British policies toward its colonies, the biography of the author and the date of the play's composition argue against it. Seven years would pass and a tax on tea would be imposed before the colonists would begin to see themselves as Native Americans, and six further years would pass after the "Indian uprising" in Boston harbor before John Smith's dialogue made overt use of the analogy in a dramatic framework. In 1766 the American Revolution was still on a distant psychological horizon. Nevertheless, in a play ostensibly so removed from questions of colonial politics, it is interesting to note that governance is a central issue. If it has no other value to American drama *Ponteach* should serve to remind us of the pervasiveness of political concerns in the eighteenth century.

As an American drama, *Ponteach* is of minimal importance. It introduces for the first time in American colonial drama a Native American protagonist and foreshadows the vogue of the "Indian play" throughout the eighteenth and much of the nineteenth centuries. As formal dramatic literature, the play is a pale imitation of the best neoclassical tragedies. Its blank verse is inflated and awkward; the plot, especially Honnyman's confession of the murder and his tearful parting from his wife and children, is melodramatic; and the characters are for the most part stereotypes. Nevertheless, these shortcomings are somewhat offset by an intriguing native protagonist and a telling social commentary.

Like colonial comedy, the tragedy of the period reflects American authors' attempts to transform the experience of colonial life into art. While the paucity of those efforts and the mediocre products are perhaps as much the result of the aesthetic standards of the day as of any deficiency of American artistry or vision, one does not sense in the tragedies of colonial America the clear voice that one hears in the comedies. The "upstart" colonists' self-consciousness about writing serious art may have inhibited them both politically and artistically. Nevertheless, as the Revolutionary War drew nearer, the foundation had been prepared for an elevated treatment of American struggles and sacrifices. If the comedies of the Revolution were to prove the literary weapons of attack, the tragedies would provide the literary definition and defense for a new people.

2

Drama and the American Revolution

As America's colonial period drew to a close, a significant, though initially imperceptible, shift in personal and collective identity occurred. While act upon act of the British Parliament compromised the political, economic, and personal rights of colonial residents, most of the colonists, who had heretofore regarded themselves as Englishmen living in North America, began to think of themselves to one degree or another as Americans. Ill-conceived policies embodied in the Sugar, Stamp, Tea, Townshend, and "Intolerable" Acts, to name only a few, steadily increased political dissatisfaction and, finally, united the majority of colonials against English policies. As the grim parity of repression enveloped the whole of colonial America and as British and American relations spiraled toward open conflict, the most radicalized Patriots sought to persuade uncommitted citizens of the necessity of independence while equally ardent Loyalists warned of the horrors of rebellion and urged conciliation. Throughout the colonies, the Tories, united through their alliance with the governing British, felt little need to join forces. The Patriots, on the other hand, seeking to replace the traditionally fragmented and parochial concerns of individual colonies with a sense of collective danger and national engagement, utilized various strategies to generate the beginnings of a national consciousness. To inform, inspire, and solicit support from Patriots in other colonies, committees of correspondence linked the merchants of Boston with the planters of Virginia, the Yankee traders of New Haven and Providence with their counterparts in Charleston and Savannah. Though events themselves probably persuaded most people to join either the Patriot or Tory causes, neither side was content to rely upon the power of "facts" alone to establish the validity of its case. Following a pattern found in most English political crises in the seventeenth and eighteenth centuries, the suasive potential of literature was exploited by both parties as each camp used the literary talent at its disposal to argue its position and to secure adherents to its particular viewpoint. American poets such as Francis Hopkinson, Philip Freneau, and John Trumbull pressed their art into the service of the Revolution, as did the more famous essayists of the period—John Dickinson, Samuel Seaburg, and Thomas Paine. Likewise, American dramatists lent their talents to the fray. The potential, and later the reality, of revolution forced both Tory and Patriot playwrights to define themselves, their opponents, and the nature of the issues in a manner that remains both powerful and intriguing more than two hundred years later.

Whig and Tory Dialogues

The most rudimentary form of colonial drama, the dialogue, continued to be popular during the Revolution. Both Patriots and Loyalists were attracted by a straightforward form which allowed the author to announce and develop arguments in an easily accesible entertainment. Like their colonial antecedents, the dialogues of the revolutionary war period are rarely subtle and only minimally significant as drama. Despite their overtly propagandistic purposes and an inclination to rely upon spokespersons rather than fully realized characters, the dialogues nevertheless do provide some rudimentary characterization and contain the bare essentials of dramatic conflict.

The most notable Whig dialogues are attributed to Thomas Paine, whose pamphlet *Common Sense* they greatly resemble. Together his two pieces offer an index to the steady radicalization of the colonists. In *A Dialogue Between General Wolfe and General Gage in a Wood Near*

Boston, which appeared in the Pennsylvania *Journal* on 4 January 1775, the British hero of the French and Indian War attack on Quebec upbraids a humbled Gage for failing to realize that each Briton is endowed with a liberty based upon "immutable laws of nature" and that therefore Americans have every right to object to a king whom they have not "approved." While Paine's intention seems most obviously to point up the flaws of the 1774 Quebec Act (which foreclosed westward colonial expansion by extending Quebec's boundaries to the Ohio and Mississippi rivers and thereby provided a Catholic neighbor for the stoutly Protestant New England and Middle Atlantic colonies), his discourse suggests the possibility of reconciliation. By the appearance of A *Dialogue Between the Ghost of General Montgomery, Just Arrived from the Elysian Fields, and an American Delegate, in a Wood near Philadelphia,* in February of 1776, Paine's vision had been modified by the events of Lexington and Concord and by his own writing of *Common Sense.*[1] Again he presents his audience with a hero whose status as a martyr to liberty makes him a worthy spokesman for the Patriot cause. But in a masterful propaganda stroke, Paine chose an American hero, Richard Montgomery, whose death at the seige of Quebec in December of 1775 had served not only to place him on the same level as Wolfe but also to suggest an ironic parallel between the tyrannical French of the French and Indian War and the English of Paine's own time. In this dialogue, Montgomery argues forcefully that reconciliation is no longer possible and that, like the liberty-loving Greeks and Romans of antiquity, Americans ought to fight for their independence. Both dialogues serve to identify qualities that Paine admired—courage, honor, and love of liberty—with the Patriot cause, while denigrating any opposition as cowardly, dishonorable, and oppressive. Though as propaganda these are effective pieces, their dramatic possibilities are poorly exploited and they are most important as a part of the culmination of the dialogue tradition begun in the earlier colonial era.

The Tory dialogues are, on the whole, a more interesting group of propaganda pieces, though their status as drama is as problematic as similar Patriot efforts. While the writers of the Patriot dialogues decided to approach the conflict through measured rhetorical argument, the Tory writers chose as their main device humor. Tory response to the steady disintegration of colonial America's ties to England was characterized by disbelief at the audacity of the Americans who presumed to dictate to the most powerful empire in the eighteenth-century world, revulsion at the prospective loss of a well-established and ordered social and political system which, from the Tory perspective, needed only minor adjustments, and scorn at the shortsighted and self-serving proponents of independence who wished to embrace a form of government little better than mob rule.

For example, in *Debates at the Robin-Hood Society in the City of New York on Monday Night 19th of July, 1774*, the anonymous author attacks the Patriot leaders in New York City (a notorious Tory bastion even after the outbreak of hostilities) as "pretended friends" whose "insidious acts" have brought the affairs of the colony and the entire continent to a crisis.[2] The author exults in the supposed demise of the Patriot faction, but warns that these "Demons" will again seek to raise the standard of "the PUBLIC, the PEOPLE, the FREE CITIZENS" as a means of advancing their seditious behavior. Though the piece may have been specifically occasioned by the late 1774 meeting of the First Continental Congress in Philadelphia, the author does not seem to be attacking particular individuals. The author relies upon generic blockheads and economic opportunists such as Peter Fight-the-Good-Fight-of-Faith, Matt-of-the-Mint, and Mr. Silver-Tongue, easily identifiable types in the period's political satire, to lampoon effectively the Patriot cause without the necessity of personal caricature. Nevertheless, the "play" remains little more than a series of self-revelatory speeches.

More amusing and in many ways more subtle is *A Dialogue, Between a Southern Delegate, and His Spouse on His Return from the Grand Continental Congress.*[3] Here the obvious purpose of criticizing the political folly of the American congress is nicely incorporated in a traditionally popular piece of farcical action, the domestic squabble. The sprightly exchanges between the henpecked husband and his sharp-tongued spouse point up both the Tory perception of the danger involved in the Patriot's stand against the English and the strong urge for stability which ran counter to the desire for independence. Relying upon a metaphor with great resonance in a century obsessed with discovering and maintaining principles of political, cultural, and familial order, Mary V. V., the ostensible author, asserts that the loyalty the colonists owe to their sovereign is like that a wife owes her husband. The sense of violated "natural order" embodied in the wife's tirade reflects the author's attitude that the Patriots are attempting to usurp a role not rightly theirs. While the piece is more overtly dramatic than other dialogues of the period, it is not good drama. The attempt to locate serious political debate in a farcical action is probably doomed to failure. And, ironically, the dramatic medium itself is rendered problematic in the course of the piece.

Despite the author's obvious sympathy with the wife's political position, her characterization as a virago violates eighteenth-century rules of decorum and undercuts her as a Tory spokeswoman. While the wife continues her indictment as the dialogue ends, her husband has already decided that her objections are "Rant, and Bombast" derived from "Romances and Plays" (38). In other words, the theatrical style of her delivery and the overblown literary sources of her ideas are both suspect.

The most elaborate of the Tory dialogues, known by its short title, *The Americans Roused in a Cure for the Spleen; or Amusement for a Winter's Evening,* was published in Boston in 1775 and is ascribed to Jonathan Sewell, a noted Tory hack.[4] The most distinctive element of the piece is the breadth of colonial society and political opinion to which we are exposed through its seven characters. Following the pattern of other Tory dialogues, intelligence and reason reside with the Loyalist characters, while Puff and Graveairs, the Whig characters, are portrayed as politically naive. The Tory spokesmen systematically answer the Patriot's grievances (poorly advanced by their Whig opponents), and the force of the argument sways the ostensible Whigs to recant their objections to English rule. The model here is obviously rhetorical debate rather than drama, and we should not be startled, therefore, that the piece seems to lack the impact or conflict requisite for good drama.

The dialogue's ability both to delineate conflicting points of view effectively and to vitalize political debate guaranteed its popularity with both Tories and Whigs. Moreover, the use of characters provided the partisan author an additional way of exalting or disparaging a political position, by indicating the types of people who adhered to that philosophy. Since politics is by its nature a collective enterprise, so the theory seems to have been, those chary of their reputations might be affected by seeing their fellow Whigs or Tories in action. While none of the writers was talented enough to transcend the dialogue's obvious limitations, there is little doubt that the dialogues performed their limited function admirably.

Patriot Attacks

The American plays written during the Revolution form, in more than the merely obvious sense of the phrase, a "revolutionary literature." With only one notable exception, the Patriot drama of the Revolutionary War is militantly biased, insists that its auditors accept the validity of its premises, and seeks to destroy its perceived opposition in any manner available. Written by members of a society in tremendous upheaval, this drama, like Soviet plays of the 1920's or the theatre of China's "cultural revolution," reflects a social, cultural, and political world self-consciously simplified by the aesthetics of revolution. To judge these plays strictly as pieces of drama, therefore, may be to guarantee disappointment in our dramatic heritage.[5] Like such seventeenth-and eighteenth-century English antecedents as Crowne's *City Politiques*, Otway's *Venice Preserved*, and Addison's *Cato*, these plays by Warren, Brackenridge, and Leacock are inextricably entwined with their historical moment and a comprehensive understanding of them may depend as much on the ability to recover Whig ideology as on a refined dramatic aesthetic.

It is one of American literary history's more intriguing ironies that the "Founding Fathers" should have found their preeminent dramatic voice in a now nearly forgotten woman, Mercy Otis Warren. Aligned by birth, marriage, and friendship with many of the leading Massachusetts Patriots, Warren wrote as many as five pamphlet plays, extending over a seven-year period, on issues springing from the Patriots' struggle for freedom. Her first play, *The Adulateur* (1772), is an indictment of Thomas Hutchinson, the last royal governor of Massachusetts before the outbreak of overt hostilities. She continued her attacks on Hutchinson, forecasting his demise in *The Defeat* (1773). After Hutchinson fled to England in 1774, Warren roundly lambasted his supporters in *The Group* (1776). Two other plays, *The Blockheads* (1776), which portrays the British occupation and later evacuation of Boston, and *The Motley Assembly* (1779), which decries effete social attitudes during the Revolution, are often attributed to her.[6] Although she never saw a play produced, her sensitive reading, especially of Shakespeare and Molière, prepared her well to deliver the first dramatic assaults of the period.

Set in Upper Servia (Boston), the original version of *The Adulateur* details the greed of Rapatio (Hutchinson) and his clique and the response of a group of Patriots headed by Brutus (Warren's brother, James Otis).[7] Although the finished product shows some signs of a rather haphazard construction, its energy and intense emotion tend to overshadow such considerations. In sum, *The Adulateur* is a scathingly effective condemnation of Hutchinson. Portrayed as a man so desirous of position and wealth that he would repudiate his heritage, betray his family, friends, and country, and ignore his own conscience, Rapatio is in effect little more than a two-dimensional personification of political evil. The Patriots, reflecting Warren's obvious bias, are little better drawn. They seem mere outraged voices of freedom lacking any significant individuality. The play reflects its neoclassical roots not only in its ideological commitments to public virtue and love of liberty embodied in the long-suffering Romans who oppose Rapatio, but also in the manifest Patriot desire for order and decorum. The play's imagery, with its reliance upon nature as an index to the relative merits of the parties, is conventional. The ending, which expresses the gloomy fear that public virtue may return only after "murders, blood, and carnage, / Shall crimson all these streets," points up at once one of the more interesting elements of Warren's plays and the dangers of using an ahistorical aesthetic to judge them.[8] Without a recognition that the press of events and a desire to influence future attitudes and actions forced Warren to end her play without resolving the conflict around which she had constructed her action, the reader is left with a sense that Warren's art failed her, that she was unable to provide an artistically satisfying closure to the piece.

Published, like *The Adulateur*, in two installments in the Boston *Gazette*, *The Defeat* is a slight effort which, because of its fragmentary nature, is often seen as an "incomplete extension of *The Adulateur*" (Franklin, xiii). In the first installment, Warren projects through a series of selected scenes the psychological and political downfall of Rapatio. She enhances her psychological portrait of Rapatio by presenting soliloquies which more fully depict her villain's internal life. Despite his obvious desire for fame and power, his greed is apparently insufficient to suppress a "natural" horror of his crimes. Rapatio himself acknowledges, "Yet spite of pride, of avarice, or revenge / I tremble at the purpose of my soul" (2). In the play's climax, Rapatio and his minions are defeated and allegorical characters of Freedom and Happiness are restored. In an obvious bit of wish-fulfillment, Warren ends her second play with Rapatio repenting as he is about to be executed. The publication of incriminating letters from Hutchinson to friends in England prompted Warren to renew her attack in a second installment. Again, she drives home her message by having Rapatio confess his desire to "Plunder, Shackle, and Oppress" (9). She also chooses this occasion to single out for special vilification one of her opposites in the Hutchinson camp, Jonathan Sewall. Implicitly arguing for a distinction between her art and that of Sewall, Warren asserts that Sewall's work flows from a "prostituted Pen / Long Hackney'd in Venality's low Walks" and that he is incited by a desire for "Lucre" which "reigns his Deity and Guide" (11). Obviously, tyranny for Mercy Warren presents as pernicious a danger to art as it does to civil government.

Warren's next effort, *The Group*, a farce in two acts, attacks the sixteen individuals who, after the abrogation of the colonial charter, accepted royal appointments to the Massachusetts Council, thereby stripping the citizenry of a cherished electoral voice in the colony's affairs. Although a bitingly effective work of political propaganda, the piece would produce relatively weak theater. As in her earlier work, her original audience's awareness of the political situation and the personalities involved may have persuaded Warren that fully dramatizing the conflict was unnecessary. Despite a lack of onstage conflict, Warren differentiates her characters a bit more carefully than hitherto. Ironically, the loss of Hutchinson (Rapatio) as a central villain has the positive effect of compelling Warren to speculate on the motivations of the other members of the Hutchinson clique. Warren reiterates her contention that these men are not truly committed to the Loyalist ideology but have selfishly betrayed their native land and their consciences. She heightens her audience's sense of the magnitude of their countrymen's treason by presenting several of the characters' feeble attempts at rationalizing away their qualms. While potentially humanizing, these episodes actually serve Warren as another opportunity to mock the greed, hypocrisy, and immorality of her opponents and to scorn their willingness to sacrifice everything for personal advancement. In the end, she seems to suggest that Hateall, the most hardened and forthright of the Loyalists, is typical when he says, "Tho' hell and all its hell-hounds should unite / I'll not recede to save from swift perdition / My wife, my country, family, or friends" (5). Her characters are occasionally hyperbolic, but their sentiments are clearly expressed in the common vein of political polemic. Warren effectively evokes the social, educational, and political distinctions among her characters, but with the exceptions of the rantings of Hateall and the literary ostentation of Beau Trumps, the dialogue is unexceptional.

Warren's last two efforts bring her keen wit and sharp tongue to bear on events following the outbreak of hostilities. *The Blockheads; or, The Affrighted Officers*, published as a pamphlet play in 1776, satirizes the English and Tory retreat from Boston after the American forces secured control of Dorchester Heights, making the British position in the city untenable. For the first time Warren turns her attention directly on the British, whom she portrays as not only cowardly and corrupt but also unwilling to keep promises made to their Tory supporters. The vaunted skill of the British army, often cited before the Revolution as a reason for caution, is portrayed as a bugbear. In fact, Warren asserts through Shallow, it is Patriot arms that are feared. In a moment of earthy candor the

British officer confesses, "I would rather sh-t my breeches than go without these forts to ease myself" (14). Warren structures the play around two distinct but related actions. The primary plot traces the British reaction to the seige, the desperate attempts of the British command to reverse the course of events, and their final ignominious retreat. The second plot centers on a Tory family, the Simples, and details their fates as British sympathizers. While not great drama, *The Blockheads* is more than a mere "conversation piece" (Anthony 93). The bickering of the Simples has a ring of farcical realism to it, and the play is strongest when Warren focuses on Simple's regrets at having lost his land and friends, on his wife's foolish determination to follow the British so that she can maintain her dubious status as a gentlewoman, and on their daughter's mercenary plan to use a marriage to the impotent Lord Dapper as a springboard to the fashionable world of London.[9]

By 1779 the major military campaigns in the northern colonies were at an end and life in Boston took on a more normal pace. To most New Englanders the fighting's shift to the south meant not only a return of commerce and trade, but also a revitalization of a social life which had been greatly restricted by the British occupation. Against this political and social situation, Warren penned her next play, *The Motley Assembly*. This work represents a shift in interest for Warren, for it is the social rather than the political world which consumes her dramatic energies. Specifically, Warren lambastes those colonials who paid lipservice to the Patriot's cause while at the same time preferring British culture to that of America. She also decries the unwillingness of these selfish individuals to acknowledge the connection between the political and the social worlds. The particular objects of her satire are the "assemblies," or dances, sponsored by prominent Bostonians. In a series of loosely connected scenes Warren reveals the hypocrisy of the ostensibly neutral socialites, the inanity of women who crave stylish parties rather than liberty, and the righteous indignation of Whig officers at the snubs of "genteel" young ladies. Careless, a navy captain, provides the final comment on the matter by hoping that on his return from sea, he may find in Boston either "a great reformation, or a thoro' extirpation" of the Tories (15). Thus Warren's satire operates against both Tories and Whigs. Since the Tory sympathies of the socialites are manifest, the folly of their effete entertainments is compounded. Not only are these assemblies intrinsically wasteful and debased activities, but they are also ineffective in deflecting Whig suspicions. But the Tory folly has its Whig counterpart. The tone of the piece as a whole and the exchange of Aid and Careless that ends the play clearly indicate the author's belief that the Whigs are foolish to vitiate their revolutionary zeal and distort their clear sense of the enemy by consorting with Tories in a social arena.

If Mercy Warren is the premiere Patriot satirist of the Revolution, then Hugh Henry Brackenridge might justly lay claim to the title of the Revolutionary War's heroic tragedian. While Warren sought to ridicule the Tories and British into submission, Brackenridge chose another tactic. As his more famous novel *Modern Chivalry* (1792–1815) indicates, Brackenridge was well aware that satire is a most effective method of anatomizing folly. But satire's strength is at once its weakness. Satire's reliance upon inference renders enunciation of its unstated norms a redundancy at best and an insult at worst. Yet a sense of collective ideals, a sense often garnered as much through imaginative rendition as through any carefully articulated presentation, is essential to the success of any revolutionary enterprise. It was this need that Brackenridge sought to redress. The results of his effort are his two sober poetic dramas, *The Battle of Bunkers Hill, A Dramatic piece of five acts, in heroic measures* (1776) and *The Death of General Montgomery in storming the city of Quebec* (1777). Both plays attempt to transform, through an American dramatic art, Patriot military defeats into triumphant testimonials to a new national spirit and to translate colonial military heroes into martyrs to American liberty.

The Battle of Bunkers Hill develops through a series of counterbalanced scenes that contrast the British and American armies before, during, and after the battle. Despite Brackenridge's testimony that his students at a Maryland school performed the play, the lack of concern for its theatricality is rather obvious. The stage direction at the beginning of the third act, "Enter GARDINER, with seven hundred men," indicates that the author is more intent upon historical accuracy than readily producible theater.[10] Although most modern readers find it cumbersome, Brackenridge's use of verse (which he handles adequately) gives the characters and events the dignity and substance the author desired. The characterizations are simplistically appropriate to the historic moment and the author's biases. The British are fighting merely "to preserve their reputation in the world," while "the Americans fight to preserve freedom and to deserve the sacrifices of their fore-fathers" (Silverman, 285). The mettle of the American fighting man is personified in General Warren who uses his last breath to admonish his fellow patriots "Be now abjur'd, never to yield the right / The grand deposit of all-giving Heaven / To man's free nature, that he rule himself" (260).

Montgomery's expedition against Quebec, the first unmitigated military disaster of the war for the Americans, was the perfect subject for Brackenridge's special talents. Like many of its epic antecedents, *The Death of General Montgomery* seeks to define the nature of a national hero and to extol him as a model. Prowess in force of arms, willingness to endure personal sacrifice for the public good, and the stoic acceptance of imminent death in the cause of liberty are lauded not only in Montgomery but also in several of his junior officers, men whose youth makes them more pathetic figures. The play insinuates that such courage and fortitude must eventually carry the day, despite the sad outcome of this battle. Against the Americans are ranged the cruel and savage British who reveal their depravity by repudiating the agreed upon terms of the American surrender and giving captured Americans to Indians to be tortured and killed. An interesting mixture of poetic and dramatic elements, the play shows some development in Brackenridge's dramatic skill. Burr's elegiac address to his dead friends and superiors suggests the oratorical genesis of the piece. But the play is not without its effective theatrical moments. For example, on the heels of Burr's funeral comments after Montgomery's death, the ghost of General Wolfe rises from the Plains of Abraham, decries British tyranny, mourns his unintentional part in extending English control in North America, and forecasts the birth of an American nation "'stablished in truth," whose history shall be one of "peerless glory and immortal acts".[11]

Lying generically somewhere between the satiric works of Warren and the heroic plays of Brackenridge is *The Fall of British Tyranny; or, American liberty triumphant. The First campaign.* (1776), authored by John Leacock.[12] Like both Warren and Brackenridge, Leacock is intent upon bringing any undecided colonists into the American camp while excoriating Britain and her sympathizers. But unlike his two contemporaries, Leacock is not content solely to extol the American cause or to ridicule the British. His formal choice of a "tragicomic" vehicle indicates the artistic decision to balance his satiric indictment of the English with an heroic, American alternative. Such a strategy provided the original audience with a psychologically soothing way of repudiating British failings while salvaging the beloved "English" tradition that George III's government seemed determined to destroy. The complex interaction of modes in the work produces a drama whose formal tensions reflect the conflicts of the era more fully than any other play of the time.

The play's prefatory material—a dedication penned by one of Leacock's alter egos, Dick Rifle, an anonymous preface and poem, "The

Goddess of Liberty," and a prologue by Peter Buckstail, another Leacock pseudonym—reveal a dialogic impulse well suited to Leacock's political purposes. Rather than relying upon a single voice of Patriot outrage, Leacock carefully creates a revolutionary chorus by harmonizing potentially disparate dictions, tones, imageries, and cultural and political perspectives. For example, Rifle's dedication is a masterful piece of personal invective rendered in the contemptuous vein of much political discourse in the period. Scornfully directed at the British officials in America, especially those working for the so-called Scottish faction at George III's court, Rifle taunts those who are now easily identified by the "American characters and letters of blood on [their] posteriors" (285). The dedication is immediately followed by a preface suffused with moral indignation. Primarily an attempt to give religious sanction to the rebellion, the preface makes its case chiefly by using carefully chosen Biblical imagery and quotations and by equating the divinely inspired wisdom of Solomon with the sentiments of Paine's *Common Sense.* "The Goddess of Liberty," as its title suggests, further broadens the suasive base of the prefatory material to include an idealistically couched appeal to classical, anti-despotic political and poetic traditions. Immediately, however, Leacock counterbalances the elevated diction and poetic elegance of his apotheosis to Liberty with the chilling menace of Peter Buckstail, the frontiersman, whose threats of hanging and tar-and-feathering suggest the more direct reality of life in revolutionary America. Having read and/or heard the prefatory material, the audience has been educated to a new, revolutionary aesthetic which seeks to subsume diverse artistic impulses to the singular ideological purpose of American liberty.

Unsurprisingly, Leacock continues his basic pattern of alternating attempts to build colonial consensus with his attacks on the British in the play itself. This is particularly true in the first two acts in which Leacock contrasts the machinations of Bute's party with the upright and public-spirited deliberations of America's friends in the English Parliament, headed by Lord Wisdom, William Pitt, the Earl of Chatham. The first act is devoted to a character study of Bute and his cabal. In scene after scene, Leacock exposes the determination of Paramount and his colleagues to reduce not only America but also England to servile dominions which they may rule in the autocratic vein of France or Spain. The effect of this expose is, of course, to diminish American responsibility for the conflict. As Paramount's last speech suggests, America has no real option—the war has been forced upon the colonies by Paramount's ambition: "The fate of England and America is now fixed, irrevocably fixed;

the storm is ready to burst; the low'ring clouds portend their fate my glory, there fall my triumph" (302). This point is reiterated in the second act discussions among America's English friends.[13] Lord Wisdom, for example, acknowledges that the pervasive corruption in English governmental and military institutions renders hopes for a peaceful political reconciliation futile.[14] Summing up his despair in highly charged Biblical style, Chatham describes England as "sheep without a shepherd."

Having expounded in some detail on the English political causes of the Revolution, Leacock turns his attention to their American consequences. The remainder of the play, set in various locales in America and Canada, serves as a Patriot chronicle of the early days of the Revolution. In the first three brief scenes, set in Boston, Leacock uses dialogues among common people to suggest the colonies' psychological and political movement toward revolution and independence. He then follows those with two scenes showing a cowardly Gage thrown into confusion by his forces' defeat at Lexington and Concord. Shifting the action to the countryside, Leacock provides a long, delightful inversion of the pastoral colloquy in which two American shepherds describe in detail the British defeat at Lexington. Returning to Boston, Leacock introduces Clarissa, a Patriot matron, the morning after the battle of Bunker's Hill. Informed that she has lost her husband, son, and brother in the battle, Clarissa reveals herself the model of patriotic fervor by insisting that she and others must take courage from her family, "martyrs to liberty," and continue the fight for independence (328).

The fourth act divides its attention between English attempts to incite rebellion among slaves in the southern colonies and the British reaction to the battle of Bunker's Hill. Leacock carefully distinguishes the British-inspired slave uprising from the Patriot revolution, both as to impetus and effect. The slaves are depicted as a subhuman species whose native savagery is no match for the duplicitous English who intend to sell them back into slavery the moment the Patriots are crushed. Though Leacock is ideologically sympathetic to the human desire for freedom, the slaves' longing for an anarchic, Hobbesean state of nature obviously distinguishes them from the colonists whose new society will be mediated by reason's civilizing influence. The British exploitation of the slaves damns them once again as oppressors whose talk of freedom is wholly self-serving. Epitomized by Lord Kidnapper, the instigator of the plan, who spends his time offstage in his cabin frolicking with his personal trollops, the British are morally little better than the savages they attempt to enlist. When the scene shifts back to Boston at the end of the act, the

British fare only slightly better. In Massachusetts, the British are not lying sensualists; they are merely cowardly and inept. Like Lord Kidnapper's starving crew in Virginia, the Boston commanders and their troops suffer most acutely not from honorable battle wounds but from hunger. Outmaneuvered by Washington and unwilling to risk their lives in battle, Gage and his fellows hide in their garrison painfully aware after their pyrrhic victory at Bunker's Hill that America will not provide them the easy victories that they had anticipated.

The brief final act traces the American campaign in Canada and the reaction of Washington and his high command to the capture of Allen and the death of Montgomery. The first two scenes contrast the heroism of Allen with the arrogance and brutality of the British commander of Montreal, General Prescott. While Allen may seem a bit overdrawn, his defiant "Shun slav'ry more than death" as he is being put into irons in a British dungeon effectively suggests the new "American" heroism (343). That theme is continued in the last two scenes of the play, which conclude Leacock's report of the Canadian campaign. Here Leacock repeats the familiar tale of Arnold's rugged trek to join Montgomery, the death of Montgomery, and the wounding of Arnold at the siege of Quebec. From these examples of courage comes new resolve for Washington and his command to renew the fight with increased vigor and to die rather than submit to British tyranny.

As the plot synopsis suggests, with its five acts, twenty-five scenes, and action on both sides of the Atlantic, *The Fall of British Tyranny* has a scope unparalleled in other Patriot dramas. While the play's subject matter naturally limits its influence, it does continue the process of defining the American hero, the man who seems somehow to supply rather than to embody national virtues. The play's heroes, not only Washington and Arnold but also the Massachusetts shepherds, presage one of the distinctive features of many American heroes—they are, in fact, people who don't really belong to American society at all. They are self-created individuals who define themselves outside of social conformity. Some American dramatists would soon attribute moral superiority on the basis of nationality, but Leacock resists the temptation to suggest that Americans, as a nation, are somehow more morally upright than other peoples. Instead, in Lord Wisdom and his colleagues, Leacock allows the British a degree of decency and idealism that is utterly lacking in any other Revolutionary play. Though it is obvious that *The Fall of British Tyranny* is propaganda, it is equally obvious that this is by far the most sophisticated example of Whig political drama in the period. Also of enduring significance is Leacock's tendency to frame national issues in terms of the lives of common people. The resulting comprehensiveness, stemming perhaps from comedy's tendency to subsume all classes and types into its world, seems particularly appropriate to the drama of a fledgling nation which loudly touted its belief in the ideals of democracy. Leacock also manages to tailor his language to his characters more consistently than other Patriot writers. Unlike too many of Warren's and Brackenridge's speeches, in which the reader/viewer hears a disembodied emotion, appropriate or not to the particular speaker, one hears in Leacock's play distinctive voices. Bute's insidious plotting, Clarissa's grief, Cudjo's eagerness to rebel, and Arnold's heroic ire all find apt expression.

The engagement of these plays with the historical situation inevitably has consequences that inform our evaluation of them. Like most political propaganda, they were produced in haste with a minimum of artistic polishing. Positions needed to be set out, and Warren, Brackenridge, and Leacock chose vehicles which did just that, often cleverly, always emphatically and uncompromisingly. Even in their own day these efforts (or those of the Patriots' Tory counterparts) would have been found artistically crude and often politically obnoxious, an estimation which on the whole seems fair two hundred years after the events. While making comparisons with the deliberately rendered and poetically dynamic chronicles of, say, a Shakespeare or Marlowe might seem preposterous, still, before dismissing out of hand a piece such as Leacock's *The Fall of British Tyranny*, we probably would be well served to speculate on how different a play *Richard II* might have been had Shakespeare been writing while Richard was in Pomfret Castle.

Tory Defense and Patriot Demur

Though the outcome of the American Revolution may seem to have reduced the Tories' literary opposition to little more than historical aberrations, Tory writers represented a sizable minority opinion during the Revolution and they did venture into the field against their Whig enemies. Naturally, Tories rarely exposed themselves to the rage of Whig mobs in Patriot strongholds such as Boston by speaking out against the Revolution, but the story was different in predominately Tory areas such as New York. Nevertheless, despite the occasional dialogue or play, Tories seemed less inclined to engage in literary warfare than their Patriot counterparts. Tory reluctance to write drama can be explained in a number of ways. As suggested in the preceding chapter, many colonial areas, including the future Tory strongholds of New York City and the interior of South Carolina, shared a deep-seated ambivalence to the theater and drama. Moreover, any theatrical cravings the inhabitants of these areas had were often supplied by British troops with well-financed and organized amateur productions. In addition, though the Loyalists who attended the theater may have become part of a devoted audience, that devotion did not translate into dramatic production (Brown, 160). Even those Loyalists who felt momentarily secure and were inclined to experiment with drama may have hesitated to engage in obvious partisan literary activity while the issue remained unresolved. In other words, like the Loyalists in Warren's *Motley Assembly*, they may well have decided that a studied neutrality was best for business. Finally, many of the Loyalists (and indeed some Whigs) were such cultural Anglophiles that they may have been psychologically unable to declare, even implicitly, their dramatic independence. Certainly such was the charge leveled at descendants of both Whigs and Tories by Emerson in 1837. For whatever reason, we have, in fact, only one noteworthy example of Loyalist drama, *The Battle of Brooklyn* (1776).

As one might expect, *The Battle of Brooklyn* has much in common ideologically with the Tory dialogues. Formally, however, this anonymous piece closely resembles the satiric plays of Mercy Warren. Taking as its subject matter the disastrous defeat of Washington by General William Howe and his brother, Admiral Lord Richard Howe, at Long Island in August of 1776, the play ridicules the high command of the Patriot army. Using techniques similar to those employed in *The Blockheads*, *The Battle of Brooklyn* is designed to undermine Patriots' faith in their leadership and to suggest that the moral failures of their commanders will inevitably translate into military fiascos such as the one portrayed.

The first of the farce's two acts establishes the debased characters of the Patriot leaders. In the play's first scene, Stirling, one of the Patriot generals, exposes himself as a drunken, dishonest coward. This is followed by a meeting between two American colonels who reveal that they have used their offices to steal horses and cattle from the inhabitants of Long Island. Dishonesty of another kind is the subject of a discussion between General Horatio Gates's wife and her maid Betty which divulges the impotence of Benjamin Harrison and adulterous lechery of George Washington. A council of the American generals reiterates Stirling's folly and exposes Washington's misgivings about the Revolution. The final scene of the act reveals that Putnam hopes to use the Revolution to impose a

Puritan theocracy on the colonists and to seize the estates of Tories. The second act, whose first three scenes describe the battle in some detail, is most interesting for its last scene, in which Stirling and Sullivan's servants congratulate themselves on having escaped the slaughter and decide to renew their allegiance "to the most admirable and virtuous Prince that ever swayed sceptre."[15] The bitter invective and author's delight in suggesting the worst of the opposition gives the farce a certain vigor.

Like most revolutions, the American fight for independence inclined to eradicating political nuance and to making simplistic patriotism a public virtue. Thus, the revolution's dramas tended to demand a political conformity which was, strictly speaking, at odds with the ideals they supposedly espoused. These contradictions were not completely lost on American writers in the period. While the literary efforts of most Patriots were given over strictly to advocating the cause of independence, one Patriot's voice was raised not only to support American liberty but also to warn that American intolerance in the name of patriotism threatened to replace British tyranny with a domestic variety that was potentially more destructive. Probably written between 1777 and 1779, Robert Munford's *The Patriots* probes the nature of loyalty to country, examines the operation of individual conscience in the highly charged atmosphere after the outbreak of hostilities, and advocates political forbearance (Baine, 74). While the play is formally indebted to the works of Farquhar and Steele, the themes of xenophobia and superpatriotism are definitely American.[16]

Munford chooses to wed his political commentary to a traditional romantic comedy plot whose three separate courtships provide him the opportunity to draw telling comparisons between affairs of the heart and the world of politics. In the farcical plot, Isabella, who is "resolved not to love a man who knows nothing of war and Washington," is successively wooed by two descendants of Plautus's Miles Glorioso and ends the play without a husband.[17] In the second plot, derived from such sentimental comedies as Steele's *The Conscious Lovers*, a disguised George Worthy attempts to seduce Melinda Heartfree through a sham marriage. When his plan is thwarted, he repudiates his evil intentions, secures Melinda's heart and hand, and then discovers (in typical romance fashion) that she is the long-lost niece of Meanwell, one of the play's tolerant heroes. In the sententious, principal plot, Trueman and Mira finally marry after overcoming the opposition of Brazen, her superpatriot father, who wrongly thinks Trueman a Tory.

Intertwined with the usual romantic comedy material is a discourse on the nature of political and personal loyalty and the necessity of tolerance in periods of crisis. Munford chooses to personify these issues in two contrasting groups—the self-proclaimed protectors of the public good and their supposed enemies. The former comprises the local Committee of Safety who have set as their task the ferreting out of all Tories. Brazen is typical of his fellows: "a violent patriot without knowing the meaning of the word" who "is fully resolved that nobody will tyrannize over him, but very content to tyrannize over others" (449). Some, like Brazen, have assumed their positions out of a misguided sense of patriotic duty. Others, like Summons, seek personal advancement. Still others, like Strut, hope to disguise their cowardice behind jingoistic bombast. Whatever their motives, they lack the political sophistication, intellectual acuity, and, perhaps most important of all in Munford's estimation, the compassion to rule well. The Committee's political naiveté is embodied in the sinister success of Tackabout, whose patriotic activities include damning the ministry, abusing the king, vilifying the parliament, and cursing the Scots. Unfortunately, Tackabout, one of the Committee's leading informants, is a Tory. Compounding the Patriots' lack of sophistication is their inability to discern that their ideals and their methods are in direct conflict. At key junctures in the action, the leaders of the Committee enunciate positions that indicate that the ideals of the Revolution are for them little more than political slogans. Strut, for example, argues that wise men should be excluded from politics because "they are always starting doubts and creating divisions; divisions are dangerous" (459). Yet, of course, the right to dissent both individually and collectively is exactly what the Patriots are fighting for. Arguments for justice, which formed the core of the Patriot indictment of English colonial policies, also seem to have little meaning for the Committee. At the examination of the Scots, an incredulous Brazen answers a demand for proof with the assertion that "suspicion is proof" (461). Finally, Munford indicts these men for their complete indifference to the suffering which they cause. The Committee's callous disarming of the innocent Scots almost guarantees that they will be the victims of mob violence.[18] Brazen's refusal to allow Mira to marry Trueman, the man she loves, is the most private injury in the play, but in the play's comic universe it is, of course, the most telling, since it aligns the Committee with the comic oppression that must be overcome.

Although the Scots are portrayed as the innocent targets of the Committee's witchhunt, Munford's most significant critique comes through his idealized comic lovers. In typical comic style, the young men and women in the play are in rebellion against the folly, political and personal, of their elders. Trueman and Meanwell are obviously the spokesmen for

Munford's ideal of moderation and tolerance. As Meanwell notes, "I hope my zeal against tyranny will not be shown by bawling against it, but by serving my country against her enemies; and never may I signalize my attachment to liberty by persecuting innocent men, only because they differ in opinion with me" (450). The political intolerance in the public world generates two temporarily disruptive social events in the private world of the play. Interestingly, both take the form of potentially compromised feminine chastity. First, Brazen's refusal to allow Mira to marry Trueman forces his daughter to choose between a daughter's duty and a woman's love. Of course, romantic love wins and the audience applauds her choice. But her danger is implicit in the language she uses to accept Trueman's proposal to elope: "I will play the obedient mistress that I may sooner learn to act the dutiful wife" (477). The second event, the near-destruction of Melinda, suggests the insidious example that is being set in the community. Although George's base actions are not directly attributable to his political persecution, there is the suggestion that had he not been forced by the political climate to assume an identity other than his own he would not have been tempted to betray his better principles. Certainly that seems to be the implication of Meanwell's comment that the influence of "political enthusiasm" may compel "social virtues" to be "hid under the disguise of time-serving civility" (497).

As the Revolutionary war drifted toward its peaceful conclusion in Paris, the former colonists began to contemplate their uncertain future. They knew well enough that they no longer wished to be British, and temporarily they could find comfort in their old colonial identities. But on the not-too-distant horizon loomed the prospect of a new nation, a nation which they would build, politically, economically, and culturally. Among the cultural tasks before the new nation was the discovery or development of a distinctly American literature of which the drama would be a part. Almost immediately the cries for American themes, American characters, American forms, and an American dramatic language arose which would become perennial in American theater circles. Though European dramatic and theatrical influences remained strong in America after the Revolution, American drama was well into its childhood when the nation was born.

3

Initial Experiments
in the New Republic

In the eight-year course of the American Revolution a group of patriots, some reluctantly, others enthusiastically, transformed thirteen fragmented colonies into a tenuously united nation. As the last vestige of English power in America marched out of New York City in 1783, America's political freedom was a reality. But its cultural independence was, as yet, a dream. Though the Revolutionary War proved as much the genesis of America's culture as its nationality, America's rebellion against British cultural hegemony continued long after the political issue had been settled.

As American dramatists turned their attentions from formative military and political conflicts to the country's emerging domestic life, they faced two contradictory demands from their audiences. On the one hand, cultural independence was the order of the day, and viewers clamored for a new drama to supplant the last vestiges of the discredited English/European influence. The citizens of the new republic wanted a nationalistic drama in which American characters in American settings would forcefully express American sentiments. On the other hand, the aesthetic sensibilities of the audience had been formed by viewing and reading European, and especially British, plays. Neither American playwrights nor their audiences were prepared for the tension that arose when a new nationalistic ideology was adapted to the dramatic conventions of a repudiated culture. Writers and audiences recognized almost intuitively that the conventional formal models available to American dramatists were, in effect, ideologically suspect. The clash between ideology and aesthetics that had been easily ignored in a revolutionary environment began to be acknowledged not only in critics' reviews but also in playwrights' prologues and prefaces. Throughout the early Republican period, American artists self-consciously sought to minimize the influence of their European dramatic heritage—or at least to claim that their plays sprang from American impulses even as the plays themselves conformed to the rules of European dramatic aesthetics. Although American playwrights would not make major contributions to dramatic form for more than a century, they were quickly able to provide an American coloring to theme, character, setting, and language. The process of developing a new drama for a new nation had begun in earnest.

Royall Tyler and Nationalistic Comedy

Like most of his contemporaries, Royall Tyler, the first major American playwright after the Revolution, was not a professional writer. Trained in law at Harvard, Tyler was by turns soldier, suitor to John Adams's daughter, lawyer, novelist, Chief Justice of the Vermont Supreme Court, and Professor of Jurisprudence at the University of Vermont. Nevertheless, throughout his varied life, Tyler maintained a strong interest in the theater. After the sojourn in New York that resulted in the production of *The Contrast* and the now lost *May Day in Town*, Tyler saw only two others of his plays (*The Farm House* and *The Georgia Spec*) mounted by professional companies (Tanselle, 82–86). Tyler nevertheless continued to write drama, adapting Molière's *The Doctor in Spite of Himself*, transforming an episode from Cervantes' *Don Quixote* into *The Island of Barrataria*, and writing at least three sacred dramas based on Old Testament material. But it is Tyler's first play, *The Contrast*, produced at New York's John Street Theatre in April of 1787, which has guaranteed his place in the history of American drama.

The theme of *The Contrast* is forthrightly nationalistic, appropriate to the post–Revolutionary War period of artistic jingoism. Americans, the play contends, are generally moral, honest, noble, unpretentious, and clear-sighted people—unless corrupted by decadent Europeans, in this case the effete English.[1] Represented in the play by the foppish Anglophile Billy Dimple, who espouses the supposedly debased tenets of Lord Chesterfield, European life is presented as morally degenerate and economically irresponsible. Dimple is an American, however, and that fact adds an interesting twist to what otherwise would have been redundant satire after the propaganda of the Revolution. Dimple's willingness to adopt an English moral and social model suggests the precariousness of the cultural identity that flowed from national independence. Overt political influence might have ended when the Redcoats abandoned their redoubts, but British social attitudes and values, long admired by Americans, still held many captive. Indeed, according to the play, English decadence had already begun to enslave a new generation. As Seibert has noted, "the play reveals the contrast between Americans who are themselves and those who try to be something they are not, between dowdy virtue and the supposedly fashionable deceit and selfishness, between independence and servility" (10).

Built around a series of counterpointed scenes and characters, *The Contrast* attempts to answer the perceived need for a new native drama by grafting American characters and attitudes on to the comedy of manners as reconceived by Sheridan. Since probity, not wit, was the dominant aesthetic criterion of early Republican drama, the central action centers on the fate of a sentimental couple, Maria and Colonel Manly, who secure each other only after Maria's engagement to Dimple, the son of an old family friend, is voided by her indignant father, who discovers that Dimple is a wastrel and a lecher. The nationalistic temper of the play is everywhere evident, but it finds its most serious expression in the action and speech of Manly. Late of the Continental Army, Manly is the first in a long series of eighteenth- and nineteenth-century embodiments of idealized American manhood whose central concern, both on and off the battlefield, is their nation's moral and political health. Unable to divorce political well-being from national morality, Manly arrives in New York seeking financial assistance for members of his wartime "family" (the soldiers whom he has commanded), only to find a world quickly abandoning duty in favor of self-gratification. Echoing *The Motley Assembly*'s indictment of vacuous social rituals and fashions, Manly quickly announces his revulsion at postwar indulgence, and such Goldsmithian lines as "Luxury is surely the bane of a nation: Luxury! which enervates both soul and body, by opening a thousand new sources of enjoyments, opens, also, a thousand new sources of contention and want" establish him as the play's moral center.[2] At the same time, however, these comments vindicate his sister Charlotte's sly observation that "His conversation is like a rich old brocade, it will stand alone; every sentence is a sentiment" (57). Manly is, thus, an ambiguous figure. Tyler seems to assert that although Manly is a genuine hero and model American, he is also more than a bit pompous and too given to fashionable sentiment.[3]

Manly's sensibility is wholeheartedly endorsed, however, by Maria Van Rough, whose father asserts that she has fallen under the spell of "your Charles Grandisons, your Sentimental Journals, and your Robinson Crusoes, and such other trumpery" (54). As the ideal sentimental female, she loathes the idea of marrying Dimple, who, she has discovered, is unworthy of her lofty ideals. But, as a dutiful daughter, she is equally reluctant to contravene the wishes of her father, who stubbornly insists that she should marry the man of his choice. Indeed, until she obtains her father's blessing to wed Manly, she hesitates even to hear the Colonel's suit. While Tyler hints at his own difficulty with Maria by permitting Letitia and Charlotte several witty comments at Maria's expense, he vindicates his heroine's sentimental virtues by uniting her with Manly at the play's end. Like Manly, she seems both the object of admiration and the butt of a gentle satire on the excesses of sensibility.

Ranged against these paragons are Tyler's fallen Americans—Charlotte, Letitia, and Dimple. The two young women are harmless gossips whose frivolities and petty slanders are never shown to do any real damage, despite Maria's and Manly's misgivings. In fact, their sharp tongues and easy wit redeem them from truly severe criticism. Charlotte's biting second-act description of her coterie's antics at the theater provides more than an opportunity for clever mimicry; it also indicates that these two young women recognize their inane social whirl for what it is. If not as overtly serious as Manly might wish, the young women do, in fact, share most of his values. Though their insight into the fashionable world of cotillions, theater parties, and weddings is astute, it does not prepare them to deal with the more serious threats posed by Dimple. His manipulations of language and social convention for his own immoral purposes distinguish him from his less sophisticated victims. He has exchanged the gossips' follies for an active viciousness that threatens to bring about the destruction of the genteel young women in the play, as well as himself. The distinction between the two groups is most obvious at the end of the play when Charlotte mouths a conventional speech of repentance while Dimple disdainfully exits, attempting to maintain the deportment of a man who "has read Chesterfield and received the polish of the world" (76). At play's end, though Dimple alone departs, both vacuity and depravity have been symbolically expunged from a renewed American social order.

Revamping Sheridan's polished Charles Surface as a brusque American warrior provides a tinge of local color to the main character of the play, but for true innovation in characterization one must turn to the subplot, which reiterates the British-American contrast in the antics of Jessamy and Jonathan, the servants of Dimple and Manly, respectively. Again the conflict arises over a woman (Jenny, Maria's maid), and again American frankness and integrity are presented as preferable to European polish and duplicity. The comic subplot suggests that Americans are in fact culturally and morally ill-equipped to adopt self-serving European social forms. Jonathan's disastrous attempts to seduce Jenny with strata-gems borrowed from Jessamy lead the first of the stage Yankees to long for the simple life and honest woman that he has momentarily forsaken: "If this is the way with your city ladies, give me the twenty acres of rock, the bible, the cow, and Tabitha, and a little peaceable bundling" (67). But the seemingly satisfying ending of this subplot fails to minimize two disturbing ironies. First, Jonathan, the idealized American yeoman, is essentially no more morally upright than his anglicized countryman, Jessamy. Only Jenny's rejection of his advances sends him back to the wilds of rural New England. Second, and even more disconcerting, Jonathan's provincial attitudes and unthinking prejudices (especially against the theater) intimate dangers implicit in Manly's assertion that "there is a laudable partiality, which ignorant untraveled men entertain for everything that belongs to their native country" (60). By counter-pointing an ignorant Yankee's homespun, rural dialect with his gentle-manly employer's slightly more sophisticated, sentiment-laden discourse, Tyler not only heightens the humor of Jonathan and the sobriety of Manly, but also defamiliarizes Manly's nationalistic rhetoric and some-what tempers his audience's unselfconscious endorsement of it. Jona-than's insistence that he is a "true blue son of liberty" (60) constitutes an ideological bond that Manly might willingly acknowledge. But Manly's and the audience's appreciation of Jonathan's patriotism is inevitably mitigated by his lack of sophistication. Therefore, despite his best at-tempts, Tyler is unable to resolve the tension between the demands of his comic aesthetic and the ideology he wishes to present.

Jonathan's naiveté also provides Tyler an opportunity to comment obliquely on the evolution of culture in America. Jonathan's famous report of going to a performance of "The School for Scandalization" provides an amusing portrait of Jonathan's backwoods ignorance. But it also reflects Tyler's realization of the cultural distinctions between his native pre-revolutionary Boston and the more cosmopolitan New York of 1787. Boston's anti-theatrical bias (itself emblematic of a pervasive colonial attitude) was an outgrowth of the seventeenth-century religious and ethical precepts that had brought the Massachusetts Bay Colony into existence. However, a new, more secularly oriented nation had emerged from the Revolution, and that nation was already demanding arts to both amuse and edify its populace. The trumpeting of a new native drama in *The Contrast*'s prologue also signals the advent of a new cultural age.

Tyler invokes easily recognizable locales as backdrops for his characters' actions, but his use of setting does provide an interesting index to one method of Americanizing the drama. Like his successors, Dunlap and Barker, Tyler perceives in the American topography a reflection of national political and social ideals. In the subplot, Tyler structures a series of contrasts which illuminate not only differences between Britain and America but also between cultural moments within American society. At their broadest, the contrasts pit countries and metropolises against one another. Jessamy, walking on the New York Mall, comments that it is a "very pretty place" though "it won't do to speak of in the same day with Ranelagh or Vauxhall" (59). The favorable comparison of the more natural mall of New York with two of London's fashionable formal gardens is inadvertently revealed by Jessamy himself: "I hope the city won't ruin it by repairs" (59). But, in turn, the criterion of naturalness suggests that New York, like all cities, is inherently inferior to the country. Jonathan's confusion when New York's "Holy Ground" proves to be the haunt of prostitutes and his longing for the "twenty acres of rock" (67) effectively reinforce the idea that cities pervert nature, rendering even solid earth morally ambiguous. The countryside, on the other hand, honestly presents itself as it is—rock is always rock.

Though Tyler's drama is in many ways imitative of English models, its language does possess an interestingly American cast.[4] Throughout the play verbal styles as much as substance are contrasted: the effusions of Dimple are paired with the terse comments of Manly; the adulterated euphuisms of Jessamy are humorously mangled by Jonathan; the arch social commentary of Letitia and Charlotte is matched with Maria's melancholic musings. The consistent counterpointing of scenes serves not only to point up discrepancies in speech patterns but also to raise questions of authenticity. Is there a native idiom? Who, if any one, is speaking American English in this play? How does American English represent American ideals? Obviously, neither Dimple nor Jessamy are serious candidates. Dimple is merely a pastiche of phrases from Chesterfield, and his servant apes his master with obvious comic results. Letitia and Charlotte are self-conscious in their use of language, but the essential disparity between their language and actions suggests that their idiom fails to embody the honesty that Tyler demands of American English. Both Maria and Manly are moral exemplars, but their speech is derived from European sentimental models and, as such, is ideologically suspect. Van Rough and Jonathan both speak with distinctly American voices, but their language lacks sophistication. Van Rough's insistence on the "main chance" identifies him as a Knickerbocker materialist whose language of acquisition and control is in direct conflict with the discourse of sentimental accommodation privileged by the plot's resolution. Jonathan's homespun Yankee idiom presents some potential as a truly national language—it is expressive, it makes minimal use of abstractions, and it embodies a democratic spirit ("servants" are replaced by "waiters," for example). Unfortunately, Jonathan's language suffers from both a lack of linguistic sophistication and a provincial orientation which restricts its potential speakers. In addition, as is evident from Jonathan's ready acceptance of Jessamy's teachings, even the idiom's native speakers lack faith in its efficacy in achieving certain goals. Linguistically, Tyler suggests, America has yet to find a voice with which to address the world. Until that is done, Americans are perhaps doomed to parrot the sentiments of others.

The Contrast strikes a major chord in the drama of the early Republic not only in its nationalistic theme, but also in its implicit commentary on the problems of creating an American drama. Tyler's comedy proved that an American playwright could create an American locale populated by at least superficially American characters. But the nagging problems of finding truly American issues and an American idiom with which to confront those issues remained an ongoing concern for the playwrights who followed.

William Dunlap:
The Professional Dramatist in the New Republic

While Royall Tyler managed fleetingly to form his republican audience's dramatic aspirations into successful theater, his truncated career provided little opportunity to seriously affect the direction of the new nation's drama. That role fell to William Dunlap, the first professional dramatist-manager in America.[5] Born in Perth Amboy, New Jersey, in 1766, Dunlap was trained initially as an artist, studying briefly in London with Benjamin West, one of the preeminent history painters of the era.[6] Although he largely abandoned the formal study of art, Dunlap remained in London for almost three years, attending the theater regularly and developing a knowledge of stagecraft which grounded his subsequent career in America. Returning to New York in 1787, Dunlap initially drifted away from the theater, marrying and settling down to work in the family glass and china import business. By 1796 his interest in drama and theater had been rekindled in the form of several produced plays and a quarter ownership in the Old American Company of Comedians headed by Hallam and Hodgkinson. Under the terms of their agreement, Dunlap became manager of the company, controlling the finances, repertoire, and cast—and also able, if he chose, to produce his own plays. While Dunlap acknowledged that his theatrical impulses were neither economically nor artistically selfless, he also asserted that an element of public-spiritedness entered into his endeavors. Quoting his own diary of 1796, he notes in his *History of the American Theater* (1832) his feeling at the time: "If the effects of the stage are as great as its friends and enemies have concurred in representing it, surely I should have the power to do much good."[7] Dunlap's optimistic belief that he could use the stage to improve the citizenry is representative of a pervasive theme in early republican speculations on culture.[8] Ironically, however, Dunlap's theatrical career offers a particularly telling commentary on the cultural pitfalls of the period.

As manager of the Old American Company from 1796 until 1805, when he was forced to declare bankruptcy, Dunlap faced conflicting demands from the public, his players and partners, and his own art. As business manager, producer, and house playwright, he was forced to balance his personal desire to write and stage his own plays with the financial demands of a struggling theatrical company torn by internal bickering and buffeted by popular neglect. In its continual search for materials which would guarantee its economic survival, the Old American Company put into production a large number of Dunlap's own works, in addition to the standard repertoire of English classics.

Short-lived though the respite proved to be, Dunlap found temporary economic salvation for his company in translating contemporary French and German playwrights, most notably August von Kotzebue. For example, in 1799–1800, his most financially successful season, Dunlap's ninety-four performances at the Park Theater were dominated by French and German plays—fifty-two of Kotzebue's melodramas alone.[9]

Dunlap is now largely remembered for this introduction and dissemination of continental drama in America, which had a chilling effect on the development of an American dramaturgy. Yet the importance of Dunlap's contribution to the shape of nineteenth-century American theater is hardly to be overestimated. David Grimsted in a tellingly entitled chapter, "The Corruption of an Enlightened Age," asserts that when Dunlap resigned his managership, "the type of play that would be popular for the rest of the nineteenth century had been acclimated to the American stage" (19–20). The type of play that Grimsted refers to is, of course, the melodrama.

Dunlap's own reservations about the quality of the melodrama were overcome by the form's financial success. These plays were immediately adopted by American audiences, who saw, in Kotzebue especially, a superficially republican ideology combined with an ostensibly egalitarian dramatic aesthetic.[10] In domestic plays such as *Menachenhass und-reve*, which Dunlap (following the British translator) renamed *The Stranger*, Kotzebue casts stories of ordinary people into an emotionally intensified relief, providing the audience endless opportunities to submerge themselves in a sea of compassion and good feeling. When he shifts to heroic concerns, Kotzebue continues to emphasize the inherent virtue of the natural self, suggesting implicitly that his heroines and heroes are merely ordinary people in extraordinary circumstances.[11]

The emphasis on dramatic emotionality was abroad in America even before Kotzebue's fame gave added impetus to the trend. Its pervasiveness is suggested in Dunlap's experimentations with Gothic drama: *Fontainville Abbey* (1795), adapted from a novel by Mrs. Radcliffe, and his original effort *The Mysterious Monk* (1796). The audience's tolerance for superficial emotionality alone might soon have waned, but the advent of the continental melodramas at the turn of century added additional elements which effectively set the direction of the theater for the next century. The financial success of tightly plotted melodramas—designed to discourage, if not prevent, audience reflection—and an appealing emphasis on theatrical effects guaranteed that American theatergoers would see intellectually superficial, emotionally charged, spectacular theater as long as profit was the motive of management.[12]

While Dunlap himself was painfully aware of the theater's economic realities, his most famous play, *André* (1798), seems to transcend the commercial demands of a struggling theatrical manager. Using as its backdrop the revolutionary war execution of Major John André, the British officer who conspired with Benedict Arnold to destroy the West Point garrison, *André* explores the internal conflicts of a young American captain, Arthur Bland. Out of personal gratitude to André, who has saved him from death on a prison ship, Bland seeks to persuade the General (a thinly disguised Washington) to pardon André. Washington is adamant, however, refusing to be moved by a succession of intercessors, including Bland, Bland's mother (whose husband is to be killed in retaliation if André is executed), and Honoria, André's lover. The play ends with André's gallant acceptance of his fate as a just punishment for a lapse in his otherwise honorable life, Honoria's descent into madness, a report that Bland's father is safe, and Bland's wretchedness at André's execution.

The revolutionary war setting, a wealth of nationalistic sentiment, traditionally popular themes of personal honor and patriotism, and an elevated treatment would seem to have guaranteed the play's success. Certainly the contemporaneous popularity of John Daly Burk's romantic verse tragedy *Bunker-Hill; or The Death of General Warren* indicates that the nation was receptive to fictionalized histories of its inception. Nevertheless, Dunlap's play closed after three performances. (A quickly mounted and weak production did not improve the play's reception.) Years later Dunlap attributed the play's failure to its being "a most unfortunate subject for the stage" (*Theatre*, 2, 17). Dunlap is perhaps being a bit disingenuous; what his audience was not ready to accept was a play which sought to examine in any meaningful way the unresolved conflicts between aristocratic personal values and the demands of democratic idealism which resided just below the surface of Federalist America.

Given the ostensibly self-conscious and seemingly collectively inspired birth of the nation in revolution, questions of national identity and direction in the post-Revolutionary War era would seem on their face easily answered. However, the arguments and compromises attendant to the drafting and ratification of the Constitution, and the ongoing battles between Federalists and Jeffersonian Democrat-Republicans made patently clear to Dunlap's contemporaries that the consensus generated by the war with England had little duration once independence had been achieved. Thus, the formulation or re-formulation of a national consciousness and character, both considered necessary to the continued survival of the new country, became a compelling necessity to Dunlap and his audience. In addition, to fulfill his own conception of his role as a public artist, Dunlap was under a particular obligation to give form and voice to his vision. In his attempt to understand and shape the future, therefore, Dunlap begins by first artistically recapturing and reevaluating the past in *André*. In the process, he constructs a complex fiction which allows him to lay out, with more sophistication than his predecessors, the emotional and intellectual ambiguities of the recent war; to suggest the conflicting values abroad in the new nation; and to delineate the ideological framework within which he hopes the new state will be constructed. Unlike Burk's *Bunker-Hill*, which emphasizes romance and theatrical spectacle, *André* focuses on the divisions within the country as a whole, rendering them in a series of debates. Dunlap obviously expects his play's arguments to educate the audience away from excesses of narrow-minded jingoism and aristocratic political solipsism toward a more "reasonable" accommodation on which the nation might function.

Although Dunlap's final goal is the education of his audience to a new order, some sense of his general attitude toward social organization is revealed in his treatment of André, the representative of the British-American world being swept away by war. Despite at least one critic's misgivings, Dunlap's choice of André as the play's hero is artistically appropriate if we remember that André was not only a historical figure but also a fictional creation whom Dunlap was free to develop for his own artistic ends.[13] Dunlap's insistence upon artistic freedom is evident in his treatment of the title character. André's treason consumes little of Dunlap's time since he can rely upon the audience's historical consciousness to supply that element of the Briton's story. What the audience lacks, and Dunlap intends to provide, is a sense of the man behind the historical facts. Not overly concerned with the historical accuracy of his portrait, Dunlap paints a predominately flattering portrait of André: his sense of his failure to adhere to his own principles, his concern for Bland's father, and his love of Honoria all suggest the accuracy of Bland's assertions to the General that André has been "as gallant soldier as e'er fac'd a foe, / Bless'd with each polish'd gift of social life, / And every virtue of humanity."[14] But as M'Donald, the author's surrogate, argues (and André himself admits), whatever his previous glories, he has been "sunk by misdeed, not fortune" (90). Though guilty, and therefore justly condemned, André becomes more than an emblem of treason within the play. His humanity emerges and he becomes an appealing and complex enemy, a man who, having compromised his personal ethics, atones for his lapse with his life. Politically, as the General makes clear, this enemy of the nation must be destroyed—but artistically, his destruction allows Dunlap the opportunity to portray that death's pathos and to suggest the moral and political complexities that arise in the ostensibly unambiguous arena of war.[15]

The ambivalence that attaches itself to André also reflects the conflicting emotions which characterized colonial responses to the Revolution, especially before and after the hostilities themselves. While revolutionary fervor during the war effectively reduced the political world to black and white, before July, 1776 many of those who would emerge as the most determined republicans acknowledged a regret at what they perceived as the necessity of separating from Great Britain. In many instances their comments suggest a sense that England, like André, had betrayed its own best instincts. In fact, André's rationalizations for his actions—the monetary enticements of corrupt superiors, promises of preferments, and a desire for personal fame—read like the colonists' indictment of British ministers of state and colonial officials in the 1760s and 1770s. By the end of the tragedy, therefore, André is more than a man whose life is ended by military justice. He has become the metaphoric representation of England and as such provides Dunlap a convenient mechanism by which to explore the other characters' political philosophies as potential bases for post-revolutionary social organization.

If André personifies the waning influence of a politically corrupt England, then Arthur Bland represents the colonists' confusing political legacy. As one might expect, Bland is stoutly republican in his sentiments. But his patriotism is of such a radical stripe that his fervor obviously troubles Dunlap. Ironically, Bland's republicanism is interpenetrated by a residual allegiance to aristocratic values and personal codes which, in the American mind, had once underpinned English society. This paradoxical combination is a volatile mixture which threatens at any moment to demand either ideological purity or a rigid classism, both of which would doom the new nation. Throughout most of the play, Bland belies his name, blustering about in one fit of passion after another. He does more than heighten the emotional intensity of the play, however. His uncontrolled passions deftly suggest what Dunlap most feared, what the political history since the Revolution had seemingly borne out, and what the partisan reception of his play itself suggested—that unrestrained, unreflective emotion, while glorious in the Revolution, now threatened to undermine the existence of a peaceful nation. Dunlap's political perspective in the play remains fundamentally nonpartisan. For Dunlap, Bland embodies uncontrolled passion, and the essential issue of the tragedy becomes the potential consequences of emotionality, not its genesis. To further the point, Dunlap undermines the audience's sympathies with the overtly emotional characters (André, Bland, and Seward) and flatteringly develops a paragon of enlightened reason in M'Donald. It is M'Donald who, through a series of debates, guides Bland (and the audience) to understand Dunlap's position on ideological issues vital to the nation's future course: the nature of man, the desirable ends of society, and the service of art in a democratic republic.

Having introduced Bland and revealed his passionate temperament, Dunlap immediately presents the audience an alternative with a discussion among the General and two officers, Seward and M'Donald, about the nature of America, the causes of the Revolution, and the future of democracy. Dunlap structures the encounter along classical lines with synthesis emerging from reasoned debate. The discussion begins with the General's portrait of America as a land of yeomen who, appropriate to the General's classical republican vision, leave their fields "and straightway play the hero" (89), defending their lands from encroaching tyranny. Seward adds that America is the vanguard of a new spirit of freedom which will, with America's shining example, sweep despotism from the world. Against the classical republicanism of Washington and the romantic republicanism of Seward, both of which are underpinned by idealistic theories of men, Dunlap posits M'Donald's rationalist vision. Like Hume and Reid, his Scottish philosophical precursors, M'Donald believes man generally lacks commitment to abstract principles, but "naturally" resists oppression out of a strong sense of self-interest which he will fight to protect or enhance.[16] The discussion shifts from man in the abstract to the fate of André in particular. Using the Wheel of Fortune trope, Seward argues that circumstances have overpowered André's generally virtuous character. M'Donald retorts that André has "sunk by misdeed, not fortune" (90). Washington, appropriately, seems to provide the synthesis by arguing that many men, including André, allow passion to subvert reason. Since the audience is aware of André's eventual fate, Dunlap is able to praise Washington in the play's dialogue while allowing history to vindicate M'Donald.

The second debate transcends the immediate situation and explores the prospective post-revolutionary society's ends and relationships with Europe. At the same time, Dunlap uses the encounter between Seward and M'Donald to hammer again on his theme of the political dangers of civil emotionality. Seward, the optimistic spokesman of the first act, has undergone an unexplained mood swing. Convinced that Europe will unleash a "herd" of corrupting individuals on the new land, Seward prays for "barriers, all impassable to man" (94) to cut off all intercourse. Unlike the aristocratic Bland, who seeks only to fulfill known obligations, Seward is willing to translate his republican nightmares into national policy. M'Donald's tempered response is that America, rather than close itself to European influence, should encourage commerce, appropriate Europe's "blest science," and thereby secure for itself a quantum cultural leap from "that simplicity / With ignorance curst, to that simplicity, / By knowledge blest" (94). Beyond pointing up the obvious contrasts in the international theme, Dunlap uses this exchange to further reinforce his audience's growing suspicions of emotionality. Seward's seemingly unmotivated philosophical transformation undermines his intelligibility as a character, aligning him even more closely with the unstable Bland and rendering his political views increasingly suspect. In addition, and supremely important in evaluating his suasive strategy, Dunlap removes Washington from the debate, leaving M'Donald as the only alternative for the audience. However, carefully using the Protean terms "blest science" and "simplicity" (the latter's importance emphasized by its repetition), Dunlap manages to evoke Washington's authority and lend its weight to M'Donald, while neatly modifying Washington's agrarian, somewhat aristocratic republicanism. By the end of the second debate, Dunlap has managed not only to suggest a model of enlightened man to contrast with the emotional Bland, but also to provide a fairly comprehensive vision of that man's prospective society—a republic giving free rein to both commerce and speculative thought.

In the final lines of *André*, Dunlap touches upon his deepest interests, art and history. In the play's prologue, Dunlap seeks to privilege his art by linking it to the country's history. At the same time, he consciously delineates the limits of historical facts in isolation: they detail past events; they provide a chronology; but they do not contain within themselves a useful perspective. Only through a "blend" of art and history may events impart "pleasure" or "mend the heart" (82). As the play draws to a close, Bland and M'Donald depart André's execution, reacting to this death in characteristically contradictory manners. For Bland, André's death is an *"act* accurst" [emphasis mine], sufficiently momentous to atone for all Americans' sufferings in the war. M'Donald, in contrast, urges that "every child be taught to lisp the *tale*" [emphasis mine]. In this masterful stroke, Dunlap ends the last debate—and the play—by translating M'Donald's judgment into necessary, just action and democratic art. André's execution serves not only to found and guarantee freedom but also to provide the play's material, grounding Dunlap's art in fact and thereby serving to perpetuate liberty by providing the proper ideological framework within which to understand history.

It may be indicative of the broader forces at work in the land that Tyler, no doubt enveloped in the continuing glow of the Revolution and excited by the statecraft being formulated in Philadelphia, wrote a comedy, while Dunlap, equally aware that the leading hero of the Revolution had stepped from the public stage and that discordant voices rang out with insistent demands for empowerment, penned a tragedy. Like Tyler before him, Dunlap surveyed art with an eye toward making it more overtly American. Also like Tyler, Dunlap sought no aesthetic innovation but attempted to infuse received forms with what he perceived as a more American spirit. The result, in the case of *André*, was a classical tragedy in the eighteenth-century tradition of *Cato*. Despite its lack of formal originality, *André* marks a significant moment in the nation's theater. For the first time in the history of American drama, a native dramatist looked critically at American history, deemed it worthy of serious treatment, and produced a play that transcended panegyric or propaganda. Dunlap's work may not reach the level of greatness, but his occasional willingness to nudge the early Republican theater audience beyond its expectations and prejudices does demand our respect.

James Nelson Barker: Republican Tragedy and Nationalistic Art

While Dunlap's financial demise indicates both the tenuous nature of the Republican theatrical enterprise and the difficulties of playwrights who sought to provide American plays that transcended pageant, the continuing desire of Republican dramatists to democratize American art is reiterated by the work of James Nelson Barker, a Philadelphia politician and amateur playwright. The son of General John Barker, a three-time mayor of Philadelphia, James Nelson Barker was formally educated in Philadelphia and politically schooled by a sojourn in Washington, D.C. (1809–10), where he observed the workings of national government and cultivated influential people both within and outside the government. He returned to Philadelphia in 1810 and married Mary Rogers in 1811. The outbreak of the War of 1812 presented an opportunity for military service, and Barker accepted a commission as a captain of artillery. After serving on the Canadian border during the war, he continued in the army until 1817 when, having risen to the rank of major as an assistant adjutant-general, he resigned. Following his father into Democratic party politics, Barker held a series of elected and appointed governmental positions at the local and national level.[17]

Like Tyler, Barker was a talented amateur rather than a working professional, and he conceived of his dramatic writings as the diversions of his idle hours.[18] His theatrical endeavors, as he detailed them in an 1832 letter to William Dunlap, include seven mature efforts: *Tears and Smiles* (written 1806, produced 1807), *The Embargo* (1807), *The Indian Princess* (1808), *Marmion* (1812), *The Armourer's Escape* (1817), *How to Try a Lover* (written 1817; played in 1836 as *A Court of Love*), and *Superstition* (1824).[19] The breadth of these efforts, which include drawing room comedies, overt propaganda pieces, historical dramas, and trage- dies, indicates a serious interest in drama, an inference further sustained by Barker's consistent interest in the theatrical world of Philadelphia.[20] In addition to writing dramas and regularly attending the theater, Barker found time to provide through his prefaces, prologues, and newspaper articles an insightful commentary on the history of the theater and drama, the nature and merits of both the classic and contemporary canons, the actors and acting techniques of the day, and, most important, his own thoughts on the nature and function of democratic art.[21]

The implicit commentary on dramatic art begins in the preface to *Tears and Smiles*, when Barker, like most of his contemporaries, complains that his plays are neglected by American audiences.[22] He amplifies the point in the preface to *The Indian Princess*, where he explains that Americans unfairly expect their native dramas to "lisp the language of Shakespere."[23] The insidious nature of British drama is for Barker more than a matter of money and aesthetics, however. In his preface to *Marmion*, Barker argues that Sir Walter Scott, whose poem forms the basis of Barker's play, has neglected his duty as a Scot by choosing as his subject the historical moment in which Scotland effec- tively lost its national independence. In the process of indicting Scott, Barker tellingly links art and patriotism: he suggests that Bruce or Wallace would have been more appropriate heroes, since their histories displayed "every object that might allure the poet or invite the patriot".[24] Barker reiterates later in the same preface the importance of the political orienta- tion when he admits that "it was not the least of the author's gratifications, on the presentation of the play, that the coincidence [between England's relationships to Scotland in the sixteenth century and America in 1812] was perceived and felt by an audience of his countrymen" (v). But the supreme function of drama, a purpose that can only be achieved in a democracy, is "to keep alive the spirit of freedom; and to unite conflicting parties in a common love of liberty and devotedness to country."[25] Here Barker stakes out an American dramatic aesthetic whose central tenet is antithetical to both British history and literature, at least as popularly conceived in Republican America. For Barker, national drama is clearly nationalistic drama. Barker's consistent use of this standard and its effects on his dramaturgy are best revealed in two of his plays, *Marmion* and *Superstition*.

Given the theatrical proclivities of early nineteenth-century American audiences, the success of *Marmion* was not difficult to forecast. A medieval setting complete with bloodthirsty prelates, spectacular court pageantry, imperiled maidens, a compellingly evil protagonist, ghostly personal combats, and pitched battles might well be expected to prove irresistible to audiences whose tastes had been formed by plays such as Cibber's adaptation of *Richard III*. In spite of its obvious appeals, Barker relates in his letter to Dunlap that William Wood and Thomas Abthorpe Cooper sought to improve the play's reception by announcing that it was the work of an Englishman, Thomas Morton. The ruse was sufficient to guarantee the play a fair hearing, and the result, Barker announces without false modesty, was a play which "ran like wildfire" through the American theaters (*Theatre*, 315). Significantly, Barker attributes much of the initial success of the play to the audience's belief that it was the work of an Englishman.

Barker's plot follows the Scott poem: before the play's action begins, Marmion, a fictitious lord, has decided to secure the hand and fortune of Clara de Clare. To that end he has accused her beloved, Ralph de Wilton, of treason and has seemingly killed him in mortal combat. Clara has fled and has taken refuge in the convent of St. Hilda at Whitby. The play opens with Marmion on his way to Scotland, having been sent as emissary by Henry VIII to the court of Scotland's James IV. On his procession north, he returns his castoff mistress, the erstwhile nun, Constance de Beverley, to the vengeance of the Roman Catholic Church. Following a combat in which he is defeated by the "ghost" of de Wilton, who has joined Marmion's train in the disguise of a palmer, Marmion arrives at the court of James. James is gathering his forces for a war with England, but his judgment is being clouded by his paramour, the Lady Heron, another of Marmion's ex-mistresses and an English agent. Marmion serendipitously gains Clara, whose ship has been forced ashore in Scotland, but before he can violate her, James attacks England and Marmion returns to the English army. James is lured from a strategically superior position by an English plot, and after great losses on both sides, the Scots are destroyed. Marmion dies in the battle, forgiven by all because of his valor during the fighting.

As the plot synopsis suggests, this play superficially shares many of the characters, situations, and devices of other "historical" plays of the period. However, in Barker's play, these conventions serve a much different end. While Barker is of course intent upon producing the best historical play that he can engineer from Scott's poem, his main interest is ideological rather than aesthetic. That a play set wholly in England and Scotland in the sixteenth century is part of an attempt to forge an American drama may seem a bit paradoxical. But as Barker's critical writings make clear, he does not demand that the action of a play concern itself with American circumstances or that the characters be Americans. Rather, he urges, a play must endorse American ideals, a more complex project.

Barker's insistence that American playwrights write for their countrymen takes the form in this play of an attempt to secure ideological and artistic room for the American writer, for he attempts to advance the development of a national drama on at least three fronts.[26] Initially, he endeavors to liberate the materials of American art from the constraints of British ideology by precipitating a re-examination of received history. He seeks to expose the reality behind the chronicled glories of England, and, that accomplished, he argues for the necessity of an American perspective by indicating the dangers of adopting the English viewpoint. In order to understand their art, Americans must re-examine events, unencumbered by English bias. In a nice bit of displacement, Scotland becomes America's precursor state and America's conflicts with Britain are metaphorically presented in the guise of the Scottish-British conflict in the sixteenth century.

Second, while a reconsideration of history is important to Barker, an examination of the chivalric values which ostensibly underpinned English actions in the period of the play is even more imperative. Barker's contention, personified in the play's title character, is that those values are merely rationalizations for aristocratic privilege. By play's end, the very word chivalry is so emptied of meaning that it is—as Falstaff says of honor—little more than a puff of air.

Third, Barker seeks to drive home the implications of his critique of British history and values for British and American art. For Barker, Scott was merely the last in a long line of artists who had forsaken liberty for profit, becoming "the mercenary minstrel of a feudal lord" (iv). In this view, the literature of England had, in large measure, inculcated generations of readers with a set of aristocratic values whose moribund and corrupt nature had remained hidden behind a veil of art. If a new democratic art was to emerge and grow, the first order of business was to reveal the truth of aristocratic life and, by implication, the art it had spawned.

Barker's tactics are easily illustrated by Act IV, scene iv, the episode in which he develops the parallels between Scotland and America and places in the mouth of James IV a stinging indictment of England. The scene begins interestingly with James kindly guaranteeing the safety of Clara and her abbess. James then compliments Marmion, "the star of chivalry" (50), and the focus shifts to Lady Heron, who sings a song of Lochinvar's securing of "fair Ellen" (51). The chivalrous action of James and the literary ideal evoked by Scott's song stand in ironic opposition to the evil and corrupt Marmion whose true nature is known to the audience, if not to the King. Realizing that the audience may assume that Marmion is an anomaly, Barker moves quickly to eradicate that comforting prospect by transcending from personal concerns to national politics. James's indictment of England's aggressive policies is all the more damning for the light it sheds on England's methods. First, says James, England "Professes but to fight for others' rights, / While she alone infringes every right" (54). Next, England attempts to find justifications for her actions by suggesting that Scotland is partial to France, which insults the intelligence of the Scots who "know who wounds us and who gives the balm" (54). Most significantly, James states passionately, England abrogates the rules of chivalry:

> It was then—
> Even in days of truce! I burn to speak it—
> Murder and pillage, England's constant agents,
> Roamed through our land, and harboured in our bays!
> Our peaceful border sacked, our vessels plundered,
> Our leigemen robbed, enslaved and slaughtered. (55)

James concludes his speech with lines whose utterance literally brought the play to a halt in one of its early performances while the audience engaged in an impromptu patriotic rally:[27]

> My lord, my lord, under such injuries,
> How shall a free and gallant nation act?
> Still lay its sovereignty at England's feet—
> Still basely ask a boon from England's bounty—

Still vainly hope redress from England's justice?
No! by our martyred fathers' memories,
The land may sink—but, like a glorious wreck,
'Twill keep its colours flying to the last. (55)

The subsequent action of the play bears out all of James' assertions. Scotland is defeated not by a morally and politically superior country, but is lured to destruction through the policy of the English. Perhaps most important, the play ends with the preeminent figures of English arms and morality, Surrey and Wilton, able to excuse Marmion's failings because he has fought bravely—in the destruction of a liberty-loving Scotland. In sum, the play vindicates Barker's estimation of chivalric society and indicts the entire galaxy of literature which has sustained it.

If *Marmion* provided a basis for an American drama, Barker's last and best play, *Superstition*, not only proved such a drama possible, but also gave it a large measure of artistic and ideological legitimacy by using domestic material but refusing to falsely glorify an unflattering incident in colonial history. Set in New England during the late seventeenth century, *Superstition* tells the story of a fanatic Puritan minister's destruction of a woman and her son who refuse to conform to the minister's narrow-minded expectations.

Isabella Fitzroy and her son Charles have fallen afoul of Ravensworth, whose implacable hatred is such that he attributes every disaster in the community to their sorcery. As the play begins, Charles is returning home from college, having been expelled for his supposed impertinence to school officials. Losing his way in the wilderness, Charles meets the Unknown, a recluse who refuses to divulge anything about himself. Charles manages to arrive home just in time to save his love, Mary Ravensworth, from the advances of George Egerton, an English courtier who has accompanied his uncle, Sir Reginald, to the New World on a secret mission. A duel ensures, and Charles wounds George in an honorable fight. In short order, the village is almost destroyed by an unexpected Indian attack, but is saved when the Unknown leads a counterattack.

The minister Ravensworth attributes both the Indian attack and the appearance of the Unknown, whom he deems a demon, to Isabella's witchcraft, and has mother and son charged with sorcery. Charles is also falsely charged with attempted murder and rape, for his sword and handkerchief have been found at the site of George Egerton's wounding and Mary has collapsed in Charles's arms when they are surprised by her father. Unwilling for Mary to appear in court and thereby ruin her reputation, Charles refuses to recognize the validity of the court. Ravensworth uses Charles's refusal to plead as a pretext for whipping the townspeople into a frenzy in which they lynch Charles. The Unknown arrives too late to stop Charles's murder, but he reveals that he is Isabella's father, a regicide who had fled to America at the Restoration. Sir Reginald discloses that Charles Fitzroy's father was none other than the king, Charles II, and that his mission has been to present Isabella's father with a royal pardon. A distraught Mary Ravensworth dies of grief, and the play ends in a tableau of despair as a storm rages outside.

Despite the melodramatic sound of the plot, *Superstition* is a play which would work effectively on the stage. The characters—especially Ravensworth, Mary, Charles, and Isabella—are well-drawn, the action is fast-paced, and the verse is well-handled. Beyond these aesthetic considerations, the play provides interesting evidence to the durability of Barker's ideological commitments and their effects on his treatment of American characters and situations. *Marmion* had provided the opportunity to excoriate English literature's tendency to mythologize its national abuses. Barker counters the literature of Scott and Shakespeare with a model of historical drama which serves to educate a democratic citizenry rather than glorify the ruling class. In this play Barker emphasizes drama's role as a uniter of factions and encourager of freedom by metaphorically presenting the effects of factionalism and tyranny on both England and America.

The central figure in the drama and the chief exponent of a new variety of American tyranny is Ravensworth, a type of the grim Puritan who would figure so prominently in the works of Hawthorne a few years later. Ravensworth, as his name suggests, is a portent of death in the play. Unable to endure what he sees as the laxity of his fellow Puritans, he is determined to "root out with an unsparing hand / The weeds that choke the soil."[28] The object of his resolve is Isabella Fitzroy, who "holds herself above her fellow creatures, / And scorn's our church's discipline" (117) and Charles, "a lewd libertine" (118). Regardless of his ostensibly disinterested rationalizations, his moral authority is undercut by the sense of personal injury and animosity that informs his comment to Mary that Isabella is "a scoffer at things sacred / At me, and at my functions" (118). Just as Marmion has sought to reject the rules of humane interaction through abuse of his rank, so Ravensworth seeks to exploit his privileged position in the community. By transforming the people's anxiety about anything alien into a terror of witches and projecting that fear on the Fitzroys, Ravensworth is able to persecute them with seeming impunity. He has, in essence, found the way to reconstitute tyranny in a democratic environment—by making the tyranny collective, by making it appear to be the "will of the people." But Walford, the choric representative of tolerance and reasoned faith, points out that Ravensworth has failed in his responsibility to educate "The unthinking crowd, in whom credulity, / Is ever the first born of ignorance" (130).

Placed in opposition to Ravensworth's new tyranny is the Old World despotism of the Stuart monarchy, highlighted through three generations of the Fitzroy family's interaction with the monarchy. Isabella's father is presented as one of those who fought the Stuarts out of conscience and religious belief, but would have suffered death had he remained in an England which could not or would not tolerate dissent. Isabella's seduction graphically suggests the moral corruption associated with Charles II. Charles Fitzroy's death represents, from Barker's perspective, the culmination of monarchist history. For Barker, the destruction of monarchy at the hands of forces that it has set in motion is inevitable. But the cost of freedom from monarchy can be very high indeed. This play ends, after all, with the best of the younger generation on a bier, and the ability of the older generation to transform itself through this experience remains somewhat problematical.

Like *Marmion*, *Superstition* argues persuasively for Barker's democratic ideology. While Americans had escaped the physical tyranny of the old world, they remained yoked to a set of attitudes which had consistently given rise to despotism. Many, like Ravensworth, seemed to have embraced the concept of freedom only superficially, wishing merely to exchange one hierarchy for another. But, Barker seems to suggest, such patterns of thought may be broken and freedom may finally triumph. For that to occur the citizenry must be constantly vigilant, must strive for knowledge, and must not give up their freedom lightly to the will of another. And they must have an art that alerts them to the dangers that they confront both from without and from within.

Perhaps inevitably, the ideological fervor associated with the Revolution tended to subside with time's passage. Though elements of the anti-European sentiment remained abroad in the culture and periodically exercised considerable sway over some dramatists and audiences, British and continental literary aesthetics and dramatic fashion held increasingly greater influence on American playwrights, especially after the War of 1812. Additionally, a growing sophistication among the American *literati* led in some quarters to a less politicized definition of the national literature than had been possible earlier. Thus, American drama between 1814 and the Civil War was much more receptive than it had been during the early Republic to formal and thematic experimentations. Nevertheless, the tentative steps of the early Republican dramatists marked paths which were to become well worn by the Civil War. The pull of native material, evident variously in *The Contrast*, *André*, and *Superstition*, encouraged the grafting of new, American subject matter onto received dramatic forms. Conversely, the dominating attraction of European literary aesthetics continued to have a powerful influence on American dramatists, reemerging most immediately in the romantic plays of Bird, Stone, Boker, and others. Consciously striving to form their nation's new culture, Tyler, Dunlap, and Barker bequeathed their successors solid models. Regardless of its eventual form or subject matter, a self-consciously American drama now existed.

Tragedy and the Drama
of High Culture

While often acknowledging the notable efforts of Tyler, Dunlap, and Barker, early nineteenth-century critics and playwrights continued to decry the general lack of a native drama. Though agreed that European plays should no longer dominate the American stage, they were at some variance about the proper focus and direction that American drama should take. Many early nineteenth-century writers and critics, concurring with the cosmopolitan Dunlap, anticipated a drama whose quality would rival the efforts of Europe's masters. America, they thought, would soon produce aesthetically superior plays along European models. This attitude, reinforced to a certain extent by the international popularity of literary romanticism and the continued influence of European models on American prose and poetry, complicated native dramatists' attempts to write distinctively "America drama" by suggesting that the nationalistic element in art was either irrelevant or the accidental consequence of the playwright's birth. Other theorists, echoing the attitudes of Barker, demanded more obviously "American" qualities in their plays and insisted that in order to establish appropriate criteria for the evaluation of American drama, that American dramatists serve an overtly political purpose by educating Americans to the nature of their country and its people, by constructing an historical mythology, and by delineating the duties of the private man in a democratic country.[1]

The tension embodied in the very phrase "American drama" resisted amelioration, and the ideological and aesthetic dichotomy that had surfaced for American dramatists, audiences, and managers in early Republican drama continued until at least the end of the Civil War. For American drama and theater in the period between 1812 and 1860, the result was the emergence of two implicit responses to the dilemma, each with legitimate claims to the title "the American drama." Each had its practitioners in the library and its supporters in the theatrical establishment and publishing houses. Each response captured parts of the audience in America and abroad, and managerial decisions to embrace one or the other alternative do not seem to have determined, ultimately, the economic success or failure of acting companies or theaters. Finally, each spawned dramatic and theatrical successors which continued to adapt its basic literary techniques and ideological vision to the changing American scene. Despite their many differences, the authors of these two varieties of drama often perceived themselves as achieving, or at least striving after, the same goal—a national drama.

The first response—the romantic, often poetic, play—represents the efforts of a relatively small group of well-educated, culturally sophisticated writers who saw American drama as capable of achieving international legitimacy only if American writers accepted as much as possible the dominant literary aesthetic. Like their European counterparts, the American romantics were fascinated by the past and the future, and had a love for the distant and exotic. Suspicious of reason and rules, these writers repudiated any slavish adherence to received principles of artistic construction. Although they tended to focus on matters of the heart, the romantic playwrights, unlike the melodramatists, sought to explore character meaningfully, and in the better pieces of the period—*The Broker of Bogota* and *Francesca da Rimini*, for example—their plays provide insightful character studies in aesthetically sophisticated forms. Since the romantics sought primarily to examine private emotion, they were imaginatively at home among all social classes and political situations, portraying events of classical and modern times with an eye attuned more to their private consequences than to their historical significance.[2]

The alternative response is less easily labeled. More heterogeneous than the romantic plays, the less literary, more popularly oriented drama of early nineteenth-century America is a hodgepodge of characters and dramatic actions. Usually centered around a contemporary political or social issue or an emerging national character type, these plays are an invaluable dramatic record of the concerns and attitudes of the period. Their writers often saw themselves as outside the mainstream of American theatrical life, and their plays tend to reflect a concern with the dispossessed and the marginal. In these plays, slavery, temperance, life on the frontier, the social idiosyncrasies of the wealthy, and the rapid transformation of America by the new capitalism are examined through the experiences of clear-thinking rural Yankees, ignorant blacks, and noble and ignoble Native Americans and frontiersmen. The multifarious and complex phenomenon of popular drama, as well as its aesthetic and ideological implications, will be discussed separately in the next chapter.

John Howard Payne and the Emergence of Romantic Drama

The first major impetus to the growth of romantic drama in America is found in the work of actor, playwright, and translator John Howard Payne. Born in New York, the son of a headmaster, Payne first achieved theatrical notoriety as a boy actor. Ambitious, he departed America in 1813 and made his London debut. Although initially successful, Payne soon found his acting career at a standstill and traveled to Paris in hopes of improving his fortunes. Upon his return to London in 1815, Payne sold *Trial Without Jury; or, The Magpie and the Maid*, his translation of the French melodrama *La Pie Voleuse*, to Covent Garden. The success of that play resulted in Payne's entering into an agreement with the Drury Lane management committee to act as its theatrical agent in Paris. This arrangement was marked by misunderstandings and ultimately proved of marginal benefit to Payne either as an actor or playwright. Thus, between 1815 and his return to America in 1832, Payne turned his talents almost exclusively to translating and adapting Parisian pieces for the London houses, for a time collaborating with his friend Washington Irving.[3] During this period, Payne produced some of his most commercially successful plays: *Thérèse* (1821), *Clari* (1823) with its famous song, "Home, Sweet Home," *Charles II* (1824), and *Richelieu* (1826). After assorted economic and artistic trials and triumphs in England, Payne returned to America, lionized by his countrymen as an actor and playwright whose works had proved successful not only in America but also in England. Although his plays remained favorites of British and American audiences and actors for most of the nineteenth century, Payne received little recompense for his efforts in a period without effective copyright laws. Abandoning the stage, he secured political appointments under Presidents Tyler and Fillmore and died in 1852 while serving as United States consul in Tunis. Although his efforts were ultimately of little personal benefit, Payne proved a significant, if short-lived, influence on the direction of American drama.

Although the majority of Payne's efforts were translations and adaptations, a dramatic sense honed before audiences in America and England guaranteed that his reworkings continued to hold the stage long after most of the originals had faded from the theatrical consciousness. With an actor's eye for a formidable vehicle, Payne produced roles which appealed to both acknowledged British masters such as Edmund Kean and emerging American stars such as Edwin Forrest. Thus, Payne's influence transcended that of more original dramatists and gave American dramatists credibility with European actors and managers. More important for contemporary American audiences and dramatists, Payne's career suggested that an American's work would be accepted by the theatrical establishment of England—provided, of course, that the Americans were willing to accede to the demands of European taste. Despite his seeming neglect of nationalistic demands, Payne's restiveness with the continuing artistic hegemony of Europe occasionally finds metaphoric expression in his plays. A case in point is his best tragedy, *Brutus; or, The Fall of Tarquin*, a work that combines the incidents, language, and effects from five sources into a double-edged discourse on the nature of tyranny and democracy.

Drawing together elements from Brutus plays by Nathaniel Lee, Voltaire, William Duncombe (who translated and adapted Voltaire), Hugh Downman, and Richard Cumberland, Payne constructs his play around two plot lines—the expulsion of the Tarquins and Brutus's condemnation of his son, Titus, for aiding Tarquinia, the tyrant's daughter. On its surface the play is a well-wrought but fairly typical indictment of tyranny, another in the long list of plays condemning despotism that thrived on the nineteenth-century stages of America and England. But Payne's choice of a protagonist is a telling one given his position in the English theatrical world. Brutus is more than simply another idealized republican mouthing the litany of freedom designed to appeal to every political perspective in the audience. He is also a variety of artist, a man who has constructed a role for himself in order to survive, and this element of his character provides Payne the opportunity for subtle commentary on the fate of American art—and American dramatists and actors—in a English-speaking theatrical world dominated by the managers of Covent Garden and Drury Lane.

As the play opens, Lucius Junius (renamed Brutus in the course of the play) is a man agonizingly divided against himself. In order to survive the bloody purge which claimed his father and brother after the Tarquins seized Rome, Lucius Junius has feigned madness. As the years have passed, however, he has not avenged his father and brother, a failure that torments him with doubts about his own ability to endure until the propitious moment. Closely aligned to his personal grief is his patriotic desire to overthrow those who have subjugated his country. Both of these aspirations are complicated by Brutus's anxieties concerning his son, Titus. Brutus dares not embrace his paternal responsibilities lest his affections reveal his true state of mind and endanger Titus and himself. As the descendent of a noble family, as a patriot, and as a father, Brutus begins the play at odds with his own enunciated ideals. While the action of the play fulfills Brutus's desires for revenge, his attempts to save Rome and Titus are only partially successful, for his revenge and the liberation of Rome are only accomplished at the expense of his life and that of his son. Titus, seduced by his love for Tarquinia to aid the Tarquin cause, is condemned by his father, who strictly observes the demands of the law but dies of a broken heart at his son's execution.[4]

By utilizing Brutus as a metaphor equating artistic creativity and paternity, Payne suggests the dilemma and possible fate of the American playwright and actor. Early in the play, Brutus reveals that he has created a role as an addle-headed fool to mask his desires for revenge and national liberty. But the entrance of Titus points out that Brutus's assumption of one character has necessarily meant the abrogation of another—his role as a father. Without the benefit of his father's wisdom, Titus has fallen under the influence of the beautiful yet morally dubious Tarquinia. The perennial conflict of generations is thus overlaid with political arguments concerning the extent that a private man's emotional life should be dictated by public concerns, as well as discord between disguised probity and naive sensuality. The alienation of father from son and the absence of a positive moral force in Titus's life has guaranteed that genuine communication is impossible and that neither will survive.

Given Payne's treatment at the hands of the Drury Lane Theatre subcommittee, his own artistic identification with Brutus must have seemed compelling, though not particularly reassuring. Whether conscious or not, the parallels between playwright and hero are instructive.

Metaphorically, *Brutus* suggests that an American author/actor must, like Lucius Junius, appear less than he is in order to survive in the theatrical environment of London. Playing to his audience's preconceptions of Americans as provincial fools and frontier barbarians, the American creates an illusion which is, like that of Lucius, doubly destructive. First, he must generate plays and characterizations which in most instances reflect alien values. At least temporarily, he must betray his principles. Then, since his artistry guarantees that his creations are effective, thereby further undermining his own ideals, he must endure the self-generated reminders of his talent's perversion. Nevertheless, when presented the opportunity, as the play's action implies he inevitably will be, the American artist must repudiate those roles and plays. The sense of wasted talent and lost opportunity that permeates *Brutus* is less obvious in Payne's other plays, but it remains part of the fabric of many of his efforts, even such light pieces as *Charles the Second*, in which Rochester's reformation merely highlights his dissipated past.

Despite his individual unwillingness or inability to reject the ideological and aesthetic demands of European managers and audiences, Payne is representative of the vast majority of romantic playwrights in the period before the Civil War who confronted in one manner or another their ambivalent artistic heritage. Drawn by an artistic allegiance which transcended national boundaries, these writers often sought to minimize the nationalistic elements in their plays by locating the action in a distant era or locale. Nevertheless, they could not escape issues and attitudes which pressed home to them their affiliation with the "American experiment." Payne's career represents one accommodation available to these writers. In addition, Payne provided a much-needed boost to American drama and American dramatists. His success upon the larger stage of Europe made Payne seem the embodiment of the thesis that America's playwrights could be accepted on the international scene. More important, his plays, especially *Brutus*, secured a permanent niche in the standing repertoire of American companies and provided a visible model for American playwrights to emulate.

Robert Montgomery Bird: Romantic Drama in the Age of Jackson

While the tide of Jacksonian democracy swept across the nation's political stage, Robert Montgomery Bird, the most talented American dramatist in the first third of the century, continued to people the theatrical stage with exotics living out their adventures in faraway lands. Born into a wealthy family in New Castle, Delaware, in 1806, Bird suffered through an unhappy early childhood after the family was separated at the death of his father. Having endured a Dickensian experience at the New Castle Academy, Bird rejoined his mother in Philadelphia and graduated from the Germantown Academy in 1824 and the medical school of the University of Pennsylvania in 1827. While still in medical school, Bird had begun writing verse and plays. After an unsatisfying year in medicine, he abandoned his practice and undertook to become a serious writer. His first professional effort, *Pelopias*, was awarded the prize in Edwin Forrest's 1830 contest for new dramas, but was never acted. After consulting with Forrest, Bird wrote *The Gladiator* (1831), which proved to be one of Forrest's most enduring successes. He quickly followed with *Oralloossa* (1832) and capped his dramatic endeavors with *The Broker of Bogota* (1834). Quickly recognizing that his plays would not provide the financial security he needed, Bird turned his efforts to novels, producing, among others, *Nick of the Woods* (1837), one of the most popular of the frontier novels. After quarreling with Forrest in 1837, Bird retired from the theater for the duration of his life. Following brief stints as a gentleman farmer in Maryland and as a professor of medicine at the Pennsylvania Medical College, Bird became active in Whig politics. He eventually joined his writing talents and political beliefs by becoming the publisher of the Whig newspaper, the Philadelphia *North American and United States Gazette*, a position he held until his death in 1854.[5]

More than those of any other American writer of romantic drama in the first half of the century, Bird's plays reveal the subtle impact of democratic ideology upon romantic tragedy. While Bird could focus on the dilemmas of nations and pivotal moments of history, as he did in *Oralloossa*, his most theatrically and aesthetically successful plays reflect a pronounced bias toward the concerns of the common man. Works such as *The Gladiator* and *The Broker of Bogota* argue forcefully that tragedy is as available to the commoner as it is to a king. Through his choice of subjects, his language, and his characterizations, Bird presented his audience with men and women who possessed a dignity historically reserved for the social, economic, and political elite. In the process, he provided another tentative resolution to the dilemma of how American playwrights might compose a tragedy pertinent to a growing democratic society without resorting to parochial subject matter.

The Gladiator is an interesting example of Bird's attempt to demystify the remote world of classical history, a fertile ground of romantic drama and one from which the common man had been almost totally effaced. Indeed, on the surface, ancient Rome would seem a particularly inhospitable setting to explore democratic ideals in any form. But the themes of freedom, slavery, imperialism, and the dignity of the natural man that Bird associated with Spartacus's rebellion against the power of imperial Rome made the play particularly pertinent only three years after Andrew Jackson's populist victory of 1828.

After his capture, Spartacus refuses to become a gladiator until he finds that his wife and child are alive and his master agrees to buy them in exchange for Spartacus's services. However, when Spartacus enters the Arena to find that his opponent is his brother and that the Romans expect them to fight to the death, he joins his brother in an uprising which soon brings much of the slave population of Rome to their cause. Having defeated several Roman forces sent against them, Spartacus and his brother disagree on strategy—Phasarius wishes to lay siege to Rome itself, while Spartacus wants to depart Italy and return to Thrace. When Spartacus insists on his proposal and, at the instigation of his wife, refuses to surrender Julia, the captured niece of praetor Crassus, Phasarius breaks with his brother and takes away his followers. Phasarius foolishly attacks a Roman army and his force is annihilated. After his brother's penitent return, Spartacus entrusts his wife and son to Phasarius and successfully escapes Crassus's forces with the remnant of his army. His triumph is rendered hollow when his dying brother enters to reveal that Spartacus's wife and son have been killed in their escape attempt. Driven to despair, Spartacus gives over Julia and renews his assault on Crassus. Spartacus dies defiantly in a final attack on Crassus's tents.

Though there is no evidence to support the supposition that Bird was writing an abolitionist tract, by 1831 the continuation of slavery was emerging as the central divisive issue between North and South. Nat Turner's failed uprising in Virginia and the beginning of William Lloyd Garrison's abolitionist newspaper, *The Liberator*, both of which occurred the same year the play premiered, indicate the pertinence of the play to the contemporary society. Jacksonian social institutions aside, Bird's choice of subject certainly insured that his audience would confront issues of slavery and freedom, elite and common culture, and imperialism and isolationism. Spartacus, of course, embodies many of the ideological assumptions of Jacksonian America—belief in a non-elitist culture, a desire for individual freedom, and, above all, a belief in the political and moral worth of the common man. But Rome—with its ideology buttressing institutional slavery, elitist culture, and ruthless imperialism—is drawn with such care that the hero's indictment seems almost superfluous. The slave auction (a scene whose emotional power was to make it ubiquitous in anti-slavery plays a bit later), the episodes of gladiatorial combat that validate Spartacus's characterization of the Arena as a "temple, where [the Romans] mock the Gods / With human butchery," and the searing portrait of Thrace rendered a wasteland by the imperialistic impulses of Rome all speak to the dangers of cultural and political tyranny.[6]

Despite the play's overtly democratic political themes, its language can initially present something of a puzzle for the modern reader. Following his day's generally accepted rules of decorum in tragedy, Bird liberally sprinkled *The Gladiator* with pronouns more common to Elizabethan England than to either Rome or nineteenth-century America, giving the play a certain stilted quality. Nevertheless, the imagery is rich and capable of conveying both great beauty and fine pieces of characterization. For example, late in the fourth act, Bird suggests the complexity of Spartacus's character in a telling speech that reveals both his humble origins and the grandeur of his imagination. In a poetic rhapsody about his youth in Thrace, Spartacus delivers his paean in appropriately bucolic verse:

> In my green youth I look'd
> From the same frosty peak, where now I stood,
> And then beheld the glory of those lands,
> Where peace was tinkling on the shepherd's bell
> And singing with the reapers; or beneath
> The shade of thatch eaves, smiled grey old men,
> And with their children laughed along the green. (265)

This deeply personal vision presented in conventionally pastoral terms is available only after Spartacus has freed himself from the limitations imposed by the mundane perspective of less daring men. He has climbed "cloud-piercing Haemus" where his only companions are "the eagles and the thunders" (265). But even as he elevates Spartacus's language, Bird is careful to portray his hero's vision in terms that would have resonated for an American audience deeply aware of the correspondences being drawn between the wilds of Thrace and the frontier of America. Bird therefore carefully utilizes images that associate Spartacus with the seemingly elemental freedom of nature. Spartacus is the heroic common man—not, as in the case of melodramatic heroes, a common man made heroic by a tragic situation. He arises from a common social station to live out his tragic life in a world in which position and privilege have become equivalent to inhumanity and oppression.

The deftness of Bird's characterizations and their ability to elevate the life of the common man are best exemplified by his portrait of Baptista Febro in *The Broker of Bogota*. This masterpiece of domestic tragedy, set in the Spanish colonial empire of eighteenth-century South America, traces the destruction of Febro and his son Ramon. Having determined that his eldest son has been guilty of ignoring business and indulging in drunkenness and riotous living, Febro resolves to bring the boy back to a life of probity. He therefore disinherits Ramon and banishes him, demanding that Ramon give over his evil companions to re-enter his father's good graces. Febro is also persuaded that his daughter Leonor has a suitor he has not approved and demands that she refuse her suitor's attentions. Beguiled by the evil Cabarero and driven by the prospective loss of his fiancée, Juana, Ramon agrees to rob his father's vaults. When Febro, on the heels of the theft, goes to pay Ramon's debts, he is accused of stealing his clients' gold. Found guilty when the son refuses to verify his father's story, Febro's life is spared, but he is stripped of his property. Leonor, unaware of her father's hardships, elopes with "Rolando," the Viceroy's disguised son, Fernando. When Febro returns to the Viceroy's palace to rescue his daughter, Juana reveals that Ramon has confessed his part in the robbery. Although tottering at the brink of insanity and despair, Febro rejoices momentarily upon discovering that his daughter has married the Viceroy's son. But this happiness is short-lived. Febro learns that Ramon has disclosed to the authorities his part in the theft and committed suicide, and he dies of a broken heart.

The central figure of this piece, Baptista Febro, is a rich dramatic character whose social position serves to increase rather than diminish his complexity and his tragedy. Like Spartacus, Febro chooses to adopt and espouse a set of values which are alien to his situation in life. Since Spartacus is forced to act in the public arena, and more particularly in the world of arms where democracy is gauged inapt, his aristocratic values seem appropriate to his situation, and the circumstances allow Bird to argue that such values are as available to a Thracian commoner as they are to a Roman patrician. But Bird's decision to locate the action of *The Broker of Bogota* in the private world invariably prescribes an entirely different set of actions and audience expectations. The authoritarianism suitable to a shepherd turned general is less becoming in a father dealing with his son's private follies. However, part of Febro's tragic makeup is his inability to recognize the necessity for just such discriminations. Febro insists on minimizing the distinctions between private and public life and seeks to impose the same standard of conduct upon both. The enlightened aristocrat the Marquis de Palmera attempts to persuade Febro that such standards are too severe ("these are such ills as gentleness / Might best reprove"), but Febro is adamant in his error.[7] As his willingness to collapse youthful indiscretions and adult crimes into the same category indicates, Febro sees the power of civil law as an extension of the private moral authority of the father. Ramon's transgressions portend in Febro's mind not merely the demise of familial order but the destruction of the social framework which has made Febro's existence possible.

A loving father whose highhanded tactics tend to obscure his real affection for his son, Febro is partially unable to recognize his error because the old verities of the hierarchical world that has formed him are no longer functional. Though their trappings remain, the military and civil foundations of colonial empire represented by the aristocrat Palmera have slowly and surely been eroded by the leveling effects of money. Febro's wealth, on which even Palmera relies, stems not from the traditional bases of military proficiency or social class but from his economic facility. Caught in a moment of historical flux, unaware of the extent of his power, and unable to act ruthlessly, Febro falls back on the only social ethic which he knows. Unfortunately, Febro's elitist, aristocratically based ideology poorly meshes with the emerging social and economic reality of bourgeois capitalism. Indeed, Febro is destroyed by his blind adherence to an outmoded style of life. Wedded to a hierarchical model of personal and political relationships, he is unable to question his own assumptions about either. Most obviously, he blindly continues to dictate to his children, though both Ramon and Leonor have revolted to one extent or another. Unlike the aristocrat Palmera whose trust in his son is rewarded by Fernando's marriage to Leonor, Febro refuses to tolerate his children's natural desires to reach beyond the family to define themselves. Ramon's weakness and his poor judgment do not vindicate Febro's actions any more than Leonor's marriage justifies the children's rebellions. Out of a desire to protect them, Febro refuses to allow his children to confront temptations—a process acknowledged by many early nineteenth-century writers about child-rearing as a necessary step toward maturity.[8] Trapped between his need for order and control and his love for his children, Febro moves inexorably toward his destiny. As Palmera poignantly notes in the last lines of the play, both the "rigid sire and disobedient son" (235) are doomed by heaven to pay for their sins and follies.

Despite his other shortcomings, Febro is incapable of adopting the wholly amoral economic ethic espoused by the manipulator Cabarero. Cabarero makes clear that he understands the operation of the new order:

"Give me gold, and I will show thee the picture of philosophy, the credential of excellence, the corner-stone of greatness" (201). Cabarero's materialist machinations indicate that he is hardly meant to serve as a model. He destroys families, perverts romances, and will blithely accept the death of an innocent man solely to obtain money. He ends the play disgraced and condemned, a portent, the play seems to suggest, of those who give over humanity for money.

The variety of Bird's works is indicative in many ways of the entire spectrum of American romantic drama in the first half of the nineteenth-century. While *The Gladiator* continues the well-established pattern of "democratizing" romantic tragedy, *The Broker of Bogota* demonstrates an increasing willingness to accept the conventions of the form on their own terms. Though it is tempting to suggest that the *The Broker of Bogota* intimates analogies between Febro's hierarchical attitude and those of tyrannic governments, the play is finally a domestic tragedy whose political component serves as the basis for a study of character, not as the focus of the play's action. At most, by dignifying Febro, the play indicates the added stature that a romantic vision of the common man—as upright, courageous, and fundamentally good—would provide to more politically oriented, "democratic" art.

George Henry Boker:
Romantic Tragedy's Quintessence

In nineteen days in 1853, George Henry Boker produced *Francesca da Rimini*, the play his biographer has called "the greatest American romantic tragedy, and one of the greatest poetical tragedies in the language."[9] Though revivals by Lawrence Barrett in 1882 and Otis Skinner in 1901 served to guarantee the play's reputation in the annals of the American theater, E. L. Davenport's initial 1855 mounting of the play in New York and Philadelphia met with only moderate success. Like Bird before him, Boker found his dramatic efforts unappreciated and turned his talents to other varieties of literary endeavor. Nevertheless, *Francesca da Rimini* remains impressive testimony to the power and artistry of American romantic drama in the mid-nineteenth century.[10]

Born in 1823 into a prominent Philadelphia banking family, Boker attended the Walker Private School and matriculated at Princeton where he studied literature and began writing poetry. Upon his graduation in 1842, Boker refused a position as secretary to the American ambassador in Vienna secured by his father, but agreed to his family's demands that he study law. He married in 1844 and continued his legal studies until his father agreed that he had no aptitude for the bar. After a tour of the Continent, he returned to Philadelphia determined to pursue a literary career. Though he continued to write poetry throughout most of his life, his produced plays were written in the brief period between 1848 and 1853: *Calaynos* (1848), *The Betrothal* (1850), *The World a Mask* (1851), *Leonor de Guzman* (1852), *Francesca da Rimini* (1853), and *The Bankrupt* (1853). The cool response of audiences and management to his plays, the politics and civic responsibilities of Philadelphia during the Civil War, and a personal preference for poetry directed his efforts away from the theater. In 1871 he accepted an appointment as minister to Turkey, a position in which he continued until he took up a similar assignment in Russia in 1875. Upon his return to private life in 1878, he became president of the Union League of Philadelphia, an organization he had helped found. After Barrett successfully revived *Francesca da Rimini* in 1882, Boker turned his hand again to drama, but none of the plays of this period were accepted for production. After enduring a prolonged illness the last three years of his life, he died in 1890.

The plot of Boker's *Francesca da Rimini* follows the outlines of the familiar story as related in Canto V of Dante's *The Inferno* and as modified by Boccaccio's *Il commento sopra Divina Commedia*.[11] In an attempt to end the feuding between Guelfs and Ghibellines, Lanciotto of Rimini is engaged to Francesca of Ravenna. Although a sensitive man and feared warrior, Lanciotto is physically deformed and argues that his courtier brother, Paolo, is more suited than he to fulfill such an alliance. When their father is adamant, Lanciotto contemplates suicide, but agrees to the marriage if Paolo will go to Ravenna to secure Francesca. Francesca, told that she must marry for political reasons, agrees to perform her duty. When Paolo arrives, Francesca mistakes him for Lanciotto and, though she soon discovers her mistake, the physical appearance of her intended husband is kept from her by her maid and Paolo. When they finally meet, Lanciotto releases Francesca and Ravenna from their pledges, but at the insistence of her father she restates her determination to marry Lanciotto. After revealing their trepidations to their confidants, Lanciotto and Francesca marry. But when Francesca shrinks from his nuptial kiss, Lanciotto recognizes immediately that she does not love him, and he eagerly embraces the news that the Ghibellines have revolted. Left alone by Lanciotto's departure for the wars, Francesca and Paolo confess their passion for one another. Having overheard the lovers' admissions, Pepe, the malicious jester who has sworn to revenge himself on Lanciotto and Paolo for beatings he has received from them, races to Lanciotto's camp and reveals what he has seen. Enraged by Pepe's story, Lanciotto seizes him. Pepe tries to kill Lanciotto with Paolo's stolen dagger, but Lanciotto stabs him. As he dies, Pepe says that Paolo has paid him to kill Lanciotto. Lanciotto returns to Rimini and confronts the lovers, who refuse to deny their love. After Paolo prevents Lanciotto from killing himself and thereby providing an "honorable" solution to the predicament of the three, Lanciotto stabs Francesca. When his brother still refuses to fight, Lanciotto kills Paolo.

While most critics agree that Boker's play is a superior achievement, they have been less than unanimous about the nature and methods of his tragedy.[12] A minority of critics read the play as a commentary on Boker's personal situation and, more generally, on the social/political conditions in nineteenth-century America. Paul Sherr, taking a cue from Edward Sculley Bradley, suggests that the intrusion into the play of certain "Americanisms" reveals Boker's disappointment with his own family for insisting that he lead a conventional life and the writer's growing dissatisfaction with Philadelphia and the nation at large for its increasing emphasis on a materialism which refused to acknowledge the importance of the arts (361–71). Paul Voelker argues that the central thematic interest of the play is a critique of the "fraudulent nature of the politics of an aristocratic system" and "the effects of such a system on those who are its instruments" (385). Both of these readings have at their hearts the seemingly prophetic figure of Pepe and, in particular, his third-act exchange with Lanciotto on philosophy and government. Sherr's argument posits an equation between Pepe and Boker as artistic "doubles," both of whom seek freedom from their society's restraints (369–70). Voelker portrays Pepe as a medieval Jacksonian Democrat committed to destroying the aristocratic world, a project that interestingly enough aligns him with a political double, Lanciotto, the only member of nobility to express any concern for the common people (390–92). Neither of these readings is particularly persuasive. As we have seen, American dramatists have rarely been reluctant to introduce political materials into their plays. Had Boker been intent upon political commentary, any number of stories would have been available. Yet, as one critic has correctly noted, "although the question of government surfaces several times, it never arises as crucial to any of Boker's four major tragedies."[13] More important, the action of play suggests that Boker, if he wished to maintain audience sympathy for

Lanciotto, would complicate the process by identifying him closely with Pepe. For all of his democratic rhetoric, Pepe's hatred of Paolo and Lanciotto does not stem from any significant class antagonisms. In the first-act monologue in which Pepe announces his intention to seek revenge, the character's emphasis is intensely personal as he viciously contrasts Lanciotto's malformed body with his own. Little that Pepe, the "natural" man, does in the remainder of the play would make an identification between the two characters desirable.

Though Boker may not have attempted to draw overt political correspondences, his own poetics suggest that he believed that the play was pertinent for its original audience. Certainly, the play's aesthetics reflect the widely held contemporary belief in the timelessness of truth and poetry, ideas given expression by, among others, Matthew Arnold in his attempt to define the educative function of the arts. Evans notes Boker's specific belief that the truth worthy of literary expression existed outside of time and place and that literature's function was to express that universal truth through a poetry whose linguistic bases were similarly eternal (Evans, *Boker*, 17–20). The import of this poetics on *Francesca da Rimini* is not only Boker's willingness to choose a medieval love affair as his subject but also his implicit assertion that a moving poetic presentation of the fate of these Italian aristocrats has significance for a democratic people living five hundred years later. Obviously Boker's attention is on three individuals destroyed by a web of fate that they themselves have fashioned, and not—or only coincidentally—on three aristocrats destroyed by a corrupt political system.

These matters aside, Boker's primary artistic contribution is his decision to shift the story's primary emphasis from the lovers to the husband, Lanciotto, thereby guaranteeing the play an original voice.[14] The traditional focus of the story is the love of Francesca and Paolo, and Boker handles this element of the story well, evoking our sympathy by suggesting their youth and beauty, the guiltless genesis of their love, their agony at the betrayal of Lanciotto, and their willingness to die rather than deny that love. Paolo begins the play a courtier, reputedly as successful in the fields of love as his brother is in battle. But his unwillingness to tolerate laughter directed at Lanciotto reveals not only his love for his brother and a keen sense of family honor, but also a clear vision of his own relative merit. His cryptic comments to Francesca in Ravenna reveal the rapidity with which his love has developed, the depths of his love, and the agony that it has brought to him: "Since I came, / Heaven bear me witness how my traitor heart / Has fought against my duty; and how oft / I wished myself in Lanciotto's place, / Or him in mine."[15] As the play progresses, Paolo, increasingly torn between his love for Lanciotto and his passion for Francesca, becomes almost paralyzed. By the final act, he is reduced to the object of Francesca and Lanciotto's competing desires.[16] Overcome by grief at his betrayal of Lanciotto and unable to find "some good cause to perish in" (364), his death, at the hands of his brother, is a merciful release from an unbearable torment.

Francesca evokes even more sympathy at the beginning of the play than does Paolo. A helpless pawn in the internecine feuding of Guelfs and Ghibellines, Francesca accepts her duty to act as agent to secure her family's safety. But the compassion she secures with her pointedly phrased reluctance at being given away "Like a fine horse or falcon" (330), merely prepares the audience for her compounded agony at discovering the deceptions that have been played upon her: "It was ill usage, gross abuse, / Treason to duty, meanness, craft—dishonour!" (334). The love she has inadvertently given to Paolo cannot be recalled, but she attempts valiantly to meet her obligations by marrying Lanciotto. Having laid the groundwork for and gained Paolo's confession of his love, she presses for the consummation of that love. The girl who leaves the stage with Paolo returns a woman ready either to die with her lover or to kill Lanciotto to preserve that love. Her dying words of love, "Here, rest thy head / Upon my bosom. Fie upon my blood! / It stains thy ringlets" (367) with its juxtapositions of tender mothering, romantic passion, and impending death epitomizes the potential denied and the merit wasted. Though each suffers individually the pangs of their situation, the tragedy of Paolo and Francesca resides finally in their inability to resolve the conflicting demands of their love for each other and the loyalty they feel toward Lanciotto (Evans, *Boker*, 77–78).

Though his portraits of Paolo and Francesca are well done, Boker's master stroke is his characterization of Lanciotto. Boker's decision to shift the center of the play to Lanciotto allows him to explore not only the perennial theme of appearance versus reality from yet another angle but also permits him to argue the power of fraternal love. Zanger has noted that Boker inverts the traditional portrait of Francesca's husband as a jealous, vengeful, and violent man by providing several speeches that indicate the depth of his compassion, his agonizing desire to love and be loved romantically, and his devotion to his younger brother (415). In a world in which surface beauty counts for all, however, he is doomed to endure his deformities alone. His despair at realizing that Francesca does not love him is compounded by his feeling of betrayal at the hands of

Paolo. Fate denies Lanciotto, as it does the lovers, any acceptable alternative. He could, perhaps, tolerate the loss of Francesca; he has, after all offered to give her up before. But the loss of Paolo is more than he can endure. Driven to name the pain which racks him, Lanciotto settles upon "family honor," but as his final words reveal, that phrase poorly expresses his pain: "I cannot cheat myself with words! / I loved him more than honour—more than life— / This man, [my] Paolo—this stark bleeding corpse! / Here let me rest, till God awake us all" (368).

Boker's accomplishment in *Francesca da Rimini* was of little immediate effect on the course of American drama. Though the productions of Barrett and Skinner provided the play lasting fame, its initial lack of success convinced Boker to turn his literary attentions elsewhere. Thus, American theater lost its most powerful and compelling romantic dramatist. Nevertheless, Boker's play provides telling commentary on the state of American romantic tragedy in the mid-nineteenth century. While the political perspectives which had once made romantic tragedy suspect had diminished through the first half of the century, the tastes of the audiences had not proved receptive to its vision. Often removed in time and attitude from the world of their audiences, these plays, especially if they lacked an overt political element to which the audience could relate, paled in comparison to the more parochially oriented popular plays. The simpler heroism of Louisa Medina's frontiersman, Nick of the Woods, though homegrown, seems to have excited audiences as much or more than did the exploits of Brutus or Spartacus. The theatrically successful poetic drama that American romantic dramatists sought to bring to the American stage remained a distant vision, but a vision American writers had proved they could grasp.

5

The Popular Drama
Before the Civil War

The forty-odd years between the end of the War of 1812 and the outbreak of the Civil War were decades in which the tenuous nature of the young republic's political accommodations, economic foundations, and social codes were sorely tried and inevitably refashioned. The development and eventual admission as states of the vast territory of the Old Northwest, the emergence of Jacksonian democracy with its concomitant economic and social tensions, the continuation of slavery and increasing impatience of abolitionists and "Free-soil" men with the South's "unique institution," and persisting international tensions—all these proved material for the popular theater. Meanwhile, the recurrent demands for the creation of an acceptably democratic American literature provided a grounding rationale for not only a poetic but also a popular drama.

If poetic drama reiterated for upper-class, educated America a set of traditional values and a sense of America's affinities with the Western cultural tradition, the "common folk" found an equally appealing reflection of their emerging ideals and identity in the popular drama of the day. In large measure eschewing the elevated language and romantic displacements of its poetic counterpart, popular drama sought to reconcile two potentially conflicting goals. Above all else, these plays aimed at entertaining their audiences, at being theatrically successful: They are pervaded with spectacle, melodramatic situations, stereotypical characters, a morally unambiguous universe, and an unabashed nationalism. At the same time, these plays face straightforwardly the immediately relevant question of the national character, reflecting Americans' often localized sense of themselves at mid-century. For an audience anxiously seeking to discover itself in the mirror of the stage, these plays represented an ongoing attempt to define America and Americans, a theatrical taking stock. Firmly rooted in their historical moment and reflecting many of the prejudices and concerns of the day, these "entertainments" explore a staggering range of moral, political and social questions about American life. The frontier, sectional differences among older parts of the union, the influence of foreign cultures on America, private and public vices, and burning social issues such as temperance and slavery all provided grist for the dramatists' mill.

Wedded to the proposition that the bustling and energetic America of the 1830s, '40s and '50s would continue its economic and political vitality, the plays explicitly asserted that the country was also capable of greater moral and cultural growth. Many of them also implicitly suggest that the economic and political events transforming both the original colonies and the western territories often compromised—and in some cases repudiated—personal and civic morality. Thus, these plays often sought to instruct both the individual and the nation, blatantly propounding their ideologies through a range of literary and theatrical devices. Though it would be a mistake to think of these plays solely as moral, political, or social tracts, many playwrights used the forum provided by the stage to engage in polemics on contemporary personalities and topics: the frontier and its inhabitants, the Yankee, city life and fashionable society, and slavery, to name only a few.

The Myth of the Frontier: *The Noble Savages of Stone and Paulding*

The continuing movement of the population west from the original colonies was one of the great events of the age and one destined to throw into relief many of the new nation's most cherished assumptions about itself. The migration of thousands of Americans to the frontiers initially east and later west of the Mississippi River marked not only a major demographic shift but also a transformation in the collective imagination of Americans toward the lands of the west. The seventeenth-century "wilderness," with its biblical overtones of moral and physical tempering, had become, by the mid-nineteenth century, the promised lands. A procession of trappers, woodsmen, farmers, and merchants lured by fur, free farmland, untapped sources of raw materials, and new markets for finished goods quickly transformed the "backwoods" into hamlets and cities. With the forced relocation or military suppression by 1840 of most of the Native Americans east of the Mississippi, later pioneers escaped one of the perennial obstacles to westward expansion. Nevertheless, the hardships of western life were still sufficiently daunting to allow those who survived and succeeded to feel that they had earned their place in the America they were settling and redefining.

The transformations were not merely economic and demographic. One consequence of the migration from the older states was an attenuation of the staid influences of Boston, New York, and Philadelphia, the old colonial bastions of high culture. Traditional versions of heroic life derived from classical history or romantic sources seemed in some ways as alien to the wilderness settlers as the tree-lined avenues of Boston. More important, for frontier writers (of both the east and west), the lands of the west and their hardy, colorful inhabitants provided a wealth of new material. There quickly emerged a series of myths collectively embodying the ideology of the frontier, whose effect was to sustain and legitimate those ideals of frontier life credited with taming the land (and its previous inhabitants) to the rough-and-ready aspirations of the newest Americans. Building upon foundations provided by earlier writers of frontier lore, John Augustus Stone and James Kirke Paulding provided the library and theater with exciting tales based upon two new American romantic figures—the Native American and the frontiersman.

The initial and purest exploitation of the frontier myth is found in Stone's *Metamora*. Responding to Edwin Forrest's nationalistic call in the New York *Critic* (28 November 1828) for a five-act tragedy with an "aboriginal of this country" as the central character, John Augustus Stone wrote *Metamora; or, The Last of the Wampanoags*. An actor himself, Stone capably tailored his play to Forrest's expansive acting style and, in the process, provided Forrest with one of his most popular and financially successful roles. Reworked by Stone and Forrest, the final version of the play presents a telling commentary on the period's assumptions concerning acting and on Forrest's prejudices in particular. More important, *Metamora* evidences the early American theater's recognition of the emerging mythology of the frontier and its dramatic potential. At the same time, *Metamora* suggests the romantic vision's resistance to cultural particularization. Without Forrest's buckskins, knife, and headband, Metamora might easily step into any number of romantic stories chronicling the demise of the superior individual in ancient Greece or Rome.[1] Forrest's stirring portrayal of the doomed primitive, the appeal of native subject matter, and a chauvinistic impulse within American theater guaranteed the play's initial success and its attractiveness as a model. When John Brougham finally hooted them from the stage with his withering parody *Metamora; or, The Last of the Pollywogs* (1847), "Indian" plays had been a staple of the American theater for almost twenty years.[2]

Metamora draws its inspiration from the legend of King Philip, or Metacom, who led the Wampanoags and Narragansetts in a short war against English settlers in Massachusetts, Connecticut, and Rhode Island (June 1675–August 1676). However, beyond meeting the demands of Forrest's contest, Metamora's historical reality is irrelevant to the play. His character owes much more to the already well-established "noble savage" tradition than to the historical record. While the play lacks the sophistication of plotting and characterization of other romantic dramas, it provides an interesting insight into American playwrights' attempts to deal with the conflict between romantic individualism and a stable social order.

Stone's double-plotted drama is standard "Indian play" fare. In the secondary plot, Oceana's regicide father bows to blackmail by offering to marry his daughter to the villainous Lord Fitzarnold, rather than to the virtuous Walter, later revealed to be the son of Sir Walter Vaughn. The main plot traces Metamora's attempts to resist English colonial expansion after he is falsely accused of murder. Having befriended Oceana, Metamora first spares the girl and her father in the midst of a general massacre and later resolves Oceana's romantic dilemmas by slaying Fitzarnold, who had previously ignored pleas for assistance from Metamora's wife and was about to compound that villainy by assaulting Oceana's virtue. Following the historical record, Metamora suffers the destruction of his tribe and the death of his infant son before being trapped by the colonists. Recognizing his doom, he stabs his wife to death and dies in a volley of muskets while cursing the English. With Fitzarnold dead, Oceana is free to marry Walter.

Metamora's cultural and moral otherness provides the basis for a series of implicit comparisons and contrasts. There is little doubt that the romantic primitive is in many ways the play's most attractive character. Unlike the English, busily carving a new country out of a resistant frontier, Metamora is at one with the rough-hewn Eden of the new world. Indeed, his very existence is indivisible from the wilderness; like Adam, he inhabits it "as if a sculptor's hand had carved him there."[3] But in the romantic world of Stone's play, Metamora's woodland existence transcends mere enviable forest-craft, for nature is fraught with moral significance. Thus Walter can contend that efforts to Anglicize Metamora would "cost him half his native virtues," and that his pagan beliefs are at least partially excusable since "his worship though untaught and rude flows from his heart, and Heaven alone must judge of it" (12). Metamora quickly emerges as the embodiment of physical nature's noblest elements, "the grandest model of a mighty man" (10).[4]

For all his perfections, however, Metamora and his way of life, as the original 1829 audience knew well, had been swept away before a seemingly inevitable tide of cultural destiny. As an heir to white colonization, Stone attempts to justify the course of history through an appeal to cultural chauvinism ostensibly grounded in divine authority. Additionally, events during Metamora's war with the English provide the occasion for the audience's revaluation of him in concrete circumstances that reveal the cultural disparities existing between the English and the Native Americans—or, at least, the white man's vision of them.

Although Metamora's love of country and family and his tactical brilliance as a military leader initially enhance his stature in the audience's eyes, his barbarism, like that of Marlowe's Tamburlaine, is obviously designed to both awe and repel. Though the English are as willing as the Wampanoags to destroy, Stone insists that the English lack Metamora's capacity to revel in the process. Against Metamora's "Drag him away to the fire of the sacrifice that my ear may drink the music of his dying groans" (28), Stone portrays reluctant English settlers realizing, "'Tis time to lift the arm so long supine, and with one blow cut off this heathen race, who spite of reason and the word revealed, continue hardened in their devious ways, and make the chosen tremble" (20). The evocation of a divinely inspired historical, political, and social order serves to accentuate the cultural differences that Stone has downplayed in the play's exposition. Like latter-day Israelites, the English stand ready to seize the land they have been promised. Ironically, even Metamora's own portentous dreams of destruction are made to support the English. Thus, while Metamora remains primarily a romantic hero, the audience is called upon to evaluate his character by standards which contradict the romantic ideology at the base of his characterization. On the one hand, Metamora makes a persuasive case for the romantic vision of man. At one with nature and the ideals which are reflected there, he is appealing as an individual. On the other hand, Metamora's unique stature and Stone's refusal to extend his qualities to other Native Americans in the play suggest that he is atypical of his culture. Religious truth and social progress reside with the English. Like biblical Israel, the America which will evolve from these colonial events is sufficient warrant to justify the destruction of Metamora and his people. By couching the conflict as one between individual potentiality and the power of countervailing cultural and historical forces, Stone is able simultaneously to heighten the pathos associated with Metamora, excuse white responsibility for his death, and celebrate the political and social institutions that are to a large extent contingent upon the destruction of the pre-European inhabitants.

To its contemporary viewers, *Metamora* proved that native materials were worthy of serious romantic treatment. To later historians, the play has testified to the domestication of the romantic impulse in the "Indian plays." Though these plays remained popular throughout the period, Stone's characterization of Metamora provides insight into one of the reasons for their eventual demise. These dramas insisted upon translating local individuals and events into universal characters and situations whose particulars are essentially irrelevant. Metamora is remarkable at the beginning of the play not because his origins in an alien culture allow the audience to see him and itself more clearly by recognizing the essential differences between two ways of life, but because his existence suggests that honesty, courage, and loyalty were indigenous to America even before the advent of the English colonies. At best Metamora is a singular individual in a defunct culture who, while intriguing, offers only limited insight into the audience's culture. Stone attempts to ameliorate this sense of uniqueness in the finale by counterpointing Metamora's death with the revelation of Walter's parentage. However, the play's suggestion that within the stable, "civilized" context of colonial society Metamora's attributes inhere in the "average" man and lead inevitably to social and economic elevation is too fragile to resist serious scrutiny. Thus, though Metamora is superficially an "aboriginal of this country," he is much more a romantic hero in the vein of Brutus or Mazeppa than a recognizable American. Although he could not finally resolve the conflicting romantic and cultural fictions, Stone was perfectly capable of exploiting their obvious appeals. His play is probably more important, therefore, as an indication of America's continued strivings for a cultural representation than for the particular artistic solution it provided.

If Native Americans provided appealing portraits of honor and courage in the face of an irresistible cultural tide, the frontiersmen who supplanted them, historically and theatrically, offered a more overtly American model of heroism. In such plays as Louisa Medina's *Nick of the Woods* (1838) and W. R. Derr's *Kit Carson, The Hero of the Prairie* (1850), the hero tamed land and savage with a daring that guaranteed his perpetuation as an American type in popular culture. In some senses only time and technology separate Nick of the Woods from Matt Dillon. But heroism is available to comedy as well as more overtly serious forms, and the plays of the period also utilized the frontiersman as comic social commentator. The most energetic and culturally penetrating of this latter group is James Kirke Paulding's brief piece, *The Lion of the West.*[5]

Originally composed for James H. Hackett's 1830 contest soliciting "an original comedy whereof an American should be the leading character," *The Lion of the West* became one of the most successful plays in Hackett's repertoire. Hackett had the play revised, once by John Augustus Stone, and again for its English premiere by William Bayle Bernard, who retitled it *The Kentuckian; or, A Trip to New York.* The play's contemporary appeal is obvious, for it relies upon two of the period's cherished comic formulas—crossed courtship and a bumptious, eccentric protagonist. This two-act farce loosely links two "romantic" actions. In the first, Caroline Freeman, an American heiress, is pursued by two Englishmen: the honorable merchant, Mr. Percival, and the false aristocrat, Jenkins. In the second, Nimrod Wildfire, the title character, turns fashionable New York society upon its head by mistakenly pursuing and trying to marry the condescending English visitor, Amelia Wollope.[6]

Paulding's effort clearly owes a debt to such plays as *The Contrast*, which established the country/city and American/English contrasts as fertile grounds for American comedy. Nevertheless, an examination of *The Lion of the West* provides insight into popular comedy's social and political functionings in the Jacksonian period. By exploring afresh the old discrepancies between England and America, Paulding reiterates the traditional American endorsement of democratic liberality over European social convention and class-consciousness. But by also developing the heretofore largely unexamined comic possibilities in the relationships among Americans from different sections of the country, Paulding points to the emergence of various "Americas" and to the tensions which reside behind the play's comic action. One of the play's major subtexts is the behind the play's comic action. One of the play's major subtexts is the nation's emerging sectional conflict, a theme which was playing itself out on the contemporary political scene in both easterners' anxieties at what many of them saw as the divisively egalitarian impulses of frontier-inspired Jacksonian democracy, as well as in discussions of the states' rights to nullify national legislation.

Paulding launches his frontal assault on English culture by caricaturing the English in Amelia Wollope and her brother, John Jenkins. Each character's actions provide the opportunity to suggest the unsuitability of English mores to a developing American nation and to question the bases of English "civility." Amelia Wollope's desire to "ameliorate the barbarism of American manners" suggests not only a willful misapprehension of most of American society but also the English cultural chauvinism deeply resented by Americans in the mid-nineteenth century (Paulding, 31).[7] Modeled on the British novelist Frances Trollope (whose 1827–1831 sojourn in America provided the basis for her scathing indictment *Domestic Manners in America*), Amelia is completely at a loss in a society which does not subscribe to her culturally derived set of decorums. Though many in the play's early audiences might well have agreed that by English standards, American society was somewhat unrefined, they could not have escaped realizing with Caesar, "a free gemman of color" who serves Amelia tea, that her insistence upon repressing the "impertinent liberty" of those she deems her social inferiors is but the social concomitant of a broader political program which would effectively "'stinguish the civil liberty" (31–32). Amelia's motivations are further called into question by her insistent linking of sensibility with money, "refinement at 500 dollars a share" (43). Indeed, her failure to secure an income, as much as her indelicate treatment at the hands of Wildfire, precipitates her indignant exit from the play and from America.

Though Amelia is finally nothing more than a presumptuous cultural interloper, it is her brother who sustains Americans' most fundamental prejudices about the English. Jenkins, who has purloined the identity of his late friend, Lord Grandby, reveals a purely mercenary interest in Caroline Freeman. Marriage, he allows, will only permit him "to escape one prison by opening the doors of another" (29). In both impulse and manner, damningly contrasted to his upright countryman, the aptly-named merchant prince Percival, Jenkins's craven nature is revealed by his "duel" with Wildfire. His plans defeated and his identity revealed, this "possum" (as Wildfire brands him) skulks from the stage at the play's end. Paulding's delineation of Jenkins's folly and villainy completes the undermining of English claims to cultural superiority.[8]

Though the English are the most obvious targets of his cultural criticisms, Americans do not altogether escape Paulding's satire. By shifting the action of the play from frontier Cincinnati (the historic locale of Frances Trollope's department store and of her attempts at cultural reclamation) to New York, Paulding is able to examine the growing disparity and tensions between the "aristocratic" pretensions of many city-dwellers and the more humble mores of their country-cousins. The effete values and social aspirations of easterners are embodied in Mrs. Freeman, who evidences a decidedly undemocratic turn of mind by declaring that her husband's reluctance to encourage the suit of Lord Grandby is nothing more than "republican infatuation" (20). She compounds her lack of judgment by sneering that the untutored but good-hearted Wildfire is a "savage" and that "so plain a person as . . . Percival" is obviously without merit (22, 37). That easterners are not beyond hope of redemption is indicated by Mr. Freeman and his daughter, Caroline. Freeman strikes the "correct" political stance by maintaining (to the disgust of his wife) that in America, the only titles are those conferred by integrity, talent and hard work. Paulding further emphasizes the democratic impulse of the play by having Caroline recognize that Percival is the appropriate choice for her husband because he is "affable, intelligent, and generous" (37). Though this view finally prevails, the elitist aspirations of Mrs. Freeman indicate that Americans must remain vigilant to avoid the lures of "fashion."

Resistance is made somewhat easier by the existence of a social litmus test in the person of Nimrod Wildfire, Jacksonian democracy personified.[9] While the romances move the action, the center of audience attention and interest resides almost solely in this character. Wildfire dominates the stage, committing an endless series of farcical *faux pas*—using the king of clubs as a calling card, asserting that he finds dangling his feet out of a window refreshing after dinner, intentionally overturning trays of food, transforming a fashionable *soiree* into barn dance, and generally ignoring the dictates of fashionable society—much to the dismay of his uncle's more refined wife and the supercilious Mrs. Wollope. But Wildfire's missteps are seemingly redeemed by his vanquishing of the villain and serendipitous rescue of Caroline. The play's action vindicates Freeman's assertions that his nephew's "whimsical extravagance of speech" and "total ignorance of conventional restraint" stem from "mere exuberance of spirits" and is more than compensated "by a heart which would scorn to do a mean or dishonest action" (22). In the comic world of the play, Wildfire's energy is more than a match for the social conventions of the Old World. In short, Nimrod Wildfire is, for his own time, the perennially appealing American iconoclast devoted to puncturing the pretensions of the social upper class.

The romantic conception of Stone and Forrest and the comic vision of Paulding and his collaborators are telling indices of the era's innocence. As these playwrights scoured the history of colonial America or cast their eyes about their own time, they seem to have been consistently drawn to characters able to transcend, however temporarily, social limitations. On the American stage, these Native Americans and white frontiersmen provided vindication for the Jacksonian democrats' repudiation of what they saw as a corrupt social order. Beyond the momentary influence that they probably had on the political attitudes of their audiences, there can be little doubt that these plays certainly aided the emergence of the American myth of rugged individualism. Certainly in these plays that individualism was beginning to take on a distinctly localized cast. While the serious "noble savage" plays were eventually propelled into dramatic oblivion by John Brougham's parodies, the comic appeals of American iconoclasts and regional eccentrics endured. Rarely afterwards, however, was the humor to be so unequivocal. Subsequently, the humor was often reduced as these characters were placed in dramatic universes more complex than Paulding's. As we shall observe in the discussion of the slavery plays, for example, the humorous antics of sectional characters would gradually lose much of their appeal. In 1830, the divisive effects of sectionalism that were to propel the country into a bloody Civil War were only beginning to emerge in the national consciousness.

Though novel in its appeal, the frontier was not the only area to provide the American stage a regional character. Indeed, at this time, New England was re-emerging with renewed vitality in the person of the indomitable Yankee. Again setting forth to see the world beyond the hills and valleys of his native Down East, the Yankee served both to remind the nation of its rural roots and to reinforce America's growing sense that those roots nurtured a practical intelligence and a basic honesty even when they had been transplanted to the city.

The Heirs of Jonathan: The Stage Yankee

Long before the frontiersman had emerged as a regional type, Royall Tyler had introduced the first distinctly American character to the national stage in Jonathan, the Vermont farmer and former soldier who journeys with his old commander from the wilds of New England to the seat of colonial culture, New York. From 1787 until the Civil War, Jonathan's dramatic progeny ventured forth to both American and foreign locales. When he had tired of America's Eastern cities, the Yankee sailed to France, England, Cuba, Poland, Algiers, Spain, and China, indulging in his usual antics to the consternation of the local populations.[10]

The development of the Yankee character is at once a tale of continuity and change. From Tyler onward, the function of the Yankee was principally comic, a role for which he was perfectly suited by his background. As the eternal country bumpkin, he is constantly amazed at the urban environment in which he inevitably finds himself. Lost both literally and figuratively in the urban crush, he is reduced to absolute confusion by the throngs of people: "No, I don't know where anybody lives in this big city, not I; for my part I believe how they all lives in the street, there's such a monstrous sight of people scourging backards and forards."[11] Though often befuddled by his surroundings and circumstances, the Yankee consistently refuses to acknowledge anyone as his superior, especially his social superior. Like his forefather in *The Contrast*, the Yankee might be in the service of another, but employment never gives him master. This social independence seemingly stems from his simple belief that rural life demands more of men than does city life. Given the opportunity, he will reel off a catalogue of accomplishments which suggested the breadth of his personal and social vision: "I'm the boy for a race, for an apple-paring or quilting frolic—fight a cock, hunt an opposum, or snare a partridge with any one.—Then I'm a squire, and a country judge, and a *brevet* ossifer in the militia besides, and a devil of a fellow at an election to boot."[12]

This vanity, at once akin to that of frontiersman yet couched in uniquely New England vernacular, is often complemented by an inquisitiveness that makes a shambles of social decorums. The Yankee's egocentricism proves especially humorous in his dealings with women. Though he always maintains that he is married or betrothed to a local deacon's daughter, the Yankee away from home is often a philanderer whose romantic ineptitude is the butt of many jokes. Despite his shortcomings, the Yankee does have a more serious side to his character which tends to emerge in the plays later in the period. While often presented as one willing to engage in rural sharp practice, the Yankee will rarely contravene basic morality. With a shift in emphasis, this fundamental honesty can propel him into the role of protector of those more vulnerable than himself.[13]

While more than a hundred pre–Civil War plays exist in which a Yankee has either a principal or minor role, the central moments in the evolution of the Yankee character and the Yankee play can be traced through references to a handful of events and people. In the period immediately after the success of *The Contrast*, the Yankee character emerged as the central figure in such works as Beach's *Jonathan Postfree; or, The Honest Yankee* (1807) and Lindsley's *Love and Friendship; or, Yankee Notions* (1809). But it was the advent of a group of actors who sought to specialize in Yankee roles—and the success of two works—which served to guarantee the character's enduring popularity. Ironically, the first actor to recognize the box-office potential of the Yankee was not an American, but an Englishman, Charles Mathews, who drew upon his experiences on an 1822–23 American tour to write (in collaboration with Richard B. Peake) *Jonathan in England* (1824). Hoping to capitalize upon the reputation of Mathews's play, the American actor, James H. Hackett adapted the English dramatist George Coleman's *Who Wants a Guinea* as *John Bull at Home; or, Jonathan in England* (1828). His success in the role encouraged other Americans, notably George Handel "Yankee" Hill, John E. Owens, Dan Marble, and Joshua Silsbee, who collectively kept the Yankee on the stage almost continually until after the Civil War.

The demand for roles encouraged the proliferation of Yankee plays of varying quality. The first major success in this resurgent genre was Samuel Woodworth's *The Forest Rose*, a comedy with music first produced in 1825. Unlike his immediate predecessors who placed the Yankee at the center of the play, Woodworth subordinated him to the main characters and used him as a counterpoint. Nevertheless, much of the humor in the play derives from Jonathan Ploughboy, whose simplicity and ineptitude in love is balanced by his "cracker-barrel" philosophy and general shrewdness, and the play's forty-year success is almost solely attributable to this one character. After Woodworth's piece had again verified the appeal of such plays, the Yankee actors found their next great role in Joseph S. Jones's *The People's Lawyer; or, Solon Shingle* (1839), a comedy typical in its manner of delighting audiences that distinguished itself by hinting at a serious element within the Yankee's character.

The action of this play has little to do with the Yankee character whose name appears in the play's subtitle. The plot actually centers around the efforts of Robert Howard, the People's Lawyer, to exonerate Charles Otis, an innocent young clerk who has been discharged and falsely accused of theft by his former employer, Hugh Winslow, after

Charles has refused to lie for him. In the play's climax, Howard wrenches a confession from the employer's accomplice, secures Winslow's arrest, and proceeds home to propose to and be accepted by Charles's sister Grace, whom Howard has wooed while disguised as a lowly mechanic. Solon Shingle's basic role throughout the play is to wander into the serious action, punctuating it with irrelevant, farcical interruptions.

While Howard is set up as the hero of the piece and Shingle "simply talks on and on," the Yankee's presence in the play need not be wholly explained as a plot device (Meserve, *Outline*, 71). Shingle serves an important thematic function by providing parallels to both of the younger men. Like Otis, Shingle has become embroiled in a legal case by refusing to settle his own dispute dishonestly; his situation in Boston thus offers a comic counterpoint to Otis's more serious dilemma. Jones also exploits the affinity between the two characters by making Shingle's curiosity and naiveté the means of delaying and eventually frustrating the villain's plans. Shingle's comic performance in the courtroom, when he mistakes the proceedings against Otis as an investigation into a missing barrel of his applesauce, temporarily reduces the case against Otis to comic confusion and foreshadows Howard's explosion of the conspiracy less than three pages later.

His relationship to Howard, though less obvious, is perhaps even more central to the play's thrust. At the play's end we learn that Howard's father has insisted that his son learn a manual skill as well as the profession of the law. Indeed, throughout most of the play Howard has appeared on stage as a simple working man, a man of Shingle's social class. The parallel may be dismissed as merely the fortuitous result of Jones's employing the "disguised prince" motif in his love story. But as Thomas Dekker's *The Shoemaker's Holiday* suggested long before, there is a significant difference between living incognito among the poor and mastering one of their crafts. Howard's adoption of his role as the People's Lawyer stems directly from his daily confrontation with those who abuse the poor, and like Shingle's namesake, Solon, Howard has attempted to use the law wisely to redress social injustice. Thus, the Puritan ethic's myth of honest, physical labor tied to social and ethical responsibility, which finds comic expression in Shingle, is given heroic stature in Howard.

And Shingle seems suggestive on a more general level. The end of the play provides the apparently irrelevant information that Shingle has been the friend of both the younger men's fathers. The generational difference that costume and makeup would have made obvious to the audience from the beginning of the play is thus made pointedly explicit for the reader. While his literal fatherhood has previously been referred to at several points in the play, his social and political paternity, suggested in passing by his comments about fighting in "the revolution" and the "last war" (the War of 1812), have been until now granted little significance. In the final scene, however, Shingle stands as the metaphoric father whose political sons and daughter have secured the blessings that his generation's sacrifices have made possible.

Though Jones does hint at the greater social and political significance of his Yankee than has heretofore been acknowledged, Shingle remains primarily a comic figure. In a similar manner, most of the dramatists and actors who figure in the history of the Yankee plays drew contrasts and make pointed satiric comments about society in the midst of otherwise amusing and light-hearted plays. To recognize the latent political and social commentary provided by this character—and to realize that today, cut off as we often are from a vivid sense of their effects on their contemporary audiences, we may have a tendency to dismiss these plays too readily—we need only remember that the meaning of a drama is finally realized most fully in production. The point is strikingly illustrated by Joseph Jefferson in his autobiography, where he was careful to note that Dan Marble played almost all of his Yankee roles in a costume that resembled "the present caricature of Uncle Sam, minus the stars but glorying in the stripes" (20).

High Society: Mowatt's Fashion

The rural character that forms the cornerstone of both the frontier and Yankee plays is utilized to more substantial purpose and with greater sophistication in the best comedy of the pre–Civil War period, Anna Cora Mowatt's *Fashion* (1845).[14] The action of the play is rather straightforward, though complicated by the usual intrigues of drawing room comedies. The Tiffany family, having risen from humble beginnings to wealth, has fallen victim to the lures of foreign fashion. Mrs. Tiffany is determined to marry her daughter Seraphina to the fraudulent Count Jolimaitre, while her husband is equally insistent that Seraphina marry his clerk, Snobson, who has evidence that Tiffany has committed forgery. The virtuous Gertrude, Seraphina's music teacher, tries to expose the false count but is temporarily compromised in the attempt. Inevitably, all comes right in the final scene when Adam Trueman, having learned Gertrude's motivations, reveals that he is her wealthy grandfather and unites her with the upright Colonel Howard. Trueman then breaks Snobson's hold on Tiffany by pointing out that the clerk is an accomplice to the forgery and agrees to save Tiffany from his creditors on the condition that he send his wife and daughter into the country.

The central issue in the play is the nature of fashionable American culture in mid-nineteenth-century New York. Like Tyler sixty years before, Mowatt comes down firmly on the side of traditional republican pieties, but unlike Tyler, Mowatt extends her vision beyond the particulars of affectation to include a pointed satire on the economic bases which contribute to it. In this way, Mowatt confronts one of the fundamental questions that has consumed American writers ever since—the relationship between culture and economics in a capitalist society. Mowatt's social satire is wide-ranging and delightful, but it is her enlivening portraits of the various American types that gives the play its power. Her single plot, while providing few scenic counterpoints, gives her play a strict focus and lends persuasiveness to the play's indictment.[15]

Following traditional satiric patterns, Mowatt sets out her targets with dispatch. The play opens with a discussion between Zeke, the newly hired black servant, and Millinette, a French lady's maid, that quickly establishes the false values abroad in the household. Zeke asserts that "it am de fixin's dat make the natural *born* gemman. A libery for ever."[16] Though the audience may initially tend to dismiss Zeke's willingness to enter servitude because of his ignorance and lack of social standing, the play's action suggests that the white, *nouveau riche* Tiffany family are no more capable of resisting the evils of fashion than is Zeke. Indeed, if anything, Zeke's position in society guarantees that the effects of his indulgence will remain purely a matter of personal folly; at most he will provide an amusing spectacle on Broadway. In the hands of Mrs. Tiffany, however, fashion has the potential of being subversive of the democratic ideology against which the characters are being judged. Fashion, Mowatt suggests, is potentially a tool for reshaping society along aristocratic lines, and it is this political element of the satire which receives increasing emphasis in the course of the play. By play's end the relationship between political freedom and moral probity has been so firmly reiterated that Trueman's reinstitution of traditional "American" values carries with it a reassurance of the political future of the nation.

Mrs. Tiffany, the antagonist of these values, is one of the most brilliant comic characters in this particular period.[17] Like Mrs. Freeman in Paulding's *The Lion of the West*, Mrs. Tiffany is obsessed with establishing a social elite within New York. Her inept French, her attempts to suppress her origins as a milliner, her shrewish insistence upon ruling her house and husband in accordance with her own idiosyncratic sense of fashion, and her total lack of culture betray her dearth of self-awareness and make her comic downfall certain. Though Mrs. Tiffany functions primarily as a butt of the social satire, Mowatt insists that the audience recognize the political groundings of the would-be *grande dame*. From the ludicrous parody of royal prerogative in changing her servant's name from Zeke to the more aristocratic sounding "Adolph," to her insistence that she dotes on titled nobility and considers herself one of the "American *ee-light*," a class that she equates with "the aristocracy," Mrs. Tiffany's pretensions are delineated with unmerciful delight—but always within a context that keeps Mowatt's political assumptions before the audience (48). That Mrs. Tiffany willfully blinds herself to American realities is made most pointedly in her dismissal of Tiffany's objection that her lust after fashion is ruining them economically. To Tiffany's catalogue of mounting debts, his wife haughtily replies that such financial concerns manifest the "grovelling ideas" of a typically "plebian" American (46). Excluded from the play's concluding moments, Mrs. Tiffany and her daughter are reduced to children whose baubles have been withdrawn in favor of a rural education in "economy, true independence, and home virtues" (61).

At the center of the play's action and values are Adam Trueman and his granddaughter, Gertrude. Trueman's names, age, rural background, and direct speech identify him with the revolutionary war era, and he strides through the play like a Founding Father purging cultural enslavement as he had earlier expelled political bondage. His characterization of Zeke's livery as "scarlet regimentals" and repudiation of them as "the *badge of servitude* in a free land," again serves to distinguish social fashion from "republican simplicity" (40). More important, it is Trueman who renders the moral criticism of fashion which is at the play's center: "And pray what is *fashion*, madam? An agreement between certain persons to live without their souls! to substitute etiquette for virtue—decorum for purity—manners for morals! to affect a shame for the works of their Creator! and to expend all their rapture upon the works of their tailors and dressmakers!" (51–52). The accuracy of Trueman's critique of Mrs. Tiffany's social climbing is itself sufficient for the satire. But his social judgment gains added weight from the audience's sense that it is grounded in the principles of the nation's founding political struggles. His role as comic hero and civic spokesman is reiterated at the end of the play when he defines the untitled American nobility for the audience: "we have honest men, warm hearted and brave, and we have women—gentle, fair, and true, to whom no *title* could add *nobility*" (62).

While Mowatt's satire is aimed primarily at social pretension and extravagance, she also weaves into her play a significant examination of the economic foundations of this fashionable world. Through the use of Snobson, Trueman's continued references to Tiffany's happier days as a simple peddler in rural New York, and Tiffany's attempts to exchange his daughter for Snobson's silence at the end of the play, Mowatt questions the object of Americans' obsession with financial success.[18] Tiffany's new wealth has provided his wife the means to indulge her folly, and in turn, her excesses have driven him to forge his accounts. Faced with ruin and prison, he is willing to sell his daughter into a marriage with the vile Snobson in order to escape punishment. Trueman, who has lost his own daughter to a mercenary cad whose desertion precipitated her death, again serves as the voice of morality, repudiating Tiffany's plan as "foul traffic" (Mowatt, 60). When the crisis has passed, Trueman sends Tiffany back to his counting house with the admonition to "let moderation, in future, be your counsellor, and let *honesty* be your confidential clerk" (Mowatt, 61). Though this moment passes quickly in the rush of the play's end, it evidences an increasing fascination with business and the businessman on the American stage, an interest that foreshadows such Wall Street plays as Bronson Howard's *The Henrietta* (1887).

For those concerned with the immoral potential of business, a more immediate problem presented itself in the combined legacy of Yankee business acumen and Southern agricultural practice—slavery. In an era when regional distinctions served as important elements of personal identity, the southern plantation gentry and the slaves whose labors guaranteed their masters livelihoods increasingly found themselves center stage in dramas which held their way of life up to the scrutiny of their countrymen.

The Slavery Plays of Aiken and Boucicault: Melodrama and Social Commentary

No topic dominated the domestic American political imagination in the first part of the nineteenth century as did slavery. All the great statesmen of the age—Clay, Calhoun, Webster, Douglas, Lincoln—expended their energies in attacking, defending, or trying to shape some political remedy to the issue. The addition of Texas and the territories secured after the Mexican War exacerbated tensions over the slavery question, and compromise after compromise emerged from Washington in an attempt to find a resolution to the sectional disputes that found their most emotional expression in slavery. More generally, the reformist impulse, which captured many of the socially minded between 1830 and 1860, focused much of its time and resources on abolition.[19] American letters stepped into this political furor with enormous impact when Harriet Beecher Stowe published *Uncle Tom's Cabin* in 1852. In relatively short order, the issue was firmly entrenched in the American theater repertoire.

The most famous of the slavery plays is George L. Aiken's adaptation of Stowe's novel, which roughly follows the life of the title character in his relationships with a series of owners until his eventual death at the hands of Simon Legree. Aiken originally composed the play that we have today as two separate pieces, and the sprawling six acts and thirty scenes are indicative both of the difficulty of dramatizing Stowe's six-hundred-page novel and of the general tendency of popular drama to evolve over time in response to audience, actor, and managerial wishes.[20] From a traditional aesthetic perspective, one could hardly argue with Quinn's assessment that "the play is hopeless" (Quinn, 1: 289). But Quinn himself recognized that the importance of this work resided beyond such criteria, for he significantly adds, "yet in the catalogue of social forces it remains probably the most potent weapon developed by the literary crusade against slavery" (Quinn, 1: 289). Thus *Uncle Tom's Cabin* must be seen not simply as a flawed drama, but as a social force, a force whose power resided not only in the usual appeals of melodramatic action but also in its ability to redefine slaves as human beings who were entitled to the dignity accorded other members of American society. It is, without any doubt, propaganda—but powerful propaganda whose rhetorical strategies are worthy of consideration.

The essential strategy of the play is to first humanize the slaves by undermining generally accepted psychological premises concerning them, and then explore alternative solutions to the issue of slavery by contrasting the fates of George Harris and Uncle Tom. After establishing the emotional affinities between blacks and whites, Aiken identifies the blacks with various American religious and political beliefs which lend stature to their demands for freedom and pathos to their fates. The denial of the "otherness" which psychologically grounds slavery leads inevitably to the humanitarian, religious, and political conclusion that slavery as an institution is indefensible.[21] At the same time, following Stowe's lead, Aiken satirizes various elements of American, and particularly southern, society.

The process of redefinition begins in the opening scene of the play, in which George's tirade effectively throws into relief three of the most repulsive elements within slavery—the conception of human beings as chattel, the denial of the individual's right to sustain himself and his family through his own initiative, and the disregard of familial links by slave owners. George's mulatto coloring, his generally educated diction, his resentment at his economic exploitation, his obvious love for his wife and child, and his thirst for freedom all serve to diminish the distance between blacks and whites and make George an ideal embodiment of the slave's predicament for a white audience. His initial plaintive cry, "What's the use of our trying to do anything—trying to know anything—trying to be anything," vents the frustration and anguish of people doomed not by inherent moral or intellectual deficiency but by circumstances.[22] When Eliza, who has internalized southern beliefs in the biblical sanctioning of slavery, argues for obedience to his master and patience in the face of suffering, George expresses his spiritual desperation by acknowledging, "I can't trust in heaven. Why does it let things be so" (361). Aiken's obvious answer is, of course, that heaven has very little to do with slavery. Since slavery is a social and economic institution conceived, implemented, and maintained by men, the play's action argues that men and women who suffer because of its operation have every right to resist. Following the British colonists who had asserted that liberty was one of humanity's inalienable rights and had taken up arms to sustain their point, George vows, "I'll be free, or I'll die" (361). This pedestrian version of Patrick Henry's more famous line indicates the depth of George's desire for freedom and thus aligns him with the most sacred of American political tenets—the inherent desire and right of all peoples for personal liberty.

The Harris's subsequent escape, evocative of the Holy Family's flight into Egypt, provides an opportunity for other Americans to respond to this personal and political course of action. Wilson, the conservative businessman who recognizes his former employee's intelligence and personal integrity, voices the traditional objections to George's repudiation of the slave laws, augmenting these with yet another appeal to the will of Providence. But in one of the most telling political and religious arguments of the play, George argues that America's unwillingness to acknowledge his humanity is sufficient warrant to justify his escape and that interpretations of Providence often depend upon the individual's circumstances. Persuaded by George's reasoning, Wilson is so moved that he forces money on George to aid in the escape. More significant in this polling of American types is Phineas Fletcher, Aiken's representative frontiersman. A former slave owner whose love for a Quaker has transformed him into a would-be abolitionist, Fletcher regards George as manifesting the same love of freedom that has always been associated with the pioneer. Fletcher's assistance in the Harris's escape to Canada, including his killing of the slave-hunter Loker, serves to align the brash, honest, and morally upright westerner with the slave in his resistance to the South's oppressive social and economic system.

Aiken presents the alternative response to slavery in his portrait of the long-suffering Uncle Tom. While George is unwilling to accede to the ostensible dictates of Providence, Tom consistently bows to his circumstances, even as his slavery becomes increasingly life-threatening. Tom's inevitable martyrdom is suggested early in the play when he refuses to join Eliza in her escape, arguing that either he must sacrifice himself or both slaves and whites will suffer. The wellspring of his attitude is a simple but devout religious faith that he constantly reiterates in the course of the play. From his initial assertion that "the Lord's given me a work among these yer poor souls, and I'll stay with 'em and bear my cross with 'em till the end," to his final defiance of Legree, "do the worst you can, my troubles will be over soon; but if you don't repent, yours won't never end," Tom remains a firm believer in a creed of Christian faith and good works (363, 396). As the exemplar of "true" Christianity, he provides a pointed contrast to the missionary spirit of the pious Yankee, Ophelia St. Claire, who is finally forced to admit that she has "always had a prejudice against negroes" (377). Tom's character also suggests the basis on which a rapprochement between the races may be accomplished. His death at the hands of the Yankee Legree provides the emotional climax to the indictment of the physical brutalities of slavery, but his apotheosis in the play's final tableau, in which Eva St. Claire assumes the role of a Protestant Virgin, reiterates the play's underlying belief in the dignity of the individual before a heavenly judge who disregards race.

Surrounding these two plots is a biting satire of the economic mechanisms that perpetuate slavery. With the exception of Wilson, the members of the white power structure are portrayed as weak-willed exploiters, conscienceless opportunists, or villains. At best these individuals tacitly accept slavery, ameliorating its nature through personal intervention. At worst they epitomize the brutal realities of the system. In the first group fall Shelby, who originally owns Tom but is forced to sell him to meet debts, and the self-indulgent St. Claire, who agrees to free Tom at the behest of the saintly Eva, but fails through negligence to fulfill his promise before his untimely death.[23] While these generally benign and well-meaning slave owners are relatively lightly chastised, the business-men who sell and recapture slaves—Haley, Marks, Loker and their ilk—are anatomized in a scathing rebuke of the "business" of slavery. Aiken reveals the moral bankruptcy of these flesh-dealers in Haley's comment, "I've got just as much conscience as any man of business can afford to keep, just a little, you know, to swear by, as 'twere" (362). The villain of the piece, Simon Legree, occupies a unique place in the play for he personifies the evil which is slavery while at the same time tempering to a small degree the play's indictment of the South. Though Legree now lives in a South which permits his cruelty, his Yankee origins both hint at the New England shipping interests which aided slavery's growth and indicate that the moral depravity of slavery is available to all men who are willing to repudiate moral good. Legree's confessional recollection of his youth testifies that he has chosen the path of evil long before Tom arrives at his plantation. That slavery has exacerbated his evil nature seems a legitimate inference, but Aiken's play refuses to suggest that slavery has been the genesis of his villainy.

Aiken's play does nothing to mitigate Stowe's propagandistic im-pulse to simplify. His moral universe is self-consciously black and white, and his political philosophizing is peripheral to the emotional appeal that he is making. In the hands of a more practiced and thoughtful playwright, sentiment might have been used to augment rather than overwhelm the ideas of the play. Certainly that is one of the major distinctions between Aiken's adaptation and Dion Boucicault's 1859 blockbuster *The Octoroon*, which traces the linked fates of the title character and a Louisiana planta-tion.

Whereas Aiken's play manipulates the audience in such a way as to discourage rational reflection about the underlying legal questions involved in slavery, Boucicault insists that his audience recognize that the fate of the slave legally denied full citizenship is merely one manifesta-tion of a broader question of the viability of law as a democratic society's framework. Slavery becomes not only a theme of the play, but also a means of examining the essential contest between the desires and rights of individuals and of the law's goal of maintaining society. The death of Zoe and the implicit marriage of George and Dora seem to affirm the traditional American faith in a society of laws. However, Boucicault undercuts the orthodoxy of the ending through repeated episodes which suggest the law's inability to withstand manipulation and its capacity for frustrating elemental human instincts toward goodness.[24]

The centrality of this concern with the law is suggested by the fact that both of Boucicault's plots—which trace the destruction of Zoe, the octoroon heroine, and the attempts by the villain M'Closky to wrest the Terrebonne plantation from the hands of Judge Peyton's widow—turn on legal issues. Indeed, by the end of the play, justice and its practical embodiment, the law, have to a large degree displaced the fates of the characters to become the center of the audience's attention. Thus, though the deaths of Zoe and M'Closky fulfill traditional emotional expectations engendered by melodrama, they also highlight the potential conflict between institutionalized reason as embodied in law and more fundamentally conceived notions of justice.

The legal subtext emerges in the initial conversation between Mrs. Peyton and her nephew George. When George wittily observes that he left Paris "amid universal and sincere regret [leaving] my loves and my creditors equally inconsolable," Mrs. Peyton replies, "George, you are incorrigible. Ah, you remind me so much of your uncle, the judge."[25] At first, this exchange seems to provide only an innocuous piece of characterization. But as the play continues, Boucicault develops a damning irony from this similarity, for Judge Peyton, the law's deceased personification, has brought destruction to the door of those he loves. His ineptitude is initially delineated by Salem Scudder, who reveals that the judge lost half of his plantation to M'Closky as a result of eight years of extravagant living. But the judge's folly is not restricted to the loss of fields of sugar cane and cotton, for this is antebellum Louisiana, and the cunning M'Closky has discovered that Zoe, legally chattel, has not been freed because of a lien on the plantation. So by the end of the first act Boucicault has managed to completely undermine the central figure of law in the play. Judge Peyton stands exposed as not only inept but dangerous. By extension, the same may be said of the law, for the law will allow the thoughtlessness of a single individual both to ruin the financial security of his family and to jeopardize their very lives. Aware that the audience might think it was merely the personal inadequacies of the judge that were being taken to task, Boucicault provides three other significant examples of the law's less-than-ideal operation.

The first of these comes in what might, in the context of slavery plays, be called the obligatory auction scene. As the gentlemen of means

Slavery is starkly depicted as a literal contest between good and evil in the auction scene of Dion Boucicault's The Octoroon *(1859).* COURTESY OF THE NEW YORK PUBLIC LIBRARY, ASTOR, LENOX, AND TILDEN FOUNDATIONS

gather to dispose of the property of their fellow aristocrat, the late Judge Peyton, a scene unfolds which tellingly contrasts humane sentiments with the requirements of the law. Zoe's fate is not yet sealed; she may still escape the villain if the Peyton family is allowed to buy her from the estate. Sunnyside, a family friend, argues that the Peytons be allowed to do so, but Pointdexter, the auctioneer, objects that "while the proceeds of this sale promises to realize less than the debts upon it, it is my duty to prevent any collusion for the depreciation of the property" (160). Such legal scruples sound above board and honorable, unless the audience remembers that, moments before, Pointdexter has allowed just such a scheme in order to preserve a slave family. The upshot of this strictness of interpretation—this following of the letter and disregarding of the "spirit" of the law—is, of course, the sale of Zoe to M'Closky.

The most overt of the legal scenes involves Wahnotee, the "noble savage," who disappears soon after the death of Paul, a young serving boy who is murdered by M'Closky. When Wahnotee reappears, he is seized by a crowd of angry citizens who demand his immediate lynching. As we might expect, Salem Scudder, Boucicault's spokesman for goodness, has some trepidations about "stringing up an innocent man." Indeed, arguing against summary execution, Scudder makes all the stock arguments about law as the foundation of civilization:

> I appeal against your usurped authority. This Lynch law is a wild and lawless proceeding.
>
> Here's a pictur' for a civilized community to afford; yonder, a poor ignorant savage, and round him a circle of hearts, white with revenge and hate, thirsting for blood; you call yourselves judges—you ain't—you're a jury of executioners. It is such scenes as these that brings disgrace upon our Western life (163).

The reaction of the crowd suggests that the speech will be totally ineffectual in forestalling the lynching, but it does have the virtue of reassuring the audience, reiterating a distinction between vengeance and law. The assurance is shortlived. At the crucial moment, Pete, another household slave, enters with the miraculous self-developing picture that shows M'Closky bending over the body of Paul. With this new piece of evidence before him, Scudder changes from defense to prosecuting attorney. With the change in role comes a similar reversal of legal philosophy. When asked who will accuse M'Closky, Scudder again volunteers:

> Fellow-citizens, you are convened and assembled here under a higher power than the law. What's the law? When the ship's abroad on the ocean—when the army is before the enemy—where in thunder's the law? It is in the hearts of brave men who can tell right and wrong, and from whom justice can't be bought. So it is here, in the wilds of the West, where our hatred of crime is measured by the speed of our executions—where necessity is law! I say, then, air you honest men? air you true? put your hands on your naked breasts, and let every man as don't feel a real American heart there, bustin' up with freedom, truth, and right, let that man step out (163).

This shift in Scudder's attitude about law and justice is one of the most disturbing elements of the play. Since it is Scudder, the author's surrogate, who shifts, the audience is left with more than a little suspicion that the law can be manipulated if one merely has the talent. Law, the structuring element in American culture, provides neither social integration nor reliable protection. To the guilty it offers merely formalized blood vengeance. To the innocent it turns a deaf ear. This latter point is made forcefully in Boucicault's treatment of Zoe, his most telling method to indict the legal system and the ideology that underpins American justice.

From the beginning of the play it is obvious that Zoe is the standard against which all other characters are to be judged. Like many another melodramatic heroine, she is the moral standard of the play. The "good" characters—Scudder, Wahnotee, Mrs. Peyton, and George— love her in ways appropriate to their positions. Even the villain M'Closky is not immune to her virtuous charm, and though M'Closky's speeches reveal that his passion is not wholly honorable, Scudder is forced to acknowledge that M'Closky's affection for Zoe is his only redeeming virtue. Although the apex of Boucicault's moral universe, Zoe has problems. She is an octoroon in a society that legally demands racial purity. The ramifications of her situation are hinted at early in the play when she is propositioned by M'Closky: Despite his willingness to set her up as the new mistress of Terrebonne, he is not inclined to contravene the miscegenation statutes by granting Zoe legal status as his wife. While these legal constraints are by no means insignificant, Zoe's greatest obstacles are the unexamined racial suppositions which ground the planter mentality.

Throughout the play, people are seen in stereotypically racial terms. Boucicault presents instance upon instance of the dehumanization of nonwhites until the audience is forced to realize that for the play's privileged white Americans, nonwhites are inconsiderable facts of existence, merely elements of the material universe within which the whites move. The audience's perceptions are given voice in this instance by George Peyton, who, though white, has spent his life abroad and thus has not internalized American racial attitudes. The disparity between George's European outlook and the American viewpoint is dramatized in the early scene in which Sunnyside and his daughter Dora appear at Terrebone for breakfast. George remarks to himself, "They do not notice Zoe," and then pointedly adds to Sunnyside, "You don't *see* Zoe, Mr. Sunnyside" (138; emphasis mine). Sunnyside's response is indicative of a man who has been informed of something so obvious that he is unconscious of it: "Ah! Zoe, girl; are you there" (138). Couched as it is in the form of a rhetorical question, Sunnyside's response suggests that he places as much importance to the existence of Zoe as he does to the table at which he sits. Zoe, like the table, exists within the same physical realm as the squire, but neither one is of such import that attention should be wasted upon the fact. That this is an American rather than southern attitude is indicated later in the play when Scudder remarks upon a noise in the cedar swamp, "it's either a bear or a runaway nigger" (167). This conjoining of "bear" and "nigger" is a perfectly natural equation for Scudder—both are subhuman creatures whose natural habitat is the wilderness.

As Scudder's comment reveals, nonwhites lack stature in American society because they are considered subhumans whose natures are circumscribed by passion. In explaining to George why their love can never be recognized in American society, Zoe articulates the grounding myth of the planter's racial code and reveals her internalization of it. Drawing George's attention to what she describes as "a bluish tinge," she continues:

> That—that is the ineffaceable curse of Cain. Of the blood that feeds my heart, one drop in eight is black—bright red as the rest might be, that one drop poisons all the flood. Those seven bright drops give me love like yours, hope like yours—ambition like yours—life hung with passions like dewdrops on the morning flowers; but the one black drop gives me despair, for I am an unclean thing—forbidden by the laws—I'm an Octoroon! (147)

Like those around her, Zoe accepts that nonwhites are bestial creatures whose lower passions and unreasonable natures make them a threat to the operation of an orderly society. Such passions place all nonwhites outside the purview of the law—an extension of reason—and, consequently, outside of an American society which is presumed to be based on law. Since they have no legal identity in themselves and since their inherent natures are antithetical to the maintenance of civilized society, it becomes incumbent on whites to restrain them so that such a society may continue. As the fate of Zoe reveals, this attitude is not without pathetic consequences.[26]

By loving George, Zoe has contravened a basic tenet of her society. She has presumed to love one who is her social and racial superior, and as she cannot reconcile herself to a society that refuses to sanction her love, she harmonizes her emotions and legal status in the only way available to her—suicide. Personally incapable of forcing her society to reexamine its racial code, Zoe sees her death as a means of reasserting the "proper" social order while simultaneously preserving her love by removing it to a plane on which justice, as opposed to law, operates. As she tells George in the last scene of the play: "I loved you so, I could not bear my fate; and then I stood between your heart and hers. When I am dead she will not be jealous of your love of me, no laws will stand between us" (169). The playwright's treatment of Zoe's death is his most poignant indictment of the American legal system, but its pathos is seemingly insufficient to justify a revolutionary rejection of the law. While the law has proven a poor ordering principle, it remains for Boucicault the only viable alternative society has. As much as he may admire the passions which motivate Zoe, Boucicault's portrayal of M'Closky's fate reveals a hearty skepticism of passion, at least as an alternative basis for society.

M'Closky, like Zoe, is driven by emotion, although in the villain's case those passions are immoral. Toward the end of the play, M'Closky, pursued by blood vengeance embodied by Wahnotee, argues that as a white man he is entitled to the operation of the white man's legal system. Scudder, having heard the plea, replies:

> Here we are on the selvage of civilization. It ain't our side, I believe, rightly; but Nature has said that where the white man sets his foot, the red man and the black man shall up sticks and stand around. But what do we pay for that possession? In cash? No—in kind—that is, in protection, forbearance, gentleness, in all them goods that show the critters the difference between the Christian and the savage. Now, what have you done to show them the distinction? for, darn me if I can find out (167).

M'Closky has failed his obligations to society; by his own actions he has repudiated his privileged status. He has reduced himself to the variety of subhuman, nonwhite beast the law is designed to curb. Ironically, of course, the suppositions which are vindicated when applied to M'Closky are proved patently false by Zoe's perfection. To Boucicault the tragedy resides in the foundations of the American legal system, which is incapable of recognizing qualitative differences in motivation. Like Ibsen's Krogstad twenty years later, Boucicault seems to say, "the law takes no account of motives" (Ibsen, 229).

Thus, in a manner which Aiken's more overtly propagandistic project had precluded, Boucicault's play simultaneously justifies and calls into question the forces of the law. The society is maintained, but only at the expense of its most exemplary member. For Boucicault, however, the sacrifice seems not only worthy but necessary. Brought on by the choices available in the legal system of the day, the death of Zoe rights the world of Terrebone (a world still part of the accepted order in 1859), guarantees the continuation of that society, and banishes the forces of chaos to the swamp. The final tableau of Wahnotee standing over the body of the slain M'Closky pointedly reminds the audience that the alternative to law is the return of the savage.

By the outbreak of the Civil War, the popular drama had proved the appeal of indigenous characters, issues, and situations. In turn, the theatrical success of these dramas provided American playwrights an opportunity to develop a national drama which could address the particular concerns of the day. In the aftermath of the Civil War, this process was to continue, fueled by a renewed desire to unify the country and to discover the "essence" of America, and aided by the emergence of a full-blown melodramatic vision which presented its insights in forms available to the humblest, least-educated native as well as the new immigrants. Though the melodramatic vision had, in some senses, always been part of the American dramatic scene, the period after the Civil War would see it rise to an ascendancy unparalleled in the history of the American theatrical scene.

6

The World of Melodrama

As the early-twentieth-century critic and playwright William Archer heralded the advent of "modern drama" in *The Old Drama and the New,* the broadside he aimed at "the old" signaled the critical demise of a variety of drama which had in one form or another dominated the English and American stage for nearly two centuries. Though most literary theorizing about drama is no longer in the hands of self-interested competitors, it is testimony to the effectiveness of the critiques of playwrights such as Shaw—and their advocates, Archer among them—that to this day melodrama remains the most misunderstood of all dramatic forms.[1] Certainly the stereotype of American melodrama remains one of a play in which a moustache-twirling villain attempts through dastardly means to compromise the personal or financial integrity of a golden-haired heroine until prevented by a white-clad hero who arrives in the nick of time to preserve chastity and rightful titles, and oversee a denouement replete with poetic justice. Though images of heroes pushed from cliffs and heroines about to be sawed in two do suggest some of the appeals of melodrama, they are at best a caricaturist's vision of the form. They do not acknowledge its durability, its cross-cultural popularity, its service as an agent of socialization, or its later function as a forum in which conflicting ideologies could confront each other and, to a certain extent, resolve the social and political tensions of the emerging western industrial-capitalist states of the nineteenth century.

As a dramatic form, melodrama provides an efficient vehicle for exploring social institutions, movements, and values, for it presents life in a simplified form, a way which "expresses the reality of the human condition as we all experience it most of the time" (Smith, 11). Analogous to the world of a child's fantasy (Bentley, 218), melodrama presents events and people without the complexity called for in other dramatic forms. As a result, easily recognizable typed characters afford audiences the means of expressing their collective identity. Replete with virtue, courage, and persistence, melodrama's heroes and heroines are pitted against external forces which threaten to overcome and annihilate their representative humanity. Uncomplicated by serious internal doubts which might divert either his or the audience's attention from the action's conflict (Heilman, 213), the hero confronts—often successively—forces ranging from environmental cataclysm to nearly overwhelming social evils to seemingly inexplicable personal antipathies. The usually more passive heroine, repository of those values which promise the perpetuation of a civilized society, provides the linkage between the hero and his antagonists. After episodes often characterized by "outrageous coincidence," the action of the drama provides only two possible resolutions—triumph or defeat (Heilman, 81).

But within these formal and emotional patterns, America's melodramatists provided numerous variations. Often drawing its materials from contemporary events and concerns, the melodrama became the projected fantasy life of an America caught up in a period of unprecedented flux. During the heyday of American melodrama, roughly between 1865 and 1900, the face of America was radically transformed in a number of ways. Despite the ravages of the Civil War, the population of the country doubled in the second half of the century, with much of that growth concentrated in about a dozen cities where immigrants, joining with recent arrivals from rural areas of the United States, sought employment in the new commercial hubs of America. Agriculture and small businesses were giving way to industry as the prime employer of the American work force, and new, more intense class consciousness was emerging as tension between the new capitalists and a fragmented and varied labor force became a fact of life. Dislocations from earlier social and economic patterns generated both a longing to return to a more established and comprehensible form of life and attempts to understand through imaginative literature the new realities of American society. On the stage, melodrama sought not only to comprehend the geneses of the new reality but also to delineate America's new outlines.

Fables of Melodramatic Identity: Augustin Daly's New America

As the works of Augustin Daly testify, the popular conception of American melodrama is not without foundation. In the period between his initial successes in the late 1860s and his death in 1899, no one exercised more influence over the American theater. Critic, producer, director, adaptor, playwright, and theatrical entrepreneur, Daly established and maintained one of the most successful theatrical companies in New York, producing a legion of actors and actresses who learned their craft under his sometimes dictatorial tutelage. His sway was felt beyond the confines of the New York theatrical scene, for he was instrumental in elevating American theater on the international stage by being the first to take an entire American company to Europe, reversing the traditional pattern of importing English actors and productions to America. A series of increasingly successful tours, and the securing of his own theater in London, provided Europeans the consistent opportunity to view American plays and Daly's adaptations of the classical repertoire.[2]

Despite his contributions to the reputation of American theater, Daly did much less to advance the development of American drama than might have been expected given his position and resources. While he persistently argued for American writers to produce material for the stage and personally encouraged writers such as Bronson Howard by providing a venue for their efforts, he blazed little new ground in his own dramatic endeavors. As even a cursory examination of his plays reveals, Daly preferred instead to rely upon proven formulas for success. Though Daly did not significantly modify the direction of American drama, his plays remain interesting not merely as indices of theatrical tastes in the latter nineteenth century but also as examples of the ways in which a skillful melodramatist might address certain crucial issues of the day without alienating a nonliterary audience. With perceptivity, Daly's plays, especially those of the 1860s and 1870s, examined America's process of redefining itself after the Civil War. Consistently drawing his audience's attention to the nexus of family, social position, wealth, and class, Daly questioned for his audience the myth of the self-made American individual while at the same time providing the readily accessible thrills associated with the melodrama.

Together with his intriguing frontier drama *Horizon* (1871) and city spectacles such as *Roughing It* (1873) and *The Dark City* (1877), Daly's contemporary reputation rested upon his early sensational melodramas that reflect the social tensions emerging in the post–Civil War era. (Felhein, 47). Just as that sectional conflict had essentially reframed the political dynamics of the country, Daly's early plays posit a moment of social redefinition in which individuals confront the northern, urban equivalent of the southern planter society. Usually choosing as the embodiment of the issue a woman—the most tenuously defined of all members of late-nineteenth-century urban, white society—Daly seeks to explore the anti-democratic and repressive impulses of industrialized high society. Through Laura Courtland and Bessie Fallon, the heroines of *Under the Gaslight* (1867) and *A Flash of Lightning* (1868), Daly brings home to his audience the forces shaping their society and the fragile nature of social being. In *Under the Gaslight* Laura is driven from polite society when her parentage is mistakenly cast into doubt. In *A Flash of Lightning* Bessie runs afoul of her father and is falsely accused of stealing a gold necklace. Though both plays end with the heroines reintegrated into their class and possessed of suitable potential husbands, the fantastic resolutions do little to relieve the audience's new anxieties concerning the myth of individual economic and social autonomy.

Since *Under the Gaslight* is typical of Daly's sensational melodramas, a description of its plot will illustrate the variety of appeals and devices that Daly utilized to guarantee his success. The play opens on New Year's Eve in the Courtland mansion, a bastion of insulated New York high society, a vapid world in which worth is contingent upon ostentatious show and social position rather than true virtue. Byke shatters this complacent world by intimating to Laura Courtland, her sister, Pearl, and Laura's fiancé, Ray Trafford, that he is her father. In a moment of weakness, Trafford decides that Laura's supposed parentage makes their marriage impossible and breaks off their engagement by means of a letter which later falls into the hands of Mrs. Van Dam, doyenne of their social circle. Dismayed at Trafford's insensitivity and reluctant to allow her presence to be an embarrassment to either Trafford or Pearl, Laura runs away.

A lithographic rendering of the famous railroad "sensation scene" in Augustin Daly's Under the Gaslight (1867).

COURTESY OF THE PHOTOGRAPHS AND POSTER DIVISION OF THE LIBRARY OF CONGRESS

The remainder of the play delineates Laura's perils as she seeks to make her way while avoiding the pursuit of both the repentant Trafford and the vile Byke. Aided by Snorkey, a one-armed Civil War veteran, and Peachblossom, an erstwhile victim of the villains, Byke and Old Judas, Laura temporarily evades both men. Eventually discovered, she is declared Byke's daughter by a misled New York judge, despite her protestations and those of Trafford. Byke decides to spirit Laura out of New York, but is confronted by Trafford and Snorkey. To secure his escape, Byke tosses Laura into the North River, but she is rescued by Trafford and carried to Pearl's country house. Time passes and Laura again decides to flee when she fears that Byke will discover her and that her continued presence will undermine a new alliance between Trafford and Pearl. In her flight she discovers Byke's attempt to murder Snorkey, and after hacking her way out of a railroad storage shed with an axe, Laura rescues her crippled protector from an oncoming train. After Byke's subsequent attempt to kill Pearl during a robbery is foiled, he secures his freedom by revealing that Pearl is actually his and Old Judas's daughter and that Laura was stolen from her crib and replaced by Pearl. The reported death of Old Judas ends the potential threats from Byke, who judiciously decides to emigrate, and the play ends with the prospect of Trafford and Laura marrying in a brighter tomorrow.

Under the Gaslight's plot and its theatrical possibilities amply suggest the grounds for its immediate success. Though Joseph Daly, Augustin's brother and collaborator, acknowledged that the first performance was plagued by more than the usual first-night accidents, he could nevertheless maintain that "the audience was breathless," a condition, he asserted, necessary to any successful drama (75). Despite the affective success of the plot, however, the importance of the play resides in Daly's intriguing treatment of several issues which are obscured in the rush of events. Like many another melodramatist, Daly deserves more careful consideration for his rendition of the social and economic premises of the world through which his characters move.

Daly's interest obviously is not the inner workings of his central characters, for they are little more than pasteboard figures whose function is to allow the events of the play to wash over them. His preoccupation is with a world of sudden danger and life-threatening events, a world in which neither family, social position, nor personal integrity is sufficient stay against potential oblivion. To speak of "a" world is in some senses misleading, for Daly carefully suggests two sets of overlapping societies, one defined by time, the other by economics, and it is at the intersection of these worlds that Daly chooses to set his play. On one level, *Under the Gaslight* acts out a conflict between aristocratically conceived romantic individualism and a more typically nineteenth-century bourgeois individualism. On another, it pits upper-class wealth against lower-class poverty. Both of these conflicts are played out in the fate of Laura, who by her unique personal circumstances eventually suggests a possible ideological reconciliation.

The play begins firmly in a romantic world. The heroine's name, Laura Courtland, is evocative of Petrarch's vision of feminine perfection and of the aristocratic world which has generated her, but Daly also drives home his point by invoking the traditional romantic plot convention of displacing the "princess" from her kingdom to allow those around her to recognize her merit. That mid-nineteenth-century New York lacks the overt romance of the woods surrounding Athens or the verdant dells of Bohemia should not deceive us for long. Laura is every bit the romantic heroine and her subsequent actions and attendants will merely reinforce our initial suspicions. Refused recognition of her inherent worth, Laura seeks the contemporary anonymity of life among the urban lowly, exchanging a shepherd's staff for the more "realistic" paintbrush. But just as her brush transforms the world of her former friends by vitalizing their dull photographic portraits, so too Laura's existence reshapes her Dorcus-like attendant, Peachblossom, weaning her from evil and preparing her for marriage to Touchstone/Snorkey. Laura's departure also provides Trafford the opportunity to realize the narrowness of his social vision and to grow emotionally. By play's end he not only acts but feels the heroic part that has fallen to him. But, like most romantic heroines, Laura's positive, transformative influence upon others is matched by a static quality within herself; she is at play's end what she was at the beginning. Her adventures have allowed her and the audience to recognize elements of her personality which were not self-evident when she was safely ensconced in her mansion—but revelation is not development. She is at the end the perfection she was at the beginning, "the long sought sunshine" (327) which she promises to Trafford in the play's closing lines.[3]

The genesis of Laura's character in romance goes far to explain how Daly conceived of Laura. For Daly, Laura personifies the ideal of romantic individualism, a flawlessness before which environment is an irrelevancy. Laura has, after all, overcome two bouts of dehumanizing circumstances, one as a child after she was stolen from her crib and before she was "reunited" with the Courtlands, another after she flees from New York high-society. Her sense of self-worth is absolute. Her assertion to Trafford that "love is all a woman has to give; but it is the only earthly thing which God permits us to carry beyond the grave" (327), simultaneously connects her with an eternal divinity and acts as a partial repudiation of the complicating social implications of the writings of Darwin and Spencer. Mankind, suggests Laura's character, need not evolve toward some future perfection; that perfection continues to exist in the present just as it has in the past.

Against the aristocratically inspired Laura, Daly posits the Van Dam family, representatives of a monied elite whose social position hides their lack of true merit. This debased class, which has assumed the prerogatives of royalty in the new world but lacks the nobility of spirit to justify their social position, is incapable of recognizing Laura's individual virtue. When confronted with Laura's supposed lower-class parentage, they fall back upon the simple expedient of economically grounded social class as a means of distinguishing excellence, thus guaranteeing the perpetuation of their privileged status at the expense of Laura's obvious worth. The perverted basis of society's values is manifest in the play's early assertion that, though they lack the economic means to do so, the Van Dams continue to move in the best circles because they successfully manage to perpetuate a facade of prosperity. Tellingly, in a period of post–Civil War economic expansion, American capitalist society's assumption that a positive correlation exists between ethics and economic success finds one of its earliest challenges in the Van Dams.

Nevertheless, Daly does not initially seem to question the fundamental connection between economics and morality because he has the Van Dams' economic indigence reflect their impoverished morality. Indeed, as Trafford's bitter imagery suggests, the Van Dams and their social cohorts are not really human at all and have no aspirations to humanity. Instead, he maintains, the society which they lead is like a pack of Siberian wolves who will devour a fallen member (289). Mrs. Van Dam's assertion that Laura has stolen Trafford's "breeding" (291) is laced with trenchant irony. As the audience has already discovered, for Mrs. Van Dam it is the social organization of the pack rather than the metaphysical excellence of the species that is of primary importance. The return of Laura to her rightful place in society at the end of the play may suggest a reassertion of aristocratic virtue, but Daly's exclusion of the Van Dams from the dénoeument renders such a conclusion problematic at best, especially as Daly is unwilling to fully question the linkage of money and morality.

In the second, purely economical world of the play, Laura and Mrs. Van Dam are ironically lumped together as members of a corrupt monied class against whom the villains, Byke and Old Judas, conspire.

In this arena, wealth is the sole determinant of identity and people function solely as economic mechanisms without reference to any other framework. For Byke and Judas, even the appearance of social propriety is irrelevant. Laura and Pearl thus become for them only a means to wealth and are used as tools of aggrandizement. Indeed, the villains' ruthlessness is conducted without the usual heat associated with evil in the period's melodramas. Never, for example, does Byke wish to indulge his sexual appetite at Laura or Pearl's expense; the sublimated rape fantasy of much melodrama finds no play here. In a peculiar manner, the straightforward, transactional attitude of Byke and Old Judas toward the Courtland women renders the ostensible violence of the play even more disturbing, for it paints that violence as merely a localized, individualized version of the violent displacements that more powerful entrepreneurs were enacting in the society at large. While the audience's sympathy for the Courtland women may generate a repugnance at Byke's actions, there is little to differentiate his actions from, for example, the practices of railroad tycoons who effectively decimated Native Americans in the process of building and profiting from the construction of the transcontinental train system.

If Byke and Judas offer an implicit criticism of economic exclusion, Daly is careful to counterbalance them with Snorkey and Peachblossom. At first, both the latter characters seem to fall roughly into the kindly comic servant category. But like their stage cousins, the genial slaves of plantation drama, these two are linked to Laura by more than admiration. In the most simple terms, Laura is the economic linchpin around which they revolve. Snorkey meets Laura when Byke hires him to bring her a bouquet, and he later continues to search for her at the behest of Byke and Trafford, both of whom are paying him. Although Peachblossom, who says she "belongs" to Laura, has exchanged the beatings and oppressions of Old Judas for less onerous poverty as Laura's servant, she still defines herself in terms of her economic status, as property. After being separated from her mistress, Peachblossom returns, seeking to propel Laura into her rightful place as the Courtland heir. Peachblossom, who is by this time romantically allied with Snorkey, protests that she does all for love of Laura, but her earlier groundings of affection in food and clothing suggest that at some level she undoubtedly hopes to profit economically from Laura's goodness.

Through its potboiling action, Daly's *Under the Gaslight* compels its audience to experience the tensions of an urban society embroiled in the process of redefinition as the forces of capitalist industrialization rework the nation in the wake of the Civil War. The railroad train which races toward the crippled Snorkey in the play's third act suggests other forces bearing down upon the society which the veteran helped to secure on the Fredricksburg battlefield. The national values of individual freedom and human dignity which the nation had seen as compromised by the existence of slavery, and which supposedly had been reaffirmed by a bloody conflict, face in Daly's play a new set of economic and class challenges. Though Daly is ultimately unable to offer a resolution of the difficulties he perceives, his restoration of Laura to her privileged social position with the prospect of a marriage to a newly sensitized Trafford and a determination to aid the now-penniless Pearl hint at a reassertion of traditional American faith in the ability of personal goodness to remain undiminished by wealth—and the willingness of the monied elite to protect the rights of the less fortunate while providing them the opportunity for social and economic advancement.

The Master Melodramatist:
Dion Boucicault at Home and Abroad

The power and durability of melodrama is exemplified most pointedly in the life and work of the transplanted Anglo-Irishman Dion Boucicault, whose career as an American playwright extended from 1855 to 1885. As the premier practitioner of melodrama in the period, Boucicault's consistent facility for gauging and playing to the popular tastes of his American audience guaranteed his financial success, no matter how much his personal idiosyncrasies may have diminished his fortunes.[4] His initial success in the United States, *The Poor of New York* (1857), bears the stamp of many of his later plays by incorporating both theatrical spectacle and contemporary events. Framed by the financial panics of 1837 and 1857, the play follows the vicissitudes of the Fairweather family whose fortune is stolen by the unscrupulous banker Bloodgood and is restored only when Bloodgood resorts to arson in an attempt to murder his clerk Badger, who has a receipt which proves Bloodgood's theft.

Though the play is in many ways merely a localization of its French original, *Les Pauvres de Paris*, Boucicault plays adeptly upon his American audience's local prejudices. American distrust of banking, raised to the level of patriotism by earlier Jacksonian animosity toward the National Bank, provided an edge to the villainy of Bloodgood, especially in the atmosphere of financial panic that enveloped New York in 1857. Boucicault augmented Bloodgood's role as socioeconomic evil by a conflagration on stage which suggested the destructive force which might at any moment be unleashed against the individual. Though Badger's role as blackmailer somewhat tempers the audience's identification with him, Bloodgood's actions are sufficiently heinous and the effects of Badger's revelations so positive for the hero and heroine that the audience's inhibitions are overcome as Boucicault uses "every stale staple of the popular theatre" (Hogan, 67).

Although Boucicault's depiction of the plights of the urban masses and slaves suggest his concern with marginal members of society, it is in his Irish plays that he speaks most eloquently for a group whose movement into American society faced significant misunderstanding and a certain amount of overt discrimination. Beginning in 1860 with *The Colleen Bawn* and continuing through *Arrah-na-Pogue* (1865), *The O'Dowd* (1873), *The Shaughraun* (1874), and *Robert Emmet* (1884), Boucicault brought to the American stage a series of incredibly popular Irish plays.[5] Ironically, though the topics and characters were Irish, only one of the plays, *Arrah-na-Pogue*, premiered in Dublin; the rest first saw the stage in America. Though Watt is no doubt correct in seeing Boucicault's melodramas as playing a major role in establishing the Irish history play tradition against which Shaw and O'Casey rebelled, it is important to remember that for a large portion of the latter nineteenth century the largest Irish audiences were to be found not in Dublin but New York (23–24).[6] For Boucicault, the plight of the American Irish was analogous to that of the Irish living in Ireland itself, and these plays became a way of not only striking a blow for Irish independence but also reconciling his countrymen with their new home in America.[7]

The Shaughraun, set in Ireland in the aftermath of the Fenian uprising of 1867, is probably Boucicault's best play and is typical in its strategies and treatment. The play's romantic hero, Robert Ffolliott, returns from transportation to Australia under sentence of death in order to be reunited with his love, Arte O'Neal. Though "Her Majesty" has pardoned Ffolliott, the Irish villains, Duff and Kinchela, conceal the pardon in order to protect their lives and secure Ffolliott's home and fiancée. Aided by the titular comic hero, Conn the Shaughraun, Ffolliott manages to escape from British custody. Eventually Conn discovers the villainy of Duff and Kinchela to both the British and the villagers, and Ffolliott ends the play reunited with Arte and blessing the prospective marriage of his sister, Claire, to Captain Molineaux, the honorable British

SCENE FROM DION BOUCICAULT'S IMMENSELY SUCCESSFUL DRAMA
"ARRAH-NA-POGUE," at the Royal Princess's Theatre.

Boucicault's Irish plays all reveal his ability to unite romantic melodrama with unabashed nationalism. In Arrah-na-Pogue *(1865), Boucicault's vision of British tyranny takes visual form as redcoats arrest the hero at his wedding.* COURTESY OF THE BRITISH LIBRARY

officer who has managed to balance his love for Claire with his duty to pursue and capture Ffolliott.

As in most comic melodramas, the genesis of the play's conflicts reside outside of the central characters. Were Ffolliott and Arte, Claire and Molineaux, and Conn and his love interest, Moya Dolan, left to their own devices, a series of nuptials would no doubt follow in short order. Certainly the play's setting in the rural County Sligo and the sparing of Molineaux and Claire suggest that Boucicault is at least partially relying upon the long-established romantic comedy pattern of private love affairs as the basis for the action (Watt, 40). But these loves serve as a given of the play's action rather than its mainspring. The focus of the play is clearly political intrigue, for it is the political situation that prevents the marriages at the play's opening, and it is not until that reality changes that the romantic design of the play can be fulfilled. These romantic couplings suggest the private basis on which the public political resolution between the Irish and the British may be sustained.

Though Boucicault was too much a hard-headed theatrical businessman to alienate his audience by writing a straight propaganda piece, he was not above utilizing his audience's melodramatic expectations to aid his play's reception. Therefore, Boucicault develops his analysis of the Irish-British problem by insisting upon the correspondence between politics and morality. Simply stated, he superimposes a political standard on the traditional melodramatic moral universe. Those who support Irish independence, or at least an end to British occupation, are portrayed as "good," while those who partake of Britain's exploitation of Ireland are "evil." Though Molineaux's personal goodness somewhat complicated the playwright's schema, Boucicault insists throughout the play upon this standard, and the indivisibility of the political and moral renders the play a powerful piece of political propaganda.

Boucicault's strategy emerges in the opening scene, which begins when the good-hearted Molineaux comes to seek permission to hunt upon what he presumes is Claire's unencumbered estate. When she disabuses him of his misconception and rehearses her poverty, Molineaux, playing, ironically, as much upon the theatrical stereotype of the Irish as English bias, opines that her diminished state is no doubt the result of "ages of family imprudence, and the Irish extravagance of your ancestors."[8] Claire's response is pointedly partisan, embodying as it does the traditional Irish vision of the inextricability of political and religious freedom: "Yes sir; the extravagance of their love for their country, and the imprudence of their fidelity to their faith" (175). This is quickly followed by a reference to her brother whose transportation to Australia has been a direct result of his Fenian activities. Though Molineaux's confusion at having caused Arte and Claire any discomfort suggests his personal merit (a verdict reinforced by his attraction to Claire and his abhorrence of Kinchela), the exchange and his visual presence in British uniform establishes the political hierarchy in Ireland and forces the audience, especially the original audience watching the play two years before the American centennial, to perceive the situation of Claire and Arte as yet another example of the results of "redcoat" oppression. The scene's political subtext is amplified by the advent of Kinchela, whose references to Dublin, the seat of British authority in Ireland, and boorish attempts to coerce Arte into betraying her love for Ffolliott unite the political evil of Ireland's colonial status with thoroughgoing melodramatic villainy. Kinchela in typical fashion threatens to evict the heroine from her home.

Father Dolan's tale of Kinchela's duplicity as Ffolliott's guardian reiterates Kinchela's personal corruption and intimates the unjust operation of an alien British law. But against the legal machinations of Kinchela, Father Dolan evokes not only the religious principles of honesty and charity one might expect from a prelate but also the ancient familial rights of the Ffolliotts and the O'Neals, an antecedent ordering principle overthrown in the "old times" by successive British conquests of Ireland (178). The exchange between Duff and Kinchela which ends the scene reveals in detail the deadly ends to which Kinchela attempts to put the British occupation and thus serves to vitiate any remaining faith the audience may harbor for an apolitical British justice, at least as it applies to the Irish.

The appearance of Ffolliott reinforces the correctness of the moral/political standard which Boucicault has established, for the Fenian hero quickly proves that his partisan views have not negated his basic humanity. In a deliciously comic meeting, Ffolliott first saves Molineaux from tumbling over a cliff, and after sharing a cordial drink rescues the Captain from potential death at the hands of Conn—who, Ffolliott maintains with biting irony, cannot bear the sight of red. This episode is followed by a series of scenes which further develop Robert's heroic character. Ffolliott's bravery, already suggested by his return from Australia, is later exemplified in his harrowing escape from the English authorities and his pursuit of Kinchela. Ffolliott's romantic rewards of both fortune and the long-suffering Arte O'Neal tend to obscure his political significance at the drama's end, but Boucicault's resolution is contingent upon the royal pardon, a device which serves to reiterate Ireland's occupied status while simultaneously giving at least partial vindication to Robert's political agenda and palliating the audience's disquietude at the earlier operation of British justice.

Ironically, it is through Conn the Shaughraun that Boucicault is able to make his most forceful political commentary.[9] In many ways derived from a whole series of comic Irishmen who had preceded him to the English and American stage, Conn is initially portrayed as little more than the traditional poacher, tippler, and general Irish ne'er-do-well. But the audience's response is quickly complicated by their recognition of Conn's sincere concern for Claire and Arte, his love for Ffolliott, his quick wit, and his obvious bravery. Conn is by inclination and long practice an Irishman who refuses to acknowledge the British law, a man given to living on the outskirts of society. As the village scoundrel, he is the bane of Father Dolan's life, especially as Conn loves Moya, Dolan's niece. But even the parish priest can cite nothing more serious than Conn's too-great love for the bottle and other people's game, and, as Hogan has suggested, there is something endearing about his intention to continue despite society's attempts to restrain him (92). By the play's end, Conn's unflinching support for Robert has aligned Conn with his friend's Fenianism. Indeed, Conn in some ways has become a breathing embodiment of that cause. For Boucicault, Conn seems to represent the "natural" Irishman, unencumbered by the fetters that the legalistically inspired British civilization has sought to impose. Like the American frontiersman, though with a longer historical and theatrical pedigree, Conn possesses a natural nobility which makes his inherent democratic spirit compelling for the audience.

Ranged against the heroes and heroines are the villains, Duff and Kinchela. For Boucicault the melodramatist, these antagonists are rather standard fare, for their greed and cruelty are to be encountered superficially in any number of Boucicault's other plays. They are unique, however, because their villainy is heightened by the sense of treason that attaches itself to their actions. This is especially evident in Boucicault's portrayal of Duff, the police informer. Though in trying to calm a Duff anxious at the prospect of Ffolliott's return, Kinchela can speak of the informer's having performed his duty. Duff is fully conscious of what his actions have produced:

> My jooty! was it my jooty to come down here amongst the people disguised as a Fenian delegate, and pass meself aff for a head centre so that I could swear them in and then denounce them? Who gave me the offis how to trap young Ffolliott? Who was it picked out Andy Donovan an' sent him in irons across the say, laving his young wife in a madhouse (190).

Trapped at the play's end by the advancing villagers, Duff falls to his knees before Conn, begging for the pity he has denied others. The Shaughraun, embodied voice of Duff's executed and imprisoned victims, himself injured in Duff's would-be attack upon Ffolliott, scornfully refuses to spare the villain: "Ay, as you spared me! As you spared them at whose side you knelt before the altar! As you pitied them whose salt you ate, but whose blood you dhrank! There's death coming down on you from above— there's death waiting for you below" (218). Duff's leap to his death and the fearful exit of Kinchela in the hands of the constabulary cleanses the Irish body politic and smooths the way for the private reconciliations of the multiple marriages. But Boucicault's argument for a unified Irish response to the British oppressor is powerfully made.

Considering the subject matter and nationalist sentiments of *The Shaughraun* and the other Irish plays, it is not surprising that critics have tended to see them solely as Boucicault's response to Ireland's continuing nationalistic struggle and the sorrows of Irish history. However, these plays also speak eloquently to the life of the Irish in America in the latter nineteenth century and, as such, are tellingly American. By the 1870s, many of the "Irish" in America were as much American as they were Irish. Two generations had sprung up on American soil since the great migrations of the 1830s and 1840s, and new immigrants continued to arrive from Sligo, Cork, and Galway. However, despite their contributions to the building of the new industrial state and their service during the Civil War, the Irish remained cut off from the mainstream of American life, "objects of contempt and discrimination" (Archdeacon, 97). Indeed, as the anti-Irish political cartoons of Thomas Nast and instances of gerrymandering of Irish political strength in New Jersey and New York testify, even their attempts to partake of venerated American democratic institutions faced fierce resistance. Linked to "the old sod" by familial ties and ethnic heritage, Irish-Americans faced a whole range of economic, political, and social biases which many saw as the moral and economic equivalents of events in Ireland.[10] An empowering drama therefore became every bit as necessary in an American context as did the performance of these plays in London, Manchester, and Liverpool. Not surprisingly, Boucicault seems to have spoken in two voices in these plays. As a native-born Irishman, he decried the fate of his homeland, showing the courage and determination of its people and the inhumanity of the British policy toward Ireland. As the adopted son of America, he pleaded that his chosen home not repeat with its newest citizens the outrages that Britain had once committed upon its American colonists and persisted in inflicting upon nineteenth-century Ireland. In this double vision, attuned at once to his heritage and his current situation, Boucicault struck a note which continues to resonate in the ethnic theatre of America.[11]

Melodrama as National History

While Daly was seeking to bring new light to the tensions of city life and class conflict and Boucicault was endeavoring to humanize Irish immigrants, another group of playwrights was busily reinterpreting recent national history in an attempt to reunite the nation emotionally by examining its most recent and most deeply felt social and political wound, the Civil War. In a series of plays in the 1880s and 1890s, American melodramatists presented plays which examined the causes of the war, the nature of its conflicts and the grounds upon which a reconciliation had been or might be accomplished. Using the strengths of melodrama—a simplified moral universe, easily comprehensible characters, and exciting action—these playwrights sought to integrate the recent past for their audiences by presenting a dramatized history which testified to the enduring values—individual dignity, political freedom, and the indivisibility of the union—ostensibly reaffirmed by the war. The results not only indicate the flexibility of melodrama as a form but also belie in substantial ways the stereotype of melodrama as a naive drama whose orientation wholly neglects political or social commentary.

In their use of history, these dramatists were in one sense continuing a tradition even older than melodrama, for from the Greeks onward, dramatists have found historical material particularly appealing (Lindenberger, 6). Ranging from what Lindenberger calls documentary drama—which purports to enact chronicled "facts"—to the "unhistorical history play"—which is concerned with historical issues but is not based upon "real" events—history plays provide a convenient method of casting the present into relief by juxtaposing it with the audience's past (14–29). The history play allows for a simultaneous examination of past and present institutions, beliefs, and values, and depicts in a condensed framework the manner in which and the degree to which continuity has been maintained. The effect is most often a psychic uniting of the audience with its past, providing viewers the opportunity to identify with those elements that are still appealing and to repudiate those which seem antiquated. Because the audience is never in doubt as to the "plot's" resolution, the audience's "interest tends to shift from the *what* to the *how*" (Lindenberger, 24). While this shift may, as in the case of such tragic histories as *Antony and Cleopatra* or *Maria Stuart*, generate complex characterizations, historical drama by no means demands them. As Brecht's *Mutter Courage* indicates, historical drama's delineation of the historical process itself may occasionally even demand a simplification of character. Thus, the melodrama's ostensibly unambiguous characterizations present no inhibition to the uniting of history and melodrama. The melding of melodrama and historical drama provides, in fact, an ideal means of uniting the public world with private affairs, personalizing the tides of history while exalting private concerns by playing them out upon a stage dignified by its concern with historical process.

Besides their use of recent history, all the Civil War plays of the 1880s and 1890s are united by their appropriation of one of the pervasive myths about the South—its uniqueness as a region. While this myth is of long duration, in the years immediately preceding the Civil War it found one of its most ardent and popular spokesmen in William Gilmore Simms. In a series of romantic novels which displaced antebellum southern cultural assumptions to the romanticized, temporally distanced and privileged past of the American Revolution and its aftermath, Simms established in copious detail the idealized pastoral and political foundations of the Old South. As Kolodny has pointed out, this bucolic vision combined the mythic Earth Mother with the pervasive American longing for a new edenic garden (115–32). For southerners, the result was a conception of the land as a surrogate mother whose nurturing power was inextricably tied to the maintenance of long-established and seemingly divinely sanctioned patterns of life. So the southern resistance to change stemmed at least in part from a subconscious desire to resist a second expulsion from the Garden. An outgrowth of this subconsciously feminized landscape was the conflation of the land with southern womanhood in a way unavailable to other sections of the country. So powerful and pervasive was this identification that Simms's admonition to his son is typical: "remember that you are to defend your mother country and your natural mother from a hoard of mercenaries and plunderers" (Kolodny, 115). The melodramatic heroine's central role as the embodiment of cultural values made the southern woman a particularly appealing focus for these dramatists. It is therefore not surprising that the plays often present the reuniting of the country as a stormy romance in which a northern hero overcomes the initial resistance of a southern heroine. The private institution of marriage becomes a metaphor for the public reuniting of the political nation after what amounts to a lovers' spat. Before the reunion, however, came the dissolution and an examination of the causes of the discord.

The thorniest issue facing postwar playwrights was the emotional wellspring of the war, slavery. As has already been noted, in the years immediately preceding the Civil War, slavery and its victims had generated a large number of plays in which both joy and pathos served an overtly political purpose. In most cases, only two alternatives were available to slaves in these dramas. In the first, exemplified by George Harris in Aiken's *Uncle Tom's Cabin*, the slave, usually a mulatto, repudiated slavery and triumphantly escaped to freedom. However, most plays traced the lives of characters who chose the other alternative, as illustrated by Zoe in Boucicault's *The Octoroon* and Uncle Tom in *Uncle Tom's Cabin*.

In these propaganda pieces, the long-suffering protagonists endured slavery until death freed them from persecution. But the plots and characters which had sustained strong abolitionist sentiment in the 1850s were not abandoned after the war. Bartley Campbell's *The White Slave* (1882) indicates the manner in which many of the prewar melodramatic devices were utilized in order to retroactively deterge slavery of its moral stigma and thereby provide an emotional warrant for post–Civil War racial prejudice, both northern and southern.

Writing after abolition and the Civil War had made slavery a moot issue—but in an America in which much of the overt racial bigotry had re-emerged in, for instance, the de facto disenfranchisement of former slaves in the South and the increasing indifference of northern politicians to the cause of blacks—Campbell effectively eviscerates the traditional political commentary of the slavery plays. By manipulating the slavery play's conventions, consciously or unconsciously, Campbell relieved late-nineteenth-century white America from meaningfully confronting its abiding racial prejudice. The conventions that had once divided northern and southern whites by arguing against the institution of slavery served, paradoxically, in 1882 to reunite regionally factionalized whites behind a resurgent myth of white moral and cultural supremacy, thus aiding in the reestablishment of the mentality that had made slavery possible.

The plot of *The White Slave* unites popular elements from two pre–Civil War slavery sensations, *Uncle Tom's Cabin* and *The Octoroon*, but links them to a totally different effect. Lisa Hardin, the illegitimate offspring of a French marquis and Judge Hardin's deceased daughter, has been raised as the child of the octoroon Nance. Supposed a slave by all except her grandfather and Nance, Lisa is inadvertently sold to the villain Lacy when Clay Britton, the judge's adopted heir, has to settle his gambling debts upon the judge's death. Though he repudiates and attempts to prevent the execution of the sale, Clay is imprisoned, and Lisa and the slaves are forced to leave their "Old Kaintucky Home" (Campbell, *White Slave*, 224) for the villain's plantation in Mississippi.[12] Rejecting Lacy's offer to become mistress of his estate, Lisa flees with Clay, only to be recaptured after escaping a burning riverboat. Lisa's true heritage is established and she agrees to marry Clay, while Lacy, who has killed his former mulatto mistress when she attempted to aid Lisa's flight, is slain by the local sheriff while trying to flee.

Campbell's major transformation in *The White Slave* is his use of a white woman rather than an octoroon as his heroine, a change which would ostensibly seem to heighten the pathos of the "slave's" situation. Following the racist assumptions of the genre, if a woman such as Boucicault's Zoe, who is only one-eighth black, is to be pitied, then how much more deplorable is the situation of a woman who, having no "black blood," is erroneously deemed a slave. By substituting a white who cannot legally be a slave for the mulatto usually found in such plots, Campbell effectively excludes blacks from the play's emotional center. The play's focus thus shifts from the institutional abuses of slavery, the genre's traditional target, to the predicament of a melodramatic heroine, a more theatrically acceptable problem in the 1880s. Indeed, Campbell's manipulation of the conventions implicitly suggests that any woman with "black blood" is unworthy to serve as a heroine. The play's logic, together with its treatment of its black characters, demonstrate its racial conservatism, even by the standards of 1882.

Campbell's handling of the genre also throws into relief certain assumptions of the slavery plays of the 1850s. The seemingly efficacious tactic used by Aiken and Boucicault of making their protagonists more sympathetic to white audiences by diminishing their racial otherness carried with it a tacit acceptance of the racist genetics of the period. While the tactic was effective in the immediate propagandistic attack upon the institution of slavery, it never touched basic white racial assumptions concerning blacks. Instead of dealing with the essential issue of human dignity, the octoroon plays seem to have "saved" blacks as an afterthought to the redemption of that portion of the character which was white. Indeed, the pathos that attached itself to the octoroons may be read as having sprung as much or more from an anxiety at the prospective extension of the ideology of slavery to individuals who were partially or wholly white as from a concern with the fates of blacks themselves.[13] By acknowledging a genetic disjunction between white and black and using "white blood" as a redemptive agent for their protagonists, Aiken and Boucicault may, ironically, have actually contributed to the perpetuation of underlying racial assumptions on which slavery itself was based. Thus, by 1882, with literal slavery gone and, concomitantly, the prospect of mixed-race children diminished by the removal of black women from the ready access of white masters, theatrical slavery had become merely another means of endangering the heroine, a plot contrivance of no real emotional or political concern to the post–Civil War audience.

Indeed, a more general examination of Campbell's treatment of the racial politics of the play indicates that he has taken painstaking efforts to diminish any anxiety at all over racial matters. For example, he is assiduous in circumventing the conventional problem of miscegenation which had troubled pre–Civil War audiences. While Boucicault was careful to withhold from George Peyton knowledge of Zoe's heritage, Campbell carefully exposes Lisa's birth early in the first act. With the audience in possession of the knowledge that Lisa is white, Campbell can allow the romantic lead to profess his love for her without generating any more anxiety in the audience than is usually felt for an oppressed heroine whose "protector" has proven to be a weak refuge from the storms of the melodramatic world. The treatment of the other blacks in the play also reveals Campbell's wariness of the slavery issue. Job, the slave preacher, echoes many of the Christian pieties that one associates with Aiken's Uncle Tom, but he ends the play happily contemplating the prospect of returning to his beloved plantation in Kentucky. Similarly, Aunt Martha and Clem, whom Campbell carefully tells us have been married forty years, provide domestic humor through their squabbling and the opportunity to indulge in festive song and dance in the minstrel tradition. The only character who casts even a cloud upon the racial horizon is Daphne, the octoroon mistress of Lacy, who is outraged at the prospect of being displaced by Lisa. Once again, Campbell carefully skirts the racial implications of Daphne's situation by presenting her as a woman who actually loves Lacy and who sees her situation almost totally as a personal competition between herself and Lisa, not as a consequence of a dehumanizing institution. Moreover, her murder by Lacy is the occasion for a bit of anachronistic fantasy in which she is elevated to the legal status of a human being whose death warrants the intervention of white justice. The status of slaves as chattel whose disposal was totally in the hands of their masters makes this plot contrivance a rather blatant attempt to disguise the realities of slavery.

Though not partaking of the overt North-South romance pattern of Howard and Belasco, Campbell does utilize the concept of a feminized South which finds fuller expression in his contemporaries' works. Lisa, like Zoe, is portrayed as the embodiment of both southern beauty and virtue; and, like her octoroon prototypes, beauty is for Lisa a bane, for it gives rise to her greatest affliction, the unwanted solicitations of Lacy. But as the embodiment of white southern virtue, Lisa's beauty is matched by her goodness. Indeed, in one of the most memorable lines uttered by a heroine in melodrama, Lisa responds to Lacy's threat to send her into the fields with a ringing denunciation of his proposition: "Rags are royal raiment when worn for virtue's sake, and rather a hoe in my hands than self contempt in my heart" (227). Her integrity sustained by the action of the play, Lisa is determined to return to Kentucky to perpetuate in the soil of the Big Bend plantation the values which she herself exemplifies.

Daly's protégé Bronson Howard sought to combine documentary history and melodrama in *Shenandoah* (1888). Though his was not the first play to deal with the Civil War (William Gillette's *Held by the Enemy* had been produced three years before), Howard's play seems to have struck a responsive chord with its audience, proving both an immediate popular "hit" and a profitable touring piece for appreciative audiences outside of New York. Despite its success, the difficulty of the play's subject matter was obvious to one of its original reviewers. Edward A. Dithmar of the *New York Times*, writing after the play's opening night, observed that "the author has spared no effort to emphasize the sentimental idea of the brotherhood of the contesting parties in our terrible war, and the recognition by individuals on either side of the natural ties which bound them to their foes" (10 September 1889, 4).[14] Dithmar reiterated his observation in his Sunday summation of the week's theatrical events, noting that Howard "handled the war with delicate care, almost gingerly," a circumstance which the reviewer attributes in some measure to Howard's recognition that the war "is still too near for the great body of Americans to view its incidents calmly and dispassionately" (15 September 1889, 3).

Howard's play is hardly serious drama in the political sense, for he avoids dealing with most of the partisan issues attendant to the war: his exclusion of blacks from the cast relieves him and his audience of dealing with the question of slavery; his rejection of sober political discussion precludes an examination of the regional differences which underpinned the conflict; and his domestication of the war by concentrating on the interwoven loves of his characters denies, for the most part, its harsher military realities. Instead, he seeks to emphasize the affinities of the combatants and to make the reuniting of the nation compelling by circumscribing the conflict within a romantic melodrama framework in which the uniting of several pairs of lovers becomes formally imperative. By refusing to adopt a "correct" political position, by doubling heroes and heroines, by counterpointing scenes of suffering, and by incorporating as many age groups and classes into his play as he can manage (with the obvious exception of blacks), Howard resists the impulse to exacerbate sectional divisions, choosing instead to suggest to his audience the nation's indivisibility even in the midst of its civil war.

The play's beginning on the eve of the bombardment of Fort Sumter allows Howard quickly to sketch the approaching conflict, but he carefully modulates his audience's response by presenting the growing discord not as the national tragedy his audience retrospectively knew it to have been but as one crossing element in the young lovers' romances. Though initially Robert Ellingham, the southern hero, speaks of a religious commitment to follow Virginia in secession, and Kerchival West, his Northern counterpart, counters by elevating the Union over his home state of New York, the pathos of their situation is driven home later when they are momentarily disquieted at the prospect of confronting each other on the battlefield. This predicament is quickly superseded, however, by the more dire prospect of losing their loves, conveniently each others' sisters. The young women themselves treat the matter with hardly more seriousness, for, after brief patriotic outbursts, Gertrude Ellingham and Madeline West fall into each other's arms, suggesting for their brothers the rewards of war's end and, for Howard's audience, the fulfillment of a postwar fantasy of national unity. For the 1888 audience, the immaturity of West and Ellingham and their fiancées on the eve of a war that would cause almost 500,000 deaths and immeasurable pain would have been intolerable unless it passed (as it does) in the rapid flow of events and was seen merely as melodramatic convention.[15] To forestall any potential revulsion, Howard denies the audience a reflective moment, deftly moving the action on to his, and the audience's, real interest, the fate of the romances. The cannonade which ends the first act places the Ellinghams and the Wests on opposite sides of the conflict, momentarily supplanting the traditionally comic battle of the sexes with a much more public and tragic struggle. Nevertheless, Gertrude's weeping at the loss of West, which closes the act, reorients the audience to the play's primarily private rather than social focus.

That Howard is little interested in the war itself is evidenced most pointedly by the structure of the play's action, which leaps across more than three years of the war's combat to settle in the next two acts at the site of one of the last major battles of the war, Cedar Creek, Virginia, where Sheridan's Shenandoah campaign culminated in October 1864. Howard carefully edits the historical record, omitting any reference to Sheridan's potentially troubling "scorched earth" policy and allowing the Ellingham homestead to represent pictorially the quaint antebellum South which by the 1880s, under the influence of such writers as De Forest, Cable, and Harris, was once again becoming a staple of popular fiction. Ironically, the Ellingham homestead becomes an island of private virtue in a sea of public conflict, a thoroughly appropriate domestic venue for the eventual repudiation of Old South militarism by its most outspoken first act supporter, Gertrude Ellingham. Again, despite the bustle of uniformed actors and realistic touches provided by authentic trumpet and torch signals, Howard directs his audience's attention to the emotional rather than political life of his characters. Gertrude's failed attempt to act as a Confederate courier, for example, serves only to confirm her love to West, whom she continues to deny she loves. Indeed, though the war is visually and audibly omnipresent—the maneuvers of Sheridan's and Early's opposing armies are constantly referred to, orders are read, reconnaissance patrols are dispatched, and prisoners are interrogated—the war retains its secondary status even for the soldiers in the field.[16] The battlefield death of General Haverill's son in an attempt to secure Confederate battle plans provides the opportunity for his father's unknowing, posthumous reconciliation with a son who had earlier brought dishonor to the family name through embezzlement. But it is the pathos of a father's, not a general's loss that Howard emphasizes. Most significant, West's wounding by the northern renegade Thornton is an act of personal vengeance, removed from any connection with the war except the villain's uniform.

Despite its subordinate position, the war is not superfluous, for through its operation Howard delineates his conception of the fundamental impulses which united the country in the midst of its internecine sectional dispute. The reality of war's horrible cost impressed upon them by the death of young Haverill, Gertrude and Madeline view the approaching battle with a heightened sense of dread. As the cannons roar to life, Madeline is the first to toss aside patriotic sentiment as she prays for the preservation of Robert Ellingham though it means the loss of the Union. In a revealing shift of attitude, West applauds his sister's passion, arguing "every woman's heart, the world over, belongs not to any country or any flag, but to her husband—and her lover. Pray for the man you love, sister—it would be treason not to."[17] This initial surmounting of patriotism by love occurs at the essential moment of the action, for Gertrude Ellingham quickly echoes the sentiment when West, bleeding from Thornton's assault, attempts to check his company's retreat in the face of Early's assault. As West staggers toward the offstage battlefield, Gertrude berates those fleeing the field: "Men! Are you soldiers? Turn back! There is a leader for you! Turn back! Fight for your flag—and mine!—the flag my father died for! Turn back!" (430). Sheridan returns, riding appropriately upon Gertrude's confiscated horse, seals the fate of the battle and symbolically guarantees the continuance of the nation. With the country again clearly apprehending its fundamental values, the war ends, and the final act, symbolically set in Washington, completes the reconciliations of North and South, husband and wife, young and old, immigrant and native-born, anticipated by the young lovers on the battlefield. Indeed, the ending is almost too pat. The good have been saved; the evil have been chastized. In the rush to fulfill the melodramatic conventions of a romantic, "happy," ending, Howard completely ignores the massive trauma of the war itself.

While Howard carefully utilized actual history to present what could pass with an accepting audience as documentary drama, David Belasco allowed himself greater freedom in his Civil War melodrama, *The Heart of Maryland* (1895). Set in an idealized Maryland, the play centers on the crossed love of the staunchly Confederate heroine, Maryland Calvert, and her former fiancé, Alan Kendrick, now a Union cavalry colonel. This ideological conflict has generated internal family schisms as well. Unknown to her, Maryland's brother Lloyd is a spy for the Union, while Alan's father holds the rank of general in the Confederate army. All of the entanglements provide abundant opportunity for the villain, Colonel Fulton Thorpe—a man cashiered from Alan Kendrick's prewar regiment for having caused the suicide of the regimental color sergeant's daughter whom he had seduced and deserted—to wreak his revenge on Alan and to continue his licentious behavior toward women, particularly, Maryland.

Following Howard's pattern, Belasco quickly feminizes his landscape, translating Maryland Calvert into the breathing embodiment of southern pastoral values. The fictional inspiration of the state song, "Maryland, My Maryland"—a song Alan has supposedly written and Maryland has sung among the trees and bushes of her home, Lilacs, during their last meeting before the war's outbreak—she becomes for Alan and the audience the archetype of southern womanhood. Belasco attributes Maryland's grace and beauty in large measure to her aristocratic heritage. Belasco's choice of his heroine's surname allows him to link mid-nineteenth-century Maryland with the state's seventeenth-century cavalier origins as a holding of the English Lords Baltimore, whose family name was, of course, Calvert. But the legacy of the Calverts has a serious political element as well, a tradition that Maryland seems intent upon perpetuating. When Maryland receives a letter from Robert E. Lee thanking her for her aid, Mrs. Gordon, her aunt, insists that it be placed in a frame next to a similar letter of appreciation from Charles the First to the first Lord Baltimore, a man who, as Mrs. Gordon remarks, "melted down his family plate to se've his king."[18] It is perhaps not surprising given this family history that Maryland, the lilac-scented heroine, is also known as "the fiercest Southerner of all" (183). Though as a woman precluded from the fighting, Maryland has sacrificed her greatest possession, her fiancé, and the play explores the emotional consequences of this offering to political ideology.

That Maryland has internalized the war, that she represents a localized and emotionally charged battleground, is evident from an early exchange with a rejected former suitor, Tom Boone. Knowing that Maryland has repudiated Alan Kendrick for his support of the Union, Boone once again broaches marriage. But Maryland's sadness at the mention of Alan's name and her refusal to accept Boone leads the frustrated beau to assert angrily to her: "You love Alan Kendrick still! You love him with all your heart and soul! You can't—you won't forget him—though he is your enemy, and has taken up arms against your cause. This cursed Yankee!" (185). Tellingly, Maryland never denies the accusation, deflecting it instead by sharply asserting that Alan has at least taken up arms to defend his principles. The accuracy of Boone's surmise is revealed later in the first act when Maryland and Alan meet. The depth of Maryland's agony is delineated in a speech to Alan that expresses the dilemma she has faced: "Oh you don't know how we feel—we women of the South! How our hearts are torn by this divided duty. On the one side, our country—oppressed, forlorn, desolate! We couldn't desert it, could we? On the other, our very own turned to foes" (194). Pressing her argument for Alan to resign his commission, she frames a choice for him, "Put down your sword and—take me" (195).

The options metaphorically represent a simplistically dichotomous view of the various possibilities of American nineteenth-century life, but one which in the context of these plays is repeatedly reiterated. On the one hand is the phallic sword, representative of the masculine, political institution of war. Since his sword is only one of thousands being mass-produced in northern factories, it also becomes a representative extension of the power of the masculine, northern world of industrialized capitalism. On the other hand is the pastoral female, representative of fertility and its private institutional structure, marriage. Couched as it is, the hero's dilemma implicitly suggests emasculation, for in the male playwright's representation of this ostensibly female viewpoint, agreement between the feminine and masculine is seemingly impossible; the man must align himself with public or private ideals, with public masculinity or private femininity. But the hero reconciles these divergent demands through a uniquely male social construction, honor. An extension of the private individual, honor demands the public expression of private principle. The hero is thus unable to repudiate his carefully considered public positions without irredeemably compromising his private being. As Maryland's upbraiding of Boone intimates, this definition of honor is so firmly grounded in the social attitudes of the time that Alan's capitulation to her would inevitably cost him her love, for, in this world of male fantasy, she has merely momentarily lost touch with the most fundamental values of her society and of her sex.

While she acknowledges her love for Alan, agreeing to be his wife when she believes that he will not return to arms as a Union officer, she repudiates him again when he reiterates his intention to return to Union service. In the end, of course, her patriotism will not allow her to stand idly by as Alan is being sent to almost certain death, and she warns Alan of the imminent Confederate attack on the Union garrison at Charlesville. She is seemingly "doomed" by her sex to elevate the private over the public, even when, in the famous scene where she clasps the tongue of a bell to prevent its ringing and alerting the Confederate forces that Alan has escaped from custody, her actions force her to contradict publicly her avowed political beliefs. Thus, Alan's attitude is vindicated not only upon the traditionally male testing-ground of the battlefield where he leads his troops in a final successful attack upon the Confederates, but also by the actions of Maryland whose essential femininity demands its pure male equivalent in a hero of Alan's stature. The play's final tableau of Alan and Maryland's embrace not only reinforces the correctness of Alan's principled refusal to accede to Maryland's demands but also evokes an almost mythic couple, "natural" and heroic progenitors of a vigorous post–Civil War society.

Though its cultural commentary is handled with more than usual deftness, Belasco's play is in many regards a traditional melodrama. This is especially evident in his treatment of the collateral conflicts and subordinate characters in the play. The crossed loves of Lt. Telfair and Nanny MacNair, and Lloyd Calvert and Phoebe Yancey, offer little more than superficial diversions from the more serious problems of Maryland and Alan. Lloyd Calvert provides Belasco the opportunity to augment the more direct battlefield action with the breathless drama of espionage. As his romantic interest, Phoebe fulfills her role adequately by innocently hanging about his neck and weeping profusely at his death. Lt. Telfair, the young Confederate officer, and Nanny, the sister of a deceased Union soldier, provide a pale imitation of Maryland and Alan's dilemma. Like Maryland, Nanny seems unable to maintain her political beliefs, confessing, against her principles, her love for Lt. Telfair after he is wounded in battle. The nascent Oedipal conflict between General Hugh Kendrick and his son Alan is never developed to any degree. Instead, it provides Belasco with another stock device of the melodrama, a father and son temporarily alienated by the father's mistreatment of his wife. Belasco uses this situation to heighten the pathos of the play by having the reconciliation followed by the father's dutiful condemnation of his son as a spy and the father's subsequent death. Hugh Kendrick's death conveniently removes the specter of an internecine family conflict, but his tenure in the play allows Belasco to reiterate the familial loss generated by the war. Among the other characters in the play, none reveal the operation of the melodramatic origins of the play more than do the villain, Thorpe, and Uncle Dan'l, the Calverts' black slave.

Thorpe is in most ways a conventional melodramatic rogue. Given to drink and lechery, he is complicated only by external circumstances. His snarling remark to Alan—"I don't care which rag I serve under. I fight for my own hand" (Belasco, 212)—may contain an oblique reference to the notorious profiteering that attended the war effort on both sides, but Belasco never pursues the point. Like Aiken's portrait of Simon Legree, Belasco's rendering of Thorpe does seek in a superficial way to suggest the prosaic notion of the villain's inevitable torment. Though bouts of drinking and the fear of being discovered to be what Alan calls "a man without a country" (212) complicate Thorpe somewhat, Belasco is content to allow Thorpe to remain the embodiment of evil without exploring, even to the limited extent that Aiken did with Legree, the genesis of the character's venom.[19] Similarly, Belasco uses Uncle Dan'l as a conventional "darkey." Though by 1895 the blackfaced minstrel tradition had largely passed from the American theatrical scene, its legacy was everywhere apparent in the popular culture. Whatever possibility of realistic portraiture had been raised by blacks' relatively more serious depiction in the anti-slavery plays, the continued postwar antics of Sambo, Jim Crow, and Mr. Bones, and their portrayals in revisionist southern fiction, had again reduced blacks to insubstantial comic figures.[20] Perhaps not surprisingly, Belasco's Uncle Dan'l operates as a stereotypical black, complete with watermelon, whose function in the play is to exit into the orchard while white folks carry on the play's substantive business, to worry about the fate of the melons and chickens at the Union army's approach, and to fetch medicine for wounded Confederate heroes. A picturesque vestige of a past which had never existed, Uncle Dan'l represents the continuing fate of blacks on the American stage in the late nineteenth century. Not until Herne's *The Reverend Griffith Davenport* (1899) and Edward Sheldon's *The Nigger* (1909)—and, much later, O'Neill's *The Emperor Jones* (1920)—would blacks again approach the dignity they had enjoyed during the heyday of the abolitionist play.

Westward Ho!
Manifest Destiny on the Melodramatic Stage

Though the Civil War dominated the collective imagination of the era's melodramatists, its temporally circumscribed reality, its concluded "plot," and its existence as a relatively well-reported national event limited its appeal as a subject matter for melodrama. Fortunately for post–Civil War American playwrights, the derring-do of war found a near equivalent in the ongoing westward expansion and settlement. Though occasionally written by authors who knew something of the West from firsthand experience (Joaquin Miller and David Belasco are obvious examples), these plays represent less a serious move in the direction of realistic regional themes and characters than a displacement of Eastern social anxieties. Furthermore, despite their use of older frontier play conventions, the melodramas of the "new" West do reflect in their characters and actions the post–Civil War Eastern society's increasing longing for a less-complicated world in which man might once again live closer to the source of his sustenance and to generally accepted rhythms of human life. While in the older, more settled East, rigid social and economic constraints had propelled the country into war, the more fundamental demands of survival in an inhospitable Western environment again freed women and men to reexamine the failures of their former home in the "States" and establish a new society—or such was the popular assumption. Initially utilized as a real but exotic geographic location, the West underwent a steady modification on the stage until the physical map seemed no longer capable of sustaining its mythic import. But as the romantic frontier of Indian wars, mining camps, gunfights, and cowboys passed from the American scene at the turn of the century, American melodramatists such as Belasco and Walter suggested the durability of the myth by marking its cultural internalization.

In some ways, of course, the post–Civil War melodramatists did rely upon older versions of the frontier and its inhabitants. The heroic frontiersman of Louisa Medina, W. R. Derr, and John Augustus Stone, for example, resurfaced in Frank Murdock's *Davy Crockett; or, Make Sure You're Right, Then Go Ahead* (1872), a play written for the popular actor Frank Mayo, who played its title character for over twenty years. Like many of his predecessors, Murdock's Crockett is a hero uncomplicated by doubt and unsullied by education. He is the goodhearted backwoodsman whose strength, valor, native dignity, and force of will are sufficient to win the heart of the heroine and to preserve her from predators of both forest and drawing room. Paulding's comic version of the same character continued to be popular, though timely changes in the character's geographic origin provided new comic and satiric opportunities. For example, Charles H. Hoyt's *A Texas Steer* (1890) provided the usual jokes about the enduring rudeness of the frontier's citizens, in this case Texans, and the disruptive effect of blunt speech and action upon polished social interchange. At the same time, Hoyt's play also delivered an oblique commentary on pervasive contemporary political corruption and Western money's growing influence on national politics by placing the action in Texas and Washington, D.C., and by having the central character virtually buy his seat in Congress.

Much the same reliance upon older conceptions is to be found in these plays' use of a generally romantic attitude toward nature. Though they may occasionally acknowledge the reality of heat and cold, dust and mud, rain and blizzard, a surprising number of characters persist in linking the spiritual and physical environment. Perhaps reflecting the abiding American faith in a transcendent element in the physical world— evidenced contemporaneously by the continuing popularity of both the Hudson River landscape painters and the nature poetry of Whittier, Longfellow, and Lowell—these plays' heroes and heroines consistently reassert the traditional belief in the closeness of man to God in unmediated nature. Typical is the heroine's apotheosis of nature in Miller's *The Danites in the Sierras* (1877), "the highest, the holiest religion that we can have, is to love this world, and the beauty, the mystery, the majesty that environs us."[21] Almost thirty years later the title character of Belasco's *The Girl of the Golden West* (1905) can comment of life in the same Sierra Mountains in much the same manner: "God's in the air here, sure. You can see Him layin' peaceful hands on the mountain tops. He seems so near, you want to let your soul go right on up."[22]

Despite the hero or heroine's occasionally lofty spiritual pronouncements, the majority of characters usually resist the temptation of voluntarily merging with the Godhead, focusing instead on the more mundane connection between the physical environment and economic survival. In this regard the post–Civil War western plays mark a distinct departure from both earlier frontier plays and most plays set in the contemporary East. More than any of the melodramas examined thus far, these plays seem sensitized to the role of place in the economic equation. The well-known pattern of western development made the linkage of western lands to individual labor and wealth readily apparent to the audience. Besides the Spanish settlers who colonized the Southwest and California for Mexico, the wandering fur trappers, and the Mormons who sought religious freedom in Utah, the white migration into the West was almost without exception initiated by a rush for gold or silver. Though the 1849 California gold strike was the first and most famous, subsequent gold and silver booms in Colorado, Nevada, Idaho, Montana, New Mexico, and the Black Hills of South Dakota between 1859 and 1876, together with profitable mining of copper, zinc, and lead, reinforced the idea of the West as the place to acquire a vast fortune through solitary or near-solitary effort. Beginning with the railroad right-of-way real estate empire of Sundown Rowse, the Congressional lobbyist in Daly's *Horizon* (1871), the West is presented again and again as a place of economic empowerment. Ironically, most of the plays present the link between land and wealth so openly, often locating their actions in the emblematic gold fields of California, that the setting's symbolic importance tends to escape the audience's notice, seeming only another element of the "local color." These plays also tend to present a rather idealized version of the miner's life. The reality of large-scale, heavily capitalized mining combines, the Western equivalent of the Eastern audience member's factory or company office, rarely make their way to the stage. Instead, stoutly independent placer-miners, the mythic remnant of a lost, economically independent labor force, work long hours for the chance at great personal wealth.

The stage pioneers (and presumably their audience) seem to expect that this wealth will facilitate the formation of a new, presumably better, social order. As in earlier frontier melodramas, there is a great deal of talk in these plays about an inherent sense of justice and order that men carry in their breasts. But on the frontier, such ideals are constantly in need of forceful reiteration by individuals and groups of citizens. No matter what its ideals may be, the frontier social reality presented in these plays has a familiar and occasionally quite disturbing anti-democratic cast. A seemingly persistent desire for a vapid social hierarchy, the shadow of ethnic and racial bias, poisonous greed, and a penchant for violence are seemingly all transported west with the settlers. Though these melodramas provided an imaginative displacement of issues which continued to plague the nation and an opportunity to examine possible solutions, their conclusions are increasingly skeptical that the unique qualities of a place will or can resolve social problems. In this regard, these plays tend to support a rather conservative moral position in the raging late-nineteenth-century debate over the basis of society's problems—though acknowledging *environment's* influence, these melodramas persistently attribute the majority of civilization's problems to the collective impact of individual moral failure.

Typical in this regard is Daly's early frontier success, *Horizon*. In Daly's play, the fundamental problem with the process of westward migration is that it is being undertaken too often by people already possessed of a debased human nature. Some of those going West are fleeing unsavory, even criminal, pasts and repeat or merely modify their offenses in the West. The ne'er-do-well Knickerbocker Wolf Van Dorp, for example, who has kidnapped his daughter and deserted his wife, remains a shiftless drunk on the frontier. Similarly, John Loder, a gambler of the type popularized by Bret Harte, is immediately suspect as one whose mercenary use of his wits is only possible outside a civilized society. Even the "noble savages" have been tainted by their contact with easterners: Wannemucka, *Horizon's* villain, has transferred his aggressive behavior from his traditional knife and gun to the deck of cards he now carries. As Loder wryly observes to Rowse, when Wannemucka "was in his native state, he went for the hair of your head. Now he's in the midst of civilization, he carries the weapons of enlightenment, and goes for the money in your pocket."[23]

But the indictment is not limited to those who obviously fall beneath the societal standards of respectable middle-class life in the East. In their western dealings, even those who retain a veneer of eastern respectability are characterized in the main as scoundrels or fools. Sundown Rowse, who in a New York drawing room suggests that he will emulate the purchase of Manhattan by taking trinkets to trade for additional land in the West, is perfectly willing to argue that his congressional land grant has effectively created a principality of which he is ruler. When the citizens of Rogue's Rest refuse to accede to his wishes, he demands that a young army officer forcibly evict them. In the context of the play, of course, Rowse's insistence upon putting the potentially violent inhabitants off his property is an amusing example of the conflict between eastern and western realities. Rowse's violence may be less overt than that offered by the gun-toting Vigilance Committee, and it may be grounded in accepted legal practice and channeled through the proper governmental institutions, but its existence implies that personal whim and individual greed can find support in law, and it is ultimately sanctioned as an acceptable basis for western social organization. While rarely presented this forthrightly, the position which Rowse represents is never really challenged in these plays.

In fact, the moral corruption of the West's inhabitants finds its most overt representation in the region's pervasive violence. Almost all of these plays, whether concerned with the "Indian wars" or the more "peaceful" life of the gold fields, contain at least one incident of physical brutality, perpetrated either by individuals or groups. In most melodramas, violence is presented as a cultural anomaly, a momentary aberration in the normal flow of society's life. Even the Civil War melodramas seem to suggest such a pattern, choosing to emphasize enduring social values rather than temporary conflicts over transitory political questions. Frontier plays, on the other hand, seem to present violence as a normal element in the life of the characters. In these plays, guns and knives are worn and used unselfconsciously, in a manner that would be remarkable only to those who, like an eastern audience, exist outside that world. Thus, the violence of the frontier melodramas is simultaneously part local-color setting, part formal necessity, and part cultural criticism.

Though less sweeping in scope, the gold field plays (*The Danites in the Sierras, My Partner,* and *The Girl of the Golden West*) still managed to provide the sense of a violent world. Given the amount of money either seen or referred to in these works, it is not surprising that they explore the proliferation and the consequences of violent and ruthless greed. Stage theft of food, drink, horses, money, gold—of almost anything and everything—is ubiquitous and is most often accomplished through violence. The frontier's rough civic response is equally notorious, and these plays are replete with actual or threatened lynchings. Often those who have violated the social code are revealed to be no worse than their executioners. Continuing the pattern of ethnocentric privileging evident in *Horizon*, the majority of the gold field plays carefully choose their villains from marginalized members of the emerging western society. In Miller's play, Mormon revenge precipitates the murders of a good Christian woman and her baby. Campbell's *My Partner* (1879) uses an old villain on the American stage, an Englishman, as the murderer and thief. Most blatant is Belasco's play, which manipulates its audience's response by giving the villain/hero two ethnically disparate names—Ramerrez/Johnson.

BARTLEY CAMPBELL'S POWERFUL AMERICAN PLAY

MY PARTNER

WITH **LOUIS ALDRICH & C.T. PARSLOE.**

The appeals of highly charged moral dilemmas played out against the grandeur of the frontier are suggested in this poster for Bartley Campbell's My Partner *(1879).* COURTESY OF THE PHOTOGRAPHS AND POSTER DIVISION OF THE LIBRARY OF CONGRESS

The individual corruption that runs rampant in these plays cannot be overcome by a recommitment to democratic ideals and institutions whose operation could potentially temper its abuses. And, despite romantic protestations to the contrary, most of the characters seem oblivious to the consolations in nature, seeking comfort instead from their fellow humans. Given this social impulse, their rudimentary society constitutes a powerfully coercive mechanism, even for characters who have no solid reason to desire or perpetuate conventional society. Ironically this western society becomes merely a rough-and-ready parody of its Eastern counterpart. A vivid example of the dangers of the mindless transferal of accepted social conventions is presented in the escapades of Capt. Tommy and Bunkerhill, two "whores-with-hearts-of-gold" in Miller's *The Danites in the Sierras* (1877). After their societal redemption, Capt. Tommy and Bunkerhill unexpectedly become champions of the new civic morality; as such, they complacently argue with the Widow (who is extending to others the same compassion she has earlier shown her "fallen sisters") that "we ladies can't afford to fly into the face of society" and "society must be respected" (395). The incongruity of strictly applying a morality to another which they themselves could not meet is apparently lost on these two "ladies." More troubling still is the persistent racial and ethnic hierarchy that Miller's play highlights. Away from the inherited historical problems of slavery and immigration, easterners nevertheless continue to indulge racial and ethnic prejudices. Native Americans, Mexicans, and the Chinese are all marginalized in the new society, usually deprived of even a modicum of dignity. Thus the Eastern problem of increasing ethnic diversity (suggested in Boucicault's Irish plays) seems to find no solution in the post–Civil War vision of the West. Nor do the traditional institutions of democracy offer much consolation, at least in the short run. Even when these institutions are generally supported, their supplanting of personal agendas can take some time. Ned Singleton in Bartley Campbell's *My Partner*, pointing up civic progress since the boom, notes that "politics are not what they were in California, when the longest knives and best shots won."[24] Coming in response to another character's failed attempt to buy votes with outlandish promises and free whiskey, the remark may merely indicate a shift of tactics rather than the approaching fulfillment of political ideals.

By the turn of the century, the long-popular assumption that a desire for social and economic justice suffused the hearts of the frontier citizenry and was being translated into institutional reality had fallen into disarray. Although reality may have failed to sustain the vision, the potency of the myth of the West is evident in its final transmutation. In *The Girl of the Golden West,* Belasco makes his most powerful case for the enduring nature of the myth through the story of Minnie Falconer, proprietor of the Polka saloon in the Sierra Nevada Mountains mining camp of 1849. Minnie, the girl of the title, is the object of the affections of a varied group of miners and their hangers-on. Pursued by all, Minnie has given her heart to no one until she falls for Dick Johnson, also known as Ramerrez, a notorious armed robber. Though Minnie feels somewhat betrayed when she learns that Johnson is an outlaw, she nevertheless tries to conceal him from a posse led by Jack Rance, the gambler-sheriff. When Rance discovers Johnson in her house, Minnie plays poker with the lawman, staking herself against Johnson's life. By cheating, Minnie wins a temporary reprieve for her lover, but he is finally captured and is doomed to hang. The couple persuade the populace to allow them a final goodbye, and that loving exchange in turn convinces the townspeople to "pardon" Johnson. He and Minnie end the play headed for a new life in the East.[25]

   Though in some ways a typical gold-field melodrama, Belasco's play is remarkable for the manner in which it finally disposes of the West. Belasco relies throughout upon the conventions of the frontier drama—swift action, a compelling heroine, beautiful natural scenery, and a seemingly unequivocal moral universe. But in his choices of Johnson as the hero and Minnie as the heroine, in his uniting of them, and in his exiling of them from the West, Belasco propels the myth in a different direction than had his predecessors. In earlier frontier dramas the hero, no matter how rough-and-tumble, had almost always been a pillar of the budding community. Here Belasco confounds matters by suggesting that an admitted thief is actually worthy of the audience's sympathy. Belasco carefully mollifies the audience's presumed uneasiness by having Johnson reveal that his father raised him without ever letting on what the family "business" was, and also by indicating that Johnson has only been working at his "profession" for six months. The character is made even more sympathetic, of course, by his love for Minnie, who unites an endearing naiveté with a firm determination to aid her lover when she has finally given her heart. Minnie is Johnson's perfect match. A rough-and-ready woman who runs a saloon and is capable of holding her own against a pack of not-so-gentlemanly men, Minnie is a new kind of heroine. Here is not the romantic embodiment of "civilization" who redeems the lapsed hero, but a woman willing to wager her sexual virtue for her man. Together Minnie and Johnson come to embody the emergence of a West in which the possibilities once associated with a physical locale become internalized as an unexplored, uncompromised psychic landscape where individual potentiality can be realized. As Minnie states toward the end of the play: "we both came out of nothin' an' we met, but, through loving, we're going to reach things now—that's us! We had to be lifted up like this, to be saved" (96). The conflation of romantic, religious, and acquisitive discourses suggests a final melding of the various elements associated with the West. The great irony of the play is, of course, that Minnie and Johnson must leave the West in order to realize their dream. The West comes to represent for them, and by extension for the audience, a place of physical and emotional dissolution. So the couple must construct their own Eden in the old world of the East. Facing the rising sun on the prairies east of California, and responding to Minnie's sorrow at the loss of the "promised land" of California, Johnson drives home Belasco's final point: "We must look ahead, Girl, not backwards. The promised land is always ahead" (97). For a nation whose citizens could no longer solve their problems by departing into a physical frontier, only the power of imagination remained as a means of overcoming the limitations and frustrations of contemporary existence.

Melodramatic Postscript: *Eugene Walter's* The Easiest Way

Though melodrama is popularly considered to have passed from the scene with the advent of Ibsen, Shaw, and Pinero, such a perception is only partially accurate. As the critical acclaim and eventual box-office successes of the early European dramatic realists in the 1880s and 1890s combined with the emerging native realist narrative movement to pave the way for a shift in direction for American drama, the dominance of melodrama certainly diminished. The sensational melodramas disappeared relatively quickly, but the erosion of the form as a whole was slow and has arguably not been fully accomplished to this day. Certainly, American drama at the turn of the century showed continuing evidence of melodramatic representation of American life. A case in point in Eugene Walter's *The Easiest Way*, a vastly successful play produced in 1909 by Belasco.

Set in Colorado and New York, Walter's play traces the demise of Laura Murdock, a Broadway actress of indifferent skill who has guaranteed her success by sexual alliances with influential theater men. On a tour of Colorado, Laura meets and falls in love with John Madison, man of the world, and they agree to marry when John has secured the necessary fortune. The one stipulation that Madison imposes is that Laura repudiate her former lifestyle and throw over her latest paramour, Willard Brockton. For his part, Brockton wishes them well, though he is less than sanguine about Laura's ability to remain faithful to Madison. Laura agrees, and she and Madison leave each other determined to fulfill their dream.

The scene shifts to New York, where Laura's increasing poverty finally impels her to make a false reconciliation with Brockton. She fails to inform Madison what she has done, leaving him to discover her weakness when he arrives ready to marry her. After confrontations with Brockton and Madison, Laura is left alone, determined "to make a hit, and to hell with the rest."[26]

Much of *The Easiest Way* represents a departure from standard melodramatic dramaturgy. First, the play has at its center an active woman who has self-consciously chosen to advance her career by morally dubious means. This is a far cry from the essentially passive "good" women of melodrama who are not usually roused to action until their chaste loves are threatened. Second, the hero of the piece is also less of a model citizen than melodrama has led us to expect in that role. Although, in the mode of Johnson in *The Girl of the Golden West*, Madison is seemingly "reformed" by the love of a "good woman," that rehabilitation is hardly permanent. His repudiation of Laura at the end of the play is grounded in a far more realistic psychology than is evident in a similar situation in Campbell's *My Partner*, for example. Third, very little happens in the play, at least by melodramatic standards. The play is essentially a series of dialogues which chart the internal struggles of the characters rather than a progression of incidents detailing the protagonists' external travails. Finally, the playwright's seeming lack of outrage at Laura or her loss, and his ostensible willingness to urge the audience to adopt his distanced perspective, represents a telling departure from the melodramatists' insistence upon traditional morality and intense emotional engagement.

Nevertheless, much of the world of the frontier melodrama remains intact in *The Easiest Way*. The East-West contrast that provided the underlying structure of the western melodrama is replicated almost without modification. The West remains the "land of opportunity," in this case romantic as well as economic, providing Laura a "real man" and Madison the economic security he needs. Though there is greater depth than in most of the earlier melodramas, Walter's characterizations rely upon many of the cherished stereotypes of the melodrama—"loose" women are still loose, businessmen remain hard-bitten, and reform is still available, apparently, only to men. Most significant, the moral universe of melodrama remains in full force. Walter's openness to moral questioning comes to an abrupt halt in the denouément of the play when the implications of the sexual politics he has seemingly accepted allow for the possibility that Laura may escape the male-engendered "double-standard" and manage to marry a "good" man, though she herself has fallen short of the accepted moral standards of the age. Walter quickly reinforces the standard male code of morality, demanding adherence to the "natural" rules (those discovered by men) in order to guarantee the protagonist's happiness.

Though touted by such influential writers of the period as William Dean Howells and James Herne, realism did not suddenly sweep away the remnants of a decayed theatrical conception. As this brief discussion of *The Easiest Way* should suggest, melodrama continued to wield considerable influence among American dramatists, even after literary realism began to make significant inroads into the theater. The meticulous attention to theatrical illusion advocated by some producers of melodramas such as Belasco actually retarded American drama's embracing of realism by confusing physical verisimilitude with realistic art. But in the last two decades of the nineteenth century, as melodrama continued to pack theaters, realistic drama and theater was moving steadily into the mainstream of American theatrical art.

7

The Development of Realism

While melodrama's primacy in the American theater from 1860 to 1900 cannot be questioned, an alternative dramatic mode was steadily developing during the same period. Driven to come to grips with the identical political, social, economic and philosophical forces which found sublimated and displaced attention in the melodrama, American realistic drama experienced its nascent critical and stage expressions in the last three decades of the nineteenth century. Though the ascendancy of realism in the wake of O'Neill, Odets, Kingsley, and Sherwood has tended to obscure such considerations, the complexities of realistic drama's emergence and the resistance of melodramatic drama to dislocation in the last years of the nineteenth century present a fascinating chronicle of the transformation of theatrical tastes and illustrate profound changes in the premises grounding dramatic representation. Led and encouraged by many of the era's most influential literary figures, including William Dean Howells and Henry James, and prodded by such theater men as James A. Herne, American writers in ever-increasing numbers began to embrace a realistic aesthetic and to transform theoretical pronouncements into concrete and actable plays. But, as we shall see, the "realisms" that emerged were finally every bit as varied as the melodramas with which they contended.

Late-Nineteenth-Century Realist Dramatic Theory

To speak of "realism" in relationship to the plays of the period is somewhat problematic for at least four reasons. First, the term "realism"—as used by both dramatic critics and theoreticians such as Howells and James and more successful playwrights such as Herne—emerged from the particular social, dramatic and theatrical context of the late nineteenth century. A comprehensive discussion of this complex period lies far beyond the scope of this study.[1] Second, even among Howells, James and their contemporaries, the term "realism" served more to evoke an unrealized aspiration than to specify an already-settled critical, dramatic, or theatrical practice. The term was used as a matter of course to describe any number of elements of drama and theater depending upon the momentary focus of the writer or the aspect of the theatrical experience that the writer wished to emphasize. Subject matter, dramatic structure, characterization, dialogue, acting style, stagecraft, and the intellectual content of the plays all received varied interpretations at the hands of theoreticians and practitioners. Third, James's and Howells's discussions of realism's major tenets are now and then colored by overtones of their own narrative projects and are, as a result, sometimes at odds with the possibilities encompassed by a dramatic framework. For instance, James and Howells occasionally seem to "forget" that the fully nuanced narrative characterizations available to the novelist are less possible in a play whose immediate experience is circumscribed by three hours in a theater rather than many more hours spent in a private study. Finally, modern discussions of the concept of realism are fraught with such interpretive baggage that returning to what is occasionally the naive and unconscious starting positions of late-nineteenth-century writers may itself seem an untutored critical exercise. Nevertheless, only by reexamining those formulations can we retrieve a sense of the radically transformative project that these writers saw themselves espousing and bringing to pass. And only by reconsidering their original conceptions can we obtain even a contingent understanding of the questions and theoretical responses which in turn spurred their dramatic and critical successors. If we would understand how later realists, from O'Neill and Odets through Williams and Miller, used and reshaped realism in the first half of the twentieth century, we must first try to understand what they saw and read on the stage and page—what formed them aesthetically, formally, and theatrically into what they became.

For such writers as Howells and James, the word "real" almost always implied a dialectic whose unstated opposite half was "ideal."[2] For them, the major failure of their contemporary drama and theater was its stubborn refusal to acknowledge the disparity between the reality the audience experientially knew existed outside of the playhouse and the dramatic illusion they saw when the lights dimmed. The target of choice for such critics was the melodrama. On several grounds—subject matter, dramatic structure, dialogue, acting styles, the deceptive effects of the stagecraft, and intellectual content—the melodrama was from their perspective a sham.

The realist's core objection to melodrama was its studied insistence upon repudiating "real life" in favor of an idealized, simplified, and neatly wrapped fantasy. Realistic drama demands instead, Howells insisted in an early review of Ibsen, playwrights who wish "to deal with questions of vital interest, to deal with them naturally, and . . . honestly."[3] Such subject matter does not lend itself to the construction of plays that are narrowly focused or that provide easily discovered solutions to the problems they raise. Indeed, Howells suggests that in Ibsen one finds a playwright who constructs plays around problems "as wide as the whole of life, and . . . seeks a solution in the conscience of the spectator for the future rather than the present." Ibsen enhances this effect by avoiding narrowly framing the issue in terms of personality (a general failure of Ibsen's English imitators, according to Howells), instead making the spectator "feel the import of what has happened civically, socially, humanly, universally" (Kirk and Kirk, 146). While Howells's idea that life, much less the representation of life, is susceptible to some variety of objective verification and judgment is far more problematic than he acknowledges, in the context of the late-nineteenth-century American epistemological pillars of empiricism and pragmatism, his position is easily understandable.

Tied to the representation of serious issues (which could be treated comically, as Shaw and Howells demonstrated) was the issue of dramatic structure, a question of some import for James and Howells, both as critics of the drama and as novelists. Of the two, Howells staked out the more radical position, seeking to reverse traditional aesthetic conceptions of dramatic structure. Deriving their authority from Aristotle's pronouncements, the neoclassicals and later the adherents of the French "well-made play" tradition had sought to impose a preconceived artistic order upon the action of the play. Though James was generally tolerant of this approach to dramatic form, for Howells such a structural principle seemed a violation of the necessity for realistic drama to find its touchstone in the inherently inconclusive material of "real life." Thus, in praising the efforts of Shaw, Wilde, Jones, and Pinero in the mid-1890s, Howells is careful to note that the "recognizable semblance of the world" which provides their subjects is matched with structures derived from the rhythms of the events themselves: "To the inward truth, or measure of truth, there is a pleasing response of outward truth; the plays have a good form."[4] Part of the explanation for Howells's and James's differences in attitude may reside in Howells's more overtly politically charged view of realism's potential as a force of social transformation. Certainly, in his longest pronouncement on realism, *Criticism and Fiction*, Howells implies as much when he argues that the realist "feels in every nerve the equality of things and the unity of men; his soul is exalted, not by vain show and shadows and ideals, but by realities, in which alone the truth lives."[5] Though James would privilege structures derived from earlier forms, for both Howells and James the final arbiter of a contemporary play's artistic value was its adherence not to imposed standards derived from other cultures and other ages, but the play's representation of the apprehensible reality experienced by a thoughtful member of contemporary civilization.

Just as the subjects of realistic plays were to be derived from "real life" and the representation was to be structured (in the Howells conception) by the rhythms derived from an "objectively" observed flow of the events themselves, so too the diction and dialogue of the characters must do nothing to destroy the illusion that the audience was hearing human beings in everyday life. Across-the-board realists demanded an end not only to the rhetorical flourishes and lyricism derived from older forms of drama, but also the disruptive techniques of asides and soliloquies. People were to speak "naturally" on the stage, even if that meant that the play would be full of colloquialisms, dialects, or vulgarities. This theoretical position often led to interesting critical comments, especially in the case of Howells, vigilantly surveying the contemporary dramatic scene from his editorial offices at *The Atlantic Monthly* and *Harper's Magazine*. Though he generally found more to decry than praise in the contemporary popular theater, Howells occasionally encouraged what he perceived as advances on the road to realism among the popular dramatists, especially when their efforts had been well received by the public. Accordingly, though the action was contrived and the structure ramshackle, Howells could praise Edward Harrigan's farcical "Mulligan Series" for its attempt to render ethnic dialects accurately.[6] Fortunately, as Howells and Herne were to demonstrate admirably, colloquial speech could reinforce more serious drama as well as Harriganesque slapstick.

The actor's craft ideally complements the dialogue provided by the playwright, and on this score there is a striking difference between the perspectives of James and Howells (Murphy 33–36). Flowing from his continued admiration of older dramatic forms, especially the classical and Shakespearean repertoires, James insisted upon a style of acting appropriate to the illusion under construction. For him, the quiet style associated with realistic plays was ill-suited to the demands of, say, *Henry V*. In *Scenic Art*, James insists that actors trained to play in realistic drama must be able to recover the Shakespearean tradition if they are to play their parts acceptably: "An actor who attempts to play Shakespeare must establish for himself a certain Shakespearean tradition; he must make sacrifices. We are afraid that as things are going, most actors find it easier to sacrifice Shakespeare than to sacrifice to him."[7] As one might expect, Howells was less compromising than was James on this score. For Howells, the evocative truthfulness of the quiet style of acting suited to writers such as Ibsen implicitly revealed the overblown and essentially false nature of the drama that had previously dominated the repertoire. The point emerges in Howells's description of actors' responses to learning to play Ibsen:

> So far as I have spoken with actors who have played Ibsen, I find that without exception, almost, they like to play him, because he gives them real emotions, real characters to express, and they feel in him the support of strong intentions. They have to forget a good deal that they have learned in the school of other dramatists. They have to go back and become men and women again before Ibsen can do anything with them, or they with him; but when they have done this, their advance toward a truer art than they have ever known is rapid and unerring. (Kirk and Kirk, 145)

Despite their disagreements over the relative merits of the quiet acting style, for both James and Howells the essential issue was the contribution that acting could make to the dramatic illusion. For both, consistency of portrayal was the ultimate index of good acting no matter what the play.

Surrounding the actors as they recited their dialogue was the machinery of the theater, the most technically advanced element of the theatrical experience in the last three decades of the nineteenth century. Ironically, the major impetus to the increasing verisimilitude of the physical action and its environs had come from melodrama itself. Pressed to compete with such elaborate nonrepresentational sensations as circuses, musicals, and variety shows, melodramatic playwrights and their managers had sought increasingly to incorporate spectacular scenes into their plays. Horses galloped through battlefields, heroines escaped over ice floes in rivers that surged across the stage, and tenements burned before the eyes of spectators. Exemplary of the refinement to which such effects finally ran are the well-known efforts of David Belasco, who rebuilt on stage an actual boarding-house room, complete with running water, for a production of *The Easiest Way*, and, on another occasion, scrapped a lighting effect for *The Girl of the Golden West*, which he had spent three months and $5,000 perfecting, because it was not sufficiently "Californian."[8] While the realists could hardly argue with the verisimilar impulse, they had a great deal of difficulty with the motive that seemed to lie behind it. Rather than enhancing the overall reality of the illusion, elaborate sets and technically demanding "sensation scenes" tended to disguise the essential falsity of the action which occasioned them. Indeed, as Howells points out in a review of Edmond Rostand's *Cyrano de Bergerac*, even such a relatively innocuous effect as "a tree, opportunely dropping its autumnal leaves" as the hero is dying is of little value in a play which is, in the end, little more than "tinsel."[9] From the realists' perspective, the artistry of the costumers, carpenters, musicians, and lighting specialists should, in the final instance, augment, not falsify, the action.

For the realist critics, the play's central idea—its intellectual content—had to underpin all the other elements. Against the escapist impulse of melodrama, the realists insisted upon serious consideration of contemporary issues. This agreement aside, the realists ranged across a wide spectrum in their attitudes toward the relative merit of "ideas versus form" in drama. Again, James and Howells assumed polar positions. For James, the aesthetic expression of thought seemed to take precedence even over the quality of the ideas themselves. Though he acknowledged the interrelated nature of the two concerns, his expression of the relationship between them makes his priorities evident: "In a drama the subject is of the essence of the work—it *is* the work. . . . if it is shapeless, the work must be amorphous."[10] For James, the aesthetic form rendered the ideas comprehensible; it provided pattern and arrangement of the various elements of the intellectual content of the play. Without such a form, the play and its ideas remained trapped in the unshaped world of potential art, undifferentiated from experience as a whole. Given, as we have already noted, to a belief in a more socially active role for the drama, Howells was not so bothered by an overtly didactic, less aesthetic form than was his friend James. Nevertheless, Howells found ideas especially pleasing when rendered deftly. In his eulogistic essay on the death of Ibsen, Howells could easily balance concerns of serious treatment with his delight in the particular form that Ibsen's expression took: "the great and dreadful delight of Ibsen is from his power of dispersing the conventional acceptations by which men live on easy terms with themselves, and obliging them to examine the grounds of their social and moral opinions," but "to my experience he is a dramatist of such perfection, he is a poet of such absolute simplicity and veracity, that when I read him or see him I feel nothing wanting in the aesthetic scheme."[11]

For Herne, the greatest realist playwright of the period, the question could be answered on different grounds. In an article contrasting the realist aesthetic with the "art for art's sake" movement, he contended that the nature of the realist aesthetic might not generate "beautiful" art, but in its truthful portait of representative reality it found an alternative which earlier art had overlooked. If its objects were not beautiful in a conventionally aesthetic sense, they did present "the latent beauty of the so-called commonplaces of life, . . . [dignify] labor and [reveal] the divinity of the common man."[12] Ultimately, this opposition—between the beautiful expression of serious thought and a belief in the primacy of the thought itself—is one which James, Howells, and Herne would all have probably agreed disappears in the greatest art.

Although theoretical and aesthetic inconsistencies and disagreements divided the advocates of realism, it was the looming specter of the melodrama that finally united them in a common cause: the transformation of the American stage. Indeed, as we shall see, the works of the playwrights of the period are hardly ever generated from a doctrinaire position, nor can they be understood simply by reference to a list of critical precepts. Instead, the realist writers (and those melodramatists who occasionally shared their social and aesthetic concerns) undertook their labor fitfully. While they produced some plays that from the distance of a hundred years might still be deemed fully "realistic," more often than not the progress, even among the most committed, was halting. One by one the contributions of the collective effort coalesced into what we, for lack of a better phrase, call realistic drama. But if we find the efforts of these late-nineteenth-century dramatists no longer fully realistic, we might fruitfully reflect upon how the continually shifting conception of literary realism has generated critical reassessments of many of those firmly ensconced in the realist pantheon of only a few decades ago— O'Neill, Odets, Williams, and others. Rather than decry with William Archer the artistic failures of these early realists, we might be wiser to acknowledge the multivalent nature of our critical terminology and accept the inevitability that each generation must reassess the cultural value of the artistic work of earlier ages.

William Dean Howells:
Radical in the Drawing Room

When speaking of the first stumbling steps of realism's rise to preeminence in American drama, one must begin, ironically enough, with a man whose current critical reputation is almost solely based upon his fiction. Bestriding almost the entire range of late nineteenth-century American literary endeavor, William Dean Howells is a figure whose influence upon the period's dramatists and audiences is difficult to overestimate. Through a series of coincidences, it was Howells's fate to become not merely the best-known spokesperson for American literary realism but the champion of realistic drama in particular. In a literary career that spanned more than five decades as editor of the *Atlantic Monthly* and *Harper's Magazine*, Howells devoted a significant portion of his time and energy to advocating, critiquing, and writing realistic drama. Though his own plays were never particularly successful in the commercial theater of the time, Howells's position as editor of two of the most highly respected mass-market periodicals of the later nineteenth century made it possible for him to expound his views on dramatic art to a broad American middle-class audience whose economic prosperity gave them the means and the time to refine their sensibilities through literature and the theater. Moreover, the forum at *Harper's* gave him free rein both to censure the continuing popularity of melodrama and to offer the public alternatives through his praise of realists like Herne, or others, like Harrigan, who were aiding the cause in more limited fashion. Though Howell's own plays made little inroads with the theater managers of the day, they proved incredibly popular with the reading public of *Harper's*, where he published them regularly, and they provided Howells a tool of some power when he renegotiated his contract with the magazine in 1889.[13] As Booth Tarkington would testify in an article on Howells, Howells's plays "began to be acted everywhere within a week or two of their publication, and a college boy of the late eighties and 'golden nineties' came home at Christmas to be either in the audience at a Howells farce or in the cast that gave it."[14] Thus, both as a critic and as a practicing playwright, Howells's shadow stretched long over the American dramatic scene.

Though his plays have received increasingly serious attention in both histories of American drama and, occasionally, in more general discussions of the American realist movement, their intellectual depth and the seriousness of the issues with which they grapple have yet to be examined fully. As several writers have noted, Howells's preference for one-act plays, which he vexingly persisted in referring to as "farces," served him ill both in his own time and later. Augustin Daly, ever able to put his finger on the public pulse, wrote that Howells's ". . . one-act pieces bring no profit & very little lasting reputation to authors, actors, or managers" (Meserve, *Howells*, xvi). If the managers could see little profit in Howells's one-acts in an era in which the one-act curtain-raiser was passing from the American theatrical scene, critics of American drama have been a bit more discerning. Murphy notes, however, that the critical obsession with generic classification has bedeviled an understanding of Howells's efforts almost from their inceptions (71–73).

The rehabilitation of Howells's reputation as a dramatist began in earnest with the publication of Arthur Hobson Quinn's magisterial *A History of the American Drama from the Civil War to the Present Day*, in which Quinn devotes an entire chapter to Howells's impact upon the dramatic scene of his day. Quinn argues that some of Howells's plays are worthy of more serious consideration because they are comedies of manners rather than pure farces (Quinn, *History*, I, 78–80). And indeed, though in several of his pieces the actions do center almost exclusively around the physical situation of the characters, the essential thrust of most of Howells's plays is "entertainment" of a much more intellectual sort than one normally attributes to situation-based farce. While revealing a healthy appreciation of the incongruities and idiosyncrasies of the social world from which they spring, these plays often generate a self-reflexive discourse which examines the very nature of the artistic process of which they are a record. Whether evoking for serious consideration the epistemological premises of realism or indulging oblique satires on melodrama, Howells's plays provide a telling commentary on the contemporary battle between dramatic alternatives.

Howells's dramatic output was greatest in the 1880s and 1890s when he wrote a series of pieces in which he refashioned many of his social circle (notably Mark Twain, Howells himself, and their wives) into the central characters of his plays. Occasionally, the object seems pure lighthearted entertainment about the complications of life in the modern world, though even in these plays the action is realistic to the extent that it is almost always heavily steeped in the physical reality of contemporary life. In *The Sleeping Car* (1882), a befuddled husband, trying to find his wife, disturbs the occupants in a Pullman sleeper; in *The Elevator* (1884), guests on the way to a dinner party are trapped in the newly installed convenience. In others, the more routine aspects of the day-to-day life of Howells's social circle are chronicled. Complications in preparing for a formal evening in *Evening Dress* (1892), the mistaken identity of a new family cook, in *The Albany Depot* (1889), securing a doctor for a sick child in *A Masterpiece of Diplomacy* (1894)—all provide grist for Howells's comic mill. The picture that emerges from these plays—providing, one suspects, their immediate appeal for readers like the young Tarkington—is of a readily identifiable middle-class world. Here there are no "great actions," but the actions presented resonate with the lived experience of their readers and viewers. The plays are, in a word, real.

Though he was adept at writing farces, Howells often used his comic talent to examine more serious issues in plays with action focused upon the dissonance between his society's professed adherence to the ideal of truth and its less-than-forthright operations. Typical of this group of plays is *The Unexpected Guests* (1893), in which Mrs. Willis Campbell (based upon Mrs. Mark Twain) is confronted with the arrival at a formal dinner party of a couple she believes has earlier declined her invitation. Coming on the heels of an opening dialogue in which she has maintained that truth is "a female virtue," the reaction of Mrs. Campbell, and others in the know, to the unanticipated arrival of Mr. and Mrs. Belfort allows Howells to explore with delicious humor the convenient "social lie."[15] To the sardonic delight of her husband, Mrs. Campbell acts as if nothing whatsoever is the matter and assures the Belforts that they were expected. When quizzed as to why she has not turned the Belforts away, the hostess stoutly maintains it was impossible when Mrs. Belfort had "literally thrown herself on my mercy. She had no business to do it, and I shall always think it was taking a mean advantage; but I wasn't going to let myself be outdone in magnanimity" (425). The disparity between the force of social convention and the absent ideal of truthfulness is neatly reflected in the play's staging, which contrasts the onstage confusion of the hosts and "in-the-know" guests with a telling recitation by William Cullen Bryant on an offstage phonograph. Willis Campbell vacillates between irrepressible enjoyment and sincere concern at his wife's discomfort; Mrs. Campbell and her friends explore the moral and social implications of the moment in the midst of trying to rearrange dinner companions; still other guests, including the absent-minded Roberts (based on Howells himself), are dispatched to keep the Belforts from finding out their true situation. All of this action is punctuated by the offstage sounds of a new Edison phonograph, ominously reproducing Bryant's recitation of a pertinent line from his poem "The Battle-Field": "Truth crushed to earth will rise again" (420). The attempted deception eventually falls apart when a servant charged with calling Campbell's club to secure more quails for the dinner shouts into a telephone loud enough for everyone to hear, "There's a lot of folks come that they didn't expect, and they got to have some more birds" (428). The final exquisite reversal comes when Mrs. Campbell discovers that in her haste to leave for another engagement, she had failed to read Mrs. Belforts' reply to her invitation carefully enough to discover that it was an acceptance rather than a regret. As the play winds to its conclusion, Campbell is left to wryly observe that his wife Amy has been correct all along in asserting women's fidelity to truth: "It's perfectly wonderful! Mrs. Campbell can't get away from it when she tries her best. She tells it in spite of herself. She supposed she wasn't telling it when she said there was no mistake on your [Mrs. Belfort's] part; but she *was*. Well, it *is* a feminine virtue, doctor" (429).

Framed as it is by the discussion of truth, the comic action proves an apt vehicle for examining a host of attitudes toward truth, for deflating women's self-righteous assumption of the role of guardians of virtue, and for exploring truth's place within the social world of Back Bay Boston. Willis Campbell, the mischievous western interloper in this terribly correct world, initially acknowledges that one potential solution to social dilemmas is the unvarnished truth. As Amy Campbell notes, if unwanted visitors appear at his door, "Willis's idea of *truth* would be to send word that he didn't want to see them" (420). She, on the other hand, argues that sending word that she is indisposed or not at home is far kinder, a proposition agreed to by Dr. Lawton. When Campbell requests what Lawton's concept of truth is, Lawton frankly admits that he has none, explaining, "I've been a general practitioner for forty years" (420). The stage is thus set for the "unexpected guests," whose arrival provides ample opportunity to test the relative merits of each concept of truth in a taxing social situation. As Amy Campbell anticipates trying to reconcile the physical reality of too few quails and too few place settings with her fabrication, the depth of the acceptable duplicity in this society emerges in her stray comment about the carefully arranged table decorations: "I'd got the violets scattered so carelessly. Now I shall just *fling them on*" (423). The linguistic incongruity of what she has said passes quickly in the play but serves to suggest that social conventions' distortion of language has rendered even the prospect of stating truth problematic. Howells brings his audience discomfortingly close to the realization that society's acceptance of the convenient social lie renders civilized life different only in degree from the type of falsity he regularly attacks on the melodramatic stage. Even more potentially troubling is the implicit critique of the gender constructions of the period, which have indoctrinated women to believe that "truth" must be sacrificed to the higher ideals of decorum and genteel kindness. Howell's denouément, which reprieves truth from its socially imposed oblivion, drives home Bryant's assertion about the resiliency of truth and simultaneously suggests Howells's faith that truth can form the basis of dramatic art.

Howells's very early play A *Counterfeit Presentment* (1877) indicates, even more forcefully than does *The Unexpected Guests*, the seriousness with which Howells could approach dramatic composition. Accepted and performed by Lawrence Barrett on tour, A *Counterfeit Presentment*'s fate on the commercial stage was finally a disappointment to Howells. Combine this circumstance with the fact that Howells's greatest financial success, *Yorick's Love* (1878), a dreadful, extravagant poetic drama which he also adapted with the aid of Barrett, violated Howells's realistic aesthetic, and one may have some clue why Howells turned to writing one-act plays for *The Atlantic Monthly* and *Harper's*. Though his interest in drama remained strong (he wrote and adapted several full-length plays between 1878 and 1885) and his desire for money would occasionally renew his interest in writing for the commercial stage (especially in the wake of the handsome royalties his friend Twain received for Raymond's adaptation of *The Gilded Age*), Howells seems to have become increasingly wary of being lured back into writing for the stage unless under contract.[16] Considering the quality of A *Counterfeit Present-ment*, it is arguable that the conditions of late-nineteenth-century Ameri-can theater precipitated the loss of a potentially fine playwright.

The plot of A *Counterfeit Presentment* revolves around the love which develops between Bartlett, a struggling painter of New England landscapes, and the bereaved Constance Wyatt, a young American who has recently been jilted in Paris. Devastated by her experience, Constance has fled Europe with her parents to recuperate in the tranquility of rural New England. The play opens in the parlor of the Ponkwasset Hotel, with Bartlett saying goodbye to his minister friend Cummings, who is returning to Boston, taking one of Bartlett's paintings with him. Bartlett, a man who combines talent and a rash temperament, tries to convince Cummings that his own misanthropic attitude is justified by his being jilted three years before. Cummings disagrees, pointing to the much more tragic case of an American girl in Paris who has been vilely abandoned by her fiancé. On cue, the two notice a hat and shawl left by a previous occupant of the room, and Bartlett sardonically proceeds to describe their owner. They are soon joined by General Wyatt, who momentarily mistakes Bartlett for the young man who abandoned Wyatt's daughter, and threatens to cane him. Constance enters and, upon seeing Bartlett, faints. Bartlett is berated by Mrs. Wyatt and beseeched to remain until Constance can be cared for and the general can return to explain the family's bizarre reactions. But Bartlett is so incensed that he storms off, leaving Cummings to face General Wyatt. Wyatt returns and explains to Cummings that Constance is the very girl of whom Cummings has heard. The general reveals that, unknown to his wife and daughter, he discovered his daughter's fiancé was a forger and forced the scoundrel to end the engagement with Constance. By a "startling" coincidence, this rogue could be Bartlett's identical twin. Wyatt pleads that Cummings relay the information to Bartlett, apologize for the general's behavior, and ask Bartlett to vacate the hotel so as not to cause Constance any additional pain. Upon Wyatt's departure, Bartlett returns and learns the whole sordid story from Cummings. Crestfallen at his own insensitivity and swearing Cummings to secrecy that he has come into this embarrassing knowledge, Bartlett is ready to depart when General Wyatt reenters and requests, at the behest of Constance, that the painter stay rather than be further inconvenienced by the Wyatts. Bartlett is determined to leave until Con-stance herself enters and begs him to stay. The first act curtain descends on the uneasy Wyatt family as Bartlett, having agreed to remain, exits the parlor. With this set of complications in place, the remainder of the play rehearses Constance's recovery, despite lingering suspicions her fiancé has somehow discovered an unworthiness in her, and the inevitable path by which Constance and Bartlett are united in the play's last act after the truth about Constance's former lover is finally revealed and Bartlett's future as a painter seems to have been assured.

Despite the implausible coincidence which generates the play's complications, the subject matter and general tone of this play are much more serious than those of the plays we have examined heretofore; they are, in fact, much closer to Howells's novels of the period than to most of his plays. Giving rein to his realist impulses, Howells generates a play that is much more in keeping with English social discussion plays than the melodramas that dominated the contemporary American stage. The plot action of the play is, of course, the path of true love, but Howells chooses this vehicle to examine collaterally two important issues—gender roles and a moral life. Through both of these concerns Howells is able to make telling comments not only about American society in the 1870s but also about American dramatic art in the same period.

For Howells, the interplay of the sexes is a constant source of inspiration, both for his plays and his novels. In this particular play, he utilizes a pattern that Alfred Habegger has argued is ubiquitous in Howells—the doubled males whose doubling allows Howells to explore the varieties of manhood available to his society.[17] Male attitudes toward women and the bases of relationships between the sexes occupies the center of the action and serves implicitly to define male and female gender roles in this world. Howells's treatment is relatively straightforward, with Cummings, a "progressive" minister, representing the feminized male that high culture seemed to be generating, while Bartlett embodies the more "manly," aggressive alternative. The striking difference between the two is suggested early in the first act when Bartlett playfully picks up the hat and shawl to gain some insight into the woman who owns them. Cummings objects, saying, "It makes me feel as if you were offering an indignity to the young lady."[18] Against this rather effete fastidiousness, Bartlett draws upon his artistic eye to provide a detailed portrait of the owner. The very physicality of the picture—her blonde hair, slight, tallish figure, and Bartlett's rapture at her perfume—sends Cummings into a paroxysm of moral indignation to which Bartlett can only reply, "I'm not worth your refined pains. I might be good, at a pinch, but I could never be truly lady-like" (75). The point is made. While Cummings may preserve the moral fiber of the culture, it is Bartlett who will fall in love and eventually obtain the object of desire, Constance.

If the role of the men is complicated by the presence of two potential suitors, the available roles of women are both simpler and more complex, for Constance presents the internalized conflict between two alternative models of womanhood. The comic action effectively weans Constance away from her culturally received role as the passive female to a more independent, active, and comically appropriate self-actualizing assertiveness. Initially, Constance (as her name implies) remains faithful to her deluded idea that her love—and indeed she herself—are worthless. Grounded as her attitude is toward the operation of the dominant patriarchy which gives to men the privilege of constituting women's worth, Constance's behavior is, ironically enough, well within the realms of male imagination. Indeed, upon hearing of her plight, Bartlett is overcome with pity at her situation, generalizing that, unlike a man, a jilted woman "can't do anything. She can't speak. She can't move as long as she lives. She must stay where she has been left, and look and act as if nothing had happened" (81). Certainly this is the role that Constance has adopted at the beginning of the play—she is emotionally static. She tells her mother in her despair at her inexplicable change of romantic fortune, "It was something odious in me that he didn't see at first. I have thought it out. It seems strange now that people could ever have tolerated me" (83). The hyperbole of the line, in the context of the audience's greater knowledge, not only allows Howells a mild satiric swipe at Constance's self-absorption, but also invites the audience's indignation at the social constraints that precipitate her undeserved suffering—the benighted male assumption that women must be "protected" from the harsh realities of life. Luckily, within the realms of comedy, the world's operation can be put right by true love and marriage, a prospect that both characters and audience will embrace within two acts.

But true love's course never runs smoothly, particularly in a case where the complications are epistemological. In a masterful stroke, Howells rejects both the villains of melodrama and comedy. For him no lecherous rivals or interfering parents will do. Instead he presents a confusion over Bartlett's appearance which plagues both the hero and heroine for most of the play. Indeed, so great is the resemblance that even in the fourth act, as Bartlett confesses his love, Constance is not really sure if she is in the presence of Bartlett or his *doppelgänger*. Bartlett's agony of being as he relates his love is truly compelling: "You must feel what a hateful burden I had to bear, when I found that I had somehow purloined the presence, the looks, the voice of another man—a man whom I would have joyfully changed myself to any monstrous shape *not* to resemble, though I knew that my likeness to him, bewildering you in a continual dream of him, was all that ever made you look at me or think of me" (105). For a realist trying to write comedy, such confusion is certainly one of the ultimate challenges. How can we know who or what to believe when the transparent evidence of our everyday experience can no longer be relied upon? How may we fashion our lives or our art if our senses cannot aid us? Howells's answer is informative, for in resolving the question he is able to suggest the fundamental difference between the physical verisimilitude of melodrama and the deeper truth that lay at the heart of his realist vision. Like his mentor, Ibsen, Howells insists that his characters get beneath the surface of experience to look at its moral essence, not so as to embrace facile idealism, but to understand the more fundamental nature of each human being. Only then can life, built upon a clear perception of physical *and* ethical reality, begin. Thus, when her father's revelation about her former lover's nature has cleared her sight, Constance can look upon Bartlett with a clarity that her self-absorbed delusion has heretofore denied her: "Oh, *you're* not like him, and you *never* were! . . . It's your soul that I see now, your true and brave and generous heart; and if you pardoned me for mistaking you a single moment for one who had neither soul nor heart, I could never look you in the face again!" (108, 109). But the conventions of comedy do not demand self-sacrifice, and Bartlett insists that she fix her gaze upon the one who has proven himself worthy of her love. With wry humor at the form he has discarded in favor of his more satisfying realism, Howells charges in his stage directions that Bartlett "(*chancing to look up, . . . discovers the Rev. Arthur Cummings on the threshold in the act of modestly retreating. He detains him with a great melodramatic start*) Hah! A clergyman! This is indeed ominous!" (109). The comedy ends, as it must, in the uniting of Constance and Bartlett. But the basis of their alliance owes more to the hard-won lessons of a moral life than to the magic of traditional romantic comedy.

Formally, Howells's art ranges from farces of life's confusions in a very specific physical and temporal universe, to comedies of love's abiding mysteries in a world beset by dilemmas of perception. The compass of Howells's work allows us a sense of the possibilities that were immediately available to his contemporaries if they had the insight and determination to recognize them. But Howells was a unique case. His editorial positions gave him a freedom and flexibility that were unavailable to work-a-day men of the theater. For them the possibilities were more limited and, until the advent of Herne, their accomplishments more modest. Still, Howells had provided a model both as an aesthetician and as a playwright, and that model would not be discarded.

Steele MacKaye and Bronson Howard: Realism of Character

For those enmeshed in the day-to-day world of the theater, the continuing popularity of melodrama in the latter nineteenth century provided great resistance to aesthetic experimentation. Despite the reluctance of managers to stage any play which moved away from the tried-and-true formulas which had packed the houses for years, despite difficulties arising from a generally uninformed audience, and despite the more than occasional reluctance of reviewers to support plays that attempted to discuss serious social issues, several playwrights began to incorporate elements of the realist aesthetic into their dramatic work. Usually seeking to draw more psychologically complex characters (sometimes specifically Americans), to diminish the worst aspects of melodramatic plotting, or to use the actions of their plays to address American anxieties, these playwrights struggled to broaden their audiences' understanding of both the world around them and the nature of its varied inhabitants. Thus, northern England, the frenzy of France during the Reign of Terror, and the world of the Wall Street financier all became canvases for realistic portraits. As we turn from the lighthearted world of Howells's comedies to the ostensibly more serious work of James Steele MacKaye and Bronson Howard, we will be able to chart some of the ways in which Howells's aesthetic pronouncements found their way to the commercial stage.

James Steele MacKaye's theatrical career as actor, manager, technical innovator, teacher and playwright stretched over almost thirty years and was shaped by more immediate theatrical concerns than that of Howells. An early advocate of the French acting coach and aesthetician François Delsarte's restrained style, MacKaye appeared on both sides of the Atlantic, winning acclaim for his quiet, natural portrayals. MacKaye's Lyceum Theatre School in New York perpetuated his vision of the actor's craft. His technical innovations included "elevator" stages that allowed for more rapid scene changes and a variety of machinery to create complex lighting effects. As a manager, he rebuilt the Madison Square Theatre into one of New York's finest companies and later did the same for the Lyceum Theatre. As a playwright, he authored enormously popular works in the late 1870s and 1880s that earned their owners, if not their writer, incredible sums. (One estimate suggests that MacKaye's *Hazel Kirke* may have grossed as much as three million dollars.)[19] Having lost the historical context in which MacKaye worked, and having failed to recognize the reciprocal influence of his technical and acting innovations upon the pieces that he and others wrote in the period, critics have tended to dismiss him as one who wrote primarily in the "old style."[20] But a brief examination of one of MacKaye's less-well-known early works and his two most successful plays suggests that his early commitment to understated acting had a distinct impact upon both the characters and actions that he sought to dramatize.[21]

Marriage (1872) had long been thought lost until found in the MacKaye family archives.[22] The play recounts the disintegration of the marriage of Margaret and Walter Brooks and the serious consideration Margaret gives to leaving her husband so that she might find love with Carroll Gray, a longtime family friend. Brooks's infidelities, his indifference to his wife, and his insensitivity to Margaret's need for the emotional companionship of Alice, their daughter, has almost driven Margaret to the brink of leaving him when Brooks decides to take Gray's advice and reform. Upon hearing his friend's intention, Gray agrees with Margaret that she has a duty to Alice's happiness and should remain married. In an attempt to recover from his heartbreak, Gray departs for a tour of Europe. The last act opens a year later, with the audience quickly discovering that Brooks is again entangled with his mistress, that Margaret is deathly ill, and that Gray is soon to return. Brooks learns of his wife's love for Gray, and upon the latter's entrance there ensues a long debate in which both men finally realize how poorly they have treated Margaret, with one offering a loveless, though socially sanctioned, marriage, and the other proposing a love tinged with scandal. With both men resolved to correct the matter, they discover that Margaret has escaped her dilemma through death.

MacKaye seems deliberately intent upon expunging the usual melodramatic trappings which might have accompanied such a plot. The action is minimal, with very little physical action and no spectacle of the sort often associated with melodrama. MacKaye restricts the action to a single interior set and calls in his stage directions for his characters to act in ways that would be appropriate to members of an upper-class Newport household in the 1870s. The dialogue is natural and eschews the usual soliloquies and asides that render emotional conflict in the traditional melodrama. Most important, *Marriage* relies for its effects upon the serious consideration of a significant American social problem—the loveless marriage. MacKaye chooses to reveal the interior lives of the characters in restrained dialogue rather than the more familiar pattern of hysterical confrontation; the moral universe of the play pits the private impulses of the characters against both countervailing private ethical considerations and the weight of social convention. Margaret balances her desire for a fulfilling life with Gray against her duty to her daughter; Gray feels deeply both his love for Margaret and his ethical responsibility not to subvert a marriage that may ultimately bring Margaret happiness. The resolution fails to achieve the full impact of a play like Ibsen's *A Doll's House*, but, in light of the alternatives on the American stage in 1872, it is certainly a step toward the realistic theater for which Howells was calling.

Turning from *Marriage* to MacKaye's greatest box-office success, *Hazel Kirke* (1880; produced originally as *An Iron Will*, 1879), we may at first be somewhat shocked to see the reappearance of such melodramatic trappings as asides, sensational incidents, and the old clichéd plot of "spoiled" female honor and potential loss of the family home. Though these elements are in evidence, the surprising aspect of the play is the manner in which MacKaye subverts their melodramatic functioning. By concentrating the action on Hazel, one of the period's most natural characters, MacKaye is able to so reorient the play that the ostensibly melodramatic elements operate quite effectively within their new, more realistic environment. In fact, the alienation of the melodramatic material from its traditional formal universe forces the viewer not only to recognize the existence of these elements but also to realize that emotional intensity is not the sole property of melodrama. Finally, MacKaye incorporates a mild satire on melodrama by including in the play a "dramatist," Pittacus Green, whose antics serve to parody the melodramatists.

Set in the countryside of England, *Hazel Kirke* follows the crossed loves of the heroine, the daughter of an iron-willed Lancashire grain mill owner, Dunstan Kirke, and her aristocratic lover, Arthur Carringford, Lord Travers. Dunstan Kirke has rescued Carringford from drowning and the latter has recuperated in Kirke's house for six weeks, falling in love with the twenty-one-year-old Hazel in the process of healing. The complications are twofold: on her part, Hazel has seven years before agreed to marry Aaron Rodney, the local squire, in lieu of her father's repaying a debt to Rodney. Carringford has likewise been committed to marry the Lady Maud, his deceased father's ward, to hide the fact that his father has misappropriated Lady Maud's fortune. When Rodney finds out that Hazel's heart is Carringford's, he graciously resigns any claim to her, but her father is adamant that she fulfill the bargain. When she refuses, he

casts her out. Carringford secretly marries Hazel in Scotland and seques-
ters her in a country estate, waiting for a propitious moment to tell his
ailing mother of his marriage. Meanwhile, Rodney has become suspicious that the marriage may not be valid (marriages contracted under
Scottish authority had no legality if they were conducted on English soil)
and has relayed his fears of a sham marriage to the Kirke household.
Pittacus Green, a madcap friend of Carringford's who loves Hazel's
cousin, transmits the rumor to Carringford who, to his horror, discovers
that his valet has actually attempted the base trick of which Carringford
is accused. Without notifying Hazel of his intentions, he goes in search
of a curate to legitimate the union. Meantime, Rodney, thinking to
secure the Carringford family's aid in forcing Carringford to fulfill his
promise of marriage, brings Carringford's mother to see Hazel. When
Lady Travers convinces Hazel that she has been duped by Carringford,
Hazel repudiates Carringford and leaves. At the mill, Kirke obstinately
has sought to pay off the debt to Rodney, but has finally admitted defeat
after he has gone blind in a fit of rage at Hazel's dishonor. Hazel returns
home, unknown to her father, only to hear him say that he has not
forgiven her and would refuse to take her back even if Rodney still wanted
to marry her (as Rodney, now content to provide fatherly protection,
does). Heartbroken at this final rejection, Hazel throws herself into the
river. She is fortuitously saved by Carringford, who has discovered that
their marriage has been valid all along, and in the final lines of the play
Hazel is reconciled with her father and husband.

Obviously, there is much here derived from the melodramatic
tradition. But the lack of a traditional melodramatic villain, the focus
upon the psychologies of the two central characters, Dunstan and Hazel
Kirke, and MacKaye's restraint in the staging of the action indicates a
movement away from the excesses of melodrama toward a more realistic,
though still highly charged, love story.[23] Though it is difficult to argue
that this play represents the full potential of realistic treatments of a serious
love story, especially in light of *Marriage*, *Hazel Kirke* does provide an
interesting example of the ways in which realism was beginning to make
inroads within the commercial theater, even in material customarily
associated with melodrama. Additionally, the play indicates the abiding
commitment of MacKaye to incorporate as much realism into his plays
as he felt was practicable given the tastes of the commercial theater's
audiences.

The successive titles suggest the playwright's dual focus. The original title, *An Iron Will*, betrays MacKaye's initial intention to investigate
the psychology of Dunstan Kirke, a part that MacKaye wrote for himself.

Kirke begins the play as yet another irascible father, a traditional blocking figure in innumerable romantic comedies. But as the play's first act draws to its close, Kirke's willfulness approaches the tragic when he misinterprets his daughter's confession that she is guilty of loving Carringford to mean that she has brought "dishonor" to the family. Refusing to listen to anyone, he histrionically booms: "Begone! Thou misbegotten bairn, begone. I cast thee adrift, adrift from thy feyther's love, and may my eyes no more behold thee."[24] Echoing both Shakespeare's Lear and Gloucester, Kirke is to get his wish, for he will temporarily lose his daughter and permanently lose the eyes with which he has been unable to see the reality of her abiding affection, even as she demands to choose the man she will marry. In light of *Marriage*, the question of a potentially loveless union with Rodney takes on a deeper significance; but even for audiences not familiar with the earlier play, MacKaye has made the point explicit by having Dolly note to Green that Hazel is "the one that's sold" (43). In an era in which wealthy Americans were routinely "selling" their daughters to titled European nobility, the prospect of such a "commercial transaction" was hardly beyond the pale of the audience's knowledge or imagination—or, one suspects, their disgust.[25] Kirke's abiding concern with his obligation to Rodney gives his character an ostensibly laudable motivation, but the lengths to which he will go to remove this "debt of honor," to maintain his personal integrity and the bourgeois ideal of economic independence, undermine any incipient sympathy that the audience may have for him. MacKaye drives the theme home when he has Kirke reveal toward the end of the play his intention to leave the mill to satisfy the claim against him that Rodney insists he has no desire to collect. Still gratifying his melodramatic inclinations, Kirke insists, "I'll do penance for my child as a beggar in the street" (466). Only when he hears that Hazel is attempting suicide does his intransigence give way, as he comprehends at last the symbolic significance of his blindness: "Oh, God! this is thy punishment! I was blind when I drove her out—and now, when I could save her—I cannot see—cannot see—I cannot see!" (467). Tellingly, MacKaye, the master theater technician for whom the task of a sensational rescue would have been an easy matter, has both the attempted suicide and the rescue occur offstage, maintaining attention upon the emotional agony of a father who realizes, too late he thinks, his folly. But the same tragicomic forces that save Hazel from death permit Dunstan Kirke to end the play in the arms of his daughter.

Ranged against Dunstan's blind will is the equally determined Hazel. A masterful part for any actress, Hazel's emotions range from delicious joy in her happy marriage to agony at her supposed betrayal and the steadfast unwillingness of her father to reconcile. While the part could easily be constructed along the semihysteric lines of many a melodramatic heroine, MacKaye carefully modulates Hazel's character through his dialogue to present us with a woman of pluck who succumbs to despair only when confronted with overwhelming opposition. Even the most melodramatically inclined elements of her characterization—her break with her father, her confrontation with Lady Travers, and her attempted suicide—are restrained by the standards of the time and are well prepared-for by MacKaye's circumspect shifts in her emotional state. MacKaye is careful to establish Hazel's reflective personality early in the play. When her mother questions her about how she has fallen in love with Carringford, Hazel's response is indicative of her characterization: "All that I know is that day by day his voice has grown sweeter, his words wiser, his very presence more precious. I did not realize how empty my life would be without him, till now the time has come for him to go" (449). Having agreed to fulfill her familial duty and send Carringford away, Hazel cannot help but agonize over her fate: "What am I going to do? Drive away the happiness that heaven sends me? Insult the man I honor most— and all for what? To keep the rash promise of a silly, thoughtless girl, and so break two harmless loving hearts! Oh, I must not think of it or I shall rebel" (449). MacKaye is thus able to pave the way for Hazel's later refusal to bow to her father's will, especially in light of Rodney's having released her of her promise. Equally compelling and convincing is Hazel's confrontation with Lady Travers. Presented with another parent willing to sacrifice a child in order to "preserve the family honor," Hazel is steadfast in her belief in Carringford until confronted with Barney's seemingly incontrovertible evidence that the marriage has been a charade. Even then Hazel insists that she will force Carringford to marry her. When Lady Travers maintains that this will kill her, Hazel lapses into the same melodramatic humor that consumes her father, refuses to add "murder" to the list of evils that she believes she has committed, and agrees to leave Carringford. But the dignity of language and action that Hazel displays in the face of her social situation is remarkable both in conveying her outrage at betrayal and in the quiet assertion of her own innocent worth:

> Madam! you have asked me to fly for his sake, the sake of the man who has so degraded me. Here is my answer. I accepted these [jewels] as token of love, given to an honored wife. I scorn them

now. He shall have all! (*About to take off her wedding ring, she stops.*) No, not this. My marriage ring! (*Kisses it.*) This I have bought with a wife's love, a woman's perdition! This I will keep! (*Going.*) The rest I leave forever.—I go to cover up his infamy with my shame—and may heaven forgive you all! (460).

Hazel's refusal to be cowed by Lady Travers, her insistence upon proof of Carringford's perfidy, and her willingness to endure the social ostracism of a "woman betrayed" rather than to live with a man she can no longer respect, reveal MacKaye's studied reliance upon Hazel's characterization to manifest the injustice of both English social class assumptions and late-Victorian conceptions of children as possessions. A less well-rounded character could not carry the weight of MacKaye's social observations, but Hazel is more than equal to the task. That Hazel is finally reconciled to both Carringford and her father is testimony to the ultimately beneficent dramatic universe in which she lives, but her ultimate happiness does not totally compromise the realism of her characterization.

Though MacKaye is most intent upon developing the psychological portraits of Dunstan and Hazel, he seems to have indulged a bit of barbed humor at the expense of the melodramatists by incorporating into the play Pittacus Green, a zany parody dramatist. Green first appears a throwback to an earlier age, a Shakespearean clown whose sole function seems to be providing amusing linguistic moments by bearing witness to language's fluid nature. Typical is his introduction of himself to Dolly: "That is my distinguished name: Pittacus Green, or, as I am called for short, Pitty Green, which is maddening! If it was Pitty Brown, Black, or Blue, but Pitty Green—it's so hanged appropriate. Of course everybody does pity Green. You may not believe it, but they say I'm cracked" (443). Relatively quickly, however, Green's significance becomes more apparent. As he says:

I'm tempted to play a new rôle, turn dramatist in real life! We've only to manage to make the play what we please. There's the stern father, Dunstan Kirke; the heavy villain, old Rod; the pretty victim, Hazel Kirke; the scheming cousin, that's you; the good-natured idiotic busy-body, [that's me].

. . . .

Confound it, there's something lacking! We'll imagine here's our Andromeda chained to a rock, and about to be devoured by a dragoon—no a dragon:—wanted, the hero, the Perseus, to deliver her. (444)

In short, as his recitation of his *dramatis personae* suggests, Green has become a typical melodramatic playwright complete with his set of stock characters and a moral universe grounded in naive assumptions about the simplicity of myth. For him, there are no troubling differences between the fictions he would create and the external "reality" around him. That Rodney is not the villain is unimportant to Green. It is a simple matter to attempt to precipitate a duel between Carringford and Rodney in order "to get Squire Rodney cremated without delay" (446). MacKaye is content to neglect developing further Green's status until the very end of the play, when he has Green deliver a rhyming epilogue on the action. Stepping forward to face the audience, Green provides the simplified commentary that would be appropriate to a melodrama: "You've seen tonight a conscientious man / Offend his soul as only conscience can: / You've seen the sufferings that he caused and felt / Ere yet his iron will was forced to melt / You guess the lesson we would fain instill, / That human heart is more than human will" (471). The dissonance between the comparatively constrained action deriving its force from the characterizations of Hazel and Dunstan and the simplistic verities that Green extols is not lost upon the audience. MacKaye is able not only to present an alternative to the usual treatment but also to incorporate a bit of aesthetic commentary for those who are sensitive to the questions at issue. Like many of the other realists, MacKaye seems intent upon educating his public to the beauties and appeals of the realist mode.

When we turn from the domestic concerns of *Hazel Kirke* to the broad canvas of public politics in *Paul Kauvar; or, Anarchy* (1887), the basis of critical assertions about MacKaye's romantic impulses find some justification. Set in the period of the French Reign of Terror, MacKaye renders the grand sweep of history with a full complement of rabid *sans culottes*, haughty *ancien regime* noblemen, time-serving republicans and aristocrats, and a pair of young lovers attempting to secure their lives and love without compromising their principles. The complex plot revolves fundamentally around the attempts of the hero, Kauvar, both to protect Diane, the wife he has secretly married, and her father, the Duc de Beaumont, from the wrath of the Revolution while simultaneously stemming the tide of blood lust that is sweeping France under Robespierre. Betrayed by Gorouc, alias the Marquis de Vaux, a turncoat

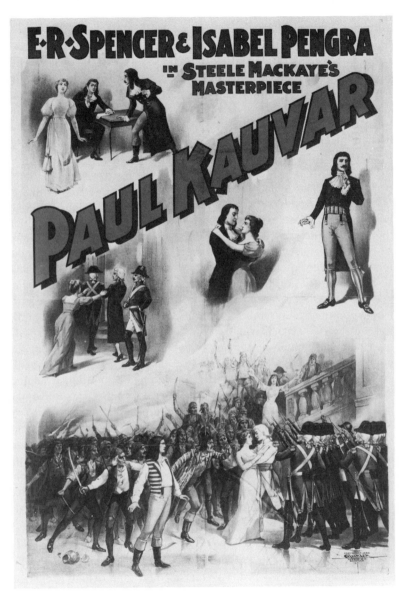

The historic sweep of James Steele MacKaye's Paul Kauvar (1887) is suggested in a turn-of-the-century poster. COURTESY OF THE PHOTOGRAPHS AND POSTER DIVISION OF THE LIBRARY OF CONGRESS

aristocrat member of the Jacobin Club, Paul narrowly escapes execution. At the end of the play, he is again able to save Diane and her father from death at the hands of the republicans after the defeat of the royalist troops at Vendée. Accused of betraying the Revolution, as he has earlier been incriminated in giving over the Duc de Beaumont to revolutionary justice, he is finally exonerated of both charges. In the wake of the news that Robespierre has been executed and a general amnesty declared, Paul is reconciled with the Duc de Beaumont and reunited with Diane.

It is perhaps a truism of the theater—at least it seems true in this period if not later—that the desire to address large social concerns too often militates against a thoroughly realistic treatment of character. Certainly that is the case in this play, for almost all of the characters are little more than pasteboard figures who represent various political positions. The two partial exceptions are Paul and Diane, who are seeking fundamentally private accommodations in a world in which public issues have all but subsumed private existence. Beneath the sweeping romantic tale, however, lurks a displaced concern with potential American class strife whose prominence was only to become evident to the play's writer in the wake of the Chicago Haymarket Riot of 1876. MacKaye, along with many others, including William Dean Howells, maintained that the public cry for blood following the riot (several anarchists were eventually executed) revealed a nearly hysterical unwillingness to seriously address the social and political inequities of the time. From this perspective, the failure of private social institutions to relieve the grinding poverty of America's underclass and the unwillingness of political institutions controlled by the entrenched wealthy to come to grips with economic exploitation were matters of the greatest moment and a subject matter that called for realistic treatment. This concern for the tensions inherent in the political world of nineteenth-century America may well have provided the subconscious genesis of the play, Percy MacKaye argues in his biography of his father:

> For a dozen years its theme—the faith in 'republican law' as a solution of 'liberty'—had taken on varied revisions of form under its author's pen. First conceived, it had probably seemed no more than a stage theme involving a deft plot, of romantic appeal as melodrama, historic and dreamily remote. Now, suddenly, its latent message leapt into a startling timeliness—as an appeal of reality, indigenous and immediate—arising to the explosion of

a bomb in Chicago, attributed to so-called 'Anarchists,' whose philosophic doctrines disclaimed any real solution for 'liberty' through 'republican law.' (*Epoch*, II, 127)

After a single production before the execution of the anarchists, MacKaye, not wanting to be accused of capitalizing upon the publicity surrounding the Haymarket incident, exchanged the play's original title, *Anarchy*, for the less provocative *Paul Kauvar*. But to assume that in doing so he wished either to avoid his audience's confronting the issues at the play's heart or to escape the public positions he had taken against executing the anarchists is clearly in error. While *Paul Kauvar* will not be confused with either the more philosophic discussions of Shaw or the grittier social portrayals of Odets, its cry for a new socially sensitive American politic is clear in the line Steel MacKaye himself cited as the theme of the play: "The infant age is threatened with miscarriage!—The torch of Liberty, which should light mankind to progress, if left in madmen's hands, kindles the blaze of Anarchy whose only end is ashes."[26]

MacKaye's importance to realism's rise on the American stage is multifaceted. His technical innovations for staging and lighting further aided in perfecting the verisimilar illusion so important to potential realistic representation. His interest in acting technique and his teaching to innumerable students the methods of Delsarte further refined the possibilities of presenting characters whose emotional depth could be rendered on stage without recourse to hysteria. Finally, his plays evidence both a desire to rely upon character as the focal point of audience interest and to tackle issues with broad implications for the America of his day. In these latter regards, MacKaye shared much with his contemporary Bronson Howard.

According to Howard, the major concern of the American stage ought to be the portrayal of American business. This opinion stemmed from his intriguing notion that business was the great master theme of the American stage, just as the caste system and marital infidelity were the central topics of English and French theater, respectively.[27] Howard first explored the theme superficially in *The Banker's Daughter* (1873) and returned to it in *Young Mrs. Winthrop* (1882). But the ultimate expression of his ideas on the subject came in *The Henrietta* (1887), a complicated mixture of realism, satire, and melodrama. The play's action centers around the complicated machinations of Nicholas Vanalstyne, Jr., to bankrupt his father (Old Nick, as he is known on Wall Street) and

Wrest possession of the Henrietta Railway and Mining Company, a conglomerate through which Vanalstyne, Sr. has manipulated the stock exchange and made a huge fortune even larger. In the climactic scene, the timely intervention of his bumbling younger brother, Bertie, foils Vanalstyne, Jr.'s plot, and the would-be tycoon dies as the ticker-tape machine rattles away in the background. Paralleling these business matters are the private love affairs of the Vanalstyne family. Bertie is in love with Agnes, the sister of Nicholas's wife Rose, but when he selflessly accepts the blame for the death of Nicholas's mistress, the romance temporarily ends. In the final act, however, Mrs. Cornelia Opdyke, pursued throughout the play by Vanalstyne, Sr., reveals the truth about Nicholas, and couples pair off with the gay abandon of a traditional romantic comedy: Old Nick with Mrs. Opdyke; Rose with the long-devoted Dr. Parke Wainwright; and Bertie with Agnes. On the periphery, providing additional comic moments, are Old Nick's daughter Mary and her newly acquired English husband, Lord Arthur Trelawny; the graspingly hypocritical clergyman, Rev. Dr. Murray Hilton; and Musgrave, Old Nick's private secretary.

The play is primarily a satire about American business, with financial wheeling-and-dealing the linchpin around which the action swirls. Howard is forthright about his intentions, embedding in the program's cast of characters a quote from Thackeray's *Vanity Fair*: "It was to combat and expose such as these, no doubt, that laughter was made."[28] But the satire of the American business community emerges from the actions of characters who are only slightly overdrawn types of the American business tycoon of the period, imminently recognizable to the original audience whose daily newspapers treated them to the exploits of men such as Gould, Vanderbilt, Carnegie and Rockefeller.[29] Indeed, in these characterizations Howard treads very delicately along the line between realistic comic portraiture and parody. For example, in the play's opening scene, the richly ornate private office in the Vanalstyne residence bustles with the business of speculation. Musgrave, the private secretary, spends most of the scene on the telephone shouting buy-and-sell orders to various agents across the country, while the Vanalstynes, father and son, contemplate the destructions of their various economic rivals with glee. The play's behind-the-scenes look at the world of high finance and its powerful central players provides Howard the opportunity to address on the stage the same issues that were beginning to become the focus of various progressive reformers. But Howard's concern is more modest than MacKaye's, and he keeps the focus sufficiently on the personalities of his characters that a thoroughgoing critique of *laissez faire* capitalism as it was practiced in the period of the great monopolies is beyond the play's orbit. Instead, Howard tries to indicate the personal destructiveness that attends such a life.

For example, Wainwright, Howard's surrogate, provides commentary in the opening scene directed not at the effects of business deals upon the country in general but upon the capitalists themselves: "You New York business men have invited Death into your own houses. The telephone and the stock indicator have enabled His Sable Majesty to move up town with the rest of the fashionable world; he used to content himself with wearing out your souls and bodies in your office" (419). Such heavy-handed moralizing, reminiscent of earlier Howard melodramas like *Shenadoah*, continues throughout the play. Indeed, at play's end it is Wainwright who provides the capping melodramatic homily: "The business interests of the country, these money transactions, these speculations in life and death, there are more sacred interests than those, and they lie deeper in our hearts" (453). Coming on the heels of the final ironic revelation that Bertie, the new "Napolean of Wall Street," makes all of his financial decisions by tossing a coin, Howard's satiric point is crashingly evident.[30] That he feels it necessary to undermine his characterization with stock sentiments and compromise the play's potential satiric force is unfortunate, but it does serve to remind us that realism's path was a convoluted one, even when America's playwrights were working with material with which they were intimately familiar.

William Gillette:
Presentational Realism and a New Hero

If in their characters and concerns MacKaye and Howard moved the American stage haltingly toward a new realism, William Hooker Gillette's contribution is less easily characterized in this context. His was a realism of the moment, a reality that sprang from the stage presentations that he provided for his audiences. Though not naive in its conception, Gillette's writing was not freighted with a deep concern for either aesthetics or social issues. He was, indeed, quite frank in admitting that his motivation was monetary reward, describing himself as a "merchant of the theatre" whose writing, producing, and acting was for the "sole and only purpose of making money in greater measure than he could make it in any other way" (Schuttler, 118). This desire to make money compelled Gillette to seek ways of satisfying his contemporary audience's taste that would set his plays apart for special attention and guarantee their financial success. Ironically, that search not only resulted in persistent attention to the quality of the productions themselves but also introduced a new version of the American hero to the stage—the cool, imperturbable, understated hero of action adventures, which became a permanent fixture of American popular drama and cinema. To trace the lineage of such later cinematic characters as Humphrey Bogart's Rick Blaine in *Casablanca* or William Powell's Nick Charles in the *Thin Man* series, one need look no further than Gillette's portrayals of such characters as Lewis Dumont/Captain Thorne in *Secret Service* or the title character in *Sherlock Holmes*, Gillette's adaptation of three Arthur Conan Doyle stories.

Gillette went "on the boards" in 1873 first as an unpaid actor and later as a journeyman portrayer of small parts in various stock companies. But he quickly recognized the advisability of writing material to serve as starring vehicles for himself. His first success was a four-act "character study" entitled *The Professor*, jointly produced by Charles Frohman and Gillette family friend, Mark Twain, in 1881. This farce traces the misadventures of the title character in his inept wooing of various women. Although the play was panned by many critics, the theatergoing public loved it. The play ran for one hundred and fifty-one nights, helping, in the process, to establish a long and mutually beneficial relationship between Gillette and Frohman. The keys to the play's success are readily understood: Gillette provides an easily appreciable set of stock jokes and situations making little or no demand upon his audience, while simultaneously insisting upon the "realism" of the action by playing it in settings meticulously rendered at Gillette's explicit instructions. Thus, as Schuttler has noted, "in *The Professor* Gillette had realized a simple, two part formula for success in the theatre: 1) give the public what it wants to see and 2) give it to them in a handsome way: realistically mounted and acted" (118).

This formula, to which he returned again and again, had its genesis in Gillette's conservative conception of the enduring nature of drama's fundamental premises. Writing on the state of the American drama for *Harper's Weekly* in the company of Augustin Daly, Edward Harrigan, Bronson Howard, and Steele MacKaye, Gillette argues:

> The trouble with most dramatic writers is that while they see and to a large extent appreciate the endless changes in methods, ideas, social relations, and personalities engendered by the progress of society, they do not, on the one hand, realize that the dramatic

laws or principles which underlie all work remain unchanged, nor on the other hand, that each age demands for its recreation the presentation in artistic form of the various elements which constitute and characterize its daily life. ("American Playwrights," 98–99)

Gillette's faith in conventional forms overlaid by a contemporary veneer led him to give his own narrow endorsement to realism: "In the development of the American drama a promising feature is the tendency toward realism as opposed to conventionalism. By realism should be inferred not actualism, but the artistic representation of reality" ("American Playwrights," 99). Thus, for Gillette, a turning away from conventional melodrama was a welcome sign of American drama's growing maturity, but that change of direction should be toward "artistic representation," a phrase which in Gillette's vocabulary almost invariably signals a combination of restrained acting and the visual components of performance. As we shall see, Gillette was to make great strides within this narrow framework, heightening both the visual and aural reality for his audiences.

Gillette's practical application of his dramatic principles is exemplified by his last two great successes, *Secret Service* (1895) and *Sherlock Holmes* (1899). In the former, Gillette returns to the period of the American Civil War which had provided the material for his earlier blockbuster, *Held by the Enemy* (1886). *Secret Service*, set during the Union seige of the Confederate capital, recounts four hours in the career of Lewis Dumont, a member of the the Union Secret Service sent into Richmond to weaken the rebel defenses in preparation for a Union attack. Before the play opens, Captain Thorne (as Dumont is known to the Southerners) has fallen in love with Edith Varney, daughter of a Confederate general, and the play's primary action traces Dumont's conflicts between his duty as a Union operative and his love for Edith. Suspected by a Confederate counterpart, Arrelsford, Thorne is confronted and captured in the telegraph office he intends to use to complete his mission. Though she now knows his true identity, Edith nevertheless saves him by producing a commission from Jefferson Davis making Thorne head of the telegraph service. Thorne in turn manages to convince General Randolph that Arrelsford is demented. After Edith and the Confederate soldiers leave and Thorne is free to complete his assignment, he refuses because to do so would compromise Edith. Escaping, he returns to the Varney house to see the body of his brother who has earlier killed himself in a staged fight while passing a message to Thorne. Captured and sentenced by drum-head court martial to death, Thorne is reprieved at the last minute

SECRET SERVICE

BY Wm.Gillette

"It Looks Like A Plot On Our Telegraph Lines !"

William Gillette's meticulous attention to scenic detail is nicely suggested by this contemporary poster for Secret Service (1895). COURTESY OF THE PHOTOGRAPHS AND POSTER DIVISION OF THE LIBRARY OF CONGRESS because he has refused to send the message that would have weakened Confederate defenses, and he exits the stage as a prisoner of war intent upon marrying the willing Edith at war's end. Counterpointing the love affair of Edith and Thorne is a lighter romance that develops between Wilfred, Edith's younger brother, and a delightful neighborhood belle, Caroline Mitford.

If recent history provided Gillette the material for *Secret Service*, he was equally adept at seeking out contemporary literary material which he could turn to advantage. In *Sherlock Holmes*, Gillette cobbled together elements of "A Study in Scarlet," "A Scandal in Bohemia," and "The Final Problem" to provide Holmes with a series of fast-paced adventures. The central plot revolves around Holmes's attempts to secure a packet of incriminating letters for a mysterious European nobleman. His mission brings him into contact with the beset heroine, Alice Faulkner, for whom he becomes a protector. Through a series of wonderfully crafted confrontations with the quintessentially evil Professor Moriarty and his henchmen, Holmes's unflappable manner and crimefighting prowess allow him to escape the clutches of evil. Eventually, the play concludes with the evil forces of the infamous Professor Moriarty in defeat and Holmes, the erstwhile misogynist, in the arms of the heroine, Alice Faulkner.

As these brief recitations of their plots suggest, neither of these plays makes use of realistic material at all, but in their performances these shortcomings were almost forgotten as the audience's imagination was immersed in a world of such physical verisimilitude that it left little room for skepticism. Augmenting the detailed settings were Gillette's studied characterizations of the plays' protagonists. Typical of his scrupulous attention to the creation of the physical world which his characters inhabited are Gillette's stage directions for the setting of the climactic third act of *Secret Sevice*. They are worth quoting in their entirety:

> *The War Department Telegraph Office. Ten o'clock. A plain and somewhat battered and grimy room on the second floor of a public building; stained and smoky walls. Large windows—the glass covered with grim and cobwebs. Plaster off walls and ceiling in some places. All this from neglect—not from bombardment. It is a room which was formerly somewhat handsome. Molding and stuccowork broken and discolored. Very large and high door or double doors up right center obliqued. This door opens to a corridor showing plain corridor-backing of a public building. This door must lead off well to right so that it shall not interfere with window*

*showing up left center. Three wide French windows up left and
left center obliques a little, with balcony outside extending right
and left and showing several massive white columns, based at
balcony outside extending up out of sight for several stories above.
Backing of windows showing night view of city roofs and buildings
as from height of second floor. Large disused fireplace with elaborate marble mantel in bad repair and very dirty on right side behind
telegraph tables. Door up center opening to cupboard with shelves
on which are Battery Jars and Telegraph Office truck of various
kinds. Room lighted by gas on right above right telegraph table,
several burners branching from a main pipe and all to turn on and
off easily by means of one cock in main pipe, just above the
telegraph table. Show evening through window up left—dark, with
lights of buildings very faint and distant, keeping general effect
outside window of darkness. (Moonlight at window on the massive
columns and the characters who go out on the balcony.) Corridor
outside door up right center not strongly illuminated. In the room
itself fair light but not brilliant. Plain, solid table with telegraph
instruments down right center. Another table with instruments
along wall at right side. Table down right braced to look as if
fastened securely to the floor. Also see that wire connections are
properly made from all the instruments in the room to wires running up the wall in the right side, thence across along ceiling to
up left and out through broken panes in upper part of windows up
left. This large bunch of wires leading out, in plain sight, is very
important. Large office clock over mantel set at 10 o'clock at
opening and to run during the Act. Two instruments A. and D. on
table right center—A. is at right end of table and is only one used
at that table, D. being for safety. B. and C. on long table against
fireplace. B. is at lower end of table, C. at upper end; one chair at
table down right center. Two chairs at table right. One chair is up
center. No sound of cannonading in this Act. At opening there are
two OPERATORS at work, one at table down right center, one at
table on right side. They are in old gray uniform, but in shirt
sleeves. Coats are hung or thrown on chairs one side. Busy click-
effects of instruments. After first continued clicking for a moment
there are occasional pauses. MESSENGERS A. and B. near door
up right center. MESSENGER 3 in front of door center talking to
MESSENGER 4. MESSENGER 2 is looking out of middle window
over left.*[31]

The details about the plaster ("All this from neglect—not from bombardment") and the columns ("extending out of sight for several stories"),
both of which are unknowable to the audience, suggest the type of visual

imagination that dominated Gillette's plays. The remarkable thing about these directions is that the action that follows renders almost every element of the stage directions pertinent: telegraphers will receive and send messages on the equipment, the messengers will come and go through the doors, Edith and Arrelsford will hide on the balcony and Edith will later be searched for there, Thorne will turn down the gas burners, soldiers will beat down the doors to the hallway, and Thorne will eventually face his greatest moment of conflict at the machinery. It is little wonder that the subtle impact of such an overpowering physical reality was to insinuate that the action being presented must be as "realistic" as the environment in which it occurred.

Complementing the detail of the setting was Gillette's acting. Gillette maintained that "excepting in those cases where the author depicts or caricatures a historical or local character, all parts are essentially types. The better the literary and dramatic work, the more comprehensive is the character drawn" ("American Playwrights," 99). While these comments might suggest a rather broad approach to the creation of character on stage, Gillette's practice ran in quite the opposite direction. Thus, in *Secret Service* Gillette is careful to provide a firm basis in his script not only for Thorne's overall characterization but also for particular actions. For instance, in the final act, Thorne must somehow convince Edith that he can both have loved her and, nevertheless, have acted duplicitously. Initially breathless from fleeing the guard and later in the scene intent upon making Edith understand his motives even as he is first verbalizing them to himself (both motivations emphasized by the dashes indicating pauses in delivery), he falteringly says:

> They'll get me in a minute—an' when they do it won't take long to finish me off! (*Looks at her.*) And as that'll be the last of me Miss Varney—maybe you'll listen to one thing! We can't all die a soldier's death—in the roar and glory of battle—our friends around us—under the flag we love!—no—not all! Some of us have orders for another kind of work—desperate—dare-devil work—the hazardous schemes of the Secret Service! We fight our battles alone— no comrades to cheer us on—ten thousand to one against us— death at every turn! If we win we escape with our lives—if we lose—dragged out and butchered like dogs—no soldier's grave— not even a trench with the rest of the boys—alone—despised— forgotten! These were my orders Miss Varney—this is the death I die tonight—and I don't want you to think for one minute that I'm ashamed of it—not for one minute! (182)

On a dimly lit stage, with the sounds of cannonading, rolling artillery pieces in the road outside, and rushing troops framing the action, this would be a moving speech. The comments of those who saw Gillette in this role make it readily apparent that Gillette's acting tended to overcome whatever weaknesses of characterization his script might have exhibited. Arthur Hornblow, writing of the original production for *Leslie's Weekly*, declares that Gillette's "acting was forceful," adding only the minimal qualification that he "carries to an extreme the air of imperturbability and unconcern which is a conspicuous feature of his methods" (Schuttler, 123–24). Arthur Hobson Quinn was even more lavish in his praise: "But above all else it is the absolute reality of the characters which is impressive. . . . By the end of the first Act we seem to have known these people always" (Quinn, *History*, I, 224–25).

If Captain Thorne provided Gillette the opportunity to translate his reticent acting methods into a dashing hero, the taciturn Sherlock Holmes seems almost to have been imagined for him. Gillette had the added advantage of bearing a striking resemblance to Doyle's description of his detective. Indeed, when Gillette went to London to present his finished script to Holmes's creator, Doyle's biographer recounts that Doyle "contemplated him open-mouthed" as Gillette stepped off the train "in a long grey cape. . . . The clear cut features, the deep-set eyes, [looking] out under a deerstalker cap; even Gillette's age, the middle forties, was right."[32] Doyle's assessment was shared by a vast number of audiences before whom Gillette was to play Holmes between his November 1899 premiere and his final stage performance in the role in March 1932.[33]

The appeal of Gillette's Holmes was in some measure an extension of his earlier accomplishment as Thorne. Again, Gillette played the hero as a man in total command of both the situation and himself, substituting as an antagonist the crafty, guileful and more clearly evil Moriarty for the tenacious and suspicious Arrelsford. Again, Gillette chose to emphasize that the hero is a man whose violations of social conventions are necessary for him to succeed in his ultimate quest for goodness. Thus, Gillette exchanges the imperative duplicity of Thorne for Holmes's deceptions of Alice Faulkner and his troubling drug use—which Gillette highlights by having Holmes inject himself on stage as Watson expresses his disapproval. Again, Gillette chooses to vindicate the actions of his hero by uniting him at the end of the play with the requisite beautiful heroine. In deliberately playing these contradictory elements of his two heroes' characters off against one another, Gillette made at least a modest contribution to American conceptions of the hero. Into the "conventional," nearly perfect male type, Gillette introduced a note of moral complexity. No longer would American playwrights feel the necessity of expunging their protagonists of all hints of moral failing. Even in the relatively simplified universe of action drama, heroes after Gillette could be drawn a bit less as moral ideals, a bit more as human beings. In this regard, at least, Gillette can be said to have forwarded the progress of realism on the American stage.

James A. Herne:
American Realism Comes of Age

The call of Howells and other realist theoreticians for a realist drama was finally answered in the last decade of the nineteenth century by James A. Herne, the actor, manager, and playwright who more than any of his contemporaries served to combine both domestic and foreign influences into a uniquely American brand of dramatic realism. In a series of plays—*Margaret Fleming* (1890), *Shore Acres* (1892), the now-lost *Griffith Davenport* (1899), and *Sag Harbor* (1899)—Herne impressed such early exponents of realism as William Dean Howells and Hamlin Garland with a vision of American life and character that could be alternatively penetrating and unrelenting in dealing with the social and moral problems of the day, or warmly affectionate without lapsing into superficial nostalgia or sentimentality. While the financial failures of *Margaret Fleming* and *Griffith Davenport* indicated a general unwillingness of the theater-going public of the "Gay '90s" to support the more sober, realistic investigation of social dynamic and character that would earn Herne the epithet of "the American Ibsen," Herne's persistence in producing them in the face of great resistance testifies to the fact that realism had taken firm root in the American drama.[34] Conversely, the popular success of *Shore Acres* and *Sag Harbor* guaranteed that a serious attempt to portray the daily life of America's rural population would not be lost to the American theater as the shift from domestic melodrama to realistic drama—much of it centered in an examination of city life—continued. Indeed, the figures of Helen Berry, Uncle Nat Berry, and Captain Dan Marble served to provide a new dignity to the American common woman and man in their contests with the forces that were reshaping America at the turn of the century and paved the way for the later writings of Fitch and Moody, and, later still, Glaspell and O'Neill.

Herne's most enduring play is *Margaret Fleming*, a realist drama with a forthright plot nuanced by small actions. The first act opens in the office of Philip Fleming at a mill in Canton, Massachusetts, in 1890. Philip, who has succeeded his father in the family business, is seen going busily about his morning routine. A conversation with Foster, one of his subordinates, reveals that Philip lives by the motto "live and let live" in his business dealings and has lost money speculating on the stock market. Philip is joined by Joe Fletcher, a former employee dismissed for drinking, who is now an itinerant salesman whose easy manner and conviviality have kept him on good terms with Philip. The conversation reveals that both are married, though Joe says his wife left him through no fault of his own. Philip complacently says that his days of "sowing his wild oats" are over now that he has a wife and baby girl. As Joe leaves, Dr. Larkin arrives and reveals that he has inadvertently discovered that Philip's mistress, Lena Schmidt, has given birth to Philip's child. After insisting that Philip see the dying Lena, Larkin suggests that Philip try to keep his wife Margaret from discovering his infidelity by taking her away "until this thing blows over."[35] Philip leaves to see Lena. The scene turns to Margaret at home, where she has just finished bathing and breast-feeding her baby. Margaret notices that the maid Maria is crying and learns that Maria's sister, though unmarried, has had a baby and is so gravely ill that she may not survive. Margaret sends Maria to be with her sister and waits sadly for Philip. He arrives, drenched from the rain. After a moment of pique at Philip's having missed their daughter's birthday party, Margaret reconciles with Philip, who immediately gives her $20,000 in government bonds for their baby daughter Lucy as well as the title to the family home and the land on which it sits. He says that these are merely measures to insure that his family is protected if his business should go badly. When Margaret presses him, he insists that nothing is the matter, and the adoring Margaret accepts his assurances.

The second act begins with Dr. Larkin examining Margaret, who complains that her eyes have been bothering her. She quickly shifts the center of concern to Philip and has Larkin prescribe some medicine. When Margaret leaves, Larkin meets with Philip and warns him that any sudden shock could blind Margaret. Philip agrees to take his wife away. Joe Fletcher appears after Larkin leaves and has an encounter with Maria, who turns out to be his estranged wife. Maria chases him off, and Philip follows. When Margaret returns, Maria asks her to go see Lena. Margaret agrees to make the visit without telling Philip.

The third act takes place in the boarding house where Lena Schmidt has just died. Margaret meets Larkin, who tries to get her to leave. Maria enters and informs Margaret that a letter to Philip proves he is the father of Lena's child. Margaret sends for Philip. As she waits, Margaret is attracted by the newborn baby's cries. Philip enters in time to watch in horror as Margaret, having failed to comfort the baby in any other way, unbuttons her dress to nurse him. She is profoundly distracted and—unbeknownst to Philip—unable to see.

The fourth act begins a week later with Maria and Larkin discussing Philip's disappearance and Margaret's blindness. Larkin and Margaret confer and then Foster, the mill manager, arrives with the news that Philip has returned. Philip enters, crestfallen, and discovers that the shock of his infidelity has blinded his wife. She assures him that an operation will restore her sight. He begs Margaret's forgiveness and she agrees. But, when he misinterprets her sentiments, she informs him that "the wife-heart has gone out of me" (543). Philip and Margaret reach an understanding that perhaps in the future their relationship can again be that of man and wife. Philip resolves to begin life anew with the intention of winning Margaret back. As he steps into the garden to visit with the children, Margaret, who has been arranging flowers, silently *"pauses in her work, gives a long sigh of relief and contentment. Her eyes look into the darkness and a serene joy illuminates her face"* (543).[36]

As one might expect from the plot synopsis, Herne had a difficult time in 1890 even getting managers to consider putting on a play that included a scene in which the title character unbuttons her blouse to feed her husband's illegitimate child—not to mention the fact that the play attacked the sexual double standard head-on. After numerous failures to secure outside backing in either Boston or New York, Herne and his wife and leading lady, Katharine Corcoran Herne, decided to take the advice of William Dean Howells and put on the play themselves. It opened in May 1891 at Chickering Hall, a small concert facility above a piano showroom in Boston, with Katherine Herne as Margaret and James A. Herne as Joe Fletcher. With the public endorsement of most of the intellectuals and literary lights of Boston and Cambridge conveyed to the public through flyers circulated by Hamlin Garland acting as an unpaid press agent, *Margaret Fleming* had its longest run in Herne's lifetime: three weeks. Though the fifty-five signers of the original advertisement liked the insightful picture of American life they saw, many returning again and again during the run, the rest of the Boston public was less than enthusiastic. After being withdrawn, the play was revived twice in 1891, once in Boston and once in New York, again in 1892 in Chicago, and in revised form in 1894 in New York. But *Margaret Fleming* remained "poison" in the theater of its time. The play was held in such ill repute, in fact, that Herne was almost prevented from getting his later plays produced. Clearly, the American public was not ready for this vision of itself.[37]

The points to which the general public most objected are, of course, the very elements that set this play apart as "unequalled in realism by any other known American drama of its century."[38] Herne's play combines into an integrated whole the various elements that we have been examining. Here are demonstrably real characters in an emotionally charged but nonmelodramatic action. Here is dialogue which is plain and direct and avoids the excesses of melodrama. Here is an action that can be represented through understated acting and performed within simple sets while using the technical resources of the theater only to facilitate a greater understanding of the characters and the situation rather than as a substitute for such exploration. Finally, here is a play which focuses squarely on an important issue. For the first time on the American stage, a playwright chooses to question seriously the assumptions of the dominant patriarchal social and moral codes.

The heart of the play is the relationship between Margaret and Philip and the transformation that occurs when Margaret discovers Philip's infidelity. In the first act, Herne carefully establishes the emotional ground of the play by counterpointing Philip's masculine business world with Margaret's domestic sphere, revealing in the process that Philip is much less capable of living up to the roles that society has provided for him than is Margaret. As either the traditional "breadwinner" or the moral head of the household, Philip demonstrates a disturbing tendency to act selfishly and unthinkingly. His conversation with Foster reveals not only that Philip has seriously compromised the financial status of his mill by taking risky stock market ventures but also that his regular business practices are rather cavalier. His motto of "live and let live" is entirely "too lenient," as Foster makes clear (522). Herne carefully suggests, through Philip's conversations with Joe Fletcher and Dr. Larkin, that this motto carries over into Philip's personal life and is grounded in a moral solipsism. Joe's casual references to Philip's promiscuity while a bachelor, and his hint that Philip might have married one of the girls from the mill with whom he has a liaison, prepare the stage for Dr. Larkin's revelations concerning Lena Schmidt. Philip's callous indifference to Lena's health and the welfare of their child, his assertion that he has tried to entice Lena to have an abortion (a felony for which, Dr. Larkin reminds the audience, the physician could have been sent to prison) or to leave town to avoid scandal, and his initial refusal to see the dying Lena—all serve to justify Larkin's outrage. Larkin's anger, it is interesting to note, is directed not at Lena, who would be the typical target of repressed melodramatic anxiety about the temptress who seeks to destroy hearth and home through sexual enticements. His view of Lena emerges from a dispassionate assessment of the social reality around him, tinged with an idealistic longing for a better world. Assuming that Lena, "a product of her environment," would "under the present social conditions . . . probably have gone wrong anyhow," Larkin directs his moral indignation squarely at Philip: "But you! God Almighty! If we can't look for decency in men like you—representative men,—where in God's name are we to look for it, I'd like to know" (525). Thus, by the end of the first scene, Herne has carefully suggested that Philip is not abnormal but a rather "representative" figure and has delineated his character and revealed his past actions so that the remainder of the play's action and Philip's responses to events seem to flow naturally from the complex characterization already provided. Our understanding of Philip may deepen, but the characterization does not take any radical new directions.

Herne is also meticulous in evoking Margaret's personality in the first act's second scene, set in the Fleming's fashionable home. The stage directions indicate the manner in which Herne has conceptually integrated the physical setting to aid his characterization of Margaret: *"the room is furnished in exquisite taste showing in its distinct character the grace and individuality of a well-bred woman"* (526). This initial visual information is reinforced throughout the scene by Margaret's action and dialogue. Herne carefully modulates the action to establish two aspects of Margaret's personality—a warm, loving nature compounded with a deeply ingrained moral rectitude. The tender stage business between Margaret and her baby not only invokes traditional visions of the purity and warmth of motherhood, but also it implicitly contrasts the sexuality sanctioned within marriage with the type of amoral intimacy that surrounds the other mother and child that have claims upon Philip. Margaret's affection for her child is a fundamental part of her personality, but her half-serious assurances that she will "punish" Lucy's "naughty, bad father" for missing Lucy's birthday dinner hints at a moral qualification to her love (527). She is seemingly incapable of indulging love without seeing it in a moral context. Her commiseration with Maria Bindley, the nursemaid, and her compassion at Lena's fate reinforces the audience's sense of Margaret's goodness, but the sternness with which she greets Philip when he enters both fulfills her earlier promise to Lucy and strengthens the two halves of the personality that we have already noted. Margaret's reluctance to accept the deed to the house serves to reinforce her naive faith in Philip while maintaining a distinction between the public and private realms which will become increasingly untenable as the play's action unfolds.

The action of the remaining acts serves to reinforce Herne's characterizations by restricting the action to the events which flow from a single antecedent reality—Philip's infidelity—and tracing the characters' reactions to that moral lapse. Each act centers upon a single revelation— the broadening knowledge of Philip's infidelity, the risk of Margaret's losing her sight, Margaret's discovery of Philip's infidelity and her consequent blindness, and Margaret's unwillingness to immediately forgive her husband and resume her previous life with him. But each of these climactic moments is carefully prepared for either in the immediately preceding action or scene. In the process, Herne carefully resists the temptation to provide sensational scenes for their own sake, notably keeping Philip's meeting with Lena off stage. Indeed, the action is, if anything, rather subdued, even in the climactic third act, owing to the natures of his characters. The act's two moments of extreme tension are deliberately defused and underplayed. In the first, when there is real threat of sensation—as Maria, in her grief at her sister's death and her righteous determination that Philip shall not escape his responsibility, pulls a pistol and threatens to kill him—Margaret, by the force of her personality and the moral outrage she herself projects, cows Maria into relinquishing the gun. Later, though terrified at the prospect of losing her sight before she can confront Philip, Margaret hardly acknowledges the onset of her blindness, focusing instead upon her growing awareness of the spiritual and emotional anguish she is feeling. Herne further unifies the play by compressing its time frame. The first three emotionally charged acts occur over the space of two days, intensifying the effect upon both characters and audience. The fourth act, set a week later, allows time for Margaret's initial anger, grief, and sense of betrayal to have been replaced by a more considered response to Philip's actions. Like Ibsen at his best, Herne uses both the relationships between the scenes and the time frame to convey the sense of a unified, wholly artistic structure appropriate to the action represented.

Complementing both the characters and the structure are dialogue that renders these characters vital human beings and textual clues about the acting and stagecraft which suggest the discreet overall effect Herne is seeking. The dialogue is completely natural, utilizing primarily the colloquial speech patterns of the upper middle class of the period; nevertheless, its flexibility is sufficient to indicate class and ethnic distinctions and even to suggest nuances of emotion within the major characters. Herne reveals a fine ear in Maria's thickly German-laced English and the grammatical lapses of Bobby, Philip's office boy. But Herne's finest dialogic achievements are found in Margaret and Philip, both of whom are notable for a lack of elevated language even in the most trying circumstances. For example, Margaret, slipping ever closer to despair at her betrayal by Philip, compares her situation with that of the dead Lena without resorting to either overblown tropes or hysterical delivery:

> You think—I—am happy because I am his wife? Why, you poor fool, that girl never in all her life suffered one thousandth part what I have suffered in these past five minutes. Do you dare to compare her to me? I have not uttered one word of reproach, even against her, and yet she has done me a wrong, that not all the death-bed letters that were ever written can undo. I wonder what I have ever done to deserve this! (538)

The single exclamation point at the end, carefully prepared for in the rising emotion of the rest of the speech, signals Margaret's momentary collapse under the weight of her discovery. But the remainder of her dialogue testifies to the subdued effect toward which the script moves. Herne could, of course, write toward a more intense effect, as Margaret's famous line "the wife-heart has gone out of me" reveals. Nevertheless, Herne is careful to select his occasions in which to amplify the rhetoric for dramatic effect.

Herne circumspectly suggests through his stage directions the quiet acting style and unostentatious, but more intellectually significant, staging he prefers. For example, after half-consciously requesting a lamp as the sunlight streams in through the windows, Margaret's final descent into blindness is rendered simply, as physical action: *She turns and slowly gropes her way to the sofa, sits on the edge of it, and feels for the child and gently pats it* (540). This scene's power is matched in its intensity by the last-act confrontation between Philip and Margaret. Garland, writing of the moment in the original version when Margaret makes her distinction between her lost "wife-heart" and her still intact "mother-heart," suggests some of the power that Katherine Herne's quiet dignity gave to her portrayal, a power not compromised by the later revision of the play:

"The wronged wife faces the shamed and broken man with a patience, kindness and yet firmness that holds the spectator literally enthralled, and Mrs. Herne plays it with such comprehension of its significance, such quiet dignity and intellectual power, that she seems inspired" (Perry, 143). In a similar manner, the play removes the usual melodramatic music, opulent sets, and impressive stage effects and allows the sets and effects to provide further insight into the characters' personalities and situations. Thus, in the same way that the Fleming house reflects Margaret's dignity and refinement, Philip's office, fitted as it is with two mirrors, suggests Philip's vanity, and the weather's progress in the first scene from sunshine to gloomy rain nicely compliments the sense of impending doom that grows throughout the scene.

The most significantly realistic element of Herne's play is its concern with the sexual double standard, a concern that emerges in the play's final conversation between Margaret and Philip. Though Margaret can forgive and says she wishes to forget, she insists she cannot return to her former relationship with Philip, at least not for some significant period. The basis of Margaret's reservation is her morality, which Herne deftly suggests the first time that the audience sees Margaret. For her, morality is a set of ethical premises that cannot be applied only to women, a point she drives home by asking Philip to imagine his reaction if she had been unfaithful. Philip's response, "Oh, Margaret!" (543), reveals at once both the moral repugnance he can feel at the idea of Margaret's unfaithfulness and his blindness at not being able to see that the same standards should apply to both husband and wife. As Margaret says: "You are a man, and you have your ideals of—the—sanctity—of—the thing you love. Well, I am a woman—and perhaps—I, too, have the same ideals. I don't know. But, I, too cry 'pollution' " (543). The halting delivery, indicative of the emotion under which she labors, betrays Margaret's realization of the inequities which the society has imposed upon her. If she were the faithful wife of a thousand melodramas, she would forget and forgive and fall into Philip's arms, rejoicing that her wayward husband had "come to his senses." But Herne's Margaret is a woman capable of resisting her own acculturation. As she tells Philip, "the old Margaret is dead. The truth killed her" (543). But the death of the old Margaret has precipitated the birth of a new woman, a woman of much greater strength and far fewer illusions. To Philip's assertion that eventually he will win her back, Margaret can only reply through her tears, "I don't know. That would be a wonderful thing. A very wonderful thing" (544). Margaret's anguish does not overturn society's insistence upon perpetuating an intrinsically dishonest and crippling sexual double standard. But like the best realistic drama, *Margaret Fleming* draws down the curtain asking its audience to address such an issue seriously.

If *Margaret Fleming* focuses the glaring light of realism on the sexual double standard associated in the late nineteenth century with the "fast life" of the city, *Shore Acres* spotlights the transformations overtaking its traditionally bucolic alternative, America's countryside. Borrowing techniques from the "local-color" narrative realists of the post–Civil War period, Herne carefully constructs an in-depth portrait of the rural byways and inhabitants of coastal Maine. Against this background, Herne plays out a traditional story of young love opposed by a hard-hearted father. The love story's usual complications are augmented not only by Herne's complex psychological characterizations but also by his dramatization of the effects of the speculative mindset upon rural America and the emerging clash between orthodox rural verities and the new, scientifically grounded thought. The resulting play provides both an updated, more complex characterization of one of America's most enduring stage figures, the "Down East" Yankee, and a dramatic model for realistic investigations of America's rural reality. Though in one notable scene Herne indulges melodramatic stage techniques to a greater degree than he had in *Margaret Fleming*, his overall staging retains his commitment to understated incident, relying upon the interplay of character to carry the force of the action.

The plot of *Shore Acres* is typical in many ways of the traditional comic love story. Helen (Nell) Berry has fallen in love with Sam Warren, a young doctor whose progressive ideas have put him at odds with most of the local inhabitants of Berry, Maine. The opposition to Warren is especially painful for Helen because her father's antipathy to one he sees as "a-learnin' my daughter a pack of lies about me an' my parents a-comin from monkeys" results in Warren's being thrown off her father's farm, at which point the young man makes his decision to move to the West.[39] Martin Berry's anger at Sam is compounded by his desire for Helen to marry a wealthy local merchant, Josiah Blake, who in the course of the play persuades Martin to subdivide his farm into lots for summer cottages in anticipation of the type of "land boom" that has previously overtaken nearby Bar Harbor. At a festive silver anniversary party attended by a quaint cross-section of the local population, Martin clashes with his wife over his intentions to develop the farm, and with Helen, who reacts fiercely to the accusation that Sam has stolen money from Blake. In the wake of her argument with her father and with the aid of her kindly uncle, Nathan'l Berry, she elopes with Sam in the sloop of Captain Ben Hutchins. Martin is so enraged when he discovers their flight that he rushes to the family lighthouse and tries to prevent Nathan'l from saving the ship in which Helen and Sam are fleeing from floundering on the coastal rocks.

Fifteen months pass. During the interim, Martin has carried out his threats to subdivide the farm, the prospective "boom" has turned into a "bust," and Martin faces the prospect of losing the farm unless he can find $1,500 to retire the mortgage. A prosperous Helen and Sam return from the West with their new baby, and a warm, though initially strained, reunion ensues. The prospect of financial ruin is averted when Nathan'l receives a letter which states that his Civil War pension will cover the family's debt. The play ends silently as Uncle Nat quietly goes about closing up the house and, carrying a single candle, climbs the stairs to exit into his bedroom.

Many of the techniques found in *Margaret Fleming* are again evident in *Shore Acres*. Once more Herne chooses to emphasize the internal conflicts of his characters rather than propelling them through a series of exciting physical actions. Even his own deviation from this pattern—the third-act fight between Martin and Nathan'l Berry and the subsequent exterior scene of the "Liddy Ann" in the storm—seems to have at its base not merely the usual increase in dramatic tension associated with such scenes, but preparation for final-act revelations about the characters of Martin and Nathan'l. The play's overall structure is tightly wrought, integrating incidents of minor significance into a tapestry designed to provide a detailed view of life in a particular Maine village. Again, the dialogue perfectly reflects the environment and personal backgrounds of the individual characters. The acting style and theatrical effects, as described in Herne's stage directions, are designed in the main to emphasize the quiet, domesticated nature of the action. Finally, though there is not the overt emphasis on social issues to be found in *Margaret Fleming*, the play exhibits a serious concern for intellectual and economic conflicts which were reshaping the American rural landscape. After *Shore Acres*, no American playwright could again turn naively to provincial America to find a simple-minded contrast to the supposedly more complex, alienating world of the city.

Though, like Steele MacKaye in *Hazel Kirke*, Herne uses the perennial generational conflict between father and daughter to propel the love plot, he seems far more interested in analyzing the psychologies of Martin, Helen and Nathan'l Berry than in simply uniting Helen and Sam. Indeed, Herne forestalls Helen's exit with Sam for two full acts in order to provide maximum opportunity for the three characters' interactions to reveal their personalities fully, and he brings Helen back in the last act only to confirm the audience's assessments. Though Martin's heritage from comedy is easily discernible, Herne goes to some pains to imbue the character with distinctly American foundations, bases which send him far beyond even his localized American Yankee prototypes. His narrow-minded, provincial attitudes are initially ascribed to the ignorant conservatism traditionally associated with the Yankee: "I don't want to know nothin'! An' I don't want *her* to know nothin' thet I don't want her to know!" (682). But confronted with Helen and Sam's insistence upon the value that they find in the new books they are reading, Martin makes evident that his is prejudice based not in ignorance but in an ideology that is besieged on every side. Against the new knowledge associated with Darwin and Spencer and promulgated by such "radical" novelists as William Dean Howells (whose *A Hazard of New Fortunes* Helen is, ironically enough, holding), Martin is determined to repose in the intellectually familiar and the emotionally reassuring: "I read the *Bangor Whig*, an' *The Agriculturist*, an' the Bible, an' that's enough" (683). Anxious about the temptation to turn his back upon farm life in order to become a land speculator, afraid of the future, and eager not to have his decisions about the land and Helen's marriage to Blake challenged by anyone, Martin finds a perfect displaced target in Sam. His abiding selfishness and his insistence upon playing the rural patriarch even as he dismantles the economic base of his authority render him a pathetic yet volatile figure as his attempt to "murder" Sam and Helen in Act 3 testifies. His eventual reconciliation with Sam and Helen in the face of his own economic failure and his begrudging awareness of the excesses he has indulged redeems him only slightly in his own eyes, and in those of the audience. His final exit lines—"She [Helen] ought to 'a' had you [Nat, as her father]. 'Twain't jes' right somehow"—rings painfully true (720).

Against Martin are ranged both his independent-minded daughter Helen and Uncle Nat, his brother, the gentle embodiment all that nineteenth-century America believed best about its rural heritage. Though neither is initially able to influence Martin about either Helen's future husband or the parceling up of the farm, both show the strength of character to resist him—and in doing so embrace alternative sets of values with which the audience can sympathize. Helen's case is the more clearcut, for in a very real sense her character is bound by the conventions of comedy. Formally, she must resist her father's wishes and align herself with a man of her own choice. She is, however, complicated by two elements of her character which give her added dimension and a real sense of humanity. First, as Uncle Nat suggests, Helen is her father's daughter; she seems compelled to confront her father and resist his will to his face in her attempt to establish her individuality. Second, she has outgrown the parochial vision represented by her father. Both intellectually and emotionally, she has been reformed by her reading and her belief in the new ideas which are part of the bond between her and Sam. She is, in other words, one of the new breed of American women who formed the central characters of so many of Howells's, James's and Wharton's novels and were to come fully to the stage in the later works of Mitchell, Fitch, Glaspell, and Crothers.

Uncle Nat, in contrast, is a remnant of fading American traditions, both dramatic and historic. Dramatically, he recalls the figures of rural virtue who intrude into the town plays of Tyler and Mowatt, dispensing equal amounts of poetic justice and republican wisdom. Historically, Nat, sixty years old when the play opens, is a vestige of rurally dominated, pre–Civil War America. He is a man who has lived through the final welding of America into a nation and has seen that reconstituted state industrialize and urbanize almost beyond his recognition. But Nat, like Helen, is more than the sum of his literary and historical influences; he is a carefully drawn human being. As the older brother and surrogate father, Nat has always looked after Martin. His sacrifices have been many and he has borne them complacently, for, unlike his brother, Nat is essentially a man of small joys and simple aspirations, a man given to rolling on the floor with children and taking enormous pride in preparing a special turkey for Martin and Ann's anniversary party. Nevertheless, as Herne notes in his opening description, though Nat *"is of the soil, yet there is an inherent poise and dignity about him that are typical of the men who have mastered their environment"* (673). This dignity and poise are combined with great empathy and a kindliness that pervades all his actions. Though all who come into contact with him are treated with great compassion, Helen is the special object of his affections. The source of this special relationship is revealed in the third act when Uncle Nat tells Martin a secret he has kept buried for thirty years:

> "Did you ever know thet I might 'a' married your wife Ann? . . . .
> I thought more o' her than ever a miser did o' money. But when I
> see thet you liked her too—I jes' went off t' war—a' I let yeh hev
> her! . . . . her child is out there—my child by rights! . . . . I give
> yeh the mother, but I'm damned ef I'm a-goin' to let yeh murder
> the child! (706)

Though he arguably hates his brother at that moment, Nat's heart is too big to hold a grudge or take an unfair advantage, as he makes clear when he reassures Martin in the fourth act that he has never told Helen of her father's malicious actions in the lighthouse. Fittingly, it is Nat who ends the play—calmly, quietly, and with infinite contentment—overseeing the welfare of the home and family that he loves so well. In Uncle Nat, Herne created his most beloved and one of his most enduring characters.

The structure of the play essentially follows the same pattern found in *Margaret Fleming*, though the shift from serious drama to comedy has significant consequences. As in the earlier play, the incidents of *Shore Acres* provide ever-more-insightful glances into the lives of the central characters. Even the incidental actions, especially those surrounding the poor neighbor Gates and his shy daughter, are integrated into the main action to form a counterpoint to the familial drama of the Berrys. But comedy is a more plot-oriented form than serious drama, and therefore the ends of each act tend to provide some momentary revelation about the progress of Sam and Helen's love. Thus, Sam's resolve to go West alone at the end of the first act is countered by Helen's decision to elope with him at the end of second, the narrow escape of the "Liddy Ann" which separates the Berry clan as the third act closes is matched by the reunion at play's end. The structure of *Shore Acres* also serves to redeem the antagonist, Martin, before its comedic conclusion. Like many another comedic villain, Martin learns his lessons through the hardships that the action provides him, and by the end of the play he is economically and emotionally ready to reconcile with Helen and Sam. Given the formal constraints of *Shore Acres*, Herne abandons the open-ended conclusion of *Margaret Fleming* and provides an appropriate comic closure. The Berrys will awake on Christmas morning once more united.

The dialogue of *Shore Acres* serves well Herne's general delineation of characters. Martin Berry's Yankee dialect nicely suggests his provincialism while providing an aurally pointed contrast to the more refined standard English of the better-educated Helen and Sam. To contrast Martin and Uncle Nat, Herne sprinkles the latter's speech with a host of homely similes and folk sayings that reflect Nat's kindliness. Herne is equally careful with his minor characters' speech patterns. Ann Berry is given the verbal tic of repeating the last word or phrase of her sentences, suggesting that this harried mother of a large family is not always sure that she has been heard or listened to; Captain Ben Hutchins intersperses his speeches with appropriate nautical and seafaring language; and Young Nat Berry, Helen's brother, spouts the language of the dime novels he reads. Herne's dialogue also facilitates his gentle satire on the acquisitive impulse that overtakes Martin Berry, Josiah Blake, and many of their neighbors. Martin's appropriation of Josiah Blake's distinctions between old-fashioned "sentiment" and the progressive world of "bustlin', go-ahead, money-makin', devil-take-the-hindermost" contemporary business, linguistically suggests the displacements of Martin's older values of thrift and monetary independence by a new capitalism based in speculation and consumption that is making inroads into the rural world (677).

The play's original acting and staging provide a masterful illustration of the impact that accrues when a simple story is combined with a confident actor's reliance upon the subtlety that flows from realistic characterizations. Herne's stage directions evidence his continuing reliance upon the small action and nuance of expression to render his characters' depth to the audience. Played against sets and amid props which strive to provide a fully realistic portrait of the Berry home, farm, and lighthouse, the effect generated is clearly evident in the reviews. Even Alan Dale, one of the most acid-tongued critics of the era, writing in the *Evening World* on 1 November 1893, just after the New York opening, was forced to concede:

> It is truth, the unerring brush with which he paints familiar colors, and his peculiar gift of being able to detect the humorous and pathetic. . . . In *Shore Acres* he has written a play so absolutely satisfying to truth that one marvels at the directness of the touches that are apparently aimed carelessly. I would take criminals in a body to see it, and rely more upon its effect than upon all the sermons that coldly inundate those unfortunates. (Edwards and Herne, 108)

Herne's faith in his acting and stagecraft is nowhere better exemplified than in the final ten minutes of the play, acted in absolute silence. Twelve years before Chekhov was to provide a similar riveting ending to *The Cherry Orchard*, Herne has Uncle Nat prepare for bed and ready the house for the night amid only silence and his own thoughts. Herne renders the scene in full detail in his script, spelling out not only Nat's actions but also his thoughts about the length of Nell and Sam's stay, what the children will say in the morning about Nell and Sam's arrival and the new baby, the storm raging outside, the difficulty of getting the farm back into shape, and, again, what the *"young uns'll say in the mornin' "* (720). The effect of this scene upon the audience was overwhelming. Indeed, one night during a performance in Boston, an un-known man seemed to speak for all who have ever fallen under the spell of Uncle Nat. As Herne mounted the stairs, candle in hand, a clear voice rang out, "Good night, old man, God bless you!" No finer tribute was ever paid to playwright or actor (Edwards and Herne, 111).

Though under the spell of Uncle Nat's exit, one is tempted to view the play as an affirmation of the traditional pieties about country life in the vein of Denham Thompson's earlier play *The Old Homestead*, *Shore Acres* is more accurately seen as an affectionate farewell to a way of life that was already passing from the American scene even as it found its last, and greatest, expression upon the stage. The picture of quiet country life with its deeply felt affinity for family and the soil, its festive turkey dinners with friends, and its enduring faith in tradition was greeted by the original audiences with such enthusiasm, one suspects, because the play's incidents were reminiscent of the origins of many in attendance who had left such an environment for the seemingly greater challenges and opportunities of the city. Although the play's ending seemingly vindi-cates traditional values, the audience's inevitable recognition that old Nat will soon pass from the scene—and that Herne's protagonists have proven the merit of their decision not to be bound by "dead men's laws and dead men's creeds"—compels the disquieting conclusion that the old patterns of life are no longer viable as the twentieth century looms on the horizon (682).[40] Like the wizened remnants of the Grand Army of the Republic who marched in ever decreasing numbers, the passing century's verities were quickly becoming the stuff of memory. Despite the persistent subse-quent appeals of advertisers and politicians to the myth of rural America, the reality, as Herne quietly pointed out, had been reshaped by the same forces that were refashioning city life. Though the physical disparities between country and city remained, the concerns that confronted the one were soon part of the other's existence as well. The same boom-and-bust cycles of the economy that had sent railroads and banks into receivership in the 1893 financial panic (and had almost kept *Shore Acres* from being a commercial success) had bankrupted family farms in the countryside. The same progressive ideas discussed among the intellectuals and literati of New York and Boston were finding their way and influence among those in the provinces. America's growth was diminishing former distinctions. This was the reality that would hereafter find expression in the drama of the new century.

The late-nineteenth-century emergence of realism as a significant influence in American drama followed a circuitous, often haphazard path. The appearance after 1900 of both playwrights and critics raised in and committed to realistic dramatic expression would eventually result in a greater number of venues in which realistic plays could be mounted and a more sophisticated audience that could appreciate these plays' explorations of American character and society. As America rang in the new century, the ascendancy of realistic drama was not yet at hand, but the first tentative steps had been taken. A new generation of playwrights—more comprehensive in their vision, more daring in their techniques, and, in some instances, more artistic in their expressions—would continue along the path that their precursors had blazed.

8

The Age of Progressive Innocence, 1900–1916

As the twentieth century began, Americans faced the future with a renewed sense of optimism, for the last decades of the nineteenth century seemed to have answered many problems left over from mid-century and the remaining difficulties seemed finally to have captured the collective attention of the nation. With the emergence of the "New South" from the ravages of the Civil War and Reconstruction, the most devastating sectional dispute in the country's history seemed to be passing into memory. Simultaneously, the reunited nation's economic base, expanding through technological innovation and a vast array of new inventions, was quickly transforming the United States into one of the small group of premier industrial states. This new manufacturing expertise fueled, in turn, a refashioning of the economic infrastructure of the country. Older manufacturing and financial centers such as New York, Boston, and Philadelphia expanded, and newer hubs including Pittsburgh, Cleveland, Chicago, Detroit, St. Louis, and Atlanta, grew up. Linked by increasingly intricate and improving rail, telegraph, and telephone systems, the older centers of capital and trade in the East found themselves ever more firmly wedded to the agricultural and raw-materials centers west of the Mississippi River. Internationally, the United States continued to dominate western hemispheric affairs and, in the wake of the Spanish-American War, realized its imperial ambitions, acquiring territories stretching from the Philippines to the Caribbean Sea. The general attitude of most Americans in light of these testimonies to national "progress" seems best expressed by George Santayana, who observed that for Americans in the latter decades of the nineteenth century,

> The world . . . was a safe place, watched over by a kindly God, who exacted nothing but cheerfulness and good-will from his children; and the American flag was a sort of rainbow in the sky, promising that all storms were over. Or if storms came, such as the Civil War, they would not be harder than was necessary to test the national spirit and raise it to a new efficiency.[1]

Despite the prevalent optimism, problems did remain. Even after the well-publicized excesses of the Grant administration, patronage and machine politics continued into the next century, and widespread corruption at every level of government seemed a perpetual fact of American political life. The country's new wealth, rather than decreasing the disparity between the wealthy and poor, actually increased and accentuated the gap between the economic classes, as few of the profits generated by increasing productivity were passed along to laborers in the form of wage increases. In addition, an unwavering faith in the social efficacy of the profit motive among the wealthy, the emergence of business trusts, and general governmental indifference guaranteed increasingly less economic competition and a perpetuation of dismal working conditions. Urban consolidation of manufacturing sites and requisite worker populations, both native and immigrant, exacerbated the abidingly dismal slums, breeding grounds for startling new levels of crime, disease, and despair. The combined effects of sixty-to-eighty-hour work-weeks, unsafe conditions on the job, depressed salaries, and wretched living environments combined to perpetuate sporadic but widespread labor violence throughout the period, a reality not always alleviated by the emergence of the organized labor movement. The situation was little better in the countryside as agriculture fell more and more under the sway of transportation combines and processing middlemen who colluded to depress prices to farmers while maintaining inordinately high retail costs for consumers. Such conditions generated continued flights from the impoverished countryside and periodic hunger among urban dwellers.

But the increasing recognition of these social ills seems, paradoxically, to have nourished the generally optimistic outlook as the new century began. The late-nineteenth-century emergence of the Social Gospel, Pragmatism, "reform Darwinism," and the economic reformulations of Ely, Patten, Commons, and Veblen combined to begin a challenge of the assumptions of *laissez-faire* capitalism and the "naturalness" of the society it had produced. Eventually, books like Riis's *How the Other Half Lives* (1891), exposing the underside of America's turn-of-the-century prosperity, and the later "muckraking" journalism of Tarbell, Steffens, Lawson, and others, which unmasked specific economic and political corruption, spurred the emergence of what has come to be called the Progressive Movement. Settlement houses, public health projects, a revitalized temperance movement, prison reforms, antitrust legislation, calls for direct, popular primary voting, the organization of self-help groups for African-Americans, and the woman's suffrage movement all appeared, determined to redress specific social ills. Individually these various movements sought to redeem the American dream, in whole or part, for specific groups. Collectively, they suggested that with national unity assured and economic prosperity an achievable goal, social justice was merely a matter of time and persistent effort. Whether these reforms and reformers were effective or not is less the issue than that they existed at all, for their emergence suggests an abiding faith in activism as a means of social change.

Such social activism seems in tune with the realist aesthetic pronouncements by Howells, James and Herne concerning the desirability of structuring plays around significant social issues. On the heels of such realists' proclamations, one might reasonably expect that American drama in the first decades of the twentieth century would be in the vanguard of examining the social conditions and transformations of the period. But such was not generally the case. Part of the reason was the economic reality that the American theater as an institution was itself in the hands of a trust, the Theatrical Syndicate, headed by Klaw and Erlanger. Controlling almost all of the major theaters in America, the Theatrical Syndicate was a notoriously conservative cartel rarely given to underwriting the dramatic experimentations of even the most successful dramatists.[2] More important, however, were the limitations that realist critiques had implicitly placed upon the type of actions that could be dramatized.

The realists' decrying of the grand sweep of romantic drama and melodrama seems to have persuaded most of the playwrights in the opening decades of the century to concentrate more upon character study than upon social movement—upon the private rather than the social world. With a few notable exceptions, the period's major playwrights chose to center their dramas in the private rather than public arena, engaging social forces, if at all, through the same techniques of displacement evident in the melodramas of the post–Civil War period. Though several of the perennial tropes of American drama—the city versus the country, the social roles and private relationships of men and women, the life of fashionable America, the contest between individuality and social conformity—continued to find expression in the period, they were to be almost totally domesticated into family romances which left little room formally or emotionally for the type of incisive social commentary that would fill the pages of crusading magazines and the novels of Norris, Dreiser, Lewis, Wharton, and Anderson. Even playwrights such as Fitch and Sheldon, for whom the social environment seems most significant, rarely provide the types of insight that one might expect in the wake of Howells and Herne. The one thematic concern which must be excepted from these generalizations is the changing role of women. The growing number of women taking their places in the business world and professions and women's persistent demand for suffrage prior to 1920 forced playwrights of both sexes to treat this fundamental shift in American social reality with a seriousness that rarely attached itself to any other topic in the period.

All of this is not to suggest that American drama was returning to the escapism that characterized the heyday of melodrama. While melodramatic elements may still be detected in the plays of this period, they are usually subservient to a more serious investigation of characters' psychologies and the social environment than had been broached in the works of Daly, Belasco, and Boucicault. Nevertheless, a certain sensationalism that has its root in melodrama persisted. While the hysteric confrontations and violence associated with melodramatic ice floes, precipices, and gothic ruins were no longer evident, similar sensations often reemerged in the studies and parlors of the upper middle class. While the discussion play—especially as it pertained to women—made definite headway in the period, the more fully realized social and psychological visions of O'Neill, Rice, Anderson, Odets, Kingsley, and Sherwood remained a distant prospect.

"Bright Lights, Big City":
The Urban Whirl of Mitchell and Fitch

The dominant position of the city in the American literary imagination at century's turn is a critical commonplace. Crane, Dreiser, Wharton, and James steeped most of their novels in the atmosphere of various cities in America and abroad, and poets as varied in technique and perspective as Sandburg and Eliot incorporated the rhythms of city life into their poetry. It should come as little surprise, therefore, that turn-of-the-century American dramatists continued to explore the city, seeking to capture for their audiences scenes of city life and the effect of the increasingly common urban life-style upon its denizens. As the countryside continued to disgorge its population into the cities, traditional American rural ideals were reexamined as they inevitably came into competition with the realities of the new urban environment. Although the representation of this conflict inevitably created a certain amount of nostalgia for the "good old days" and reinforced a sense of the important difference between country and city, the plays suggest an increasing urban bias, a desire to face the realities of city life without recourse to a simpleminded repudiation of urban evil. The treatment given to the city is remarkably varied, ranging in the serious drama from the grim, semi-deterministic environment pictured in plays by Eugene Walter and Edward Sheldon to the nearly opposite point of view expressed by Clyde Fitch. Complementing these examinations is Langdon Mitchell's *The New York Idea* (1906), a sparkling comedy of manners which utilizes its city setting to slyly indict the extension of upper-class, urban consumerism to the most sacrosanct of America's private institutions, marriage.

Given the contemporary public's fascination with the world of the wealthy and the popularity of the play's female lead, Mrs. Fiske, *The New York Idea*'s initial popularity is easily understood. But as a series of successful revivals has testified, the play's reliance upon proven comedic devices and techniques—witty dialogue, generational conflict, the introduction of an eccentric foreigner, and sexual antagonism as the linchpin of the action—has guaranteed it an abiding place in the American theatrical repertoire. Mitchell's play is at heart a comedy of manners whose central complications arise from the cross-wooings of a group of socially elite, divorced New Yorkers. As the play opens, Cynthia, the horse-crazed ex-wife of John Karslake, is about to marry the dour Judge Philip Phillimore. Simultaneously, Vida, the judge's ex-wife, is on the prowl for a new husband and sets her sights on, alternatively, John Karslake or Sir Wilfrid Cates-Darby. After a series of complications turn the too-proper world of the Phillimore family on its head, reveal John and Cynthia's continuing love for one another, and establish Vida's vampiric nature, the play ends with Vida and Sir Wilfrid's marriage and John and Cynthia's reconciliation—after the revelation that they have never actually been divorced.

The primary interest of the play is, of course, the life of the *beau monde*, rendered in the style of a Congreve or Sheridan. As adept as his precursors were at discovering the quintessential metaphor for the sexual politics of the day, Mitchell updates his comedy to allow his social critique to flow not from the sexual dance which in earlier periods preceded union but rather from divorce. From Mitchell's traditionalist viewpoint, this contemporary mechanism tragicomically signals both the lamentable dissolution of one marriage and the humorous potentials of a subsequent union, and provides the means of intervening artistically in the growing controversy surrounding the realignments of male and female relationships. Mitchell's interest in manners is every bit as serious as that of earlier playwrights, a fact he made clear in a letter to the critic Montrose Moses:

> When I was writing the play, I had really no idea of satirizing divorce or a law or anything specially temperamental or local. What I wanted to satirize was a certain extreme frivolity in the American spirit and in our American life—frivolity in the deep sense—not just a girl's frivolity, but that profound, sterile, amazing frivolity which one observes and meets in our churches, in political life, in literature, in music; in short, in every department of American thought, feeling and action.[3]

Though Mitchell's discourse reveals the satirist's typical repudiation of current local folly by appealing to the supposedly shared outrage of author/reader/audience at violations of an implicitly timeless morality and social custom, the force of his social critique resides, just as much as Congreve's or Sheridan's, in a quite specific time and place. Though New York may still be the locus of moral corruption, it is not the same corruption that one finds in, say, Tyler or Mowatt. Similarly, though New York's frivolity may have its analogues in Boston or Philadelphia, the specifics of this locale are not merely incidental to the play's action.

In sum, Mitchell's play seeks to investigate the manner in which this particular milieu shapes and reflects the ideology of a precise segment of America's social elite.[4] In this manner, *The New York Idea* recovers locality for an American comedy newly sensitized to realism's demand that setting serve as a means of furthering character rather than merely as a backdrop to the action.

The specific, historically contingent synergy between character and the fashionable city environs is disclosed in the opening scene of the play, set in, as the stage directions specify, "the old-fashioned, decorous, comfortable interior" of the Phillimore's "old-fashioned" Washington Square house. Like Daly's *Under the Gaslight*, Mitchell's *The New York Idea* relies upon the immediate affinity created between its original New York audience and the characters neatly ensconced within their fashionable Manhattan residences, emblematic of the metropolis's world of privilege. However, unlike Daly's play, which tantalized its audience with contrasts between the worlds of the upper and lower classes, Mitchell's comedy remains firmly entrenched within the parlors, boudoirs, and paneled studies of the wealthy. In place of Daly's class conflicts, Mitchell substitutes the clashes between successive generations of the elite. This New York becomes the battleground on which the older, staid relics of Victorian propriety are fighting a rear-guard action against the effronteries offered to civilized society by the new, "smart set" generation. But, as is typical of much comedy of manners, the characters who serve to indict the foibles and follies of a passing generation are themselves held up to a certain amount of ridicule. Thus, as Mitchell's comments to Moses suggest, the play is not an unambiguous endorsement of "modern" attitudes.

As representatives of the passing order, the Phillimore clan provide easy targets and furnish Mitchell with an appropriate set of satiric butts whose discomfiture is justly applauded by the audience. Indeed, the opening scene, in which the Phillimore family's supercilious stuffiness is revealed as they agonize over the wording of invitations to Philip's approaching remarriage, immediately aligns the audience's sympathies with Cynthia, the quintessential "smart set" woman, before she ever appears on stage. The subsequent tea-table discussion of the approaching nuptials between Philip's dowager aunt, Miss Heneage, his hypochondriacal mother, and his supremely pompous cousin, William Sudley, economically completes the dramatist's sketch of the stultifying family into which Cynthia is about to marry. As Mitchell quickly reveals, moving in their circles is an exercise in nuanced decorum, for even the calendar is permeated with an inviolable sense of appropriate place and position. Not even the exuberance of youth is proof against this rigidity: Philip's twenty-year-old sister Grace objects to the wedding on no other basis than "the fact is the nineteenth of May is ridiculously late to be in town." Without further elaboration, Mitchell deftly evokes for his audience the effete lives of the wealthy whose spectral summer houses on Long Island or Cape Cod stand as offstage testaments to the complex and confining material reality of the fashionable world.

The initial entrances of Cynthia and Philip provide Mitchell the opportunity to complete his indictment of an older order lacking in either vitality or redeeming humanity and to introduce its younger alternative. The family's disapproval which has lurked just beneath the surface of the decorous conversation, is readily exposed by Cynthia, who notes with withering irony that Cousin William "couldn't have received me with more warmth if I'd been a mulatto."[5] But Cynthia's outspoken personality and status as a divorcée is seemingly more than compensated for by her respectable family name and considerable fortune—inheritances which, the Phillimores hope, will perpetuate their economic privilege and reinforce their position as social and moral arbiters. The family's constant insistence upon the relationship between money and the "natural" social and political order is revealed not only by Miss Heneage's refusal to send the wedding invitation to anyone who isn't "really *in* society" (641) but also by Philip's aristocratic reading of the newspaper. Philip's interpretation of President Theodore Roosevelt's "trust busting" as a "shocking attack on vested interests" and his assertion that "the people insisted on electing a desperado to the presidential office—they must take the hold-up that follows" (620) lays bare the ideological formulations of the wealthy who equate any disturbance in their "natural order" with criminality. From the Phillimores' perspective, Philip's position as a superior court judge and his brother's situation as a respectable cleric represent legal and moral bulwarks against the encroaching anarchy associated with the newly wealthy, the socially unacceptable, and the politically dangerous. From the perspective of Mitchell and the audience, however, the brothers provide enticing targets for satiric barbs directed at a hidebound legal system bent only upon perpetuating the prosperity and station of the class it represents and religious institutions determined to salve the consciences of its self-satisfied members.

The two younger couples—Vida and Sir Wilfrid, and John and Cynthia—are themselves rendered less as ideal alternatives to the older order than as problematic options. The character who most closely resembles the Phillimores in attitude is, not surprisingly, Philip's ex-wife, Vida.

In many ways another incarnation of the dark seductress, a perennial representation of women in American literature, Vida is clearly the woman of the older order's nightmares.[6] Obsessed with money, position, and sexuality, Vida floats through the play in diaphanous gowns, attempting to seduce every man in sight, except Philip whom she describes with withering insight as "a tomb" (696). A master of sexual gamesmanship, Vida attempts to attract John and, when that fails, expertly entices Sir Wilfrid into proposing. She ends the play securely married once again, having temporarily recaptured some of the excitement, if not innocence, of her youth. As she exclaims to Cynthia, "I've just been through [the marriage ceremony] again, and I feel as if I were eighteen. There's no use talking about it, my dear, with a woman its never the second time!" (695). Even as she sweeps from the Karslake home, however, one suspects that Vida's joy will be short-lived and, having sated herself on the temporary thrill of the experience, she will soon find herself bored again. Her new husband, Sir Wilfrid, is Vida's match in his narrow vision of what constitutes a happy relationship between men and women. The direct descendent of the rural squires of Restoration comedy, Sir Wilfrid is quite clear about the roles of men and women. None of the modern "nonsense" about companionship and mutual affection for him: "Never was a friend to a woman—thank God, in all my life. . . . Might as well talk about being a friend to a whiskey-and-soda" (636). For Sir Wilfrid, an Englishman contemplating marriage "expects three things: love, obedience, and five children" (682). That Vida will almost surely fail to fulfill any of Sir Wilfrid's announced marital goals is, of course, part of the humor of their alliance. Nevertheless, one suspects that their marriage will not be boring and thus will be a definite improvement over the lifeless alternatives associated with the Phillimores.

Cynthia and John Karslake represent Mitchell's most sanguine estimation of contemporary marital possibilities among this class. John, the romantic lead and ostensible voice of reason in the play, serves primarily as an instrument for anatomizing the foibles of the smart set of which he is a member. Conventionally in love with Cynthia, though loath to reveal it to her for most of the play, Karslake gives comic voice to male anxiety about the new freedom that women have obtained through more liberal divorce laws. As he says to Philip:

> The new woman has a new idea, and the new idea is—well, just
> the opposite of the old Mormon one. Their idea is one man, ten
> wives, and a hundred children. Our idea is one woman, a hundred

husbands, and one child. . . . The fact is, Judge, the modern American marriage is like a wire fence. The woman is the wire—the posts are the husbands. One—two—three! And if you cast your eye over the future you can count them, post after post, up hill, down dale, all the way to Dakota! (675)

John's selection of Dakota as the terminus for his vision is ironic in context, for it was the site of Cynthia's divorce proceeding against him. Thus, Karslake not only inadvertently reveals his personal suffering at the hands of this new order, but also suggests that the process leads inevitably from the cultivated life of New York to the chaotic flux of frontier Dakota, from the refined and orderly parlors of traditional marriage to the matrimonial "badlands."

From Karslake's point of view, part of the major reason for the demise of marriage is that the new American woman is incapable of honest emotion. Railing at Cynthia in the third act, Karslake asserts, "I begin to understand our American women now. Fireflies—and the fire they gleam is so cold that a midge couldn't warm his heart at it, let alone a man. You're not of the same race as a man! You married me for nothing, divorced me for nothing, because you *are* nothing!" (685). Of course, his pique is grounded in a rather traditional romanticism, a fact rendered visually in the fourth act set. As the stage directions and dialogue make clear, the jumbled library of Karslake's house has been meticulously maintained in the exact state it was on the day that Cynthia, angered that John would not drop his business matters to take her to the racetrack, marched out to obtain a divorce. Not surprisingly, John's romanticism makes him fully capable of reversing himself when Cynthia returns to "save" him from a marriage to Vida. With Cynthia broken to marriage, he is magnanimously willing to allow her to "chuck chairs around till all's blue" (703). Though Karslake obviously wishes to reunite with his wife, he is also clearly unwilling to reconsider the relatively standard foundations upon which society feels marriage should be grounded. However disconcerting, a few tossed chairs are apparently a small price to pay in order to maintain male dominance.

Cynthia Karslake is the most complex character in the play. Derived in some measure from the strong-willed heiresses that peopled earlier comedies of manners, she realizes much of her depth from her struggle with two alternative visions of women's possibilities. Early in the play, Cynthia acknowledges that her options are somewhat limited as "a divorcée has no place in society" and to choose such a path leaves one feeling "horribly lonely" (625). Given that reality, a woman can either "marry on prudent, sensible grounds" or wed for love, which Cynthia describes as "a wild, mad, sensitive, sympathetic—passion and pain and fury—of, I don't know what—that almost strangled me with happiness!" (626). Cynthia's experience with love has left her spent and wary of repeating her "error." When Sir Wilfrid tells Cynthia she is marrying Philip not "because it's the sensible thing" but because "of all the other men you ever saw he's least like Jack Karslake," Cynthia's agitated response—"That's a very good reason"—barely hides her continuing affection for Karslake (662). By the end of the play, Cynthia can no longer resist what Cates-Darby bluntly suggests is the most fundamental reason for marriage—the demands of sexual attraction. Repeating one of the equestrian metaphors that permeate the play, Cynthia decides at the last minute to call off her marriage to Philip and instead to throw "the reins on nature's neck—up anchor—and sit tight!" (688). The equation throughout the play of Cynthia with the horse which bears her name gives this line more than a bit of irony, for the subsequent reconciliation between John and Cynthia suggests that rather than being the jockey who controls her emotions, Cynthia is in reality the thoroughbred who must be bridled for her own good. Assured that she is once again at home in Jack's heart, Cynthia joyfully accepts the return of her wedding ring, the social token that brands her as Karslake's every bit as much as Cynthia K's lip tattoo signifies the horse's status as property.

Mitchell's play, while touching upon the changing role of women and the narrower issue of divorce, is finally not a thoroughgoing analysis of these issues, nor was it intended to be such. For Mitchell, the satiric dramatist, these people and the city which shapes and is shaped by them are part of the abiding comedy of human life. That he resolves his play with the reaffirmation of youthful vitality and the insinuated passing of the older, spent order fulfills the demands of his form. But the play's dénouement, which reveals that John and Cynthia have never actually been divorced, suggests that Mitchell has been circumspect in portraying charmingly daring behavior that is ultimately pointless. That he cannot conceive the restructuring of the premises of the social elite whom he portrays suggests the limits of his vision.

If Mitchell's comic vision allows him to ultimately accede to the social premises of the city world which he delineates, other playwrights were more troubled by the operations of the city upon its inhabitants. The period's most complex examination of urban influences is provided by Clyde Fitch in his appropriately titled play, *The City* (1909).[7] This story of the rise and fall of two generations of the Rand family, from their beginnings in a small town in New York state to the destruction that overtakes them in New York City, is laced with melodramatic moments— Rand Sr.'s heart attack, his son Hannock's murder of his sister/wife upon discovering that their marriage is incestuous, and Rand Jr.'s reconciliation with his fiancée after his realization that his life has been a fraud. But Fitch masterfully situates these moments within a realistic framework that renders the whole an effective investigation of the interrelationship between individual moral liberty and the effects of environment. Like other playwrights writing in the wake of the realists, Fitch is sensitive to the power of environment to mold and distort human beings, but he is ultimately unwilling to attribute deterministic weight to that influence. Finally, he insists, the city is more a mechanism for refining and exposing the inherent character of an individual than a determinant of that character.

Fitch's concern with the relative merits of small town and city life is disclosed in the play's opening act, set in the small town of Middleburg, where the Rands' preeminent position is undercut by a general family dissatisfaction with the humdrum existence they lead. Mrs. Rand objects that socially she has done all that Middleburg will allow her to do. Cicely Rand is excited at the prospects of New York and longs to "escape the social starvation" of Middleburg.[8] George Jr. longs for the financial challenges and political opportunities that New York City can provide. Finally, Teresa longs for the fast life as the wife of Donald Van Vranken, the "fastest fellow going" in New York (830). The only exception to this discontent is George Rand, Sr., the local banker and pillar of Middleburg society, who stoutly defends life in a small town against the indictments put forth by his children and wife. When pressed by his son to explain his antipathy, Rand Sr. renders the standard indictment of the city as an arena of narrow economic specialization and inevitable greed: "There, no matter what you get, you want more! and when you've got more, at God knows what price sometimes, it's not enough! There's no such thing as being satisfied! First, you want to catch your neighbor; then you want to pass him; and then you die disappointed if you haven't left him out of sight!" (825).

Fitch's own skepticism of the nostalgia for small-town simplicity and virtue is adeptly revealed through his systematic debunking of Rand Sr. and the revelation of Middleburg's own underside. Though Rand Sr. can assert that his business dealings have always been "to the right side of the line" separating legality from illegality, he grudgingly admits that "the line may be *drawn* differently" in New York. But the exchange between Rand Sr. and Hannock, his illegitimate son, reveals that even by the ostensibly less rigid Middleburg standards, Rand Sr. has been guilty of criminal activity. Of course in the context of the time, that Rand Sr. has an illegitimate son at all suggests a moral laxity that finds its counterpoint in his business dealings. A drug-taking villain with a past history of debauchery and crime, Hannock is himself an interesting comment upon Middleburg life. Though Fitch's use of Hannock suggests the possibility that genetics may have a powerful influence on character, the point remains that Hannock is a product of the lifestyle which Rand has extolled to his son. By the time he expires at the end of the first act, Rand Sr. and the insular, hypocritical world of nineteenth-century Middleburg that he epitomizes have been thoroughly compromised in the eyes of the audience. Though the audience may be somewhat shocked at George Jr.'s quick shift from grief at his father's death to selfish excitement at the prospect of moving to New York, the revelations of the act have made his decision to move morally neutral.

The remaining two acts of the play are set in New York City five years later. For most of the family, the promise of New York City life has fallen woefully short. Mrs. Rand has found herself snubbed by most of New York society; Teresa has been unhappily married to a philandering Van Vranken; Cecily has turned into a selfish, headstrong girl bent upon her own pleasure.[9] Only George seems to have fulfilled his ambitions. Having become a successful businessman, he stands on the verge of being nominated for the governorship by a group of reform-minded New Yorkers, including his longtime friend Burt Voorhees. As a progressive candidate, George's nomination is contingent upon his ability to maintain his reputation for integrity and to keep his family from embarrassing the party until he is elected. Quizzed by Burt as to whether he can withstand the rigorous public scrutiny of a political campaign, George quickly responds that he can. Though he shows some momentary hesitancy when Burt asks about his business affairs, George avers that he has not "deviated from a single principle" that his father taught him (834). Pressed about his private life, George conjures the traditional twin pillars of American political respectability—an honorable family background and the love of a good woman: "I was brought up in a small town, in the old-fashioned family life that's almost ancient history in the bigger cities. I loved my father and my mother, and their affection meant everything to me. From their influence, I went under Eleanor's. You needn't worry about my private life" (834). The tenuous, self-deluding reality of George's assurances is quickly revealed, however, by a series of incidents that fully expose the moral decay permeating the Rand household.

The first episode concerns Teresa and her husband. Don Van Vranken insists that if Teresa follows through with her intention of divorcing him for his latest infidelity, he will countersue her and name Jim Cairns as her lover. Voorhees argues that things between Teresa and Don must be patched up or the party will have to remove its "Purity of Family Life" plank from its platform. Eventually George convinces Teresa to live with Don until after the election, suggesting that she can "change her mind" after the election and divorce Van Vranken when it can no longer do Rand or the party any damage. When Teresa suggests that it is dishonest to mislead Van Vranken and Rand's political allies as to her true intentions, George responds that "It's just election tactics! the others'd do it; we must fight them with their own weapons" (839).

The second complication to George's ambition centers around Cicely and Hannock. George has provided his half-brother with a job as his private secretary, and has unwittingly forwarded a romance between Cecily and Hannock, which he discovers when Eleanor Voorhees intercedes with him on Cecily's behalf. Horrified at the prospect of an incestuous union between his sister and half-brother, George attempts to dissuade Cicely from continuing her liaison with Hannock. Cicely at first refuses to accede to his authority as head of the household and then reveals that it is too late, as they have married that very afternoon. Desperate to end the union before it can be consummated, George confronts Hannock and reveals the family secret. Hannock at first refuses to believe Rand, but when Rand calls Cicely into the room to tell her the truth, Hannock, driven mad by drugs and frustration, shoots and kills Cicely. Hannock tries to turn the gun on himself, but George prevents his suicide. Hannock then plays his trump card, threatening to expose all of Rand's illegal business practices, thereby ending his political and public ambitions and costing him the woman he loves. Torn between political ambition and love on the one hand and a desire for justice for his sister's death on the other, Rand vacillates between allowing Hannock to kill himself and holding him for the authorities. Realizing that "God knows, nobody's been more deceived in me than I've been myself," Rand ultimately resists Hannock's temptations and declares, "This is my *only chance to show I can be on the level*! That *I can be straight*, when it's plain what *is* the right thing to do! God help me *do it*!" (848–49).

The play's dénouement rehearses George's determination to set things right and to recoup, if possible, his self-respect and reputation. With Hannock's threats rendered moot by his own decision to reform, George resolves to return all his ill-gotten profits, expose the forms of graft by which he has profited, and endure the public humiliation that will attend these acts. George's sincerity and his fortitude in the prospect of his disgrace secures Voorhees's renewed admiration. As the Rand family contemplates its collective failures, Mrs. Rand, Teresa and even Van Vranken embrace the comforting rationalization that the city has been responsible for their misery. But George refuses to agree and provides Fitch's ultimate vindication of the city:

> *No!* You're all wrong! Don't blame the City. It's not her fault! It's our own! What the City does is to bring out what's strongest in us. If at heart we're good, the good in us will win! If the bad is strongest, God help us! Don't blame the City! *She* gives the man his opportunity; it is up to *him* what he makes of it! A man can live in a small town all of his life, and deceive the whole place and *himself* into thinking he's got all the virtues, when at heart he's a hypocrite! But the village gives him no chance to find it out, to prove it to his fellows—the small town is too easy! *But the City!!* A man goes to the gates of the city and knocks—New York or Chicago, Boston or San Francisco, no matter *what* city so long as it's big, and busy, and selfish, and self-centered. And she comes to her gates and takes him in, and she stands him in the middle of her market place—where Wall Street and Herald Square and Fifth Avenue and the Bowery, and Harlem, and Forty-second Street all meet, and there she strips him naked of all his disguises—and all his hypocrisies,—and she paints his ambitions on her fences, and lights up her skyscrapers with it!—what *he wants* to be and *what he thinks he is!*—and then she says to him, Make good if you can, or to Hell with you! And what is in him comes out to clothe his nakedness, and to the City he can't lie! I *know,* because I *tried!*
> (852–53)

Not surprisingly, the moral voice of the play, Eleanor Voorhees, refuses to repudiate George when he repeats his intention to reform. Like the forgiving wife that she will soon become, Eleanor discerns the moral purpose behind Rand's trials: "You needed a test, though we didn't know it! And at the same time we found that out, you had to go through it;

and thank God, your real self triumphed! *To-day* you *are* the man I loved yesterday!" (854). As the curtain falls, George Rand, reunited with both his integrity and the good woman who loves him, faces the challenges of the City with a renewed sense of his own moral responsibility and the moral indifference of his environment.

That much of the play reflects the melodramatic disposition that guaranteed Fitch's perennial popularity on Broadway is beyond denying. Certainly the sensational incidents and characters, the occasionally hysteric dialogue, and the rather straightforward moral assumptions of the play owe much to melodrama. Despite these elements, Fitch's play concerns itself finally with the moral education of a protagonist whose attitudes reflect not a corruption engendered by the city, but a more pervasive malignancy that permeated American society, especially business, in the latter part of the nineteenth century. Significantly, Fitch is careful to suggest that George Rand has learned his profession from a father who, not unlike Howard's Nicholas Vanalstyne, allows the longing for profit and success to seduce him into compromising his most publicly cherished beliefs. Unlike Howard's characters, however, George Rand, Jr. is called to account for his actions, suffers for his misdeeds, and is seemingly capable of change. The existence of Voorhees and the references to Theodore Roosevelt serve to suggest Fitch's belief that the American public at the turn of the century would no longer tolerate the types of dishonesty that characterized American society during the heyday of the "Robber Barons." In this regard, Fitch shares many of the assumptions of Edward Sheldon, whose plays around social topics gave the fullest expression to the spirit of reform that was at least one element of this period's drama.

Progressivism on the Stage: Edward Sheldon's Social Plays

The Progressive movement emerged as a major force in American politics and society at the turn of the century. Given increased credibility and visibility by the forceful national leadership of Theodore Roosevelt, progressivism became a potent force in both national and local politics. The spectrum of social and political concerns that progressivism embraced ranged broadly across American society, including not only the problems of the urban centers but rural populations as well. Machine politics and business practices, temperance and education, racial discord and poverty all found their reforming champions. Inevitably, such concerns found their way to the American stage. Though overt social drama in the vein of Odets or Kingsley was not to be found in this period, at least one playwright, Edward Sheldon, proved quite adept at structuring his character studies in a way that allowed social issues of the day to receive serious attention, if not to become the center of audience engagement. Sheldon's plays arrived on the New York stage during Roosevelt's second term, a tenure marked by the passage of a wave of progressive legislation, and three of them—*Salvation Nell* (1908), *The Nigger* (1909), and *The Boss* (1911)—achieve notable success.

Both Sheldon and his contemporary Eugene Walter focused on the lower classes, seeking to evoke the oppressive reality which overtakes citizens less prosperous than Mitchell's Phillimores and Karslakes or Fitch's Rands. Relying upon what might be termed a scenic social Darwinism, Walter and Sheldon depended on the set designer's art to provide an external, visual counterpart to the spiritual and emotional status of their central characters. Walter's *The Easiest Way* (1909) uses the setting of Laura Murdock's desolate rented room in New York City to suggest the character's mounting despair. Similarly, Sheldon's *Salvation Nell* (1908) counterpoints Sid McGovern's seamy Empire Bar with Nell's "neat and clean, homely but comfortable" room after she has come under the influence of the Salvation Army.[10] Nell's transformation from morally dubious scullery maid to soldier in the Salvation Army suggests that environment is not absolutely deterministic. But Sheldon's point that Nell's fate, and eventually that of her boyfriend, Jim Platt, might have been quite different had Nell accepted a prostitute's offer to work a local bordello is powerfully rendered. That Sheldon is finally more interested in the melodramatic intensity of Nell's emotional experience than in making a definitive artistic statement concerning life among the lower classes does not lessen his recognition of the powerful impact that the urban environment has on his characters.

After the favorable reception of his gritty portrait of New York City life in *Salvation Nell*, Sheldon turned his attention to the persistently vexing question of American racial attitudes in *The Nigger*. The story of the bigoted Philip Morrow's rise to the governorship of a nameless southern state and his decision to resign from office upon discovering that his paternal grandmother had been a slave, *The Nigger* manages to provocatively link commentaries on one-party southern politics, business's influence on government, temperance, and "the Negro question." Acknowledging the political reality of the solid Democratic South that had emerged in the wake of Reconstruction, Sheldon explores and ultimately decries the lack of real political choice in local governments. Closely connected to his critique of politics is his examination of the manner in which business interests, in this case the distillery industry, attempt to subvert the commonweal. The choice of the distillery industry as the power against which Morrow fights as governor conveniently allows Sheldon to endorse temperance as a civilizing force which can eliminate liquor-induced violence. Finally, resurrecting certain of the racial themes which had found expression in the anti-slavery plays of the pre–Civil War period, Sheldon explores slavery's racial, legal, and political legacies in the South. Though the shifts of African-American population from the rural South into the urban centers of the North and West were only beginning as Sheldon's play reached the stage, the flood of immigrants to those cities made Sheldon's concern with societal self-definition based on race analogously pertinent to the nation as a whole.

Sheldon's first target—the one-party political system associated most often with the South but in reality a problem throughout the country during the period—is presented as anathema to the nation's democratic heritage. Sheldon evokes images of southern patricians attempting to resolidify the political power they had once held in the South. He provides a masterful example of the type in Morrow, whose cotton plantation, black tenant farmers, and southern-belle fiancée all immediately locate him for an audience educated to the southern caste structure by writers such as De Forest, Murfee, Cable, and Harris. While Morrow is the candidate, the real power resides in the brokers who control the party machinery. This group is represented by Noyes, whose ownership of the most powerful newspaper in the state allows him to assert that he and his newspaper "could elect a ten-months-old baby."[11] Noyes's motivation for supporting Morrow is revealed early in the play when he asserts that Morrow's ideas on race and prohibition make him an ideal candidate—especially as the election of the other potential candidate, the prohibition-ist Senator Long, would guarantee the ruin of Noyes and his distillery cronies.

Sheldon's use of the local distillery cartel as the corporate antago-nist against which Morrow will eventually rebel allows the playwright not only to address a pervasive American concern with the influence of business upon politics but also to enunciate, through Morrow, a temper-ance position strongly tied to questions of race relations. Sheldon disposes of the issue of the intermingling of business and politics early in the play. When Noyes proposes that his cousin run for governor, Morrow is suspicious that the distillers are attempting to bribe him with the governorship solely in order to maintain their interests. Noyes admits his business interests, but quiets Morrow's qualms by reassuring him that he will be autonomous after his election. Noyes does not stop there, however. In a blatant appeal to Morrow's racism and regional chauvinism, Noyes notes that the distillery industry is essential to the maintenance of a way of life that Morrow has always championed, for "the niggahs need drink t' make 'em know their place. If they couldn't spen' their wages in liquoh, d'you think they'd keep on wukhin'? Not much! An *then* where'd we be?" (43). By linking social stability, racial control, and liquor, Sheldon manages to suggest at least one manner in which business interests seek to perpetuate themselves and the society from which they have sprung by controlling the populations to whom they ostensibly cater. By maintaining and expanding their sales, Noyes and his colleagues are not only engaging in good business practices, they are also assuring a measure of control over the oppressed, drinking blacks who are prevented from securing the aid of white temperance reformers. The rub comes when Morrow, who has always believed in the individual's right to consume alcohol, embraces a prohibitionist position after a post-election riot in the capital and thereby precipitates the crisis of the play. Driven to desperation by Morrow's change of heart, Noyes informs his cousin of Morrow's heritage and attempts to blackmail the governor into vetoing a bill to render the state dry. Determined to sign the bill, Morrow engages in a species of racist paternalism that seems to have changed very little since similar sentiments were uttered by Salem Scudder in Boucicault's *The Octoroon*, and would certainly have been more than acceptable in the era of 1909: "We brought the niggahs ovah t' this country, Clif—an' I reckon we're responsible fo' them while theah heah. If we've kept 'em like children, we've got to treat 'em like children. An' we're not in the habit, Clif, o' porin' liquoh down the throats of our infants" (138).

Despite his collateral interests in one-party politics, business ethics, and temperance, Sheldon's central concern is the racial politics of Morrow and the state which he epitomizes. Morrow's position at the beginning of the play is unambiguous—he is the traditional southern racist, leavened only by a self-styled compassion which can demonstrate love for individuals while despising as a whole the race to which they belong. Personally complacent, he can contentedly observe that "While I'm good to my niggahs . . . I don't think they ought to have the franchise and I won't treat 'em as equals" (43). Nevertheless, at least a tacit believer in the equal protection clause of the Fourteenth Amendment to the U.S. Constitution, Morrow, as a county sheriff, can demand the equal application of the law to all citizens regardless of race. When Joe White, the grandson of Morrow's "mammy" Jinny, confesses to rape and murder and is pursued by a lynch mob, Morrow attempts to save White from sure hanging. Though in the face of overwhelming odds Morrow is ultimately unsuccessful in saving Joe, his stature with the audience is increased by his demand that the law be respected and given a chance to operate.

In spite of this moment of evenhandedness, Morrow persists in his racist attitudes, even after he is confronted with his own lineage. Speaking to his new ally Long, he can still maintain, "When you come right down to't, the niggah's not a man, he's an animal—he's an African savage—all teeth an' claws—it's monkey blood he's got in him, an' you can't evah change it—no, not in a thousan' yeahs!" (212). Long, the voice of the era's "liberal" pietistic thought, rebuffs such a view, asserting instead that:

> Ev'ry niggah's a man. You an' me have had mo' time t' push ahead—that's the only diff'erence between us! We're all men an' we're all doin' the same thing—stumblin' an' fallin' t'gethah, on our jou'ney t' God. So theah's no use sayin' the las' ranks ain't got no business t' go wheah the fir'st are leadin' em. I reckon, suh, that ain't square play! (212–13)

Long's appeal to popular concepts of racial evolution sets the stage for Morrow's ultimate transformation. Explaining his decision to resign and work for the betterment of blacks to Georgie Byrd, his now-former fiancée, Morrow acknowledges for the first time the legacy of slavery: "You see, what my gran'fathah did t' my gran'mothah isn't all—it's what ev'ry white man has done t' the niggahs fo' the last three hundred yeahs! An' it's time some one had to pay up, even if he wasn't extra keen on bein' the pa'ticulah chosen man" (256). Sheldon's evocation of the Christian myth of the reluctant Christ sacrificed for the sins of mankind pushes the play in the direction of Aiken's adaption of Stowe, with its final tableau of the transcendent Eva and Uncle Tom.

Sheldon's play, while undeniably racist by today's standards, made a powerful appeal in 1909 for a reexamination of slavery's social and political heritage and the racial tensions which continued to plague the nation. Implicitly, Sheldon's refusal to fulfill the romance between his hero and heroine argues strongly for the accepted "separate but equal" doctrine, and Morrow's final rejection of Georgie circumvents deep-seated fears of miscegenation which remained codified in the laws of most states in the period. Nevertheless, in a stronger way than Boucicault or Aiken had dared in the 1850s, Sheldon drives home his argument of environment's impact upon the potential of individuals within American society. Morrow's obvious intelligence, integrity, and willingness to embrace self-sacrifice in the cause of the downtrodden are, the play suggests, as much the fruits of the milieu in which he has been raised as any inherent nobility of character. That he can sacrifice himself for those less fortunate suggests that Morrow represents a path, though a narrow one, to alleviating the legacy of slavery which continued to haunt the country at century's turn. That the country as a whole would refuse to legally sanction Sheldon's arguments for another sixty years suggests both the glory and shame of the era's politically engaged drama. While it could provide a vision, it could not significantly influence legislation.

In *The Boss*, Sheldon returned to a Northern urban environment to examine the ills associated with municipal political machines and the bosses who ran them. Modeling his central character, Michael Regan, on the notorious Buffalo, New York boss William James "Fingy" Connors, Sheldon not only exposes the mechanisms of control employed by the bosses and the boss system's destructive impact upon the public welfare but also intriguingly suggests the corrosive effect of the system upon the bosses themselves.[12] While utilizing material garnered from journalistic exposés for some of the details of Regan's operation, Sheldon goes beyond the muckrakers by presenting the human face of the system and suggesting the political and social realities out of which it sprang. Though highly charged with telling portraits of the boss, his antagonists, and his allies, the play is much more than another propaganda piece about the evils of big-city corruption. *The Boss* is at once a call for political reform and a subtle rejection of demands to return to the bygone days of the "virtuous" political oligarchy of white Anglo-Saxon Protestants. As in his earlier plays, Sheldon discusses these issues within the structure of a domestic drama which finally allows him to proffer a critique that weds public policy to private morality. The final reconciliation of Regan and his wife, Emily, née Griswold, provides an apt metaphor for the new political and private beginnings that, Sheldon intimates, the nation seems to be striving for in this era.

Sheldon adeptly situates the history of the demise of his title character within a political context which paints a detailed picture of the changing political realities of the American urban landscape at the turn of the century. Fundamentally, the urban boss system, which emerged in the urban centers of the northeastern United States, reflected a shift in governmental power during the latter nineteenth and early twentieth century from the control of established elites who had dominated American politics from the time of the American Revolution to the new immigrant communities, whose cohesive ethnic identities and shared sense of political marginality provided a powerful electoral base for political organization. These shifting power relationships were most obviously possible within urban areas where the concentration of immigrant voters made wrenching power from the entrenched elites more feasible than in broader, state-wide contexts. The subsequent emergence of state machines, such as those in New York and Pennsylvania, were often merely extensions of the power held by a coterie of urban politicians. The ascension of bosses demonstrably displaced the older order, but arguably did little to redeem the aspirations of the immigrant groups upon whose support these bosses depended. This is the thrust of Sheldon's political critique, and he spends a fair amount of the play's time detailing the consequences of the boss system on the lives of the very individuals it ostensibly represented.

Not surprisingly, Michael Regan is in many respects a stereotypical Irish machine politician. Uneducated, cunning, grasping, and crude, Regan is the archetypal street tough who has risen through the ranks of the party machinery to control it and to make its political and economic operations serve his personal desires. As the play opens, he has finally cornered the last segment of the wheat distribution system which is the basis of the nameless town's prosperity. But the anticipated benefits to the Irish community from which Regan has sprung are not realized. Indeed, Regan is as callous toward his constituency as any outsider could be. Without knowing that Regan is the source of the problem, Emily Griswold early in the play describes the pathetic existence of Regan's Fourth Ward constituents: "The men spend all their wages on drink, so of course the women can't feed the children and they haven't any shoes or coal—think of it!—with the winter coming on."[13] But as her brother points out, this wretchedness is a direct result of Regan's "liquor system" which compels each employee either to spend half of the wages Regan pays him in one of Regan's saloons or to face unemployment. Though Regan more often relies upon such manipulations of the economic system to perpetuate his control, he is not above utilizing methods from his earlier, street-brawling days. For example, Regan's orders to "discipline" a local bar owner result not only in the destruction of his saloon but also a nearly fatal assault on the owner by Regan's henchmen. Eventually, cornered by the forces of reform, Regan is perfectly willing to foreclose on the mortgages of the Fourth Ward "scoopers," sell his local interests, and move across the border to Montreal to set up his operation again. As he tells his wife, "Revenge! That's it! I've got 'em all like that! (*Holding out one hand with slowly closing fingers.*) I'm goin' t' squeeze 'em till I hear their bones a-crackin'!" (879). Regan ultimately reverses his attitude and intentions, overpowered by one of the oldest clichés of melodramatic literature—the love of a good woman. However intriguing Regan's transformation may be, by the time it occurs, Sheldon has accomplished one of his primary goals, vividly portraying the effects of the boss system on America's cities.

Despite the general indictment of Regan and the boss system he exemplifies, Sheldon's play is by no means a reactionary political tract suggesting a return of the older oligarchy that Regan has displaced. Represented by James and Donald Griswold, this older order is as politically and morally bankrupt as the new order that has precipitated its demise. Replete with class antagonisms and ethnic animosities that border on xenophobia, the Griswolds symbolize a passing order whose newfound commitment to progressive reform is at best tenuous. James Griswold's assertion that his business practices have been grounded in a sense of "public responsibility" (851) smack of a self-justifying noblesse oblige, but Regan is probably closer to the truth when he alleges that Griswold's borrowings from three banks on which he sits as a director represented an attempt to "float [his] business" rather than an impartial loan based upon the depositor's best interests. Similarly, while Donald Griswold is absolutely correct in asserting that "every penny" Regan owns "he's ripped out of a human heart," the cavalier nature of the Griswolds' banking practices suggests that though their tools may be less overtly violent, they too use mechanisms to guarantee their own economic and social position regardless of the potential effects upon others. Donald's campaign to bring down the man he describes as an "Irish tough" (851), though it implicitly has the possibility of improving the lives of the inhabitants of the Fourth Ward, is driven by the same desire for personal revenge and benefit that the audience is asked to repudiate in Regan. Capable of asking Emily to betray her husband, Donald is ultimately the object of sympathy when he is almost killed by a brick thrown by "Porky" McCoy. But by play's end, his potential as the heroic alternative to Regan has been irredeemably compromised.

While none of the men in the play can escape the ideology of control, acquisition, and power which Sheldon insists traditionally grounds both American politics and business, the play is not without its progressive, reforming zeal. That element of the play's political and social spectrum is embodied in Emily Griswold, who begins the play as a selfless reformer, a woman who has used her position and wealth attempting to aid the poor. When she is confronted with Regan's proposal that she marry him in exchange for his guarantee of her family's solvency and protection of the savings of the poor she has been helping, the rather abstract spirit of reform she has demonstrated takes on a more immediate, personal dimension. In a revealing extension of the tradition of sacrifice and nurturing routinely associated with women on the stage, Emily strikes a bargain in which she agrees to marry Regan, giving him an entrée to social respectability through her family's name and reputation. Tellingly, however, she refuses to treat him as her husband in any but a social sense; there will be no sexual relations between the two. Sheldon's insistence upon maintaining his heroine's chastity while allowing her to sell herself into a loveless marriage creates the appearance of a reformist saint. But this gesture allows Sheldon to establish firmly the acceptable parameters of social reform by taking this seemingly selfless act one further step. Late in the play, when Regan insists that he will move his business to Montreal, Emily seeks to renegotiate her arrangement with Regan. Refusing to allow her earlier "sacrifice [to be] turned into an absolutely useless thing," Emily insists that she will grant Regan's sexual desires in exchange for his remaining to face his accusers and not ruining the town (879). Ironically, Regan rejects her offer in a burst of Irish romanticism that sets the stage for their ultimate reconciliation as husband and wife:

> Sellin' yourself! Payin' me cash down! Goin' cheap! (*In a kind of rage*) Gawd, d'ye think I want ye, if that's how ye come? D'ye think I'll take my wife that way? I guess ye don't know much about real men! If ye did, ye'd a never try t' pull off such a deal. Ye'd never a' made me feel ashamed o'ye—yeah, *ashamed!*—like I'm feelin' now— . . . I tell ye' my kids are goin' t' be born 'cause I loved their mother will all me body an' mind an' soul, an' cause she loved me back will all o' hers! An' if such things as that can't be, why then, so help me Gawd, I'll have no kids at all!" (880)

Regan's sudden shift of focus from the public world of business and politics into the private world of marriage and family presages the end of his power and the ascendancy of a suddenly feminized and private reform impulse. Relying upon the cultural myth of the civilizing power of woman, Sheldon concludes his play with the conjoining of public and private affairs in a literal new spring of hope rendered dramatically by Regan's emergence from the tomb of his imprisonment with his newly loving wife at his side.

As social drama, Sheldon's *The Boss* argues for grounding political and social reform in personal rehabilitation rather than governmental programs. Though Sheldon explicitly denies neither the need for action nor the efficacy of reformers, he complicates his central characters to such an extent that they, rather than the social and political systems of which they are a part, become the focus of the audience's attention. Like *Salvation Nell* and *The Nigger*, *The Boss*'s implications fall much more within the realms of traditional morality than within the social arena. Ironically, then, the plays which most overtly seek to address the progressive impulse eventually settle for a representation that the dramatic vision of the period renders possible—the individual moral life. Seemingly precluded from envisioning the social scene in the broad manner of the romantic and fully melodramatic dramatists of earlier ages, Sheldon instead relies upon his evocation of particular social and political scenes to provide the critique which would justify political intervention. Yet he inevitably draws back from the implications of his critique, settling for the reassuring reformations of his individual central characters rather than the enunciation of a specific program of social reform. Sheldon's willingness to utilize contemporary social situations as the wellsprings of his dramatic actions places him squarely in the tradition of the American social play, and the historical coincidence of his plays' productions during a period of great social flux give them a historical significance rivaled perhaps only by the anti-slavery melodramas of the 1850s. But his equivocal vision suggests both the abiding conservatism of the American commercial theater of the period and the necessity of moving outside the commercial theater in order to address America's social and political failings.

Neo-Romanticism and the New Individualism: Thomas, MacKaye, and Moody

The same dissatisfaction that prodded Sheldon and, in more oblique ways, Fitch and Mitchell to dramatize the country's shortcomings at century's turn induced other playwrights to seek alternative solutions unavailable within the nation's social and political structures. Consistent with ideological assumptions firmly entrenched within American culture and literature, these playwrights sought to examine yet again the status of the individual in America. In a host of works, these playwrights explored not only the very nature of human existence but also the individual's relationship to society and to possible transcendent realities. While their postulations were tentative and often contradictory, writers such as Augustus Thomas, Percy MacKaye, and especially William Vaughn Moody sought to suggest resources within the individual and collective humanity which might make life in the increasingly complex and dehumanizing modern world not only possible but fulfilling. Their explorations of humanity's connection to forces denied or repressed by the ostensible rationality of modernity suggest a persistent, increasingly acute tension between the needs of individual citizens and the social, commercial, and political institutions whose operations constrained their individuality and elevated the corporate and material while diminishing private and spiritual concerns. Through their persistent focus on the individual at odds with society, these plays reveal a variety of counter-politic to the emphasis on collective problems explored in social plays and progressive drama. Dramatically, these works evidence a fascination with sources of characterization which seem to extend beyond the parameters established by conventional dramatic realism of the era. While these plays reveal neither the psychological depth associated with the early Strindberg nor the radical formal experimentation of his later works, they do share the Swede's interest in nontypical characters and situations and his insistence upon expanding the field of the dramatist's vision beyond the mundane realities of domestic realism. By doing so, these plays point up the increasing diversity of material that was finding its way on to the American stage.

In some ways the most exotic play of this group is Augustus Thomas's *The Witching Hour* (1907), which deals rather sensationally with telepathy, hypnotism, and, more generally, the power of the human mind. Throughout most of his career a rather thoroughgoing melodramatist, Thomas had an abiding interest in spiritualism that found its most complete expression in *The Witching Hour*. The play speculates in detail on the power of unconscious motivations on characters,[14] asserting that actions may arise not only from within the individual but from without through the force of other persons' thoughts. Ironically, *The Witching Hour* aligns itself with the externalizing world of melodrama rather than with the internalized worlds of psychological or social realism, in which characters are motivated either by individualized psychologies or by their internalized responses to compelling social conditions.

The play's central character, Jack Brookfield, is a gentleman gambler whose chosen profession has ended an earlier romance with Helen Whipple. Still devoted to Helen, Brookfield comes to her aid when her son Clay accidentally kills a man who has tormented him with a cat's-eye stone of which Clay is irrationally frightened. Having discovered that the attorney prosecuting Clay, Frank Hardmuth, has been involved in the assassination of the governor, Brookfield releases his accusations to the newspapers while a jury contemplates Clay's fate. Suspecting that the collective outrage of the citizenry at Harmuth will precipitate sympathy for Clay, Brookfield seeks to harness the collective mental energies of the population to guarantee Clay's acquittal. Disgraced and realizing that he faces the gallows, Harmuth comes to the gambler's house seeking to kill Brookfield, but is prevented when he is instantaneously hypnotized by Brookfield and his friend, United States Supreme Court Justice Prentice. In a final sensational plot twist, Brookfield aids Harmuth's escape from immediate justice out of a sense of personal moral responsibility. Revealing that he himself had once thought that the governor deserved killing and had contemplated the exact method that Hardmuth had employed, Brookfield speculates that he might have unintentionally, telepathically motivated Harmuth to commit the murder.

The preposterous incidents of the play notwithstanding, Thomas's concern for the suggestive power of the human mind reflects the general public enthusiasm for psychology and paranormal phenomena at the turn of the century. Not surprisingly, this common interest in hypnotism, clairvoyance, telepathy, and a host of other spiritualist activities soon found its way into the literature of the day. From James's *The Turn of the Screw* (1898), with its real or imagined ghosts, to Frank Norris's *The Octopus* (1901), which weaves speculations about reincarnation into its dissection of railroad monopolies in California, the supernatural received serious consideration from almost every literary perspective. Conceived alternatively as an escape from or a transcendence of the forces of modern life, spiritualism in its various forms seemed to offer a means of reasserting the power of the individual in the face of increasingly oppressive and alienating social and economic realities. Though Thomas's play is finally a melodrama with an aura of the metaphysical, its use of the supernatural reflects the increasing skepticism at the traditional wellsprings of dramatic characterization and provides an early instance of the expanding investigation by dramatists of the roots of human motivation.

If Thomas's play preserves at least the facade of a reality situated in the normal world, Percy MacKaye's *The Scarecrow* (1908), his most enduring play for the traditional stage, blithely launches its audience into the world of unmitigated fantasy. Borrowing his plot from Nathaniel Hawthorne's short story "Feathertop," MacKaye combines Hawthorne's original satiric examination of fashionable Puritan society's willingness to embrace a scarecrow brought to life by a witch's spell with a more general, philosophical exploration of the nature of humanity itself. Though the play still effectively makes use of the satirical power of Hawthorne's original story, the emergence and examination of Ravensbane's soul becomes, ultimately, the central focus of the play. The result, as Quinn has noted, is a tragedy grounded in the heroic struggle of the human spirit in the face of inevitable doom (*History*, 2: 33).

Given both the realists' injunctions concerning typicality of character and situation and the progressive drama's demands for the verisimilar evocation of the contemporary world, MacKaye's decision to set his drama in seventeenth-century Massachusetts reveals his belief in the pertinence to his audience of the temporally and culturally unfamiliar.[15] Beyond the collapsing of psychological and spiritual distance between Americans from two markedly different periods, MacKaye's use of the historical setting and fantastic action of *The Scarecrow* provides him a dramatic warrant for the economical characterizations of his minor characters and the generation of an action fraught with metaphysical import. Within such a dramatic universe, witches and demons are easily understood and readily acceptable; Puritan officials and clerics are transparently hypocritical and superstitious; and scarecrows are effortlessly brought to life. Conversely, the unrealistic action inevitably forces his audience's attention to the timeless question eventually posed by the play's central character.

Befitting the satiric import of the play's first three acts, MacKaye takes pains to minimize the complexity of his minor characters and maintain the play's ironic tone. Relying upon such traditional emblems of greed and vanity as money, fashionable clothing, and mirrors, MacKaye quickly sketches both the grasping Goody Rickby and the supercilious Rachel Merton. Similarly, the guests at Merton's reception for the erstwhile scarecrow Lord Ravensbane are little more than the traditional satiric gallery of fops, fools, and religious hypocrites. Ironically, it is only Dickon, the familiar who serves Rickby and acts as Ravensbane's mentor, who receives anything approaching the psychologically complex characterization of the central character. A fiend whose delight in trickery encourages the audience to see him more as an amoral imp in the vein of Shakespeare's Puck than a spiritually depraved demon, Dickon serves as the mordant wit whose anachronistically modern sensibilities nicely counterpoint the historically appropriate spiritual aspirations of Ravensbane. Typical of his humor is Dickon's dismissal of Ravensbane's question of life's purpose: "When a man questions fate, 't is bad digestion. When a scarecrow does it, 't is bad taste."[16] Despite the fanciful presuppositions of the action, MacKaye does not totally repudiate the demands of motivation. Thus, picking up a hint from Hawthorne's story, MacKaye has Goody Rickby send her scarecrow child forth to humble Justice Merton, her former lover, and to secure through Ravensbane's marriage to Rachel Merton the financial security his earlier abandonment had denied her.

After delighting for three acts in the ironic world of his source, MacKaye places his mark upon the story by radically shifting the play's focus and tone. The fourth act analyzes Ravensbane's achievement of humanity. Having been confronted with a reflection of his true nature in the enchanted mirror Rachel has earlier purchased from Goody Rickby, Ravensbane seeks to understand not only his predicament but also what he initially supposes is the dual nature of all men. Conducting an inquiry of his mirror image, he eventually comes in anguish to seek answers from God for the disparity between his physical and spiritual realities:

> A flail and broomstick! a cob, a gourd and pumpkin, to fuse and sublimate themselves into a mage-philosopher, who discourseth metaphysics to itself—itself, God! Dost Thou hear? Itself! For even such as am I—I whom Thou madest to love Rachel. Why, God— haha! dost Thou dwell in this thing? (840).

This final query becomes the basis for MacKaye's definition of true humanity. Ravensbane's brief existence provides MacKaye the chance not only to heighten the pathos of the scarecrow/man's situation but also to present in condensed form a range of poetic responses to life that suggests the emergence of a soul and elevates Ravensbane from the sum of his ludicrous parts to a man in the best traditions of romantic torment:

> Between the rising and setting of a sun, I have walked in this world of Thine. I have been thrilled with wonder; I have been calmed with knowledge; I have trembled with joy and passion. Power, beauty, love have ravished me. Infinity itself, like a dream, has blazed before me with the certitude of prophecy; and I have cried, "This world, the heaven, time itself, are mine to conquer," and I have thrust forth mine arm to wear Thy shield forever—and lo! for

my shield Thou reachest me—a mirror, and whisperest: "Know
thyself! Thou art—a scarecrow: a tinkling clod, a rigmarole of
dust, a lump of ordure, contemptible, superfluous, inane!" Haha!
Hahaha! And with such scarecrows Thou dost people a planet! O
ludicrous! Monstrous! Ludicrous! At least, I thank Thee, God! at
least this breathing bathos can laugh at itself. Thou hast vouchsafed
to me, Spirit,—hahaha!—to know myself. Mine, mine is the consummation of man—even self-contempt! (840–41)

Ravensbane's anguish suggests that he has already superseded the
limits of his creation and has achieved a sensitivity of soul that marks
him as an exceptional being. Reversing the thrust of Hawthorne's original
metaphor, MacKaye urges his audience to accede not to the satirist's
vision of humanity as "tinkling clod[s]" attempting to delude itself with
false dignity, but to embrace the romantic idealist vision of humanity as
beings whose grandeur emerges in their attempt to transcend their "inane"
physicality through their appreciation of beauty and ability to love one
another and God. The validity of this latter conception of mankind is
rendered dramatically in Ravensbane's decision to sacrifice himself to
Rachel's happiness. Overcome by his love of Rachel, a love which he
asserts to her is "the night and day of the world—the *all* of life, the all
which must include both you and me and God, of whom you dream"
(844), Ravensbane breaks the pipe which guarantees his existence and
dies in Rachel's arms—a man.

MacKaye's vision in *The Scarecrow* is markedly romantic and
represents an even greater departure in treatment and tone from the more
conventional plays of the period than does Thomas's *The Witching Hour.*
Despite the play's moderate success, MacKaye's dramatic formulation did
not become a pattern for his contemporaries. With the notable exception
of Josephine Peabody's recasting of the Pied Piper of Hamlin story as *The
Piper* (1910), the American stage of the period continued to be dominated
by varieties of what passed in the era for psychological and social realism.
Though he would champion calls for a reformed theater which might
make use of fantasy, MacKaye himself seems to have realized the inhospi-
tality of the commercial stage to his vision. While he continued to write
occasional plays for commercial production, he increasingly abandoned
the traditional theater to write folk plays, civic masques, and community
dramas, forms which allowed him greater freedom to render in concrete
production his ideas about the function of drama in the modern world.[17]
Despite its lack of widespread influence, *The Scarecrow* is noteworthy for

its abiding faith in romantic individualism, an idea that was to find its fullest dramatic expression in the works of the best poetic playwright of the period, William Vaughn Moody.

Moody came to the theater after having established himself as a poet of significant gifts. The same qualities that mark his poetry—expansive vision, appreciation of the American landscape, and seriousness of purpose—marked the only two plays he wrote for the commercial theater, *The Great Divide* (1906) and *The Faith Healer* (1909). In both plays, Moody attacks elements of American society that he felt inhibited the emotional and spiritual fulfillment of his fellow citizens. Though it is appropriate to place him in the company of reform-minded dramatists like Sheldon, Moody envisioned the great questions of his day as a fundamental conflict between the individual and forces so deeply embedded in the national psyche and social fabric that they were not readily accessible to political or social reform.[18] Rather than the social whirl, or the intricacies of politics, or the complexities of urban life, his two plays are carefully positioned in the rural world with actions which emphasize the personal and spiritual rather than the collective and temporal. Seeking answers to the questions of individual fulfillment and happiness, Moody's plays are meticulous studies of characters in crisis. They generally seem to suggest that particular human beings must willingly reaffiliate themselves with primal forces whose operation—whose very existence—has been ignored or repressed by America's development. Against the oppression of the modern world, Moody posited a mystical union between the individual and a Life-Force more reminiscent of the gods of his beloved Greeks than the God of traditional Christianity. Moody struck out at both the conventional, emotionally stultifying religious foundations of the country as well as the assumptions associated with economic, biological, and social determinism. For Moody, the reaffiliation of man and God could provide the basis for a rapprochement not only between man and nature but also between man and woman. Ironically, on the issue of the conflict between the sexes, Moody was at once one of the most outspoken critics of the double standard and a man whose conservative, mythic vision precluded women from full equality with men. Nevertheless, his plays are marked by some of the period's most intriguing women characters.

The Great Divide, originally entitled *A Sabine Woman*, explores the troubled love of Ruth Jordan and Stephen Ghent from its violent inception in the Arizona wilderness to its eventual blossoming in a staid New England drawing room. Ruth Jordan and her brother, Philip, have mortgaged their mother's estate to begin a cactus fiber business in the wilds of Arizona. When Philip leaves to see his wife off on a trip to San Francisco, Ruth is attacked by three drunken ruffians. Pleading with the least despicable of them, Stephen Ghent, Ruth swears that if she is spared the rape the three have contemplated, she will willingly become "his woman." Ghent, having bribed one companion and wounded the other in a gunfight, refuses to listen to Ruth's renewed objections, and she agrees to honor her pledge after leaving a note for her brother to suggest that she has eloped with a fictitious lover. Eventually, Ruth's family and friends discover her living with Ghent, who, having married her on the trip to his home in the Cordilleras Mountains, has become a wealthy gold-mine owner. After a painful reunion with her relatives, Ruth reveals to Ghent that she despises him and herself for the life that they have led. She pleads to be freed of their union, revealing in the process that she is pregnant. Ghent refuses to let her go, but Ruth defies him and leaves with Philip to return to her family home in Massachusetts.

As the last act opens, months have passed and Ruth has delivered a baby for whom she seemingly has no affection. Having lost the will to live, she is sinking toward death. Ruth's mother and sister-in-law, believing Ghent to be still in Arizona, have appealed to him to save the family from destitution by paying off the family debts and revitalizing the cactus business. Unknown to them, he had immediately followed Ruth to Massachusetts and has been biding his time until he might attempt a reconciliation. In a tense final-act confrontation, Ruth reveals the nature of her "courtship" to the horror of her family and refuses to have anything to do with Ghent. Eventually swayed by Ghent's appeals to the truth of Nature's order and realizing that Ghent actually loves her and that she loves him, Ruth finally reconstitutes their past and accepts Ghent as her husband and the man who can teach their child to live a truly happy life.

As the title suggests, Moody's play returns to the theme of the frontier that has played itself out recurrently on the nation's stage almost since American drama's inception. However, unlike most of the earlier plays on this topic, Moody's East-West contest is more than a simple contrast between the restrictions of civilization and the greater freedom and naturalness of the frontier. Like Joaquin Miller and David Belasco, Moody insists upon the spiritual nature of the West, but his assertion is so carefully modulated and persistently serious that it rises above the mere rhetorical flourishes of these melodramatists. Developing his thesis through the plot's extended conflict between the embodied representatives of East and West, Moody argues that the frontier provides man the last possibility of apprehending "Almighty Nature" without the constricted vision imposed by a rigid moralism derived from traditional religion, especially Calvinist Christianity.[19] Moody first engages the frontier myth in its popular, romanticized version and then slowly dismantles the fiction for his audience, propelling them into an awareness of a less tidy, more disturbing reality, a reality which had been domesticated by a host of previous western melodramas. Through the spiritual progress of Ruth Jordan, Moody is able to sustain the sublimity of the West itself; through Ruth's ultimate acceptance of Ghent, he is able to vindicate the type of man who can exist, even thrive, in such an environment. Additionally, the alliance of Ruth and Steve provides Moody the means of suggesting an appropriate basis for the uniting of men and women without reference to threadbare social conventions or outworn creeds. The implicit reconciliation of these sectional representatives allows Moody to offer one of the most compelling figurations of national reconciliation ever produced on the American stage. Indeed, it is not exaggeration to suggest that Moody provides a dramatic bridge over the sectional Great Divide that continued to haunt the American imagination even as the vestiges of the physical frontier were disappearing from the map of the country.

At the play's beginning, the West is presented as merely a stimulus, uniting a revitalized aesthetic pleasure with a concomitant desire for freedom from social convention. As the independent-minded Ruth tells her sister-in-law Polly, "Since Phil and I came out, one day has been more radiantly exciting that the other" (729). Ruth's linkage of physical brilliance with emotional intensity not only divulges the inherent tension in the proper New Englander between the physical and spiritual but also foreshadows the ironic incarnation of the West that Moody will provide in the person of Ghent. Indulging her own configuration, Ruth associates the West with a specific type of man, an "unfinished" man who embodies the "sublime abstraction—of the glorious unfulfilled—of the West— the Desert" (730). The evocation of this "sublime abstraction" smacks distinctly of the idealist "natural man" whose earlier, Native American incarnations had been driven from the stage nearly sixty years before. But Ruth's qualification of that sublimity as "unfulfilled" suggests that, though she is attracted to the idea of such a "noble savage," she expects that she will be the instrument of his moral redemption. Like a Puritan Pygmalion, Ruth wishes the raw materials of her perfect man sufficiently malleable to be ethically shaped by her. The potential for conflict is apparent to Polly, who wryly observes while pointing to Polly's heart, "If Massachusetts and Arizona ever get in a mix-up in there, woe be!" (729).

Moody's vision of this potentially perfect man is more subtle and more disconcerting than Ruth's fantasy. Ghent is certainly a savage, but initially he is anything but noble. At the play's beginning he even surpasses Belasco's Ramerrez/Johnson as an unsympathetic character. Ghent is, fundamentally, the barabaric ur-man of male fantasy and of female fantasy—at least as projected by the male playwright. Moody attempts to vindicate the primal appeal of Ghent through Polly, who says to Ruth upon meeting him after the marriage, "I see what you mean about wanting one that wasn't finished. This one certainly isn't finished. But when he is, he'll be grand!" (744). Like the frontier which has spawned him, Ghent is presented as a primal force, a kind of caveman in chaps whose dynamism is warrant against the senseless and effete dogmas of a desiccated New England Puritanism. Forced in the last act to vindicate himself before Ruth's abiding revulsion at the manner in which he has secured her, Ghent can only argue that the result of their union has been good:

> Some of it has been wrong, but as a whole it has been right—right! I know that doesn't happen often, but it has happened to us, because—because—because the first time our eyes met, they burned away all that was bad in our meeting, and left only the fact that we *had* met—pure gold—pure joy—a fortune of it—for both of us. (755)

Ghent reiterates this veiled appeal to the authority of natural sexual energy later in the scene when he repudiates her Puritan ancestors' ideology of self-denial and mortification in a telling image whose sensuality irredeemably compromises the meeting-house pulpit:

> What have we got to do with suffering and sacrifice? They may be the law of some, and I've tried hard to see it as our law, and thought I had succeeded. But I haven't! Our law is joy, and selfishness; the curve of your shoulder and the light on your hair as you sit there says that as plain as preaching. (755).

For Moody the intensity of Ghent's passion more than offsets the "indelicacy" of his manners. Though he can momentarily falter in his belief in his code of nature, he finally remains faithful to the truth that a West stripped of subtleties and foolish conventions has revealed to him. Having offered his suffering at her absence and his willingness to give up his fortune, Ghent inevitably claims the woman whom "Almighty Nature" has destined for him. As Polly has said earlier, "Even I believe that now and then a marriage is made in Heaven. This one was. They are predestined lovers!" (751).

While Ghent is the catalyst of change, the fertile battlefield of this sectional war is the heart of Ruth Jordan. In a manner reminiscient of the heroines of post–Civil War reconcilation melodramas, Ruth Jordon resists the assault upon a Puritan ideology that reaches to her deepest psychic roots, an ideology that has been lately reinforced by the conventions of Victorian sexuality. Her decision to live rather than take her life when she has the opportunity hints at Ruth's eventual embracing of the life impulse represented by Ghent, but her final decision comes only in the wake of enormous torment. Torn violently from her fantasies of the "sublime abstraction," Ruth vainly attempts to hold on to her dream only to have it shattered in her initiation into the world of adult sexual knowledge:

> That night, when we rode away from the justice's office at San Jacinto, and the sky began to brighten over the desert—the ice that had gathered here—[*She touches her heart*]—began to melt in spite of me. And when the next night and the next day passed, and the next, and still you spared me and treated me with beautiful rough chivalry, I said "He has heard my prayer to him. He knows what a girl's heart is." As you rode before me down the arroyos, and up over the mesas, through dazzling sunlight and the majestic silence, it seemed as if you were leading me out of a world of little codes and customs into a great new world.—So it was for those first days—And then—and then—I woke, and saw you standing in my tent-door in the starlight! I knew before you spoke that we were lost. You hadn't enough strength to save us! (746)

The sense of catastrophe that permeates Ruth's discourse in this passage, supplanting the glories of the natural surroundings and Ghent's "rough chivalry" with failed prayers and spiritual loss, represents one of Moody's finest expressions of the legacy of Puritanism. Ruth eventually recognizes that her warped desire for spiritual purity has nearly destroyed the love she has shared with Ghent. Beset by a Puritan conscience that hears Heaven demanding that the lovers "Cleanse yourselves," Ruth has attempted to purify their love in the only way known to her: "the only way my fathers knew—by wretchedness, by self-torture, by trying blindly to pierce your careless heart with pain" (756). Invoking an imagery of light that now dissolves her earlier dichotomous vision and melds the spiritual and physical into an integrated, invigorating whole, she embraces the possibility of happiness without guilt represented by Ghent:

> And all the while you . . . had risen, in one hour, to a wholly new existence which flooded the present and the future with brightness, yes, and reached back into our past and made of it—made of it all—something to cherish. You have taken the good of our life and grown strong. I have taken the evil and grown weak, weak unto death. Teach me to live as you do! (756)

The reconciliation is completed with the East accepting the now apparent limitless possibilities of the West. Ruth's repudiation of her fathers represents the rebirth of the myth of the West, a myth whose physical reality lies beyond the Great Divide but whose emotional truth resides within the hearts of all who will throw off the shackles of convention and welcome a spiritual liberation which incorporates rather than repudiates the body.[20]

The sense of liberation that attends the end of the play is, ironically enough, based upon the reconstitution of the social roles of men and women along lines which are radically at odds with contemporary practice but, in the final analysis, reiterate longstanding assumptions about gender difference. While the force of Ghent's argument depends upon the acknowledgment of the sexuality of women in a way which was seen as quite liberal in the period, at its root it again invests women with the role of repository of moral values.[21] While asserting that most "good women" are taken "by main strength and fraud," and specifically that wives are all "paid for in some good coin or other," Steve is quite explicit in attributing to Ruth the moral transformation that has overcome him:

> And as for you, I've paid for you not only with a trumpery chain, but with the heart in my breast, do you hear? That's one thing you can't throw back at me—the man you've made of me, the life and the meaning of life you've showed me the way to! (755)

While it would be too much to suggest that Moody is arguing again for the sexual double standard, it seems fair to say that he has not divested himself of the moral presuppositions which in large measure were used to underpin the double standard in the period's ongoing debate on the topic. While men may seize their Sabine women, the effect of such an action, Moody's play suggests, is the inevitable cultivation of the men and the reinvigoration of the women through their association with the vitality of men capable of and willing to violate social convention in order to remain true to the "Almighty Spirit" that prompts them.[22]

While *The Great Divide* was an enormous success, running for more than two hundred performances in its original Broadway production, Moody's *The Faith Healer* did not meet with popular or critical acclaim either in its St. Louis premiere in 1909 or its New York opening the following year. Begun as early as 1895, the play charts the story of a rural faith healer who first loses and then regains a divinely inspired power to heal as he is torn between a sense of divine mission and a newly awakened sense of the possibilities of worldly love. Around this crisis of faith swirls subordinate opposition from representatives of conventionally narrow religion and scientific skepticism. Though Quinn thought *The Faith Healer* the superior of Moody's prose plays "because its theme is the largest and the treatment the most secure," the work is on the whole less artistically satisfying than *The Great Divide*, primarily because of its untenable linking of irreconcilable romantic and realistic elements (*History*, 2: 16).

The play opens on the day before Easter in the midwestern farmhouse of Matthew Beeler, a rural skeptic who adorns his house with portraits of scientific men, notably Darwin and Spencer, cut out of periodicals. Into this environment has come the mysterious figure of Ulrich Michaelis, a man whose very physical description reflects his ascetic nature: "Michaelis is a man of twenty-eight or thirty, and his dark, emaciated face, wrinkled by sun and wind, looks older. His abundant hair is worn longer than common. His frame, though slight, is powerful, and his way of handling himself has the freedom and largeness which come from much open-air life."[23] Michaelis reveals to Rhoda Williams that he has long been aware that he has been chosen to undertake a special spiritual mission which he has prepared for by a long sojourn in the wilderness as a shepherd. Eventually, Michaelis tells her, God informed him that his period of preparation was finished and he walked out of the countryside to perform his first miracle—the raising of Lazarus, the Indian boy who travels with him, three days after the boy's death. When Rhoda responds with mild skepticism, positing that the boy may only have been in a trance, Michaelis reveals his own nagging doubts about his "gift." But he quickly reasserts its truth and, at the end of the first act, in what seems almost an attempt to vindicate himself, succeeds in having Mary Beeler, an invalid for four years, rise from her wheelchair. Michaelis's anxieties, however, are still evident, even in this moment of triumph, for in response to Mary Beeler's insistence that he heal the multitude that has gathered around the house, he nervously asserts, "I have waited so long. I have had such deep assurances.—I must not fail. I must not fail" (787).

The second act brings a crisis of faith which temporarily renders Michaelis spiritually exhausted, unable to exercise the healing power which has been his. Increasingly aware of his growing love for Rhoda and having been subjected to the persistent challenges of Dr. Littlefield, a local physician, and the haughty indignation of the neighborhood minister, Reverend Culpepper, Michaelis strives desperately to maintain the faith that undergirds his healing power. Confronted with an acutely ill baby, Michaelis feels himself unworthy and fails to heal the child. In agony at his failure, he tells the assembled faithful, "He brought me to this house, and He raised up the believing multitude around me. But in that hour I failed Him, I failed Him. He has smitten me, as his enemies are smitten—As a whirlwind He has scattered me and taken my strength from me forever" (798). The final act charts the course of Michaelis's recovery of his powers in his embracing of the love that he feels for Rhoda and his recognition that "I had thought love denied to such as had my work to do, and in the darkness of that thought disaster overwhelmed me—I have come to know that God does not deny love to any of his children, but gives it as a beautiful and simple gift to them all" (804).

Like *The Great Divide*, *The Faith Healer* is essentially an examination of the nature and power of love as a redemptive agent. Although Moody's plot again maps the resolution of a false dichotomy in the mind of his central character, the latter play's focus on the uniting of explicitly divine love with its human analogue foregrounds a concern that had only been implicit in the story of Stephen Ghent and Ruth Jordan. For Moody, Michaelis's initial, erroneous belief in the inherent division between spiritual and physical love evidences a variety of false consciousness which has blighted the root of Christian spiritual life in general and American religious life in particular. Exacerbated on the one hand by the abiding legacy of puritanical Protestantism and on the other hand by the emergence of a post-Darwinian skepticism that questions the very existence of the divine, American spiritual life, as dramatized by Moody, flounders between alternatives which are individually alienating and collectively divisive. For Moody the answer resides in a reconstituted sense of the relationship between the human and the divine sufficiently expansive to encompass both transcendent spiritual aspirations and immediate emotional needs. The play argues passionately for that possibility, but Moody fails, finally, to provide a convincing dramatization of his theology's actualization. Part of the difficulty rests in the very nature of the issue under scrutiny and the medium through which Moody seeks to convince his audience. But the greater failure resides in Moody's inability to provide sufficiently compelling central characters who are capable of psychologically coexisting within the play's competing realistic and romantic worlds.

The initial difficulty arises from Moody's attempt to dramatize a reality which cannot be represented on stage, a conundrum that the playwright implicitly acknowledges when he has Michaelis assert that telling Rhoda the difference between two moments in his spiritual evolution is impossible because "there are no words to tell of it" (782). When she insists that he try, Michaelis relates his wilderness vision of "The living Christ!" (783). Therein, of course, lies the problem: Michaelis can only narrate his experience—he cannot render it dramatically. Rhoda's skepticism—"It was a dream," she suggests—pointedly emphasizes not only her reasonable incredulity but also the limitations of Moody's dramatic aesthetic (783). While the spiritual reality that Moody is attempting to render can be evoked inferentially (Mrs. Beeler's recovery) through poetic use of stage devices (the disappearance at play's end of the fog that has hung over the Beeler farm in the earlier acts of the play) or auditorily (a swelling, offstage song of joy as the play ends), there is simply no way of providing a representation of spiritual truth without recourse to techniques inaccessible to the realistic aesthetic that Moody ostensibly embraces. While Rhoda can assert with the utmost conviction, "I do believe!" in the play's concluding lines, personal belief—even belief as potentially appealing as that for which the play argues—does not meet the common-sense standard of proof that the play's form implicitly attributes to the audience (805).

Though precluded from rendering the divine on stage, Moody valiantly attempts through his two central characters to reveal the reconciliatory potential of love. Unfortunately, both in language and action Rhoda and especially Michaelis suffer from an essential bifurcation which ultimately renders them unconvincing either as realistic lovers or as spokespersons for a supra-rational reality. Simultaneously occupying the straightforward world of a midwestern farmhouse and a world suffused with spiritual energy, they finally seem neither to exist wholly in one or the other, nor to be able to harmonize the two. One of the play's great strengths is Moody's keen ear for language appropriate to region, class, race, and education—like the play's minor characters, Michaelis and Rhoda speak, in the main, as actual people might. Nevertheless, Moody permits both Michaelis and Rhoda to break free from their moorings in common speech to sail off on flights of rhetorical flourish which are distinctly jarring. For example, Michaelis acknowledges his love for Rhoda in such a highly charged vein that even for him it seems extreme:

> All my life long I have known you, and fled from you. I have heard you singing on the hills of sleep and have fled from you into the waking day. I have seen you in the spring forest, dancing and throwing your webs of sunlight to snare me; on moonlit mountains, laughing and calling; in the streets of crowded cities, beckoning and disappearing in the crowd—. . . . (797)

If such utterances were part of a thoroughly poetic drama, they might be more suited to the characters. But as the play develops, speeches with such intensely romantic language and metaphysical cast seem imposed upon the characters rather than emerging from the individuals we have seen.[24] On the other hand, when pressed to speak of explicitly sacred matters, either language fails them altogether (as in Michaelis's attempt to relate his vision) or they are reduced to clichéd combinations of traditional and contemporary Christian religious discourses. For instance, Michaelis says to Mary Beeler at the end of the play, "I have shaken off my burden. Do you shake off yours. What is pain but a kind of selfishness? What is disease but a kind of sin? Lay your suffering and your sickness from you as an out-worn garment. Rise up! It is Easter morning" (803–04). Neither for lovers in a realistic vein nor for exemplars of a new spiritual reality does the language of these characters ring true.

The mediating device through which Moody seeks to unite the disparate philosophical and linguistic elements of the play is a conventional love plot. The initial meeting of the two lovers, related retrospectively by Rhoda, suggests the distinctly romantic ground on which this element of the play begins: "When you met me on the road, and walked home with me, and said those few words, it was if, all of a sudden, the dead dream was shattered, and I began once more to live" (779). In a conventional romantic comedy, such a transfiguring experience would be well within the bounds of generic acceptability. But the play has repudiated that model and its psychological topography in favor of the more realistic and mundane world of the American Middle West. The love plot's action is ultimately unconvincing, perhaps because it reflects Moody's insistence upon reconstituting traditional social roles which the liberating premises of his play effectively call into question.

Though Michaelis and Rhoda are supposedly exemplars of a new order of love, they begin and end the play entrenched within a social order whose gender configurations will in large measure continue to determine the nature of the characters' lives. Particularly conspicuous is the fact that the prevalent suppositions concerning gender seem to have been little touched by the transformative power of this newly understood love. While Moody again explicitly repudiates the double standard, which is the source of the villainous Littlefield's coercive power over Rhoda, the social pattern of dominant male and subordinate female emerges from the play's action with a new, seemingly divinely sanctioned imprimatur. As Michaelis's speech about having known her forever suggests, Rhoda initially embodies all of the pulls of the flesh, desires which promise to supplant his holy mission. However, the fluid, chaotic nature of his sexual desires is finally harnessed in his emergence as social protector. Thus, his own life can be safely transformed when he recognizes that Rhoda "needed me. . . . You needed what the whole world needed—healing, healing" (804). The power structure implicit in the doctor-patient/male-female metaphor is bolstered further in Michaelis's next speech in which, accompanied by the paternalistic gesture of putting his hand *on* her head as gazes into her face, he distinguishes between the sexual power she has once possessed over him and a new dynamic: "I gazed into your eyes once, and they were terrible as an army with banners. I look again now, and I see they are only a girl's eyes, very weak and very pitiful" (804). Once again, woman has been constituted a helpless creature requiring male physical and spiritual protection. Despite her natural "wildness" and her history of sexual liberality, Rhoda has appropriately internalized the social understanding of her "fallen" state and has sunk into spiritual despair. While Michaelis can both socially and spiritually redeem her, her need for "redemption" suggests Moody's vision of the potential negative effects of the women's movement's call for greater female freedom. Indeed, as Gottlieb has persuasively argued, the play reveals a latent tension between the pre–World War I women's movement and the other critiques of American life in the same period.[25]

With the early death of Moody and the redirection of MacKaye's dramatic endeavors primarily toward civic pageants and masques, only Augustus Thomas remained active in the commercial theater after the first decade of the century. Although the American theater would be forced to await the arrival of O'Neill to again be presented with plays as concerned with essential ontological questions, these three playwrights had nevertheless provided a needed complement to the socially oriented works of their contemporaries. With the exception of Moody's *The Great Divide*, the quality of these plays does not propel them into the first rank of American drama—yet they insisted on refocusing American dramatic expression upon abiding questions of the nature of humanity and its relationship to the transcendent. In doing so, they affirmed the abiding fascination of American dramatists with questions that, in whole or part, go beyond or displace particular social circumstances. Moreover, in their resurrection of a less deterministic conception of character, they point toward the penetrating character studies in the masterpieces of O'Neill, Miller, and Williams.

Engendered Stage: Crothers, Glaspell, and The "New Woman" Question

In a general sense, it is difficult to discover a play in the first two decades of the new century which does not deal with issues of gender. Mitchell's comedy included an examination of male and female mores in the course of its satire of turn-of-the-century America; MacKaye's fantasy operated from the unexamined premise that his scarecrow/man was an allegorical representative of all of humanity; and Moody's plays decried the sexual double standard in the process of dealing with humanity's relationship to the transcendent. But another group of dramas focused explicitly on the situation of women in America. The causes for interest in gender issues are not difficult to discover. The growth of women's educational opportunities after the Civil War, women's major roles in a host of reform projects, the entrance of women into the professional ranks and business, reformation of divorce laws, the persistent agitation for the franchise before 1920—all of these resulted in the redefining of American women and acute concern for their social, economic, and even moral status. General assumptions that had underpinned private relationships between men and women and served as the foundations for their social roles were suddenly available to scrutiny. It was hardly surprising then that American dramatists should take notice of the question—and even less surprising that Rachel Crothers and Susan Glaspell should make it the particular focal point of their dramas.[26]

Crothers, firmly entrenched within the commercial theater, and Glaspell, affiliated with the most avant-garde theater group of the time, both had long, successful careers that stretched into the 1930s, well beyond the scope of this current study.[27] Nevertheless, the plays that they wrote and produced before World War I provide a provocative index to the manner in which gender issues were construed in the early part of the century and, in some measure, the conceivable resolutions available in the period. Examining Crothers's and Glaspell's plays from this period also provides an intriguing insight into the influence of commercial and experimental theaters upon both the representations of women and the degree of experimentation acceptable to each venue.

While it is tempting to conceive of Crothers and Glaspell strictly as crusaders for social justice for women, both were primarily literary artists whose dramas reflected social and political struggle rather than polemicists who utilized art to effect social change. In a 1941 interview, perhaps evincing her disenchantment with the women's movement in the 1920s and 1930s, Crothers explicitly resisted the critical perception of her dramas as simple feminist political tracts: "I've been told that my plays are a long procession reflecting the changing attitudes of the world toward women. If they are, that was completely unconscious on my part. Any change like that, that gets on the stage, has already happened in life."[28] That both Crothers and Glaspell sought to focus audience attention upon women characters and upon gender issues which American drama had in large measure marginalized or presented only from a male perspective is undeniable. But, either from conscious political choice or from an inability to escape the influence of the patriarchal ideology which held the country (and, more important, the theatrical audience) firmly within its grip, Crothers's and Glaspell's dramatic approaches had a disconcerting tendency to recapitulate at least partially the period's gender assumptions.[29]

Crothers's first success, *The Three of Us* (1906), reworks many of the stock situations and characters of frontier melodrama that remained so popular at the beginning of the century. Set in a mining town in Nevada, the play delineates the difficulties of Rhy MacChesney, the twenty-five-year-old heroine, as she attempts simultaneously to maintain her individuality, find an acceptable basis for uniting with her lover Stephen Townley, and save her brother, Clem, from entering upon a morally compromised life. Opposed by the villainous Louis Berresford, who tries to undermine her economic and romantic future with Townley, Rhy is finally able to secure a husband who loves her, a gold mine that makes her economically secure, and a male who can provide Clem an appropriate model. Though Crothers obviously draws upon elements from such successful frontier melodramas as Campbell's *My Partner*, Daly's *Horizon*, and Belasco's *The Girl of the Golden West*, her choice of her central character and the variety of complications that she provides set her play apart from its antecedents.

Crothers's major modification of the frontier melodrama model is the shifting of the dramatic focus from the male to a female protagonist. Rhy MacChesney is in many ways a tentative version of the New Woman. As the stage direction which introduces her indicates, Rhy is hardly the traditional, passive heroine of melodrama. As *"forceful and fearless as a young AMAZON, with the courage of belief in herself—the audacity and innocence of youth which has never known anything but freedom—the lovableness of a big nature and sunniness of an undying sense of humor,"* Rhy is a forceful figure capable of carrying the action of the play.[30] Perhaps because of the frontier setting, Rhy's status as the head of the household, and later revelations that Rhy earns part of the family income by breaking horses, Crothers seems to feel compelled to reassure her audience about the fundamental femininity of her protagonist. Thus, after deeming her an Amazon, Crothers continues her stage direction: *"What she wears is very far from fashion, but has charm and individuality and leaves her as free and unconscious of her strength and beauty as an animal"* (11). The contradictory impulses evinced in this stage direction, which overlays a traditionally unself-conscious masculine personal freedom with the social conventions of feminine dress, extend throughout the play. For most of the drama, Rhy insists upon her right to live her life as she deems best, just as men are allowed to do. Constantly resisting the efforts of men to belittle her endeavors or assert that she should allow them to "take care of her," she confronts with a force rarely presented before on the American stage the social restrictions which would constrain her. In the climactic moments of the play's third act, having been manipulated into a socially compromising situation by Berresford and having temporarily lost the faith of Townley, Rhy rejects the two men's shared assumption that her honor is or can be compromised by any man: "Don't you dare speak to me of my honor and my good name! Don't you dare to say you'll 'take care of it.' My honor! Do you think it's in your hands? It's in my own and I'll take care of it, and everyone who *belongs* to me. I don't need you—either of you. 'Love—protection—trust!' Why I have to fight you both" (81). Despite its fierce intensity, this moment marks the end of Rhy MacChesney as the self-assured New Woman.

Though she forcefully rejects Townley's and Berresford's attempts to judge her according to a sexual double standard, Rhy nevertheless embraces another aspect of the dominant gender ideology of the period. As Clem's surrogate mother, she accepts the idea that she must put his moral well-being ahead of her own personal happiness. Having discovered that information furnished by Clem has allowed Berresford to thwart a mining deal that Townley was putting together, she spends much of the fourth act convincing Clem that his actions are ethically repugnant and that she will need his strong arm to survive the approaching social storm that threatens to accrue from her having innocently visited Berresford. Only when Clem's male ego has been salvaged and he has again, at least temporarily, embraced an acceptable ethic is Rhy able to face Townley and attempt to rescue her own happiness. Intriguingly, after submerging her independence in her previous interview with Clem, Rhy assumes an almost aggressive posture in this scene, insisting, against all his objections, that Townley must accept on faith her assertion that her presence at Berresford's house was innocent. Additionally, though her language is a tempered version of traditional assurances of devotion rendered by unjustly accused romantic heroines, she ends the speech with a decidedly atypical gesture.

> Just because I love you. Just because my love is so great that it must move everything else. It must make you know that I've never cared for anyone but you; that I would have married you long ago, if you'd asked me; that I want you to ask me now; that I've never been anything but true to you with my whole soul—my whole self; that I love you—love you—love you, and I know that you love me, Steve. (*She kisses his lips in a long kiss.*) (98)

Though Rhy seems to have regained at least a portion of her former fieriness, her appeal to Townley and his affirmation of his love and acceptance of her as his bride paradoxically vindicates the very gender roles that Rhy has earlier rejected. What she has not been able to secure earlier in the play through quiet independence and self-assertiveness, she acquires within moments of reverting to her "proper" role as a woman more concerned with love, marriage, and family than with personal integrity. Indeed the play's final lines—"We must make a good man of [Clem]. I have you to help me" (100)—seem to emphasize her complete return to the domestic, motherly role which renders her an appropriate spouse for Townley. Though Crothers explores the possibilities of a truly independent woman, the formal conventions of her essentially comic plot and the social realities of the era will seemingly not allow her protagonist to have both autonomy on her own terms and the man she loves. Flowing from Crothers's decision to focus the play's action upon a woman is a concomitant reorientation of the plot's complications and development to reflect her concerns with gender issues. Unlike the action-laden frontier melodramas of Campbell, Daly, and Belasco, *The Three of Us* develops primarily through emotional and ideological conflicts between the characters themselves, rendered through the dialogue rather than physical confrontation. In fact, there is little "action" in the traditional sense. But the concern with gender issues seems to infuse even the plot itself. As the major complication of the play (Clem's informing Berresford of Townley's plans) clearly indicates, Crothers's method is fundamentally to dramatize the distinctions society draws between male and female actions. Clem comes into possession of the knowledge that Townley has discovered a rich vein of gold ore running through three contiguous mines by eavesdropping on a supposedly private conversation between Townley and Rhy. Berresford uses that information to secure one of the mines and thereby scuttle the deal between Townley and an eastern syndicate dealer, allowing the former owners of the mine to announce the sale only after he has manipulated Rhy into promising that she will not reveal one of his business secrets, which he proposes to tell her as an indication of his great faith in her integrity. Of course, the secret Berresford reveals is that it is he who has bought the mine. Because Townley believes Rhy is the only possible source of information which would have precipitated a sale, he suspects that Rhy has betrayed his plans to Berresford. This complicated pattern of secrets, reminiscent of the well-made play, assumes more than mere plot significance in the context because of the social conventions which sanction Berresford's actions and restrict Rhy. Essentially, Crothers seems to assert, Berresford's bribery of the willing Clem constitutes good business—the securing of information which guarantees his economic success in the male world of commerce. For Rhy, the matter is more complicated. On the one hand, she can keep her promise to Berresford and vindicate the trust usually reserved for male confidants, perhaps guaranteeing in the process her own and Townley's economic destitution and her loss of her lover. On the other hand, she can break her promise and justify the general assumption that women cannot be entrusted with matters of substance. In other words, she can act as Clem did and be labeled a gossip, or she can remain silent and be complicit in elevating business over personal relationships by destroying both economically and emotionally the man she loves.

When she chooses another path by trying to persuade Berresford to release her from her pledge, she falls victim to an even more pernicious peril— the social assumption that she must be Berresford's lover if she visits his house unchaperoned in the late evening. By contriving a way of dramatizing the social construction of meaning and forcing the audience to confront the different ways in which society views the similar actions of men and women, Crothers provides a means of transforming issues of gender from the abstract realm of ideas into the tangible world of actions.

In *A Man's World* (1909) Crothers provides one of the most pointed indictments of the sexual double standard in the period, centering the play's action upon the issue and providing a rich array of characters through which to explore the nuances of the topic. Again, Crothers's plot is rather spare. Frank Ware, a progressive woman writer who lives with her adopted son Kiddie in a bohemian apartment house in New York, comes under suspicion of being sexually involved with Malcolm Gaskell, a newspaper publisher who lives in the same building. Several of her friends and fellow residents, having noticed a resemblance between Kiddie and Gaskell, surmise either that Kiddie is Frank and Malcolm's child or that Gaskell is the father. Knowing that she is not Kiddie's mother but anxious to discover if the man she has fallen in love with is the child's father, Frank confronts Gaskell. Gaskell comes to the realization that he is Kiddie's father, but refuses to acknowledge that his actions are in any way reprehensible, arguing that he has merely "lived a man's life."[31] Heartbroken that the man she loves can not perceive his moral failing, Frank breaks off her relationship with him as the play ends.

As in *The Three of Us*, Crothers again centers her play upon a woman, but in *A Man's World* she more fully embraces the concept of the New Woman, not only by making her protagonist an independent-minded woman unwilling to live according to the conventional social code, but also by giving her a career and an active interest in the status of women generally. Crothers's greater commitment to exploring the emerging, independent woman is announced early on in both the description of Frank's apartment and the stage direction which accompanies her initial entry. The prominence of books, magazines, newspapers, art works, and, especially, the desk at which Frank works at various points in the play suggests a woman whose emotional life encompasses the satisfactions of an active career, delight in her child, and pleasure in the friends who lounge on the furniture as the play opens. This balance is reflected in the stage direction for her entrance: *"She smiles at them all with the frank abandon of being one of them—strong, free, unafraid, with* the glowing charm of a woman at the height of her development. Her clothes are simple and not new—but have a certain artistic individuality and style" (18). Although Crothers again utilizes costumes to provide insight into her protagonist, in this instance the clothes seem more fully an extension of Frank's personality than was the costume of Rhy, for Frank's "individuality" and "style" are substantiated by the total action of the play. But the more careful use of costume and set are merely the most observable alterations of method evident in *A Man's World*. Crothers's more significant decision is to abandon a modified ingénue in favor of a more mature and experienced woman as her central character. The maturity of Frank allows for a greater development of character throughout the play—and generates a greater depth of pathos when Frank must ultimately reject Gaskell.

Because she willingly ends her romance with Gaskell, Frank seems in many ways Crothers's most optimistic version of the New Woman in her early plays. Raised abroad by her writer father, who has encouraged her "to see—to know—to touch all kinds of life," Frank has explored the fate of men and women, discovering in the process that "the women had the worst of it" (35). In a tellingly self-reflexive gesture, Crothers portrays Frank's artistic commitment to women by having one of the other characters read aloud an unintentionally condescending review of Frank's latest novel:

> "The Beaten Path" is the strongest thing that Frank Ware has ever done. Her first work attracted wide attention when we tho't Frank Ware was a man, but now that we know she is a woman we are more than ever impressed by the strength and scope of her work. She has laid her scenes this time on the East side in the wretched poverty of the tenement houses, and the marvel is that any woman could see and know so much and depict crime and degradation so boldly. Her great cry is for women—to make them better by making them freer. (12–13)

As the reviewer's comment on her name hints, Frank's artistry is perceived as masculine, a circumstance that Frank, ironically enough, perceives as flattery since it suggests that people perceive her work as "too good for a woman to do" (33). Though apparently willing to let her work eventually redefine the nature of the "woman's novel" and despite even her friends' suspicions that her works are being ghost-written by a male lover, Frank is determined to persist in this new subject matter, for, as she tells her confidant Fritz Bahn, "You don't suppose I'm going to give up all my chances of seeing and knowing and understanding just because a few silly people are talking about me?" (34).

This fixity of purpose and resistance to social convention is nicely contrasted through two of Frank's fellow boarders, Lione Brune, a successful but temperamental opera singer, and Clara Oakes, a mediocre miniature painter. If anything, Lione is even harsher in her general assessment of men than is Frank: "Men are pigs of course. They take all they can get and don't give any more than they have to. It's a man's world—that's the size of it. What's the use of knocking your head against things that you can't change?" (94). But despite detesting the injustice of the situation, she, like Gaskell, can assert, "When it comes to morality a woman never holds anything against a man. . . . What are you going to do about it? Throw him over—because you happen to find a little incident in his life that doesn't jibe with your theory? Where will you be? What becomes of you? Um? Not much fun for you for the rest of your life" (94). Lione's fear of abandonment by the very men she despises is somewhat tempered by her revelation that she is madly in love with Fritz, a man whose actions put him well outside the generalizations which Lione has indulged. Nevertheless, Lione serves to suggest that even those women who are willing to live a bit more independently than would normally be accepted in the society at large eventually feel socially and economically compelled to capitulate to men whom they may not respect. This point is made even more forcefully through Clara. Having lived a hand-to-mouth existence for ten years, Clara is quite willing to give up her independence for any husband. As she says:

> I—I've always been superfluous and plain. Absolutely superfluous. I'm not necessary to one single human being. I'm just one of those ever-lasting women that the world is full of. There's nobody to take care of me and I'm simply not capable of taking care of myself. I've tried—God knows I've tried—and what is the use? What under Heaven do I get out of it? If I were a man—the most insignificant little runt of a man—I could persuade some woman to marry me— and could have a home and children and hustle for my living— and life would mean something. Oh, I can't bear it, Frank. (86–87)

Clara's self-loathing at her plain physical appearance represents one of Crothers's most salient critiques of patriarchy's mechanisms of control.

Acculturated to configure value solely within domestic parameters of ornamentation and reproduction, even those women who seek or are forced by circumstance to break the traditional roles of women in their society are nagged by the spectre of a life whose primary justifications—marriage and motherhood—are beyond their grasps. Intriguingly, Crothers has Frank respond to Lione and Clara in sensitive but contradictory ways which acknowledge the realities and desires of each woman but represent only half of the ideal that Frank holds out for herself. For Lione, Frank devises a plan to secure Fritz; for Clara, Frank proffers a job as an art teacher and resident adviser at a women's club that Frank is starting on the East side to reclaim "fallen" women. Implicitly, Crothers seems to suggest that not all women are as yet ready to embrace the full economic and emotional independence embodied by Frank (Gottlieb, *Crothers*, 45).

Though Frank can empathize with both Lione and Clara, she insists that any man who wishes to love her must accept her own comprehensive reformulation of herself and the reordered principles for relationships between men and women which she espouses. Thus, Frank's determination to pursue her art on her own terms is matched by an equal resolution to ground any emotional attachment in mutual respect. When Gaskell asserts that Frank's ideals will be swept aside by love, that she "won't give a hang for anything [she] ever believed," Frank is adamant in maintaining that she will not succumb to the pull of romance, that she "will care what he believes" (42–43). Frank's insistence is in some senses bravado which disguises her fear of love, for, as she admits to Gaskell later, "I've tried to resist it because it means so terribly much to me. My life has been filled with other things you know—with Kiddie—and my work. They absorbed me and satisfied me . . . It seemed almost like being a traitor to myself" (82). The basis of Frank's fear is revealed in the highly charged language of her admission of her love for Gaskell which discloses the tenacious appeal of romantic love even for women as strong and independent as Frank: "Oh, don't ever disappoint me. Be big and fine and honest always—let me lean on you and worship you" (82–83). Having brought her protagonist to the edge of self-dissolution in the man she loves, Crothers forcefully argues through Frank's ultimate rejection of Gaskell that the configurations of love espoused by both Gaskell and Lione need not be determinative in women's lives. As Frank tells Gaskell, "Love isn't the only thing in the world" (110). Significantly, Frank repudiates Gaskell not for his previous affair but for his refusal to acknowledge that his actions were morally corrupt.[32] "Oh, I want to forgive you. If you could only see. If your soul could only see. Oh, dear God! Malcolm, tell me, tell me you know it was wrong—that you'd give your life to make it right. Say that you know this thing was a crime" (112). When Gaskell asserts that he will not be judged "by a standard that doesn't exist," Frank resolutely declares, "It is the end" (112–13). While the play was not greatly successful (it closed after seventy-one performances), it occasioned widespread discussion and at least one explicit defense of the double standard, Augustus Thomas's *As a Man Thinks* (1911). Crothers's increasing artistry in costume, set, plot, and dialogue accounts for part of the power of *A Man's World*, but the real strength of the play exists in her portrait of Frank Ware. For the first time on the national stage, the battle between older versions of womanhood and the New Woman are embodied in such a way as to reveal the agonizing choices that women constantly face in American society.[33] And for the first time, a woman is portrayed as having the force of character to resist the weight of her acculturation and opt for personal integrity over the enticements of romantic love. While her portrait of Frank Ware provides a powerful affirmation of a woman's right to personal independence and integrity—and to establish before marriage the foundation upon which she will live with a man—Crothers's next play was to reveal the dangers of even the most liberally constituted unions.

In *He and She* (1911) Crothers presents the story of Ann Herford, a talented sculptor who has struggled, with the support of her fellow-sculptor husband, Tom, against resistance from almost every other quarter of life. At the enthusiastic urging of her friend Ruth Creel, and with the reluctant encouragement of Tom, Ann decides to enter a contest to which all the best (and presumably male) sculptors, including her husband, are submitting pieces. When Ann's frieze wins the commission and Tom's piece finishes second, Tom's disappointment and jealousy precipitate a clash over what Tom now argues is Ann's overarching ambition. Their heated exchange ends only at the appearance of their daughter Millicent, who arrives unexpectedly from boarding school to say that she has left and has no intention of returning. Eventually, Ann discovers that the sixteen-year-old Millicent has fallen in love with the school chauffeur and intends to marry him. Perceiving such a marriage as disastrous, Ann persuades Millicent to accompany her to Europe with the pretense of recovering from a feigned case of exhaustion. When she reveals her plan to Tom, he initially resists her decision, apologizing that he has earlier been unfair in his criticism of her. But eventually he accepts her trip and agrees to complete the commissioned frieze for her. The play ends with

Millicent saved from a calamitous marriage, with Tom's primacy as the economic head of the household reestablished by Ann's withdrawal from the competition, and with Ann attempting to reconcile herself to the loss of her career and her concomitant dwindling into the narrowly defined, conventional roles of wife and mother.

In some senses, *He and She* represents an extension of the discussion begun in *A Man's World*, for the play commences on the premise that Ann and Tom have established the type of egalitarian marriage denied to Frank Ware. Crothers again centers her play on an artistic woman and again provides an external validation of her protagonist's endeavors, this time in the form of the commission. But while the unattached Frank is free to repudiate Gaskell, Ann Hereford's circumstances are more complicated. The emotional stakes are higher, for Ann has married what the play initially suggests is the "right" man, one capable of supporting all elements of her life. Thus, the ideological threads of the play are intricately interwoven into a fabric which includes marriage and parenthood. Ann faces the most deep-seated and difficult dilemma for women in a culture which has elevated motherhood to iconic status while paradoxically segregating it from activities, generally reserved to men, whose value is immediately and broadly acknowledged. While Ann can accept competing with her husband, she can not dismiss the needs of Millicent.

The ideological conflict over the role of women is neatly handled by pitting Ann and Ruth Creel against a range of antagonists, all of whom question the propriety of the Hereford's way of life in general, and Ann's in particular. At the most antediluvian level is Tom's assistant, Keith McKenzie. Engaged to Ruth Creel, McKenzie evidences a pervasive anxiety at the prospect of women moving into arenas previously controlled by men. While he can agree with the general proposition that women ought to be able to do whatever they want, "when it's the girl you love and want to marry, it's different," for "the world has got to have homes to live in and who's going to make them if the women don't do it?"[34] He denigrates Ann's work not on its own merits but because it is the work of a woman: "She has more imagination than the governor, but, great Peter, when it comes to execution and the real thing she isn't *in* it with him. How could she be. She's a woman" (902). Tom's sister Daisy is reminiscent of Clara Oakes. Although a model of efficiency as the Hereford's secretary, she is secretly in love with Keith and longs to leave her job for a home and family. Not surprisingly, she shares many of McKenzie's attitudes about the proper role of women and the true source of their happiness.

Trapped within a changing economic reality which is propelling her into the business world, she represents, she says, a vast number of women who long for the more familiar role of wife and homemaker: "there are lots and lots and lots of women taking care of themselves—putting up the bluff of being independent and happy who would be so glad to live in a little flat and do their own work—just to be the nicest thing in the world to some man" (916). For Daisy, Crothers suggests, the new freedoms are a burden rather than a liberation. The most insidious antagonist in the play is Ann's father, Dr. Remington, who embodies the pulls of tradition clothed in the rational mantle of science. Though Remington is naturally enough concerned for his daughter's happiness, he is wedded to the idea that the social advances of women run contradictory to "the laws of creation." For him, the "sensitive—involved—complex elements of a woman's nature" are being perverted from their original and intended end, motherhood, a state that is "as near divinity as we ever get" (905, 924). Although he recognizes the great attraction that Ann's work has for her, he is more interested in what he conceives as her more fundamental identity, insisting earnestly to Tom that "I'd rather see her happy—as a woman—than *the greatest artist in the world*" (923). Despite Crothers's obvious disagreement with Remington's premises, she gives to him the line which sums up the dilemma for both Tom and Ann: "Men and women will go through hell over this before it shakes down into shape. You're right and she's right and you're tearing each other like mad dogs over it because you love each other" (923).

Separated from the other antagonists is Tom, who, Crothers suggests, though he will momentarily espouse a traditionalist view on the issue, is fundamentally aware of the inequities of the conventional social order and, despite his lapse, is sympathetic at a deep level to overturning them. Nevertheless, like Ann, Tom is a product of his social environment and unable to escape its force when he confronts a fundamental challenge to the self-conception that he has internalized. His initial repudiations of McKenzie's traditional sexism establish him as a sympathetic figure, almost an ideal of a New Man who can accept a reconstituted basis for male-female relationships. But his reaction to Ann's critique of his work and her suggestion that he substitute her model for his reveals a latent bias disturbingly akin to that of Keith. Contrasting his frieze with Ann's alternative drawings, he notes, "I don't know what's got into you. This is imaginative and charming and graceful—full of abandon and fantasy and even vitality—but ye gods, child, it isn't in *this* class" (909). When Ann wins the prize, Tom's sense of self is so immediately undermined that he reverts to male form, first refusing to accept any of the prize money, then asking Ann to give up the commission to "prove" her continuing commitment to him and Millicent, and finally demanding that she do so as testimony to her acceptance of his status as head of the household. Caught up in the emotions of the moment, Tom sounds like a cross between McKenzie and Remington: "You're a woman and I'm a man. You're not free in the same way" (921). Though he will eventually recant, acknowledging both that he has been unfair and that Ann's decision to forego the frieze in order to take Millicent abroad will gnaw at her, the audience is left with the nagging suspicion that his words and actions are testimony to remaining psychic work to be done before men and women can truly enter into a mutual relationship, either in the workplace or the domestic sphere.

Against these reactionary forces are ranged Ruth and Ann, women who have entered the business and artistic worlds and have succeeded on grounds where men have established the rules. Ruth, a woman rising quickly up the career ladder in the magazine for which she works, is by far the most radical figure in the play. Arguing that "being a mother is the most gigantic, important, and thankless thing in the world," she has decided not to have children and to put her energies instead into her career (911). In addition to presenting the most revolutionary position on reproduction in the play, Ruth also serves as a spur to Ann's talents, insisting that Ann not give over her artistic work to the service of Tom's career. Instead, asserts Ruth, Ann has a duty to herself to present her work on its own terms and under her own name:

> It belongs to *you*—and if you don't take care of it and give it its chance, you kill something which is more important than you are. Don't forget *that*. You're not just the talented woman, you've got *downright genius*, and you ought to make everything give way to that. *Everything*. If you don't, you're weak. (908)

The gender solidarity represented by Ruth is of key importance to Ann's decision to submit her work to the contest, but its efficacy is, given Ann's circumstances, limited to the sphere of work. Ruth's break with Keith and her disappearance from the play leave Ann to face her ultimate dilemma alone.

Crothers's major achievement in the play is her characterization of Ann Hereford, another independent yet feminine artistic woman who embodies the dilemmas that face American women. Artist, wife and mother, Ann spends most of the play valiantly attempting to negotiate the demands of others and her own sense of personal self-worth. Initially reluctant to tell Tom that she has reservations about his project, she carefully broaches the subject, selflessly offering to give up her own project in an attempt to guarantee the success of the man she loves. Confronted by his condescension, however, she rebels against the presumption that her work is inferior because of her gender. In tellingly broken phrases indicating her own emerging sense of the importance of her work, she defiantly responds to her father's query as to why she intends to submit her work:

> Because I *made* it. Because it's my work. You all say it's good. Why shouldn't I send it? I don't mind failure. I only want it to stand its little chance with the rest. I love it. It means more to me than I can possibly—why shouldn't I? I *want* to. (910)

Ann's capturing of the prize precipitates a major crisis in her marriage, but Ann resists Tom's attempts to characterize her actions as selfish, pleading that he not ask her to give up her work: "Don't ask it! Don't ask it for your own sake. I want to keep on loving you. I want to believe that you're what I thought you were. Don't make me think you're just like every other man" (921). But what Tom cannot accomplish through bullying, Millicent manages to perform without effort. Confronted by the prospect of her daughter's precipitous decision to marry, Ann is overwhelmed by guilt when she learns that Millicent has fallen in love with the chauffeur when she has been forced to stay at the boarding school while her mother has been working on a project over a school vacation. Having rushed home to the security of her mother, Millicent inadvertently taps in to all of Ann's latent suspicion that there just might be a grain of truth in Tom's criticism. Forced into a choice between career and child, Ann can see no alternative to her dilemma.[35] Nevertheless, she is fully aware of the cost of the choice that she is making. Acknowledging Tom's assertion that at times she will eat her heart out to be at work on her art, she agonizes: "And I'll hate you because you're doing it—and I'll hate myself because I gave it up—and I'll almost—hate—her" (928). But for Ann the anguish extends beyond her personal disappointment, for her sculpture has come to represent for her, and presumably for Crothers, not merely the personal accomplishment of an individual woman but concrete evidence of the potential of all women. Still, for Ann there is no choice, for Millicent is "part of my body—part of my soul" (928). With her dream overtaken by events that within her culture leave her no acceptable alternative to the choice she makes and effectively kill her attempts to reconcile career, marriage and motherhood, Ann leaves the stage ironically echoing another cultural outsider unable to accommodate his ideals to his perceived circumstances. As the lights dim on the emotional wreckage of her life, she says with Othello, "Put out the light" (928). But for Ann, Crothers suggests, the possibility of tragic self-assertion does not exist. Even that has been taken from her by the ideological force of a culture unwilling to provide a place for women, even women of genius.

He and She represents Crothers's bleakest prewar picture of the fate of women. Acculturated to roles as wives and mothers, women are, the play suggests, forced either to opt for the emotionally sterile life of complete independence or to face the prospect of foregoing their careers at pivotal moments to fulfill obligations which the culture insists are finally theirs alone. Though Crothers can dignify the struggle of women in ways that had heretofore not been accomplished by any writer, male or female, she cannot completely escape (any more than her characters can) the cultural assumptions which ground her experience. Her vision of the human dilemma, because it focuses almost exclusively upon women and takes as a given the cultural presumption that men will not change, places her squarely within the feminist movement of the period. Crothers's view, reflected in her configuration of the issue, in her use of dialogue, in her reliance upon the commercial theater as a vehicle for disseminating her vision, is that the central obstacle for women is their lack of uninhibited access to the patriarchy's seats of power. For Susan Glaspell the issue is far more fundamental. Do women have an alternative means to construct an authentic existence?

Though usually remembered today primarily as one of the founding members and guiding forces of the Provincetown Players, Susan Glaspell is also a playwright of significance to the development of twentieth-century American drama.[36] While Crothers chose to work within the commercial theater with its constant economically driven restrictions, Glaspell's association with the Provincetown Players allowed her much greater artistic freedom. Ironically enough, this freedom was grounded in the economic and physical limitations of the Wharf Theatre in Provincetown, Mass. and its New York City successor, The Playwrights' Theatre. Small acting spaces, limited resources for sets and costumes, and a dearth of actors were in Glaspell's hands tools for composing tight one-act plays whose small casts and restricted action allow for forceful examinations of the confining daily realities encountered by the women who are the plays' centerpieces. Indeed, when Glaspell expands her cast of characters to deal with "larger" themes, as in *The People* (1917) and *Close the Book* (1917), her efforts fall flat, and the plays seem little more than a series of idealistic set speeches or opportunities for witty dialogue. In effect, they lose their dramatic essence. It is in *Trifles* (1916) and *The Outside* (1917) that Glaspell proves herself a master of the short form, developing intriguing social and psychological explorations of women frozen in a world which threatens to overwhelm them. But, as Ben-Zvi has cogently argued, Glaspell's plays accomplish this by providing a new structure and language, which combine to render characterizations appropriate to their new subject matter.[37]

Trifles, Glaspell's best-known work, was not in fact her first effort for the Provincetown Players. Collaborating with her husband, George Cram "Jig" Cook, Glaspell had earlier written *Suppressed Desires* (1915), an amusing satiric sketch of Freudian enthusiasts who discover complexes and phobias in every innocent action. With *Trifles*, Glaspell displays the power that was to be repeated only sporadically in such later plays as *The Verge* (1921) and her Pulitzer Prize-winning *Alison's House* (1931). Situated during a murder inquiry at the isolated farmhouse of the victim, John Wright, *Trifles* examines the emerging self-awareness of two women who have accompanied their husbands, the investigators of the strangulation. While the men disappear upstairs, where the murder occurred, the women remain downstairs in the kitchen, discovering as they survey the scene the motivation for the murder—and impulsively deciding to suppress the evidence. While action in the traditional sense is minimal, Glaspell is nevertheless able to rivet attention on the two women, wed the audience to their perspective, and make a compelling case for the fairness of their actions. Existing on the margins of their society, Mrs. Peters and Mrs. Hale become emotional surrogates for the jailed Minnie Wright, effectively exonerating her action as "justifiable homicide."

Trifles is carefully crafted to match Glaspell's subject matter—the action meanders, without a clearly delineated beginning, middle, or end. This resistance to approaching matters directly is rendered visually as the play opens. Emerging from the outside cold, the men move directly across the stage to a stove, while the women initially remain on the periphery of the set, standing close to the door. Having cursorily surveyed the kitchen and decided that nothing of consequence to their investigation exists within its confines, the men depart the scene, and the women begin to collect Mrs. Wright's personal belongings, which are the occasion for their presence. As they construct from the artifacts of Minnie Wright's life a psychological portrait of her, their random observations begin to form themselves into a pattern: Minnie's shabby clothes testify to her husband's miserliness; a bit of erratic stitching on some quilting material bears witness to her agitation; the broken birdcage and the dead bird provide evidence to the cruelty of John Wright. The women have discovered evidence pointing to the despair which has finally exploded from within Minnie. Surrendering themselves empathetically to the desperate loneliness that they have shared with Minnie, they are forced to rely upon a transparent fiction—"We don't know who killed him. We don't *know*"—in order to deal with the magnitude of what they have discovered.[38] Though in some sense they long to return to the safe ground of patriarchial authority in which the law rightly punishes crime, the women nonetheless discover in their own hearts the greater crime of having neglected Minnie, and realize that that crime is beyond the legality which their husbands embody. The men discover nothing which explains the crime and retreat from the farmhouse bewildered. The wives leave with the dead bird securely in Mrs. Hale's pocket and a new awareness that "We all go through the same things—it's all just a different kind of the same thing" (27).

The action and structure of *The Outside* may seem even more meager than that of *Trifles*. A group of men intrude upon a former life-saving station on the outside shore of Cape Cod in a vain attempt to save a drowning victim. The new owner of the house, Mrs. Patrick, resents the trespass as she has deliberately cut herself off from people in an attempt to deal with the pain of having been abandoned by her husband. As the men strive to resuscitate the drowned man, Mrs. Patrick becomes more and more agitated. Seeking to flee the house in the wake of the rescuers' temporary departure, she is arrested by the voice of her maid, Allie Mayo, heretofore known for her perpetual silence. The discussion which follows explores one of Glaspell's favorite themes, the struggle between the conflicting impulse toward life and death.[39] Metaphorically exploring the conflict between the creeping dunes and vegetable life which seeks to transform the dunes' useless sterility into the base for a renewed vitality, Allie reshapes Mrs. Patrick's emotional topography. Transforming her own twenty-year odyssey as a widow on the edge of life into a healing balm for her employer, Allie reaches out and rekindles a sense of the possibilities which Mrs. Patrick's pain has forced her to deny. Though what she says is itself tentatively formed, the authenticity of Allie's voice cannot be denied, and as the curtain descends, Mrs. Patrick embraces her pain and the prospect of life which its acceptance holds.

Just as Glaspell has developed a new structure for her action, so too the language of her plays reflects the emerging consciousness of her central character. Most of Glaspell's women characters find speech difficult either from long silence or from a particularly traumatic set of circumstances. When they do speak, especially in the transformative moments which are the center of these two plays, they do so tentatively. The dashes which pervade Glaspell's dialogue graphically suggest women's silenced past and, often, the apprehension these women feel at verbalizing thoughts which are well beyond the psychic limits they have previously known. As Ben-Zvi notes,

> Appropriately it is a language of stops and starts, with lacunae—dashes—covering the truths they still cannot admit or are unused to framing in words. What the audience sees and hears are people learning to speak, constructing a medium of expression as they go. The way is not easy, and the language they frame is awkward. But it is clearly their language, no longer the words of others which they have been taught to speak. (157)

Part of this new linguistic awareness is seen in the elevation of the domestic matters of their daily lives from their previous position as mere trifles to instruments of significant insight. In *Trifles*, for instance, the central image of the play is derived from quilting.[40] Three times in the course of the play, the men and women discuss the means of uniting the various pieces that Minnie Wright had formed for a quilt. When Mrs. Peters first innocently inquires, "I wonder if she was goin' to quilt it or just knot it" (17), she is embarrassed by the laughter of the men. On the second occasion, immediately after the women have discovered the bird with its neck wrung, they are condescendingly asked by the county attorney if they have reached a conclusion, and they inadvertently reveal their growing suspicion that Mrs. Wright has committed the murder by answering "We think she was going to—knot it" (24). Significantly, Glaspell returns to the image in the final line of the play when Mrs. Hale again repeats to the Attorney's inquiry, "We call it—knot it, Mr. Henderson" (30). The homely quilting phrase has become a means of at once answering and refusing to answer patriarchal authority, for the women, having discovered both the motive and the reason for the method Mrs. Wright employed, are intent upon negating the men's investigation. In a grotesque play on words, they will simultaneously name "it" but dispute its existence, "k(not) it," denying the patriarchy the very mechanism of power—language—which it seeks to wield against Minnie Wright in the form of Hale's recitation of his conversation with Mrs. Wright the previous day.

The construction of plots which violate traditional rules of dramatic structure, the centering of action on characters who are either not physically present (Minnie Wright) or are emotionally absent (Mrs. Patrick), and the development of means of providing women an idiom— all are accomplishments which establish Susan Glaspell as a central figure in early twentieth-century American drama. Within the liberating circumstances of the avant-garde theatre which she helped to form and guide, Glaspell was able to explore through new means the nature of the woman's life in America. If her women lack the exceptional abilities and force of will of Crothers's protagonists, they are in some ways better indexes of the toll that patriarchy's operation had taken on the women of America. And in her striving after a language for women, Glaspell, more than seventy years ago, anticipated a search that continues today.

As the world plunged headlong into the cataclysm of World War I, the American drama—led by a handful of theater groups dominated by Glaspell and Cook's Provincetown Players, and especially its most famous member, Eugene O'Neill—ended the provincialism of its early history and abruptly entered an entirely new artistic phase. The social, political, and gender assumptions which had underpinned American drama—both those persisting from an earlier era and those that had emerged in the period immediately before the war—were swept aside. The first and most significant casualty of that war was the loss of America's isolated innocence, its conviction that the nation could remain aloof from and somehow unaffected by the carnage being unleashed by the ancient antagonists of European nationalism.

Destroyed in the process was the equally innocent belief in an American drama which was finally and quintessentially American. The world, which America had for so long resisted acknowledging, had intruded upon the American consciousness with such force that never again could the national drama ignore its reality as a reflector of experience that extended far beyond the shores of America. Dramatists such as Glaspell and Crothers continued to write for the stage, but their plays were inevitably colored by the experience of the war and its aftermath. Important new writers arose to give voice and form to new American realities—and the ideas, themes, and forms in the dramatic expression of those realities were firmly linked as never before to life elsewhere.

chronology

Date	Drama, Literature, Art*	World and National Events
1665	*Ye Bare and Ye Cubb,* first recorded dramatic performance in America (Virginia).	New Jersey colony founded; Great Plague of London.
1714	Robert Hunter's *Androboros* (p).	Queen Anne dies; George I succeeds to English throne.
1716– 1718	William Levingstone erects first colonial playhouse, Williamsburg, Va.	1718: Quadruple Alliance formed; New Orleans founded.
1752	Lewis Hallam's acting company produces first professional performance in America, *The Merchant of Venice,* Williamsburg, Va.	Franklin performs electricity experiment using kite; Great Britain adopts Georgian calendar.

*Unless marked (p) for publication, dates indicate production of plays.

1753	Lewis Hallam builds first theater in New York City.	
1764	*The Paxton Boys* (p).	British Parliament passes Sugar Act and American colonies protest; Dr. Johnson and others found The Literary Club.
1766	Robert Rogers's *Ponteach* (p).	Mason-Dixon Line drawn; William Pitt created Earl of Chatham.
1767	Thomas Godfrey's *The Prince of Parthia*.	Townshend Acts places duties on tea, glass, and paper in American colonies; New York Assembly refuses to support quartering of British troops.
1771	Robert Munford's *The Candidates* composed; *The Trial of Atticus*; Benjamin West paints "The Death of General Wolfe."	Russia and Prussia agree about partition of Poland.
1772	Mercy Otis Warren's *The Adulateur*	Samuel Adams leads formation of Committees of Correspondence.
1773	Warren's *The Defeat*; Theater opens in Charleston, S.C.	Tea Act incites Boston Tea Party.
1775	Thomas Paine's *A Dialogue Between General Wolfe and General Gage in a Wood Near Boston*.	Skirmishes at Lexington and Concord begin American Revolution; Battle of Bunker Hill.
1776	Paine's *A Dialogue Between the Ghost of General Montgomery, Just Arrived from the Elysian Fields, and an American Delegate, in a Wood near Philadelphia*; Hugh Henry Brackenridge's *The Battle of Bunker's Hill*; John Leacock's *The Fall of British Tyranny*; *The Battle of Brooklyn*.	Paine's *Common Sense*; American Declaration of Independence signed. British capture New York; Washington defeats Hessians at Trenton.

1777	Brackenridge's *The Death of General Montgomery*.	Washington defeats British at Princeton, N.J., but loses at Brandywine and Germantown. Washington sets up winter quarters at Valley Forge.
1777–79(?)	Munford's *The Patriots* composed.	1778: France allies itself with American colonies.
1779	John Smith's "A Dialogue between and Englishman and an Indian."	John Paul Jones wins naval encounter off English coast.
1783	First daily newspaper in U.S., *The Pennsylvania Evening Post* begins publication.	Treaty of Paris ends American Revolution.
1787	Royall Tyler's *The Contrast*; John Burk's *Bunker-Hill*.	Congress enacts Northwest Ordinace; U.S. Constitution drafted and sent to states for ratification.
1798	William Dunlap's *Andre*.	On brink of war with France, Congress passes the Alien and Sedition Acts.
1812	James Nelson Barker's *Marmion*.	War of 1812 begins; ends with Treaty of Utrecht (1814).
1818	John Howard Payne's *Brutus*.	Andrew Jackson leads U.S. forces against Seminoles in Fla.; *Savannah* becomes first steamboat to cross Atlantic.
1824	Barker's *Superstition*	U.S. presidential election ends without an electoral winner; Jedediah Smith discovers passage through the Rockies.
1825	Samuel Woodworth's *The Forest Rose*; Thomas Cole founds Hudson River School of landscape painting.	House of Representatives elects John Quincy Adams U.S. President; Congress adopts policy of removing eastern Native American tribes to territory west of the Mississippi River.
1829	John Augustus Stone's *Metamora*.	Andrew Jackson introduces spoils system.

1830	James Kirke Paulding's *The Lion of the West*; Daniel Emmet composes popular minstrel song, "Old Dan Tucker."	Congress passes Removal Bill, establishing Indian Territory in modern-day Oklahoma; Joseph Smith founds the Church of Jesus Christ of Latter-day Saints (Mormon).
1831	Robert Montgomery Bird's *The Gladiator*; Poe's *Poems by Edgar Allan Poe* (p); Paulding's *The Dutchman's Fireside* (p).	Nat Turner's rebellion; William Lloyd Garrison founds *The Liberator*.
1832	Bird's *Oralloossa*; Boston Academy of Music founded.	Black Hawk War in Ill. and Wisc.; Jackson reelected; Cholera epidemics in most major American cities.
1834	Bird's *The Broker of Bogota*; Dunlap's *History of the Rise and Progress of the Arts of Design in the United States* (p).	Whig Party founded; Cyrus McCormick patents automatic reaper.
1838	Louisa Medina's *Nick of the Woods*.	Cherokee nation forcibly removed from Georgia to Indian Territory; Morse Code introduced.
1839	Joseph S. Jones's *The People's Lawyer*; Longfellow's *Voices of the Night* (p).	Charles Goodyear accidentally discovers vulcanized rubber. Chartist riots in England.
1845	Anna Cora Mowatt's *Fashion*; Margaret Fuller's *Woman in the Nineteenth Century* (p).	Texas annexed; Smithsonian Institution founded; Elias Howe patents lock-stitch sewing machine.
1847	John Brougham's *Metamora; or, The Last of the Pollywogs* ends "Indian" play vogue; Melville's *Omoo* (p); Christey Minstrels at Mechanics Hall on Broadway.	Mexican War (1846–48); California under American control; Women's Rights Convention held Seneca Falls, N.Y.
1850	W. R. Derr's *Kit Carson*; Hawthorne's *The Scarlet Letter* (p).	Compromise of 1850; Fugitive Slave Act.
1852	Harriet Beecher Stowe's *Uncle Tom's Cabin* (p).	Pierce elected President; French Second Empire established by plebiscite.

1853	George Aiken's adaptation of *Uncle Tom's Cabin*.	Commodore Perry arrives in Japan; Gadsden Purchase.
1855	George Henry Boker's *Francesca da Rimini*; Whitman's *Leaves of Grass* (p).	"Bleeding Kansas" becomes site of violence between abolitionist and pro-slavery forces.
1859	Dion Boucicault's *The Octoroon*; Daniel Emmet writes "Dixie."	John Brown's raid on Harper's Ferry.
1860	Boucicault's *The Colleen Bawn*.	Lincoln elected President; South Carolina secedes.
1865	Boucicault's *Arrah-na-Pogue*; Whitman's *Drum Taps* (p).	Civil War (1861–1865) ends; actor John Wilkes Booth assassinates President Lincoln.
1867	Augustin Daly's *Under the Gaslight*; Horatio Alger's *Ragged Dick*, first rags-to-riches story (p).	Congress passes Reconstruction Acts; U.S. buys Alaska.
1868	Daly's *A Flash of Lightning*.	President Johnson impeached; Fourteenth Amendment to U.S. Constitution ratified.
1871	Daly's *Horizon*; Whitman's "Democratic Vistas" (p).	"Boss" William Marcy Tweed of Tammany Hall indicted.
1872	Steele MacKaye's *Marriage*; Frank Murdock's *Davy Crockett*.	*Alabama* claims settled; Grant reelected President.
1874	Boucicault's *The Shaughraun*.	First Chautaqua Assembly meets at Chautaqua Lake, N.Y.: Women's Christian Temperance Union formed in Cleveland, Ohio.
1876	Twain's *The Adventures of Tom Sawyer* (p); James's *Roderick Hudson* (p).	Battle of Little Bighorn; Hayes elected President.
1877	Joaquin Miller's *The Danites in the Sierras*; William Dean Howells's *A Counterfeit Presentment*.	Reconstruction ends; First national railway workers' strike.
1879	Bartley Campbell's *My Partner*; James's *Daisy Miller* (p); George	U.S. returns to gold standard; Mary Baker Eddy founds the

	Washington Cable's *Old Creole Days* (p).	Church of Christ, Scientist in Boston.
1880s and 1890s	Howells writing popular one-acts in *Harper's* and *The Atlantic Monthly*.	
1880	MacKaye's *Hazel Kirke*; Joel Chandler Harris's *Uncle Remus* (p).	Garfield elected President; Andrew Carnegie begins establishing libraries.
1882	Campbell's *The White Slave*; Bronson Howard's *Young Mrs. Winthrop*; Ibsen's *A Doll's House* performed in English in Milwaukee, Wisc.	Congress passes Chinese Exclusion Act and act barring "undesirables"; first Labor Day celebrated.
1886	William Gillette's *Held by the Enemy*; James's *The Bostonians* (p).	Presidential Succession Act; Geronimo surrenders; Haymarket Square Riot in Chicago.
1887	MacKaye's *Paul Kauvar; or, Anarchy*; Howard's *The Henrietta*; Doyle begins writing stories about Sherlock Holmes.	Interstate Commerce Act; Melvil Dewey founds State Library School in Albany, N.Y. and devises Dewey decimal system for libraries.
1888	Howard's *Shenandoah*; Edward Bellamy's *Looking Backward* (p).	Benjamin Harrison elected President; Department of Labor established.
1890	Charles H. Hoyt's *A Texas Steer*; James A. Herne's *Margaret Fleming*; Howell's *A Hazard of New Fortunes* (p).	Congress passes Sherman Antitrust Act and McKinley Tariff Acts; U.S. troops massacre 200 Sioux at Wounded Knee, S.D.
1891	Jacob Riis's *How the Other Half Lives*; Dickinson's *Poems: Second Series* (p).	Circuit Courts of Appeal established; University of Chicago founded from endowment of John D. Rockefeller.
1892	Herne's *Shore Acres*.	Populist Party formed; strike against Carnegie steel plant in Pennsylvania erupts into

		violence; Cleveland elected President.
1895	David Belasco's *The Heart of Maryland*; Gillette's *Secret Service*; Crane's *The Red Badge of Courage* (p).	Supreme Court declares income tax unconstitutional; Sears, Roebuck Company opens a mail-order business.
1898	Henry James's *The Turn of the Screw*; Paul Laurence Dunbar's *The Uncalled* (p).	U.S. battleship *Maine* blown up in Havana harbor; Spanish-American War.
1899	Gillette's *Sherlock Holmes*; Herne's *Griffith Davenport* and *Sag Harbor*.	U.S. fights guerrilla war in Philippines; U.S. annexes Wake Island.
1901	Clyde Fitch's *The Climbers*; Frank Norris's *The Octopus* (p).	President McKinley assassinated; Theodore Roosevelt becomes President.
1905	David Belasco's *The Girl of the Golden West*; Augustin Daly arrested for producing Shaw's *Mrs. Warren's Profession*—he is later acquitted.	President Roosevelt mediates end to Russo-Japanense War; International Workers of the World (Wobblies) founded by Eugene Debs in Chicago.
1906	Langdon Mitchell's *The New York Idea*; William Vaughn Moody's *The Great Divide*; Rachel Crothers's *The Three of Us*.	Pure Food and Drug Act and Meat Inspection Act passed by Congress; Troops quell Atlanta race riot; San Francisco earthquake.
1907	Augustus Thomas's *The Witching Hour*.	U.S. intervenes in Honduras; Second Hague Conference again upholds Monroe Doctrine; Panic of 1907.
1908	Edward Sheldon's *Salvation Nell*; Percy MacKaye's *The Scarecrow*.	Supreme Court rules labor boycott is illegal; Taft elected President; Henry Ford produces the Model T.
1909	Eugene Walter's *The Easiest Way*; Clyde Fitch's *The City*; Sheldon's *The Nigger*; Moody's *The Faith Healer*; Crothers's *A Man's World*.	National Association for the Advancement of Colored People (NAACP) founded in New York; Perry expedition reaches North Pole; Freud lectures in U.S. on psychoanalysis.

1910	Josephine Peabody's *The Piper*.	Interstate Commerce Commission gains jurisdiction over telephones, telegraph, and cable companies; Boy Scouts of America founded.
1911	Sheldon's *The Boss*; Thomas's *As a Man Thinks*; Crothers's *He and She*.	National Progressive Republican League founded; Supreme Court orders dissolution of Standard Oil Company.
1915	Susan Glaspell's *Suppressed Desires*.	*Lusitania* sunk; U.S. Marines intervene in Haiti.
1916	Susan Glaspell's *Trifles*.	Gen. John J. Pershing sent into Mexico to pursue Francisco ("Pancho") Villa; President Wilson sends ultimatum to German government concerning continued sinking of U.S. ships.
1917	Glaspell's *The Outside*.	U.S. purchases Virgin Islands from Denmark; U.S. declares war on Germany; draft established by Selective Service Act.

notes and references

Prologue

1. Eric Mordden, *The American Theatre* (New York: Oxford University Press, 1981), 346.

Chapter 1

1. *The Poems and Letters of Andrew Marvell*, H. M. Margoliouth, ed., 2 vols., 3rd ed. (Oxford: Clarendon Press, 1971), 1: 18.

2. The psychological and epistemological roots of the Puritan antipathy to the drama are explored by Leverenz and Tichi, respectively.

3. John Smith, "A Dialogue Between an Englishman and an Indian," *Dramas from the American Theatre, 1762–1909*, Richard Moody, ed. (Cleveland: World Publishing, 1966), 8. All quotations from this play cited in the text are from this edition.

4. Smith's benign attitude toward Native Americans and his interest in their education seems natural as Dartmouth College had evolved from a charity school for Native Americans originally situated in Connecticut.

5. In the wake of the Glorious Revolution of 1688, Jacob Leisler led a revolt against Lt. Governor Francis Nicholson, the subordinate of James II's royal governor for the Dominion of New England. Having seized the fort at New York, Leisler established a revolutionary government which ruled the colony until March 1691, when Leisler finally surrendered authority to representatives of William and Mary. Despite his having surrendered the fort, Leisler, along with his son-in-law, Jacob Milbourne, were hanged for treason in May 1691. For a complete discussion of this episode see Jerome R. Reich, *Leisler's Rebellion: A Study of Democracy in New York, 1664–1720* (Chicago: University of Chicago Press, 1953).

6. Robert Hunter, *Androboros, Satiric Comedies*, Walter J. Meserve and William R. Reardon, eds. (Bloomington: Indiana University, 1969), 17. All quotations from this play cited in the text are from this edition.

7. Robert E. Moody, ed. [Boston's First Play]. *Proceedings of the Massachusetts Historical Society* 92 (1980): 139. All quotations from this play cited in the text are taken from this edition. The original manuscript is located in the Massachusetts Historical Society.

8. *The Paxton Boys: A Farce*. Translated from the Original *French* by a Native of *Donegall*. (Philadelphia: Anthony Ambuster, 1764), 7. All quotations from this play cited in the text are from this edition.

9. *The Trial of Atticus, Before Justice Beau, for a Rape. Satiric Comedies*. Walter J. Meserve and William R. Reardon, eds. (Bloomington: Indiana University, 1969), 49. All quotations from this play cited in the text are from this edition.

10. For an extensive discussion of the recurrent themes and techniques of political satire employed in the period, see Bernard Bailyn's magisterial *Ideological Origins of the American Revolution*, especially on the issues of elections and their attendant corruptions, 94–159.

11. Robert Munford, *The Candidates, Or the Humours of a Virginia Election, Dramas from the American Theatre, 1762–1909*, Richard Moody, ed. (Cleveland: World Publishing, 1966), 18. All quotations from this play cited in the text are from this edition.

12. I can find no textual evidence to support Quinn's speculation (*Beginnings*, 55), repeated by Richard Moody (12) and Vaughn (23), that Ralpho, Wou'dbe's servant, is a slave. Since Munford owned slaves, was familiar with their speech patterns, and carefully distinguished linguistically among various social classes in the play, it seems improbable that he would not suggest that Ralpho was a slave through his speeches. The distinction of being the first African-

American in the American drama should probably fall to Raccoon, who appeared in Forrest's comic-opera *The Disappointment*, published in 1767. Caesar, who appears briefly in *The Trial of Atticus*, is the first African-American in a nonmusical.

13. The influence of Whig history on the political thinking of pre-revolutionary America is examined at length in both Colburn and Bailyn.

14. The literary borrowings of Godfrey are discussed at length by Pollock and McCarron.

15. Thomas Godfrey, *The Prince of Parthia, Representative American Plays, From 1767 to the Present Day,* Arthur Hobson Quinn, ed., 7th ed. (New York: Appleton-Century-Crofts, 1957), 38. All quotations from this play cited in the text are from this edition.

16. For a contrasting opinion as to the play's contemporary relevance see Meserve (50).

17. In the subsequent discussion, I have retained Rogers's original phonetic spelling, though his central character has generally been known to students of American history as Pontiac.

18. Robert Rogers, *Ponteach; or, The Savages of America, Representative Plays by American Dramatists,* Montrose J. Moses, ed., 3 vols. (New York: Dutton, 1918–21), 1: 118. All quotations from this play cited in the text are from this edition.

Chapter 2

1. Originally published in the *Pennsylvania Packet* 19 February 1776, it was quickly reprinted by Robert Bell as a pamphlet in the same year.

2. The charade of the radical Whig Club is maintained on the title page which asserts that the pamphlet has been "Printed by Order of the Robin-Hood Society."

3. The original 1774 edition was published by Rivington, the well-known New York Tory. My source is the reprinted edition in *Trumpets Sounding: Propaganda Plays of the American Revolution,* Norman Philbrick, ed. (New York: Blom, 1972), 27–38. All quotations from this play cited in the text are from this edition.

4. The complete title continues, *"Being the substance of a conversation on the times, over a friendly tankard and pipe between Sharp, a country parson, Bumper, a country justice, Fillpot, an inn-keeper, Graveairs, a deacon, Trim, a barber, Brim, a Quaker, Puff, a late Representative. Taken in short-hand by Sir Roger de Coverly."*

5. Philbrick makes a similar point, 1–3.

6. The issue of Warren's authorship of these two plays is discussed by Katharine Anthony, *First Lady of the Revolution: The Life of Mercy Otis Warren* 1958; Rpt. (Port Washington, New York: Kennikat, 1972), 108–15, Benjamin Franklin, V, ed. *The Plays and Poems of Mercy Otis Warren* (Delmar, New York: Scholar's Facsimiles and Reprints, 1980), xvii–xviii, xxiii, and Philbrick, 137–42, 341–344. While the data is inconclusive, I am persuaded sufficiently by the internal and external evidence to treat them as Warren's in lieu of other compelling candidates.

7. Her brief effort was expanded by an unsolicited collaborator, who added two acts and shifted the dramatic focus to the Boston Massacre of 1770. On the question of Warren's collaborator, see Franklin and Anthony.

8. Mercy Otis Warren, *The Adulateur, The Plays and Poems of Mercy Otis Warren*, Benjamin Franklin ed. (Delmar, New York: Scholars' Facsimiles and Reprints, 1980). All quotations from Warren's plays cited in the text are from this edition.

9. John W. Teunissen, "Blockheadism and the Propaganda Plays of the American Revolution," *Early American Literature* 7 (1972): 157.

10. Hugh Henry Brackenridge, *The Battle of Bunkers-Hill, Representative Plays by American Dramatists*, 3 vols., Montrose J. Moses, ed. (New York: Dutton, 1918–21), 1: 253. All quotations from this play cited in the text are from this edition.

11. Hugh Henry Brackenridge, *The Death of General Montgomery in Storming the City of Quebec, Trumpets Sounding*, Norman Philbrick, ed. (New York: Blom, 1972), 246.

12. The title continues *A tragi-comedy of Five Acts. As Lately Planned at the Royal Theatrum Pandemonium at St. James's. The Principal Place of Action in America.* John Leacock, *The Fall of British Tyranny; or, American Liberty, Representative Plays by American Dramatists*, 3 vols., Montrose J. Moses, ed. (New York: Dutton, 1918–21), 1: 279. All quotations from this play cited in the text are from this edition. Despite Philbrick's demur, 41–42, I am convinced by Dallett's argument in "John Leacock and THE FALL OF BRITISH TYRANNY," *Pennsylvania Magazine of History and Biography* 78 (1954): 456–75, that Leacock was the author of *The Fall of British Tyranny*.

13. In addition to Chatham, Leacock specifies as America's allies the Bishop of St. Asaph (Lord Religion), the Earl of Camden (Lord Justice), John Wilkes (Lord Patriot), Edmund Burke (Bold Irishman), and Colonel Barre (the Colonel). The most comprehensive discussion of the political events and personalities to which the play refers can be found in Philbrick (42–56).

14. Lord Religion and Lord Justice extend Wisdom's indictment, respec-

tively, to the churches and the courts, suggesting that neither moral suasion nor constitutional mandates will provide any stay against the evil of Paramount. The conversation among Lord Patriot, Bold Irishman, and the Colonel in the act's second scene provides the opportunity not only to reflect in detail on the public statements of Brazen (Wedderburn), one of Bute's most vociferous lieutenants, but also to expand the sense of English support for America's cause.

15. *The Battle of Brooklyn, Satiric Comedies*, Walter J. Meserve and William R. Reardon, eds., vol. 21, *America's Lost Plays* (Bloomington: Indiana University Press, 1969), 101. All quotations from this play cited in the text are from this edition.

16. These formal debts are suggested by Calhoun Winton, "Theater and Drama," *American Literature, 1764–1789: The Revolutionary Years*, Everett Emerson, ed. (Madison: University of Wisconsin Press, 1977), 97. Another, perhaps even more pertinent, source for the play is Sir Robert Howard's *The Committee* (1662), which similarly refuses to resolve the political tensions it examines in the closure provided for the romantic action. An analogy between the Commonwealth Puritans and the radical Whigs of his own day would no doubt have appealed to Munford.

17. Robert Munford, *The Patriots*, Courtlandt Canby, ed., *William and Mary Quarterly*, 3d ser. 6 (1949): 452. All quotations from this play cited in the text are from this edition.

18. For a discussion of reasons for the anti-Scotch feeling in Munford's Virginia see Canby, 438–39, n. 1.

Chapter 3

1. The contrast of American and European lifestyles, always to the advantage of America and her citizenry, became a popular formula in the years after independence. Other examples include the anonymous *The Better Sort* (1789), which again indicts the English; James Nelson Barker's *Tears and Smiles* (1807), which suggests that the Gallic influence is potentially as pernicious as that of the British; and Joseph Hutton's *Fashionable Follies* (1815), which generalizes the accusation to all of Europe.

2. Royall Tyler, *The Contrast, Representative American Plays from 1767 to the Present Day*, Arthur Hobson Quinn, ed. 7th ed. (New York: Appleton-Century-Crofts, 1957), 67.

3. For general agreement on the satire directed at Manly, see Ada Lou Carson and Herbert L. Carson, *Royall Tyler* (Boston: Twayne, 1979), 32.

4. In fact, Stein argues that critics have generally overlooked or misun-

derstood "the extent to which *The Contrast* is thematically concerned with questions of language" (455).

5. The standard biographies of Dunlap are Oral Sumner Coad, *William Dunlap* 1917; Rpt. (New York: Russell & Russell, 1962) and Robert H. Canary, *William Dunlap* (New York: Twayne, 1970).

6. Dunlap relates his brief tenure with Benjamin West in his *History of the Rise and Progress of the Arts of Design in the United States*, 3 vols. (New York, 1834), 1: 303–310. All quotations from this play cited in the text as *Arts* are from this edition.

7. William Dunlap, *History of the American Theatre*, 2 vols. 1832; Rpt. (New York: Burt Franklin, 1963), 1: 287. All quotations from this play cited in the text as *Theatre* are from this edition.

8. On the issue of cultural attitudes in the period after the Revolution see Joseph J. Ellis, *After the Revolution: Profile of Early American Culture* (New York: Norton, 1979).

9. For an exploration of popularity of Kotzebue, among others, see Francois Jost, "German and French Themes in Early American Drama," *JGE: The Journal of General Education* 28, 3 (Fall, 1976): 190–222.

10. Typical is Dunlap's observation that Kotzebue's talent "was not uniformly exerted in strengthening those moral restraints which are the safeguards of society and the foundation of human happiness; his pen was in early life devoted to wild and pernicious views of morals and manners, and afterwards to the defense of a system [monarchy] which can only be supported upon the debasement of the human race" (*Theatre*, 2, 88). For a quite different view of Kotzebue, see Jack Zipes, "Dunlap, Kotzebue, and the Shaping of American Theatre: A Reevaluation from a Marxist Perspective," *Early American Literature* 8 (1974): 272–289.

11. Kotzebue's influence on Dunlap is discussed at length in Grimsted, 8–15.

12. Dunlap recognized the potential problems for dramatic art in an open-market arena and argued that the theatre should be supported by government, *Theatre*, 2, 358–64.

13. See Norman Philbrick, "The Spy as Hero: An Examination of *Andre* by William Dunlap," *Studies in Theatre and Drama: Essays in Honor of Hubert C. Heffner* (The Hague: Mouton, 1972), 98.

14. William Dunlap, *Andre, Representative American Plays from 1767 to the Present Day*, Arthur Hobson Quinn, ed., 7th ed. (New York: Appleton-Century Crofts, 1957), 96. All quotations from this play cited in the text are from this edition.

15. The range of responses to Andre's dilemma is relatively straightfor-

ward and critics have generally agreed that Dunlap has neatly posited reason (M'Donald) against sentiment (Bland) and has reconciled them through justice (the General and, ironically, Andre). On this point see, Canary, 92.

16. Jay Martin, "William Dunlap: The Documentary Vision," *Theater und Drama in Amerika*, Edgar Lohner and Rudolf Haas, eds. (Berlin: Ench Schmidt Verlay, 1978), 181, has noted the importance of Scottish philosophers. For a more detailed discussion of both the debate structure and Dunlap's epistemology see Martin's essay.

17. The definitive biography of Barker remains Paul H. Musser, *James Nelson Barker* (Philadelphia: University of Pennsylvania Press, 1929).

18. Indicative of this attitude is Barker's comment to William Dunlap in 1832 (eight years after Barker had written his last play) that since he is writing to Dunlap on Sunday, the "work-day world cannot find fault, however I may deserve the censure of *holy*-day folks." Dunlap, *Theatre*, 2, 308.

19. This letter is reproduced in Dunlap, *Theatre*, 2, 308–16.

20. Musser cites, for example, Barker's going to the expense of securing passes in the 1820s to both the Olympic and Chestnut Street theaters in Philadelphia (83).

21. For a more comprehensive discussion of Barker's dramatic commentaries as indices of his dramatic aesthetic, see Gary A. Richardson, "In the Shadow of the Bard: Republican Drama and the Shakespearean Legacy," *When They Weren't Doing Shakespeare*, Judith L. Fisher and Stephen Watt, eds. (Athens: University of Georgia Press, 1990).

22. James Nelson Barker, *Tears and Smiles*, Rpt. Musser, 141.

23. James Nelson Barker, *The Indian Princess, Representative Plays by American Dramatists*, Montrose J. Moses, ed., 3 vols. (New York: E. P. Dutton, 1918–21), 1: 576.

24. James Nelson Barker, *Marmion* (New York: Longworth, 1816), iii. All quotations from this play cited in the text are from this edition.

25. James Nelson Barker, "The Drama," *Democratic Press* [Philadelphia] 18 December 1816: 2. Barker published a series of these articles all under the same title between 18 December 1816 and 19 February 1817.

26. My discussions of both *Marmion* and *Superstition* are obviously indebted to Harold Bloom's various discussions of "the anxiety of influence." While it is tempting to think that Barker's "readings" of previous English literature were too overt to partake of that phenomenon, it is perhaps wise to remember Bloom's pointed observation that "any poem is an inter-poem, and any reading of a poem is an inter-reading." *Poetry and Repression: Revisionism from Blake to Stevens* (New Haven: Yale University Press, 1976), 3.

27. For the intriguing details, see Musser, 47.

28. James Nelson Barker, *Superstition, Representative American Plays from 1767 to the Present Day*, Arthur Hobson Quinn, ed., 7th ed. (New York: Appleton-Century Crofts, 1957), 117. All quotations from this play cited in the text are from this edition.

Chapter 4

1. For a comprehensive analysis of the contemporary critical commentary see Walter J. Meserve, *An Emerging Entertainment* (Bloomington: Indiana University Press, 1977), 224–32.

2. The most insightful analysis of the romantic phenomenon remains Richard J. Moody, *America Takes the Stage: Romanticism in American Theatre and Drama, 1750–1900* (Bloomington: Indiana University Press, 1955). For the current discussion, see especially pp. 1–31.

3. Irving ended his work with Payne when it became apparent that neither monetary reward nor literary reputation would accrue from his investment of time and effort. For a detailed discussion of Payne and Irving's collaboration see the standard biography of Payne, Grace Overmyer, *America's First Hamlet* (New York: New York University Press, 1957), 223–238.

4. Payne's heartbroken Brutus dying of grief at Titus's loss contradicts not only the story as rendered by Livy and Plutarch but the import of the story's best-known visual rendition, Jacques-Louis David's "Brutus Receiving the Bodies of his Sons" (1789).

5. The definitive biography of Bird remains Clement Foust, *The Life and Dramatic Works of Robert Montgomery Bird* (New York: Knickerbocker Press, 1919). An abbreviated discussion is available in Curtis Dahl, *Robert Montgomery Bird* (New York: Twayne, 1963).

6. Robert Montgomery Bird, *The Gladiator, Dramas from the American Theatre, 1762–1909*, ed. Richard Moody (Cleveland, Ohio: World Publishing Company, 1966), 251. All quotations from this play cited in the text are from this edition.

7. Robert Montgomery Bird, *The Broker of Bogota, Representative American Plays From 1767 to the Present Day*, ed. Arthur Hobson Quinn, 7th ed. (New York: Appleton-Century-Crofts, 1957), 204–05. All quotations from this play cited in the text are from this edition.

8. On the changing familial roles and attitudes in early nineteenth-century America, see Robert Wiebe, *The Opening of American Society* (New York: Vintage, 1984), 265–72, 275–81.

9. Edward Sculley Bradley, *George Henry Boker, Poet and Patriot* (Philadelphia: University of Pennsylvania Press, 1927). For a comprehensive contemporary estimation of Boker's entire literary career see Oliver H. Evans, *George Henry Boker* (Boston: Twayne, 1984), hereafter cited as Evans, *Boker* in the text.

10. For the theatrical history of Boker's masterwork, see Arthur Hobson Quinn, *A History of the American Drama from the Beginning to the Civil War* 2d ed. (New York: Crofts, 1943), 348–50; and Claude R. Flory, "Boker, Barrett, and the Francesca Theme," *Players* 50 (1975): 58–61, 80.

11. On Boker's use of English and Italian sources for his plot and characterizations, see Arthur Noel Kincaid, "Italian and English Sources of Boker's 'Francesca Da Rimini'," *American Transcendental Quarterly* 1 (1969): 91–100; Jules Zanger, "*Francesca da Rimini*: The Brothers Tragedy," *Educational Theatre Journal* 25 (1973): 410–19; and Oliver H. Evans, "Shakespearean Prototypes and the Failure of Boker's *Francesca da Rimini*," *Educational Theatre Journal* 30 (1978): 211–19; hereafter cited as Evans, "Shakespearean".

12. The lone exception to the general praise for the play arises from Evans, who contends in both "Shakespearean" (219) and *Boker* (131) that the play fails because the disparate elements of Lanciotto's characterization are never brought together to form a consistent character.

13. Kent G. Gallagher, "The Tragedies of George Henry Boker: The Measure of American Romantic Drama," *ESQ* 20 (1974): 194.

14. Joseph Wood Krutch, "George Henry Boker," *Sewanee Review* 25 (1917): 463.

15. George Henry Boker, *Francesca da Rimini, Representative American Plays From 1767 to the Present Day*, Arthur Hobson Quinn, ed., 7th ed. (New York: Appleton-Century-Crofts, 1957), 337. All quotations from this play cited in the text are from this edition.

16. Zanger notes that the inversion of the seducer-seduced sexual roles borders on the comic when Paolo begins to bewail his lost virtue after he has made love with Francesca (415).

Chapter 5

1. It is worth noting that Forrest's characterization of Metamora, which no doubt reflected his firsthand knowledge of Native Americans, may have modified in performance the force of the literary conventions within which Stone worked. For an account of Forrest's 1825 interlude among the Native Americans of Louisiana, see Richard A. Moody, 47–48.

2. The popularity of the "Indian" plays is suggested by the list of forty-

seven plays produced between 1821 and 1858 (Peavy). Ironically, as Native Americans increasingly found a metaphoric home on white America's stage, they were being systematically forced from their tribal lands east of the Mississippi throughout the 1830s and 1840s. The intersection of economics and racism in this period is tellingly explored by Slotkin.

3. John Augustus Stone, *Metamora*, in *Metamora and Other Plays*, Eugene R. Page, ed. vol. 14 of *America's Lost Plays*, 21 vols., 1940 (Bloomington: Indiana University Press, 1965), 10. All quotations from this play cited in the text are from this edition.

4. On the romantic drama's treatment of nature see Grimsted, 211–20.

5. Herold's remains the only modern biography of Paulding. Reynolds briefly surveys not only Paulding's life but also his diverse literary efforts.

6. The relative parts of the contributors is at best speculative. For convenience, I refer to the play as Paulding's, recognizing that while he provided the broad outlines of the action, particular elements of the satire may well have been added later. The history of the play's composition and its various revisions are discussed in Tidwell's introduction.

7. James Kirke Paulding, *The Lion of the West*, James N. Tidwell ed. (Stanford, California: Stanford University Press, 1954), 31. All quotations from this play cited in the text are from this edition.

8. Since throughout the play it is Percival's mercantile, rather than national, background that Paulding chooses to emphasize, the extent of the playwrights' intentions remain somewhat ambiguous.

9. The potential use of Colonel David Crockett as a model for Wildfire is discussed by Mason.

10. The most comprehensive examination of the stage Yankee is found in Hodge. Dorson and Eich provide useful supplements.

11. Samuel Low, *The Politician Outwitted, Representative Plays by American Dramatists*, Montrose J. Moses, ed., 3 vols. (New York: Dutton, 1918–21), 1: 363. All quotations from this play cited in the text are from this edition.

12. Mordeciah M. Noah, *She Would Be a Soldier, Representative Plays by American Dramatists*, Montrose J. Moses, ed., 3 vols. (New York: Dutton, 1918–21), 1: 649. All quotations from this play cited in the text are from this edition.

13. For examples of both villainous and heroic Yankees see the discussion of Jacob M'Closky and Salem Scudder in Boucicault's *The Octoroon* below.

14. For an examination of *Fashion* as an instance of the continuing fascination with upper class life, see Miller.

15. The most comprehensive analysis of the play and its relationship to the social comedy of this particular period appears in Havens, 129–48.

16. Anna Cora Mowatt, *Fashion, or Life in New York, Drama from the American Theatre, 1762–1909*, Richard Moody, ed. (New York: World, 1966), 34. All quotations from this play cited in the text are from this edition.

17. As satiric comedy, *Fashion* continues to be entertaining and pertinent as New York City revivals in 1959 and 1973–74 testify. Intriguingly, the latter production recast Mowatt's play as a musical.

18. The pervasiveness of the man who utilizes business to evil purposes is suggested by the fact that four of the plays discussed in this chapter have such characters: Tiffany in *Fashion*, Winslow in *The People's Lawyer*, Legree in *Uncle Tom's Cabin*, and M'Closky in *The Octoroon*.

19. The dedication of its opponents and the duration of the struggle is suggested by noting that William Lloyd Garrison's *Liberator*, the most famous of the abolitionist newspapers, was established in 1831.

20. For a discussion of this evolution see Birdoff.

21. The dangers of this tactic and its problematic racial assumptions are examined in the discussion of Bartley Campbell's *The White Slave* in Chapter 6.

22. George L. Aiken, *Uncle Tom's Cabin, Drama from the American Theatre, 1762–1909*, Richard Moody, ed. (Cleveland: World, 1966), 360. All quotations from this play cited in the text are from this edition.

23. His acknowledgment of Tom's worth, his transformation after the death of Eva, and his death in a selfless act seem sufficient to Aiken to guarantee St. Claire's place with Tom in the final tableau of adoration. Nevertheless, as St. Claire's penultimate speech foreshadows, his negligence is the direct cause of great suffering and Tom's eventual death.

24. For a more extensive examination of this issue see Richardson.

25. Dion Boucicault, *The Octoroon; or, Life in Louisiana, Plays by Dion Boucicault*, Peter Thomson, ed., British and American Playwrights, 1750–1920 (Cambridge: Cambridge University Press, 1984), 136. All quotations from this play cited in the text are from this edition.

26. The pathos of Zoe's fate proved too powerful for the London audiences whom Boucicault treated to the play in 1861. The English audiences demanded that Zoe be allowed to marry George, and, after slight resistance, Boucicault reworked the ending, advertising his revised play as having a new final act, "composed by the public and edited by the author."

Chapter 6

1. While the recent critical literature devoted to melodrama remains minimal in reference to other dramatic forms, it is almost universally of superior

quality. Among major works on the general topic are a chapter in Bentley's *The Life of the Drama*, and full-length studies by Heilman, Rahill, and Smith. Though chronologically restricted, Grimsted remains the best book on American melodrama.

2. For discussions of Daly's career on the theatrical scene in the latter nineteenth century see Meserve, *Outline*, 135–37; Wilmeth and Cullen, 1–38; and Felheim.

3. Augustin Daly, *Under the Gaslight*, *Hiss the Villain: Six English and American Melodramas*, Michael Booth, ed., (New York: Blom, 1964), 327. All quotations from this play cited in the text are from this edition.

4. Boucicault's life and works are discussed by Walsh, Hogan, Fawkes, and Molin and Goodfellow.

5. In a very concrete sense, Boucicault's long agitation for copyright laws bore fruit in the monetary success he earned from these plays. Fawkes notes that *The Shaughraun* alone earned Boucicault half a million dollars in the United States (195).

6. I do not mean to suggest that Boucicault was unconcerned with matters in his native Ireland. As Fawkes makes evident, Boucicault felt strongly about such issues as the Fenians (195–97). I merely wish to point out that Boucicault had a more immediate political and financial reason for seizing on his Irish material than has been acknowledged. That Boucicault may well have seen these plays as serving two audiences is perfectly within reason.

7. Foner explores the complex relationship between Irish-Americans and America and Ireland in his chapter, "Class, Ethnicity, and Radicalism in the Gilded Age: The Land League and Irish-America," 150–200.

8. Dion Boucicault, *The Shaughraun*, *Plays by Dion Boucicault*, ed. Peter Thomson, British and American Playwrights, 1750–1920 (Cambridge: Cambridge University Press, 1984), 175. All quotations from this play cited in the text are from this edition.

9. As Krause has noted, Boucicault apparently coined the term "shaughraun" by changing the Gaelic participle *seachran*, meaning "wandering," into a noun suggestive of a wanderer or a tramp (37).

10. John Bodnar has noted, for example, the tendency of such Irish-American newspapers as the *Irish World* to link the "land struggle in Ireland with American social issues" such as slavery and the monopolization of capital (111).

11. This double focus is reminiscent of Boucicault's approach to slavery in his most lasting melodrama, *The Octoroon*. See Chapter 5 for a discussion of Boucicault's strategies.

12. Bartley Campbell, *The White Slave*, *The White Slave and Other Plays by Bartley Campbell*, Napier Wilt, ed., vol. 19 of *America's Lost Plays*, Barrett

H. Clark, ed., 20 vols. Princeton: Princeton University Press, 1940–41 (Bloomington: Indiana University Press, 1963–65), 224. All quotations from this play cited in the text are from this edition.

13. Even the play most widely recognized as calling for the abolition of slavery, *Uncle Tom's Cabin*, seems to partake to some degree of this attitude. While it would contravene the tenor of the play to suggest that Aiken is indifferent to the fate of Tom, the pattern does seem to operate in the instance of George Harris. Moreover, it is interesting to note that in 1856, four years after the publication of Stowe's novel and three years after Aiken's adaptation, George Fitzhugh, one of the most radical of southern racial thinkers, still attracted large northern audiences on a speaking tour in which he advocated both black and white slavery.

14. Two years later William Dean Howells agreed, noting, "the swiftly moving history is expressed from the patriotic point of view in such terms and characters as do justice to the high motives and unselfish heroism on both sides" (*Harper's Monthly* 155).

15. Apparently such was the case, for the reviewers are mute on the characters' attitude toward the war, and the viewing public flocked to see the play.

16. Howard manages to maintain the distance between the war and his audience by a variety of techniques. One of the most intriguing is his use of characters who narrate offstage action for the audience, occasionally with disquieting results. For instance, Jenny's early third-act description of the armies' maneuvers tends to recast the horror of war into a beautiful sport played by colorful paladins on magnificent horses.

17. Bronson Howard, *Shenandoah*, *Representative American Plays*, Arthur Hobson Quinn, ed., 7th ed. (New York: Appleton-Century-Crofts, 1957), 428. All quotations from this play cited in the text are from this edition.

18. David Belasco, *The Heart of Maryland*, *The Heart of Maryland and Other Plays*, Glenn Hughes and George Savage, eds., vol. 18 of *America's Lost Plays*, Barrett H. Clark, ed. 20 vols. Princeton: Princeton University Press, 1940–41. (Bloomington: Indiana University Press, 1963–65), 184. All quotations from this play cited in the text are from this edition.

19. Howard may here be deliberately echoing Edward Everett Hale's extremely popular nationalistic short story of the same title, appropriately published in 1863 when the possibility of any American's belonging to "a country" hung in the balance.

20. Thorough examinations of minstrelsy in America can be found in Richard Moody, *America Takes the Stage*, 32–60, and Toll.

21. Joaquin Miller, *The Danites in the Sierras*, *American Plays*,

Allan Halline, ed. (New York: American Book Company, 1935), 389. All quotations from this play cited in the text are from this edition.

22. David Belasco, *The Girl of the Golden West, Representative American Dramas, National and Local,* Montrose J. Moses, ed. (Boston: Little, Brown, 1925), 76. All quotations from this play cited in the text are from this edition.

23. Augustin Daly, *Horizon, Plays by Augustin Daly* Don B. Wilmeth and Rosemary Cullen, eds. British and American Dramatists, 1750–1920 (Cambridge: Cambridge University Press, 1984), 119–20. All quotations from this play cited in the text are from this edition.

24. Bartley Campbell, *My Partner, The White Slave and Other Plays by Bartley Campbell,* Napier Wilt, ed., vol. 19 of *America's Lost Plays,* Barrett H. Clark, ed., 20 vols. Princeton: Princeton University Press, 1940–41. (Bloomington: Indiana University Press, 1963–65), 65. All quotations from this play cited in the text are from this edition.

25. The emotional appeal of Belasco's story proved irresistible even when it was adapted to another medium. Puccini's 1910 opera of the same name remains one of the most popular pieces in the operatic repertoire.

26. Eugene Walter, *The Easiest Way, Representative Plays by American Dramatists,* Montrose J. Moses, ed., 3 vols. (New York: E. P. Dutton, 1918–25), 3: 814.

Chapter 7

1. The wealth of material on the general topic of American realism is so broad that reference here is possible to only a few representative, book-length studies. Among the most useful are Vernon L. Parrington, *The Beginnings of Critical Realism in America, 1860–1920* (New York: Harcourt, Brace, and World, 1930); Everett Carter, *Howells and the Age of Realism* (Philadelphia: Lippincott, 1950); Werner Berthoff, *The Ferment of American Realism: American Literature, 1884–1919* (New York, Free Press: 1965); Harold H. Kolb, *The Illusion of Life: American Realism as a Literary Form* (Charlottesville: University Press of Virginia, 1969); Edwin Cady, *The Light of Common Day: Realism in American Fiction* (Bloomington: Indiana University Press, 1971); Donald Pizer, *Realism and Naturalism in Nineteenth-Century American Literature,* rev. ed. (Carbondale: Southern Illinois University Press, 1984). On the more limited topic of American drama in the period, particularly helpful volumes include: Arthur Hobson Quinn, *A History of the American Drama from the Civil War to the Present Day,* 2 vols in 1, rev. ed. (New York: Appleton-Century-Crofts, 1936), cited hereafter as Quinn, *History*; Morris Freedman, *American Drama in Social*

Context (Carbondale: Southern Illinois University Press, 1971); J. L. Styan, *Modern Drama in Theory and Practice. Vol. I: Realism and Naturalism* (Cambridge: Cambridge University Press, 1981); and Brenda Murphy, *American Realism and American Drama, 1880–1940* (Cambridge: Cambridge University Press, 1987), cited hereafter as Murphy.

2. Brenda Murphy's excellent discussion of the theoretical underpinnings of realist aesthetics provides the starting point for my own discussion. For a more fully developed examination of some of the topics I raise here, see Murphy, 24–49.

3. William Dean Howells, "The Ibsen Influence," *Harper's Weekly Magazine* 39 (April 27, 1895): 390. Reprinted as "Ibsenism" in *Criticism and Fiction and Other Essays*, Clara Marburg Kirk and Rudolph Kirk, eds. (New York: New York University Press, 1959), 146, hereafter cited as Kirk and Kirk.

4. William Dean Howells, "The Play and the Problem," *Harper's Weekly Magazine* 39 (March 30, 1895): 266.

5. William Dean Howells, *Criticism and Fiction*, in *Criticism and Fiction and Other Essays*, Clara Marburg Kirk and Rudolf Kirk, eds. (New York: New York University Press, 1959), 15.

6. William Dean Howells, "Editor's Study," *Harper's Monthly Magazine* 73 (July 1886): 314–19.

7. Henry James, *The Scenic Art: Notes on Acting and the Drama*, Allen Wade, ed. (New Brunswick, N. J.: Rutgers University Press, 1948), 34. Hereafter cited in the text as James.

8. The first of these stories is recounted in John Perry, *James A. Herne: The American Ibsen* (Chicago: Nelson-Hall, 1978), 52, cited in the text hereafter as Perry; the latter comes from David Belasco's own memoir, *The Theatre Through Its Stage Door*, 1919, rpt. (New York: Blom, 1969), 173.

9. William Dean Howells, "The New Poetic Drama," *The North American Review* 172 (May 1901): 794–95.

10. Henry James, "Mr. Tennyson's Drama," *Galaxy* 20 (September 1875): 398, qtd. in Murphy, 38.

11. William Dean Howells, "Henrik Ibsen," *The North American Review* 183 (July 1906): 3, 4.

12. James A. Herne, "Art for Truth's Sake in the Drama," *Arena* 17 (1897): 361–70, rpt. in *American Drama and Its Critics*, ed. Alan S. Downer (Chicago: University of Chicago Press, 1965), 9.

13. Meserve makes this point in William Dean Howells, *The Complete Plays of W. D. Howells*, Walter J. Meserve, ed. and intro. (New York: New York University Press, 1960), 611, hereafter cited as Meserve, *Howells*.

14. Booth Tarkington, "Mr. Howells," *Harper's Monthly Magazine* 141 (August, 1920): 348.

15. William Dean Howells, *The Unexpected Guests* in *The Complete plays of William Dean Howells*, Walter J. Meserve, ed. and intro. (New York: New York University Press, 1960), 420. All quotations from this play cited in the text are from this edition.

16. Howells's attitude in the 1880s is at least partially indicated by a letter to Augustin Daly (March 19, 1884) suggesting that he would adapt a German comedy for "$2000 cash on delivery, if it is to appear without my name. If you want my name with yours you must pay me more." Cited by Meserve, *The Complete Plays of W. D. Howells*, xxiv.

17. Alfred Habegger, *Gender, Fantasy and Realism in American Literature* (New York: Columbia University Press, 1986), 91–96.

18. William Dean Howells, *A Counterfeit Presentment* in *The Complete Plays of W. D. Howells*, Walter J. Meserve, ed. (New York: New York University Press, 1960), 74. All quotations from this play cited in the text are from this edition.

19. Percy MacKaye recounts his father's long legal battle with the owners of the Madison Square Theatre, George and Marshall Mallory, over the rights to *Hazel Kirke* in his biography of his father, *Epoch: The Life of Steel MacKaye*, 2 vols. (New York: Boni and Liveright, 1927), I, 333–400, cited in the text hereafter as MacKaye, *Epoch*.

20. For example, Murphy lumps MacKaye with David Belasco and comments that both were "temperamentally and artistically romantics, not realists, and for the most part, they aimed to heighten the sensational, the exotic, and the unusual in their productions rather than to create the recognizable illusion of everyday life that the realists were seeking" (20).

21. Meserve echoes this point in "American Drama and the Rise of Realism," *Jahrbück for Amerikastudien* 9 (1964): 155.

22. Debra J. Woodard recounts her discovery of the manuscript and provides some penetrating arguments concerning the play in "Steel MacKaye's *Marriage*: The Beginning of a Movement toward American Realism," *Theatre Survey* 23 (1982): 189–95.

23. Meserve agrees with this assessment, noting that *Hazel Kirke* is basically "a sentimental melodrama very carefully crafted and made flesh and truthful by the realistic characters of Hazel and Dunstan." See Travis Bogard, Richard Moody, and Walter J. Meserve, *The* Revels *History of Drama in English*: Vol. VIII, *American Drama* (London: Methuen, 1977), p. 193.

24. Steele MacKaye, *Hazel Kirke* in *Representative American Plays*, 7th ed., Arthur Hobson Quinn, ed. (New York: Appleton-Century-Crofts, 1953), 451. All quotations from this play cited in the text are from this edition.

25. See, for example, the story of Consuelo Vanderbilt's forced marriage in 1895 to George, the eighth Duke of Marlborough, conveniently rendered in Arthur T. Vanderbilt, II, *Fortune's Children: The Fall of the House of Vanderbilt* (New York: William Morrow, 1989), 163–74.

26. Steele MacKaye, *Paul Kauvar; or, Anarchy*, in *Representative Plays by American Playwrights*, 3 vols, Montrose J. Moses, ed. (New York: Dutton, 1918–21), 3: 265–66.

27. See Howard's thoughts on this and other matters pertaining to the American stage in "The American Drama," *Sunday Magazine* (New York), Oct. 7, 1906; rpt. in *Representative Plays by American Dramatists*, Montrose J. Moses, ed. 3 vols. 1918–25, rpt. (New York: Blom, 1964): III, 364–70.

28. Bronson Howard, *The Henrietta*, in *American Plays*, Allan G. Halline ed. (New York: American Book Co., 1935), 414. All quotations from this play cited in the text are from this edition.

29. For a further delineation of this character type in Howard see Maxwell Bloomfield, "Mirror for Businessmen: Bronson Howard's Melodramas, 1870–1890," *Mid-Continent American Studies Journal*, 5 (1964): 38–49.

30. Howard's satire was sufficiently realistic that William Gillette could comment that *The Henrietta* was "In many respects . . . a series of photographs." "American Playwrights on The American Drama," *Harper's Weekly* 33 (Feb. 2, 1889): 99, cited hereafter as "American Playwrights."

31. William Gillette, *Secret Service*, in *Plays by William Hooker Gillette*, Rosemary Cullen and Don B. Wilmeth, eds. (Cambridge: Cambridge University Press, 1983), 147–48. All quotations from this play cited in the text are from this edition.

32. John Dickson Carr, *The Life of Sir Arthur Conan Doyle* (New York: Harper, 1949), 117.

33. The exact number of performances is in some dispute. Cullen and Wilmeth, 16, suggest "over 1300 times" while P. M. Stone in "William Gillette's Stage Career," *The Baker Street Journal*, NS 12 (1962): 19, asserts 4,400. Though Gillette's capacity for performance was legendary, the lower number seems more credible.

34. John Perry uses this phrase as the subtitle of his book on Herne.

35. James A. Herne, *Margaret Fleming*, in *Representative American Plays*, Arthur Hobson Quinn, ed., 7th ed. (New York: Appleton-Century-Crofts, 1953), 526. All quotations from this play cited in the text are from this edition.

36. The current ending represents a reconstruction undertaken by Herne's widow of the second version of the play. In the original version, the last act takes place four years later. Philip meets Joe on Boston Common and relates that his wife has disappeared, his business has failed, and he has lived a life of misery and regret. Joe becomes convinced that the child Maria has maintained was her sister's

is actually Lucy Fleming, and takes Philip off to show him the child. Meantime, the still-blind Margaret has accidentally discovered Maria and Lucy. Maria at first denies that Lucy is Margaret's daughter but then confesses. Margaret takes away the child. When Philip arrives, Maria maintains that she has sold the child. The final scene takes place in a police station where Maria, Joe, Lucy, Philip and Margaret meet. When the police inspector leaves them alone to reconcile, Margaret tells Philip that "the wife-heart has gone out of me" and they agree to part. The play ends as the police go back to their usual routine. Perry, 143–44, reprints Hamlin Garland's review for the July 8, 1890 *Boston Evening Transcript* of the original production as the source of this ending.

37. For the stage history of the play see Herbert J. Edwards and Julie A. Herne, *James A. Herne: The Rise of Realism in the American Drama* (Orono: University of Maine Press, 1964), 57–72, hereafter cited as Edwards and Herne.

38. Arthur Hobson Quinn, *The Literature of the American People* (New York: Appleton-Century-Crofts, 1951), 805.

39. James A. Herne, *Shore Acres*, in *Dramas from the American Theatre, 1762–1909*, Richard Moody, ed. (Cleveland and New York: World Publishing, 1966), 683. All quotations from this play cited in the text are from this edition.

40. Claudia Johnson makes much the same point, seeing in the speculations which fuel Warren's desire to go west a force that undermines the assumptions on which Herne ends the play, and pointing the way "beyond the realism of O'Neill to the Absurdism of the existentialist playwrights." "A New Nation's Drama," in *The Columbia Literary History of the United States*, Emory Elliott, ed., *et al.* (New York: Columbia University Press, 1988), 338.

Chapter 8

1. George Santayana, *Character and Opinion in the United States* (New York: Norton, [1920]), p. 14.

2. For a thorough discussion of the effects of the Theatrical Syndicates upon this period, see Poggi.

3. The letter is reprinted in *Representative American Plays*, Montrose J. Moses, ed., 3 vols. (New York: E. P. Dutton, 1918–25), III: 600.

4. Ironically enough, Quinn himself acknowledges the necessity for such specificity when he comments that Mitchell has revealed that the models for the Phillimores were Philadelphians rather than New Yorkers, for "nowhere else could be found quite the same profound self-contentment and surety of standards as the Phillimores represent" (*History*, 2: 64). While it may be interesting to speculate why Mitchell would provide an assurance that violates so much

else in the play that clearly acknowledges the compelling necessity of the play's New York locale, the fact remains that the obsession with horseracing and Cynthia and Sir Wilfrid's third-act offstage trip to Belmont Park are only physically possible if the play is set in New York.

5. Langdon Mitchell, *The New York Idea*, *Representative American Plays*, Arthur Hobson Quinn, ed., 7th ed. (New York: Appleton-Century-Crofts, 1957), 619. All quotations from this play cited in the text are from this edition.

6. Vida's derivation from Eve is made explicit in the second act when she offers to "join hands and stroll together into the Garden of Eden" (647) with John.

7. Fitch, the country's first internationally recognized dramatist, also carefully utilizes urban environment in several of his earlier plays, notably his satire on social ambition, *The Climbers* (1901); his case study of jealousy, *The Girl with the Green Eyes* (1902); and his examination of a pathological liar, *The Truth* (1907).

8. Clyde Fitch, *The City*, *Dramas from the American Theatre 1762–1909*, Richard Moody, ed. (New York: World, 1966), 823. All quotations from this play cited in the text are from this edition.

9. Lois C. Gottlieb argues persuasively that the general dissatisfaction of the Rand women is part of a broader pattern of patriarchal recovery associated with drama in this period, which seeks, among other things, to undermine women's growing independence. See "The Perils of Freedom: The New Woman in Three American Plays of the 1900's," *The Canadian Review of American Studies* 6 (1975): 90–92.

10. Edward Sheldon, *Salvation Nell* in *Best Plays of the Early American Theatre*, John Gassner, ed. (New York: Crown, 1967), 575.

11. Edward Sheldon, *The Nigger* (New York: Macmillan, 1910), 40. All quotations from this play cited in the text are from this edition.

12. For the identification of Regan with Connors, I am indebited to Loren K. Ruff, *Edward Sheldon* (Boston: Twayne, 1982), p. 94.

13. Edward Sheldon, *The Boss*, *Representative American Plays*, *From 1767 to the Present Day*, Arthur Hobson Quinn, ed., 7th ed. (New York: Appleton-Century-Crofts, 1957), 852. All quotations from this play cited in the text are from this edition.

14. For a more detailed analysis of Thomas's theories concerning the supernatural and their development in this play, see Ronald J. Davis, *Augustus Thomas* (Boston: Twayne, 1984), 86–89.

15. On this point MacKaye may have been greatly influenced by the example of his father, Steele MacKaye, whose play *Paul Kauvar* adopts a similar

stance. For the elder MacKaye's attitude on this issue, see the discussion of *Paul Kauvar* in the preceding chapter.

16. Percy MacKaye, *The Scarecrow, Representative American Plays*, Arthur Hobson Quinn, ed., 7th ed. (New York: Appleton-Century-Crofts, 1957), 841. All quotations from this play cited in the text are from this edition.

17. MacKaye's career was marked by an increasing interest in drama which transcended the confines of the traditional stage. Later in his career, he was increasingly associated with community drama and large public masques such as *Sanctuary: A Bird Masque* (1912), *Saint Louis: A Civic Masque* (1914), and *Caliban, by the Yellow Sands* (1916). Convenient summaries of MacKaye's dramatic speculations on the proper role of drama in a democracy are found in Michael J. Mendelsohn, "Percy MacKaye's Dramatic Theories," *Bulletin of the Rocky Mountain Modern Language Association* 24 (1970): 85–89, and D. Heyward Brock and James M Walsh, "Percy MacKaye: Community and the Masque Tradition," *Comparative Drama* 6 (1972): 68–84.

18. Jordan Y. Miller's comment that the timelessness of *The Great Divide*'s central idea, "the affirmation of the right of a person to establish and maintain his own individual character in the face of an opposing tradition," seems in many ways a fair assessment of both of Moody's prose plays. *American Dramatic Literature* (New York: McGraw-Hill, 1961), 50.

19. William Vaughn Moody, *The Great Divide, Dramas from the American Theatre*, Richard Moody, ed. (New York: World Publishing, 1966), 747. All quotations from this play cited in the text are from this edition.

20. Halpern's insistence that Moody demands Ghent's expiation of his part in the attack on Ruth through his suffering and willingness to forego both the economic (the gold mine) and the emotional (Ruth herself) fruits of his action reflects a privileging of the Puritan perspective which the play itself does not seem to sustain. Ghent's willingness to attempt to live according to Ruth's spiritual heritage may be an index of his devotion to her, but it is not an acknowledgement that his basic values are in need of refashioning. Ruth finally accepts Ghent because she recognizes the life-denying reality of the legalistic spiritual code which has framed her. See Martin Halpern, *William Vaughn Moody* (New York: Twayne, 1964), 127–30.

21. See, for example, John Corbin's review of *The Great Divide* for *The New York Sun*, reprinted in *The American Theatre as Seen by Its Critics, 1752–1934*, Montrose J. Moses and John Mason Brown, eds. (New York: Norton, 1934), 176–178.

22. For a more detailed analysis of the gender configurations of this play, see Lois C. Gottlieb, "The Double Standard Debate in Early 20th-Century American Drama," *Michigan Academician* 7 (1975): 441–452.

23. William Vaughn Moody, *The Faith Healer, Representative American*

Plays, Arthur Hobson Quinn, ed., 7th ed. (New York: Appleton-Century-Crofts, 1957), 778. All quotations from this play cited in the text are from this edition.

24. A comparison to the halting formulations of a Stephen Ghent or the anguished outbursts of a Ruth Jordan is instructive. In the earlier play, Steve and Ruth, more firmly rooted in temporal reality, maintain speech patterns warranted by their backgrounds and emerging circumstances.

25. Gottlieb argues that the tension is between the women's movement and a generally conceived Progressive Era. Though I would distinguish Moody's neo-romantic individualism from the more overtly political project of the Progressives, her point is otherwise well taken. See Lois C. Gottlieb, "The Perils of Freedom: The New Woman in Three American Plays of the 1900's," *The Canadian Review of American Studies* 6 (1975): 84–98.

26. Despite the growing interest in the issue generally, Florence Kiper could still maintain with some justification in 1914, "In a drama whose themes are almost entirely those of contemporary life, few among our playwrights are attempting to interpret to us the meaning of the growing divorce 'evil,' of the suffrage agitation, of women in the professions, of young girls in industry, of the sudden awakening of the sheltered woman to a knowledge of prostitution and venereal diseases." "Some American Plays: From the Feminist Viewpoint," *The Forum* 51 (1914): 921.

27. For full length studies of the careers of Crothers and Glaspell, see Lois C. Gottlieb, *Rachel Crothers* (Boston: Twayne, 1979), cited hereafter in the text as Gottlieb, *Crothers*; and Arthur E. Waterman, *Susan Glaspell* (New York: Twayne, 1966).

28. Interview with Catherine Hughes, "Women Playmakers," *New York Times Magazine* 4 May 1941: 27.

29. For convenient discussions of the role of Crothers's and Glaspell's art in the general cultural debate concerning women, see Deborah S. Kolb, "The Rise and Fall of the New Woman in American Drama," *Educational Theatre Journal* 27 (1975): 149–160; Cynthia Sutherland, "American Women Playwrights as Mediators of the "Woman Problem," *Modern Drama* 21 (1978): 319–36; Sharon Friedman, "feminism as theme in twentieth-century american women's drama," *American Studies* 25 (1984): 69–89; and Judith L. Stephens, "Gender Ideology and Dramatic Convention in Progressive Era Plays, 1890–1920," *Theatre Journal* 41 (1989): 45–55.

30. Rachel Crothers, *The Three of Us* (New York: Samuel French, 1916), 11. All quotations from this play cited in the text are from this edition.

31. Rachel Crothers, *A Man's World* (Boston: Badger, 1915), 111. All quotations from this play cited in the text are from this edition.

32. Gottlieb notes quite correctly that Crothers carefully avoids implying

that Frank rejects Gaskell because of his past by utilizing the structure of the play. Frank learns that Gaskell is Kiddie's father at the end of the third act, but dismisses him only after the fourth-act confrontation in which Gaskell persists in his belief that he has done nothing wrong (*Crothers*, 47).

33. As Florence Kiper commented, "The conflict of the drama is waged not so much without as within her own nature, a conflict between individual emotion and social conviction. What many of our writers for the stage have missed in their objective drama that uses the new woman for protagonist is a glimpse of that tumultuous battlefield, her own soul, where meet the warring forces of impulse and theory, of the old and the new conceptions of egotism and altruism." "Some American Plays: From the Feminist Viewpoint," *The Forum* 51 (1914): 928.

34. Rachel Crothers, *He and She*, *Representative American Plays*, Arthur Hobson Quinn, ed., 7th ed. (New York: Appleton-Century-Crofts, 1957), 898–99. All quotations from this play cited in the text are from this edition.

35. As Murphy phrases it, "Crothers states that a woman's life is compromise. Marriage *and* career means inadequacy in both; marriage *or* career means giving up an entire sphere of life (99–100)."

36. For a history of the Provincetown Players and Theatre, see Helen Deutsch and Stella Hanau, *The Provincetown: A Story of the Theatre* (New York: Russell and Russell, 1931); and Robert K. Sarlos, *Jig Cook and the Provincetown Players: Theatre in Ferment* (Amherst: University of Massachusetts Press, 1982).

37. Linda Ben-Zvi, "Susan Glaspell's Contributions to Contemporary Women Playwrights," *Feminine Focus: The New Women Playwrights*, Enoch Brater, ed. (New York: Oxford University Press, 1989), 148. Much of the following discussion is informed by Ben-Zvi's persuasive analysis of Glaspell's career.

38. Susan Glaspell, *Trifles*, *Plays* (New York: Dodd, Mead and Company, 1920), 26. All quotations from this play cited in the text are from this edition.

39. For a fuller examination of this element of Glaspell's drama, see Christine Dymkowski, "On the Edge: The Plays of Susan Glaspell," *Modern Drama* 31 (1988): 91–105.

40. Karen F. Stein provides a useful gloss on the importance of quilting to women's culture in "The Women's World of Glaspell's *Trifles*," *Women in American Theatre*, Helen Krich Chinoy and Linda Walsh Jenkins, eds. (New York: Crown, 1981): 251–254.

selected bibliography

Primary Works

Following the practices of the day, many of the eighteenth and early nineteenth-century works cited in the text were published only in newspapers, in inexpensive editions such as *French's Modern Standard Drama*, or in acting editions such as *French's Standard Drama* (New York) and *Dick's Standard Plays* (London) intended for professional and amateur companies. The degree of authorial supervision of the preparations of any of these editions is, at best, problematical. Fortunately, most of the better-known works have received the attention of modern scholarly editors and have been reprinted in readily accessible collections and anthologies. The specific source of the plays discussed in the text are noted in entries under their individual authors or, in the case of anonymous works, the play's title.

Major anthologies of Drama, Colonial to 1917

Booth, Michael, ed. *Hiss the Villain*. New York: Blom, 1964.

Clark, Barrett H., gen. ed. *America's Lost Plays*. 20 vols. Princeton, N.J.:

Princeton University Press, 1940–41. Reissued in 10 vols. plus an additional (21st) volume. Bloomington: Indiana University Press, 1963–65, 1969. The major source of less well-known plays in the period, the volumes contain material stretching from the Revolutionary War plays to the turn of the century, with brief introductions and notes on the plays included.

————, ed. *Favorite American Plays of the Nineteenth Century.* Princeton, N.J.: Princeton University Press, 1943.

Coyle, William, and Harry G. Damaser, eds. *Six Early American Plays, 1798–1900.* Columbus, Ohio: Charles E. Merrill, 1968.

Downer, Alan A. *American Drama.* New York: Thomas Y. Crowell, 1960.

Gassner, John, and Mollie Gassner, eds. *Best Plays of the Early American Theatre.* New York: Crown, 1967.

Halline, Allan G., ed. *American Plays.* New York: American Book Co., 1935.

Jacobus, Lee A., ed. *Longman Anthology of American Drama.* New York: Longman, 1982.

Matlaw, Myron, ed. *The Black Crook and Other Nineteenth-Century American Plays.* New York: Dutton, 1967.

————, ed. *Nineteenth-Century American Plays.* New York: Applause Theatre Book, 1985.

Moody, Richard, ed. *Dramas from the American Theatre, 1762–1909.* Cleveland: World, 1966. Excellent bibliographies and introductions.

Moses, Montrose J., ed. *Representative American Dramas, National and Local.* Boston: Little, Brown, 1925.

————, ed. *Representative Plays by American Dramatists.* New York: Dutton, 1918–21.

Philbrick, Norman, ed. *Trumpets Sounding: Propaganda Plays of the American Revolution.* New York: Blom, 1972.

Quinn, Arthur Hobson, ed. *Representative American Plays, From 1767 to the Present Day.* 7th ed. New York: Appleton-Century-Crofts, 1953.

Works by Individual Playwrights

Plays are listed in alphabetical order under each playwright's name with the first entry referring to the specific source used in this text. If the source is one of the anthologies cited above, a shortened citation is used. Otherwise, a full citation is provided the first time a new source is included. Next, other anthologies in which these plays may be found are indicated. This is followed by volumes of the dramatist's collected plays. Anonymous plays are listed by title.

Aiken, George L. (1830–76)

Uncle Tom's Cabin (1852); Moody, *Dramas from the American Theatre*, 349–96. In Gassner, Jacobus, Moses, *Representative*; Quinn, *Representative American Plays*.

Barker, James Nelson (1784–1858)

The Indian Princess (1808); Moses, *Representative*, 1: 565–628.

Marmion (1812); New York: Longworth, 1816.

Superstition (1824); Quinn, *Representative American Plays*, 109–140; In Gassner, Halline.

The Battle of Brooklyn (1776)

The Battle of Brooklyn. Satiric Comedies. Walter J. Meserve and William R. Reardon, eds. Vol. 21 of *America's Lost Plays.* Bloomington: Indiana University Press, 1969. 81–102. In Philbrick.

Belasco, David (1859–1931)

The Girl of the Golden West (1905); *Representative American Dramas, National and Local*, Montrose J. Moses, ed. Boston: Little, Brown, 1925. 47–97.

The Heart of Maryland (1895); *The Heart of Maryland and Other Plays.* Glenn Hughes and George Savage, eds. Vol. 18 of *America's Lost Plays.* 171–250. In Clark, *Favorite American Plays.*

Six Plays. Intro. Montrose J. Moses. Boston: Little, Brown, 1929.

Bird, Robert Montgomery (1806–1854)

The Broker of Bogota (1833); Quinn, *Representative American Plays*, 193–235.

The Gladiator (1831); Moody, *Dramas from the American Theatre*, 229–276. In Halline.

The Cowled Lover and Other Plays by Robert Montgomery Bird, Edward H. O'Neill, ed. Vol. 12 of *America's Lost Plays.*

Foust, Clement. *The Life and Dramatic Works of Robert Montgomery Bird.* New York: Knickerbocker Press, 1919.

Boker, George Henry (1823–90)

Francesca da Rimini (1855); Quinn, *Representative American Plays*, 313–368. In Halline, Matlaw *Black Crook*, Moody, Moses *Representative.*

Glaucus and Other Plays. Edward Sculley Bradley, ed. Vol. 3 of *America's Lost Plays.*

Plays and Poems. 2 vols. 1856. New York: AMS Press, 1967.

[Boston's First Play] (1732)

"[Boston's First Play]." Robert E. Moody, ed. *Proceedings of the Massachusetts Historical Society* 92 (1980): 117–39.

Boucicault, Dion (1820–90)

The Octoroon; or, Life in Louisiana (1859); *Plays by Dion Boucicault*, Peter Thomson, ed. British and American Playwrights, 1750–1920. Cambridge: Cambridge University Press, 1984. 133–169. In Coyle, Matlaw *Black Crook*, Jacobus; Quinn, *Representative American Plays*.

The Shaughraun (1874); *Plays by Dion Boucicault*. Peter Thomson, ed. 171–219.

The Dolmen Press Boucicault. David Krause, ed. Dublin: Dolmen Press.

Forbidden Fruit & Other Plays, Allardyce Nicoll and F. Theodore Clark, ed. Vol. 1 of *America's Lost Plays*.

Brackenridge, Hugh Henry (1748–1816)

The Battle of Bunkers-Hill (1776); Moses, *Representative Plays*, 1: 233–76.

The Death of General Montgomery in Storming the City of Quebec (1777); Philbrick, *Trumpets Sounding*, 211–254.

Burk, John Daly (1776?–1808)

Bunker-Hill (1797); Moody, *Dramas from the American Theatre*, 70–86.

Campbell, Bartley (1843–88)

My Partner (1879); *The White Slave and Other Plays by Bartley Campbell*. Napier Wilt, ed. Vol. 19 of *America's Lost Plays*. In Clark, *Favorite*.

The White Slave (1882); *The White Slave and Other Plays by Bartley Campbell*; Napier Wilt, ed. Vol. 19 of *America's Lost Plays*. 199–248.

Crothers, Rachel (1878–1958)

A Man's World (1909); Boston: Badger, 1915.

He and She (1911); Quinn, *Representative American Plays*, 892–928. *The Three of Us* (1906); New York: Samuel French, 1916.

Daly, Augustin (1838–99)

A Flash of Lightning (1868); *Plays by Augustin Daly*; Don B. Wilmeth and Rosemary Cullen, eds. British and American Dramatists, 1750–1920. Cambridge: Cambridge University Press, 1984. 49–102.

Horizon (1871); *Plays by Augustin Daly*; Don B. Wilmeth and Rosemary Cullen, eds. 103–151. In Halline.

Under the Gaslight (1867); *Hiss the Villain: Six English and American Melodramas*, Michael Booth, ed. New York: Blom, 1964. 271–341.

Man and Wife and Other Plays, Catherine Sturtevant, ed. Vol. 20 of *America's Lost Plays*.

Dunlap, William (1766–1839)

Andre (1798); Quinn, *Representative American Plays*, 79–108. In Coyle, Halline; Moses, *Representative American Dramas*.

The Dramatic Works of William Dunlap. 3 vols. Philadelphia: Palmer, 1806–16.

False Shame and Thirty Years, Oral Sumner Coad, ed. Vol. 2 of *America's Lost Plays*.

Fitch, William Clyde (1865–1909)

The City (1909); Moody, *Dramas from the American Theatre*, 813–854. In Moses, *Representative*.

Memorial Edition of the Plays of Clyde Fitch, Montrose J. Moses and Virginia Gerson, eds. 4 vols. Boston: Little, Brown, 1915.

Gillette, William (1855–1937)

Secret Service (1895); *Plays by William Hooker Gillette*, Rosemary Cullen and Don B. Wilmeth, eds. Cambridge: Cambridge University Press, 1983. 101–191. In Gassner.

Glaspell, Susan (1882–1948)

The Outside (1917); *Plays*. New York: Dodd, Mead and Company, 1920.

Suppressed Desires (1914); *Plays*. In Jacobus.

Trifles (1916); *Plays*.

Plays by Susan Glaspell, C.W.E. Bigsby, ed. New York: Cambridge University Press, 1987.

Godfrey, Thomas (1736–63)

The Prince of Parthia (1767); Quinn, *Representative American Plays*, 1–42. In Moses, *Representative*.

The Prince of Parthia. McCarron, William E., ed. Colorado Springs, Color.: United States Air Force Academy, 1976.

Herne, James A. (1839–1901)

Margaret Fleming (1890); Quinn, *Representative American Plays*, 515–44. In Coyle, Matlaw *Black Crook*.

Shore Acres (1892); Moody, *Dramas from the American Theatre*, 659–720. In Downer.

The Early Plays of James A. Herne, Arthur H. Quinn, ed. Vol 7 of *America's Lost Plays*.

Shore Acres and Other Plays by James A. Herne, Mrs. James A. Herne, ed. New York: Samuel French, 1928

Hopkinson, Francis (1737–1791)

"An Exercise Containing a Dialogue and Ode." Moody, *Dramas from the American Theatre*, 5–6.

Howard, Bronson (1842–1908)

The Henrietta (1887); *American Plays*, Allan G. Halline, ed. New York: American Book Co., 1935: 407–53.

Shenandoah (1888); Quinn, *Representative American Plays*, 473–512. In Coyle, Jacobus, Matlaw *Black Crook*, Moody; Moses, *Representative*.

The Banker's Daughter & Other Plays, Allan G. Halline, ed. Vol. 10 of *America's Lost Plays*.

Howells, William Dean (1837–1920)

A Counterfeit Presentment (1877); *The Complete Plays of W. D. Howells*, Walter J. Meserve, ed. and intro. New York: New York University Press, 1960. 69–109.

The Unexpected Guests (1893); *The Complete Plays of W. D. Howells*. 420–29.

The Complete Plays of W. D. Howells, Walter J. Meserve, ed. and intro. New York: New York University Press, 1960.

Hunter, Robert (?–1734)

Androboros (1714); *Satiric Comedies*, Walter J. Meserve and William R. Reardon, eds. 1–40.

Jones, Joseph S. (1809–1877)

The People's Lawyer; or Solon Shingle (1839); Moses, *Representative Plays*, 2: 381–424.

Leacock, John (1729–1802)

The Fall of British Tyranny; or, American Liberty (1776); Moses, *Representative Plays*, 1: 277–350. In Philbrick.

Low, Samuel (?–?)

The Politician Outwitted (1788); Moses, *Representative Plays*, 1: 351–429.

MacKaye, Percy (1875–1956)

The Scarecrow (1908); Quinn, *Representative American Plays*, 807–844. In Gassner; Moses, *Representative American Dramas*.

MacKaye, James Morrison Steele (1842–94)

Hazel Kirke (1880); Quinn, *Representative American Plays*, 439–71.

Paul Kauvar; or, Anarchy (1887); Moses, *Representative Plays*, 3: 235–354.

An Arrant Knave and Other Plays. Percy MacKaye, ed. Vol. 11 of *America's Lost Plays*.

Miller, Joaquin (1841?–1913)

The Danites in the Sierras (1877); Halline, *American Plays*, 377–405.

Mitchell, Langdon (1862–1935)

The New York Idea (1906); Quinn, *Representative American Plays*, 675–727. In Moody; Moses, *Representative*.

Moody, William Vaughn (1869–1910)

The Faith Healer (1909); Quinn, *Representative American Plays*, 773–805.

The Great Divide (1906); Moody, *Dramas from the American Theatre*, 721–756. In Downer, Gassner.

Mowatt, Anna Cora (1819–70)

Fashion: or, Life in New York (1845); Moody, *Dramas from the American Theatre*, 309–437. In Coyle, Halline, Jacobus, Matlaw *Black Crook*; Moses *Representative*; Quinn *Representative American Plays*.

Munford, Robert (ca. 1737–83)

The Candidates, Or the Humours of a Virginia Election (1771); Moody, *Dramas from the American Theatre*, 11–26.

The Patriots (1777/79), Courtlandt Canby, ed. *William and Mary Quarterly*, 3d ser. 6 (1949): 448–503. In Philbrick.

Noah, Mordeci (1785–1851)

She Would Be a Soldier (1819); Moses, *Representative Plays*, 1: 627–678. In Moody.

Paulding, James Kirke (1778–1860)

The Lion of the West (1830). James N. Tidwell, ed. Stanford, Calif.: Stanford University Press, 1954.

The Paxton Boys (1764)

The Paxton Boys: A Farce. Translated from the Original *French* by a Native of *Donegall*. Philadelphia: Anthony Ambuster, 1764.

Payne, John Howard (1791–1852)

Brutus (1819); Moses, *Representative*, 2: 87–175.

The Last Duel in Spain and Other Plays. Codman Hislop and W. R. Richardson, eds. Vol. 6 of *America's Lost Plays.*

Trial without Jury and Other Plays. Codman Hislop and W. R. Richardson, eds. Vol. 5 of *America's Lost Plays.*

Rogers, Robert (1731?–95)

Ponteach; or, the Savages of America (1766); Moses, *Representative Plays*, 1: 115–208.

Sheldon, Edward (1886–1946)

Salvation Nell (1908); *Best Plays of The Early American Theatre*, John Gassner, ed. New York: Crown, 1967. 557–616.

The Boss (1911); Quinn, *Representative American Plays*, 845–890.

The Nigger (1909). New York: Macmillan, 1910.

Stone, John Augustus (1800–34)

Metamora (1829); *Metamora and Other Plays.* Eugene R. Page, ed. 1–40; 401–13. In Clark, *Favorite*; Coyle, Moody.

Thomas, Augustus (1857–1934)

The Witching Hour (1909); Quinn, *Representative American Plays*, 729–770. In Moses, *Representative American Dramas.*

Thompson, Denham (1833–1910)

The Old Homestead (1886); *S.R.O.: The Most Successful Plays of the American Stage.* Comp. Bennett Cerf and Van H. Cartmell. New York: Doubleday, 1944. 167–221.

The Trial of Atticus (1771)

The Trial of Atticus, Before Justice Beau, for a Rape. Satiric Comedies. Walter J. Meserve and William R. Reardon. eds. 41–79.

Tyler, Royall (1757–1826)

The Contrast (1787); Quinn, *Representative American Plays*, 43–78. In Downer, Gassner, Halline, Jacobus, Moody; Moses, *Representative.*

Four Plays by Royall Tyler. Arthur Wallace Peach and George Floyd Newbrough, eds. Vol. 15, *America's Lost Plays.*

[V., Mary V.]

A Dialogue, Between a Southern Delegate, and His Spouse on His Return from the Grand Continental Congress (1774). Philbrick, *Trumpets Sounding*, 27–38.

Walter, Eugene (1874–1941)

The Easiest Way (1909); Moses, *Representative Plays*, 3: 706–814.

Warren, Mercy Otis (1728–1812)

The Plays and Poems of Mercy Otis Warren. Benjamin Franklin, V, ed. Delmar, N. Y.: Scholar's Facsimiles and Reprints, 1980.

Secondary Sources

General References

The abundance and easy availability of critical and historical material in periodicals, histories, textbooks, and anthologies, has made compiling a complete reference bibliography impossible. Periodical references have been limited to those of particular note. Titles that do not clearly indicate contents or those of special value have been annotated.

"American Playwrights on The American Drama." *Harper's Weekly*. 33 (February 2, 1889): 97–100.

Archdeacon, Thomas J. *Becoming American: An Ethnic History*. New York: Free Press, 1983.

Archer, William. *The Old Drama and the New*. London: Heineman, 1923.

Bailyn, Bernard. *The Ideological Origins of the American Revolution*. Cambridge: Harvard University Press, 1967.

Bentley, Eric. *The Life of the Drama*. London: Atheneum, 1964.

Berthoff, Werner. *The Ferment of American Realism: American Literature, 1884–1919*. New York, Free Press: 1965;

Bloom, Harold. *Poetry and Repression: Revisionism from Blake to Stevens*. New Haven: Yale University Press, 1976.

Bodnar, John. *The Transplanted: A History of Immigrants in Urban America*. Bloomington: Indiana University Press, 1985.

Bogard, Travis, Richard Moody, and Walter J. Meserve. *The Revels History of Drama in English*: Vol. VIII, *American Drama*. London: Methuen, 1977.

Brown, Jared. "British Military Theatre in New York, 1780–81." *Theatre Survey* 23 (1982): 151–62.

Cady, Edwin. *The Light of Common Day: Realism in American Fiction*. Bloomington: Indiana University Press, 1971.

Carr, John Dickson. *The Life of Sir Arthur Conan Doyle.* New York: Harper, 1949.

Colburn, H. Trevour. *The Lamp of Experience: Whig History and the Intellectual Origins of the American Revolution.* Chapel Hill: University of North Carolina Press, 1965.

Corbin, John. Review of *The Great Divide* by William Vaughn Moody. *The New York Sun* 4 Oct. 1906. Rpt. in *The American Theatre as Seen by Its Critics, 1752–1934,* edited by Montrose J. Moses and John Mason Brown. New York: Norton, 1934. 176–178.

Deutsch, Helen, and Stella Hanau. *The Provincetown: A Story of the Theatre.* New York: Russell and Russell, 1931.

Dorson, Richard M. "The Yankee on the Stage—A Folk Hero of the American Drama." *New England Quarterly* 13 (1940): 467–93.

Dunlap, William. *History of the American Theatre.* 2 vols. 1832; Rpt. New York: Burt Franklin, 1963.

———. *History of the Rise and Progress of the Arts of Design in the United States.* 3 vols. New York, 1834.

Eich, Louis M. "The Stage Yankee." *Quarterly Journal of Speech.* 27 (1941): 16–25.

Ellis, Joseph J. *After the Revolution: Profile of Early American Culture.* New York: Norton, 1979.

Foner, Eric. *Politics and Ideology in the Age of the Civil War.* New York: Oxford University Press, 1980.

Ford, Paul Leicester. "The Beginnings of American Dramatic Literature." *New England Magazine* n.s. 9.6 (1894): 673–87.

Freedman, Morris. *American Drama in Social Context.* Carbondale: Southern Illinois University Press, 1971.

Freneau, Philip. *Poems of Freneau.* Edited by Harry Hayden Clark. 1929; Rpt. New York: Hafner, 1960.

Friedman, Sharon. "feminism as theme in twentieth-century american women's drama." *American Studies* 25 (1984): 69–89.

Gottlieb, Lois C. "The Double Standard Debate in Early 20th-Century American Drama." *Michigan Academician* 7 (1975): 441–452.

———. "The Perils of Freedom: The New Woman in Three American Plays of the 1900's." *The Canadian Review of American Studies* 6 (1975): 84–98.

Grimsted, David. *Melodrama Unveiled: American Theater and Culture, 1800–1850.* Chicago: University of Chicago Press, 1968), 19–20. Excellent chapter on the structural characteristics of melodrama.

Habegger, Alfred. *Gender, Fantasy and Realism in American Literature.* New York: Columbia University Press, 1986.

Havens, Daniel F. *The Columbian Muse of Comedy.* Carbondale: Southern Illinois University Press, 1973.

Heilman, Robert B. *Tragedy and Melodrama: Versions of Experience.* Seattle: University of Washington Press, 1968.

Hodge, Francis. *Yankee Theatre: The Image of America on the Stage, 1825–1850.* Austin: University of Texas Press, 1964.

Hughes, Catherine. "Women Playmakers." *New York Times Magazine* 4 May 1941: 10, 27.

Ibsen, Henrik. *A Doll's House.* Vol. 5 of *The Oxford Ibsen*, translated and edited by James Walter MacFarlane. London: Oxford University Press, 1961.

James, Henry. *The Scenic Art: Notes on Acting and the Drama.* Edited by Allen Wade. New Brunswick, N.J.: Rutgers University Press, 1948.

Jefferson, Joseph. *The Autobiography of Joseph Jefferson.* New York: The Century Company, 1890.

Johnson, Claudia. "A New Nation's Drama." *The Columbia Literary History of the United States*, edited by Emory Elliott, *et al.* New York: Columbia University Press, 1988. 324–341.

Jost, Francois. "German and French Themes in Early American Drama." *JGE: The Journal of General Education*, 28, 3 (Fall, 1976): 190–222.

Kiper, Florence. "Some American Plays: From the Feminist Viewpoint." *The Forum* 51 (1914): 921–931.

Kirk, Clara Marburg, and Rudolph Kirk, eds. *Criticism and Fiction and Other Essays.* William Dean Howells. New York: New York University Press, 1959.

Kolb, Deborah S. "The Rise and Fall of the New Woman in American Drama." *Educational Theatre Journal* 27 (1975): 149–160.

Kolb, Harold H. *The Illusion of Life: American Realism as a Literary Form.* Charlottesville: University Press of Virginia, 1969.

Kolodny, Annette. *The Lay of the Land: Metaphor as Experience and History in American Life and Letters.* Chapel Hill: University of North Carolina Press, 1975.

Leverenz, David. *The Language of Puritan Feeling: An Exploration in Literature, Psychology and Social History.* New Brunswick: Rutgers University Press, 1980.

Lindenberger, Herbert. *Historical Drama: The Relation of Literature and Reality.* Chicago: University of Chicago Press, 1975.

Margoliouth, H. M., ed. *The Poems and Letters of Andrew Marvell*. 2 Vols. 3d ed. Oxford: Clarendon Press, 1971.

Martin, Jay. "The Province of Speech: American Drama in the Eighteenth Century." *Early American Literature* 13 (1978): 24–33.

Meserve, Walter J. "American Drama and the Rise of Realism." *Jahrbüch für Amerikastudien* 9 (1964): 152–200.

————. *An Emerging Entertainment: The Drama of the American People to 1828*. Bloomington: Indiana University Press, 1977. Together with its companion volume, *Heralds of Promise*, the most detailed theater histories currently available.

————. *Heralds of Promise: The Drama of the American People During the Age of Jackson, 1829–1849*. New York: Greenwood Press, 1986.

————. *An Outline History of American Drama*. Totowa, N.J.: Littlefield, Adams, 1965.

Miller, Jordan Y. *American Dramatic Literature*. New York: McGraw-Hill, 1961

Miller, Tice L. "The Image of Fashionable Society, 1840–1870." *When They Weren't Doing Shakespeare*, edited by Judith L. Fisher and Stephen Watt. Athens: University of Georgia Press, 1989. 243–252.

Moody, Richard A. *Edwin Forrest: First Star of the American Stage*. New York: Alfred A. Knopf, 1960

Moody, Richard J. *America Takes the Stage: Romanticism in American Theatre and Drama, 1750–1900*. Bloomington: Indiana University Press, 1955.

Moody, Robert E. "Boston's First Play." *Proceedings of the Massachusetts Historical Society* 92 (1980): 117–39.

Moses, Montrose J., and John Mason Brown, eds. *The American Theatre as Seen by Its Critics, 1752–1934*. New York: Norton, 1934

Murphy, Brenda. *American Realism and American Drama, 1880–1940*. Cambridge: Cambridge University Press, 1987.

Parrington, Vernon L. *The Beginnings of Critical Realism in America, 1860–1920*. New York: Harcourt, Brace, and World, 1930.

Peavy, C. D. "The American Indian in the Drama of the United States." *McNeese Review* 10 (1958): 68–86.

Philbrick, Norman, ed. *Trumpets Sounding: Propaganda Plays of the American Revolution*. New York: Blom, 1972.

Pizer, Donald. *Realism and Naturalism in Nineteenth-Century American Literature*. Rev. ed. Carbondale: Southern Illinois University Press, 1984.

Poggi, Jack. *Theater in America: the Impact of Economic Forces, 1870–1967*. Ithaca, New York: Cornell University Press, 1968.

Quinn, Arthur Hobson. *A History of the American Drama*. 2d ed. 2 vols. New

York: Crofts, 1951. Though critically dated, still an excellent place to begin. Extensive bibliographies.

————. *The Literature of the American People*. New York: Appleton-Century-Crofts, 1951.

Rahill, Frank. *The World of Melodrama*. University Park: Pennsylvania State University Press, 1967.

Rankin, Hugh F. *The Theatre of Colonial America*. Chapel Hill: University of North Carolina Press, 1965.

Reich, Jerome R. *Leisler's Rebellion: A Study of Democracy in New York, 1664–1720*. Chicago: University of Chicago Press, 1953.

Rugg, Harold G. "The Dartmouth Plays, 1779–1782." *The Theatre Annual* 1 (1942): 55–57.

Santayana, George. *Character and Opinion in the United States*. New York: Norton, [1920].

Sarlos, Robert K. *Jig Cook and the Provincetown Players: Theatre in Ferment*. Amherst: University of Massachusetts Press, 1982.

Silverman, Kenneth. *A Cultural History of the American Revolution*. New York: Crowell, 1976.

Slotkin, Richard. *Regeneration through Violence*. Middletown, Conn.: Wesleyan University Press, 1973.

Smith, James L. *Melodrama*. London: Methuen, 1973.

Solberg, Winton U. *Redeem the Time: The Puritan Sabbath in Early America*. Cambridge: Harvard University Press, 1977.

Stephens, Judith L. "Gender Ideology and Dramatic Convention in Progressive Era Plays, 1890–1920." *Theatre Journal* 41 (1989): 45–55.

Styan, J. L. *Modern Drama in Theory and Practice. Vol. I, Realism and Naturalism*. Cambridge: Cambridge University Press, 1981. Contains material on better-known early American realists.

Sutherland, Cynthia. "American Women Playwrights as Mediators of the 'Woman Problem.' " *Modern Drama* 21 (1978): 319–36.

Tichi, Cecelia. "Thespis and the 'Carnall Hipocrite': A Puritan Motive for Aversion to Drama." *Early American Literature* 4 (1969): 86–103.

Toll, Robert C. *Blacking Up: The Minstrel Show in Nineteenth-Century America*. New York: Oxford University Press, 1974.

Vanderbilt, Arthur T. II. *Fortune's Children: The Fall of the House of Vanderbilt*. New York: William Morrow, 1989.

Vaughn, Jack A. *Early American Dramatists: From the Beginnings to 1900*. New York: Ungar, 1981.

Wiebe, Robert. *The Opening of American Society*. New York: Vintage, 1984.

Winton, Calhoun. "The Theatre and Drama." *American Literature, 1764–1789: The Revolutionary Years.* Edited by Everett Emerson. Madison: University of Wisconsin Press, 1977. 87–104.

Wright, Louis B. *The Atlantic Frontier: Colonial American Civilization.* New York: Knopf, 1947.

Books and Articles on Individual Playwrights

Aiken, George L. (1830–76)

Birdoff, Harry. *The World's Greatest Hit: Uncle Tom's Cabin.* New York: Vanni, 1947.

Barker, James Nelson (1784–1858)

Barker, James Nelson. "The Drama," *Democratic Press* [Philadelphia] 18 December 1816–19, February 1817.

Crowley, John W. "James Nelson Barker in Perspective." *ETJ*, 24 (1972): 363–69.

Musser, Paul H. *James Nelson Barker.* Philadelphia: University of Pennsylvania Press, 1929.

Belasco, David (1859–1931)

Belasco, David. *The Theatre Through Its Stage Door.* 1919; rpt. New York: Blom, 1969.

Bergman, Herbert. "David Belasco's Dramatic Theory." *University of Texas Studies in English* 32 (1953): 110–22.

Marker, Lise-Lone. *David Belasco: Naturalism in the American Theatre.* Princeton, N.J.: Princeton University Press, 1975.

Winter, William. *The Life of David Belasco.* 2 Vols. New York: Moffat, Yard, 1918.

Bird, Robert Montgomery (1806–1854)

Dahl, Curtis. *Robert Montgomery Bird.* New York: Twayne, 1963.

Foust, Clement. *The Life and Dramatic Works of Robert Montgomery Bird.* New York: Knickerbocker Press, 1919.

Boker, George Henry (1823–90)

Bradley, Edward Sculley. *George Henry Boker, Poet and Patriot.* Philadelphia: University of Pennsylvania Press, 1927.

Evans, Oliver H. *George Henry Boker.* Boston: Twayne, 1984.

————. "Shakespearean Prototypes and the Failure of Boker's *Francesca da Rimini.*" *Educational Theatre Journal* 30 (1978): 211–19.

Flory, Claude R. "Boker, Barrett, and the Francesca Theme," *Players* 50 (1975): 58–61, 80.

Gallagher, Kent G. "The Tragedies of George Henry Boker: The Measure of American Romantic Drama." *ESQ* 20 (1974): 187–215.

Kincaid, Arthur Noel. "Italian and English Sources of Boker's 'Francesca Da Rimini.' " *American Transcendental Quarterly* 1 (1969): 91–100.

Krutch, Joseph Wood. "George Henry Boker." *Sewanee Review* 25 (1917): 45–58.

Sherr, Paul. "George Henry Boker's *Francesca da Rimini*, a Justification for the Literary Historian." *Pennsylvania History* 34 (1967): 361–71.

Voelker, Paul. "George Henry Boker's *Francesca da Rimini*: An Interpretation and Evaluation." *Educational Theatre Journal* 24 (1972): 383–95.

Zanger, Jules. "*Francesca da Rimini*: The Brothers Tragedy." *Educational Theatre Journal* 25 (1973): 410–19.

Boucicault, Dion (1820–90)

Degen, John A. "How to End *The Octoroon.*" *ETJ* 27 (1975): 170–78.

Fawkes, Richard. *Dion Boucicault.* London: Quartet Books, 1979.

Hogan, Robert. *Dion Boucicault.* New York: Twayne, 1969.

Kaplan, Sidney. "*The Octoroon*: Early History of the Drama of Miscegenation." *Journal of Negro History* 20 (1951): 547–57.

Krause, David. Introduction. *The Doleman Boucicault.* Dublin: Dolmen, 1964. 9–47.

Molin, Sven Eric, and Robin Goodfellow, eds. *Dion Boucicault: A Documentary Life.* Newark, Delaware: Proscenium, 1979.

Richardson, Gary A. "Boucicault's *The Octoroon* and American Law." *Theatre Journal* 34 (1982): 155–64.

Walsh, Townshend. *The Career of Dion Boucicault.* New York: The Dunlap Society, 1915.

Watt, Stephen M. "Boucicault and Whitbread: The Dublin Stage at the End of the Nineteenth Century." *Eire-Ireland* 18.3 (1983): 23–53.

Crothers, Rachel (1878–1958)

Gottlieb, Lois C. *Rachel Crothers.* Boston: Twayne, 1979.

Daly, Augustin (1838–99)

Daly, Joseph Francis. *The Life of Augustin Daly.* New York: Macmillan, 1917.

Felhein, Marvin. *The Theatre of Augustin Daly.* Cambridge, Mass.: Harvard University Press, 1956.

Wilmeth, Don B., and Rosemary Cullen, eds. *Plays by Augustin Daly*. British and American Playwrights, 1750–1920. Cambridge: Cambridge University Press, 1984. 1–38.

Dunlap, William (1766–1839)

Canary, Robert H. *William Dunlap*. New York: Twayne, 1970.

Coad, Oral Sumner. *William Dunlap*. 1917; Rpt. New York: Russell & Russell, 1962.

Martin, Jay. "William Dunlap: The Documentary Vision." *Theater und Drama in Amerika*. Edited by Edgar Lohner and Rudolf Haas. Berlin: Ench Schmidt Verlay, 1978. 170–193.

Philbrick, Norman. "The Spy as Hero: An Examination of *Andre* by William Dunlap." *Studies in Theatre and Drama: Essays in Honor of Hubert C. Heffner*. The Hague: Mouton, 1972. 97–119.

Zipes, Jack. "Dunlap, Kotzebue, and the Shaping of American Theatre: A Reevaluation from a Marxist Perspective." *Early American Literature* 8 (1974): 272–289.

Fitch, William Clyde (1865–1909)

Bell, Archie. *The Clyde Bell I Knew*. New York: Broadway Publishing, 1909.

Gillette, William (1855–1937)

Nichols, Harold J. "William Gillette: Innovator in Melodrama." *Theatre Annual* 31 (1975): 7–15.

Schuttler, Georg W. "William Gillette: Marathon Actor and Playwright." *Journal of Popular Culture* 17 (1983): 115–29.

Stone, P.M. "William Gillette's Stage Career." *The Baker Street Journal*, NS 12 (1962): 8–16.

Glaspell, Susan (1882–1948)

Ben-Zvi, Linda. "Susan Glaspell's Contributions to Contemporary Women Playwrights." *Feminine Focus: The New Women Playwrights*. Edited by Enoch Brater. New York: Oxford University Press, 1989. 147–166.

Dymkowski, Christine. "On the Edge: The Plays of Susan Glaspell." *Modern Drama* 31 (1988): 91–105.

Stein, Karen F. "The Women's World of Glaspell's *Trifles*." *Women in American Theatre*. Edited by Helen Krich Chinoy and Linda Walsh Jenkins. New York: Crown, 1981. 251–254.

Waterman, Arthur E. *Susan Glaspell*. New York: Twayne, 1966.

Godfrey, Thomas (1736–63)

Pollock, Thomas Clark. "Rowe's *Tamerlane* and *The Prince of Parthia*." *American Literature* 6 (1934–35): 158–62.

Herne, James A. (1839–1901)

Bucks, Dorothy S., and A. H. Nethercot. "Ibsen and Herne's *Margaret Fleming*: A Study of the Early Ibsen Movement in America." *American Literature* 17 (1946): 311–33.

Edwards, Herbert J. and Julie A. Herne. *James A. Herne: The Rise of Realism in the American Drama*. Orono: University of Maine Press, 1964.

Herne, James A. "Art for Truth's Sake in the Drama." *Arena* 17 (1897): 361–70. Rpt. in *American Drama and Its Critics*, edited by Alan S. Downer. Chicago: University of Chicago Press, 1965. 1–9.

Perry, John. *James A. Herne: The American Ibsen*. Chicago: Nelson-Hall, 1978.

Howard, Bronson (1842–1908)

Bloomfield, Maxwell. "Mirror for Businessmen: Bronson Howard's Melodramas, 1870–1890." *Mid-Continent American Studies Journal.* 5 (1964): 38–49.

Dithmar, Edward A. Review of *Shenandoah* by Bronson Howard. *New York Times*, 10 September 1889: 4.

———. Review of *Shenandoah* by Bronson Howard. *New York Times*, 15 September 1889: 3.

Howard, Bronson. "The American Drama." *Sunday Magazine* (New York), October 7, 1906. Rpt. in *Representative Plays by American Dramatists*, edited by Montrose J. Moses. 3 vols. (New York: Dutton, 1918–21) III, 365–70.

Howells, William Dean (1837–1920)

Carter, Everett. *Howells and the Age of Realism*. Philadelphia: Lippincott, 1950.

Howells, William Dean. *Criticism and Fiction*, in *Criticism and Fiction and Other Essays*. Edited by Clara Marburg Kirk and Rudolf Kirk. New York: New York University Press, 1959.

———. "Editor's Study." *Harper's Monthly Magazine* 73 (July 1886): 314–19.

———. "Henrik Ibsen." *The North American Review* 183 (July 1906): 1–14.

———. "The Editor's Study." *Harper's Monthly*, June 1890: 152–57.

———. "The New Poetic Drama," *The North American Review* 172 (May 1901): 794–800.

———. "The Play and the Problem." *Harper's Weekly Magazine* 39 (March 30, 1895): 266

Kirk, Clara Marburg, and Rudolf Kirk. *William Dean Howells*. 1950; rev. ed. New York: Hill and Wang, 1961.

Tarkington, Booth. "Mr. Howells." *Harper's Monthly Magazine* 141 (August, 1920): 346–50.

Hunter, Robert (?–1734)

Leder, Lawrence H. "Robert Hunter's *Androboros.*" *Bulletin of the New York Public Library*. 60 (1964): 153–60.

Leacock, John (1729–1802)

Dallett, Francis J., Jr. "John Leacock and THE FALL OF BRITISH TYRANNY." *Pennsylvania Magazine of History and Biography* 78 (1954): 456–75.

MacKaye, Percy (1875–1956)

Brock, D. Heyward, and James M. Walsh, "Percy MacKaye: Community and the Masque Tradition," *Comparative Drama* 6 (1972): 68–84.

Mendelsohn, Michael J. "Percy MacKaye's Dramatic Theories." *Bulletin of the Rocky Mountain Modern Language Association* 24 (1970): 85–89.

MacKaye, James Morrison Steele (1842–94)

MacKaye, Percy. *Epoch: The Life of Steel MacKaye*. 2 vols. New York: Boni and Liveright, 1927.

Woodard, Debra J. "Steel MacKaye's *Marriage*: The Beginning of a Movement toward American Realism." *Theatre Survey* 23 (1982): 189–95.

Moody, William Vaughn (1869–1910)

Halpern, Martin. *William Vaughn Moody*. New York: Twayne, 1964.

Mowatt, Anna Cora (1819–70)

Mowatt, Anna Cora. *Autobiography of an Actress; or, Eight Years on the Stage*. Boston: Ticknor, Reed, and Fields, 1854.

Munford, Robert (ca. 1737–83)

Baine, Rodney M. *Robert Munford*. Athens: University of Georgia Press, 1967.

Beeman, Richard R. "Robert Munford and the Political Culture of Frontier Virginia." *Journal of American Studies* 12 (1978): 169–83.

Noah, Mordeci (1785–1851)

Goldberg, Issac. *Major Noah: American-Jewish Pioneer*. New York: Knopf, 1937.

Paulding, James Kirke (1778–1860)

Herold, Amos L. *James Kirke Paulding: Versatile American*. New York: Columbia University Press, 1926.

Mason, Melvin Rosser. " 'The Lion of the West': Satire on Davy Crockett and Frances Trollope." *South Central Bulletin* 29 (1969): 143–45.

Reynolds, Larry J. *James Kirke Paulding*. Boston: Twayne, 1984.

Payne, John Howard (1791–1852)

Overmyer, Grace. *America's First Hamlet*. New York: New York University Press, 1953.

Saxon, Arthur H. "John Howard Payne, Playwright with a System." *Theatre Notes* 24 (1969–70): 79–84.

Rogers, Robert (1731?–95)

Anderson, Marilyn J. "*Ponteach*: The First American Problem Play." *American Indian Quarterly* 3 (1977): 225–41.

Sheldon, Edward (1886–1946)

Ruff, Loren K. *Edward Sheldon*. Boston: Twayne, 1982.

Thomas, Augustus (1857–1934)

Davis, Ronald J. *Augustus Thomas*. Boston: Twayne, 1984.

Tyler, Royall (1757–1826)

Carson, Ada Lou, and Herbert L. Carson. *Royall Tyler*. Boston: Twayne, 1979.

Lauber, John. "*The Contrast*: A Study in the Concept of Innocence." *English Language Notes* 1 (1963): 33–37.

Seibert, Donald T., Jr. "Royall Tyler's 'Bold Example': *The Contrast* and the English Comedy of Manners." *Early American Literature* 13 (1978): 3–11.

Shuffelton, Frank. "The Voice of History: Thomas Godfrey's *Prince of Parthia* and Revolutionary America." *Early American Literature* 13 (1978): 12–23.

Stein, Roger. "Royall Tyler and the Question of Our Speech." *New England Quarterly* 38 (1965): 454–74.

Tanselle, G. Thomas. *Royall Tyler*. Cambridge: Harvard University Press, 1967.

Warren, Mercy Otis (1728–1812)

Anthony, Katharine. *First Lady of the Revolution: The Life of Mercy Otis Warren*. 1958; Rpt. Port Washington, New York: Kennikat, 1972.

Teunissen, John W. "Blockheadism and the Propaganda Plays of the American Revolution." *Early American Literature* 7 (1972): 148–62.

Index

315

The Author

Gary A. Richardson, Associate Professor of English at Mercer University, received his B.A. and M.A. from Northeast Louisiana University in 1971 and 1975, respectively, and his Ph.D. from the University of Illinois at Urbana-Champaign in 1983. He held a Fulbright lectureship in English literature and American Studies in Nijmegen, The Netherlands (1987), and has published and lectured widely on nineteenth-century American drama both in the United States and abroad. He is currently at work on a volume dealing with representations of the Irish and Irish-Americans on the English speaking stage from the eighteenth century until the current day.

ACS-7318   2/22/95